The Nature of Narrative

THE NATURE
OF NARRATIVE

FORTIETH ANNIVERSARY EDITION,
REVISED AND EXPANDED

ROBERT SCHOLES
JAMES PHELAN
ROBERT KELLOGG

OXFORD
UNIVERSITY PRESS

2006

OXFORD
UNIVERSITY PRESS

Oxford University Press, Inc., publishes works that
further Oxford University's objective of excellence
in research, scholarship, and education.

Oxford New York
Auckland Cape Town Dar es Salaam Hong Kong Karachi
Kuala Lumpur Madrid Melbourne Mexico City Nairobi
New Delhi Shanghai Taipei Toronto

With offices in
Argentina Austria Brazil Chile Czech Republic France Greece
Guatemala Hungary Italy Japan Poland Portugal Singapore
South Korea Switzerland Thailand Turkey Ukraine Vietnam

Copyright © 1966, 2006 by Oxford University Press

Published by Oxford University Press, Inc.
198 Madison Avenue, New York, NY 10016
www.oup.com

Oxford is a registered trademark of Oxford University Press

Library of Congress Cataloging-in-Publication Data
Scholes, Robert E.
The nature of narrative / Robert Scholes, James Phelan,
Robert Kellogg.—Fortieth anniversary ed., rev. and expanded.
p. cm.
Includes bibliographical references and index.
ISBN-13: 978-0-19-515175-6 (cloth)
ISBN-10: 0-19-515175-5 (cloth)
ISBN-13: 978-0-19-515176-3 (pbk.)
ISBN-10: 0-19-515176-3 (pbk.)
1. Fiction—History and criticism.
I. Phelan, James, 1951–
II. Kellogg, Robert.
III. Title.
PN3451.S3 2006 809.3—dc22
2006009443

1 3 5 7 9 8 6 4 2
Printed in the United States of America
on acid-free paper

In Memory of
Robert L. Kellogg
(1928–2004)

Contents

Preface to the Second Edition
by Robert Scholes

Forty years is a long time for an academic book to remain in print—especially one written by a couple of brash young scholars with no academic standing to speak of. But that is the case of the present volume. The book began in discussions between Bob Kellogg and myself about a sophomore course we had invented at the University of Virginia, in which we spent a year covering narrative literature from Homer to Joyce. We taught the course more than once and used to walk home together talking about it nearly every day. The book emerged from those classes and those conversations—and from the studying the course required on our parts, which was considerable.

In some ways, we were the ideal people to have done such a course. Kellogg had gone to Harvard for graduate study, driven by an interest in James Joyce. Since he was a thorough person, he started his studies with the middle ages—and never emerged from them. When we met he was working on Old Icelandic literature in particular, but his mastery of both medieval European literature and literary modernism was impressive. I had gone to Cornell, partly because their graduate program allowed for a concentration in the novel as a genre, which was quite rare in the 1950s. My MA thesis and doctoral dissertation were in twentieth century American and English fiction, but my training covered the novel as a whole, and at Virginia I taught everything from eighteenth century British fiction to twentieth century American. Together, Bob and I had more historical range in narrative literature than any single person our age could have had.

We had been talking about collaborating on a book for a while, when I won a year's fellowship to the Humanities Center at the University of Wisconsin in Madison with a proposal for studying the history and theory of narrative literature. This opportunity meant that I would try to draft as much of our projected book as I could, leaving gaps for Bob to fill using knowledge that I didn't have. Deep in my own past were five and a half years of Latin study in the public schools of Garden City, NY, and I undertook to learn at least the rudiments of ancient Greek while in Madison. Bob knew a number of the languages of medieval Europe, and we both knew some modern languages. Neither of us knew Russian, but I had taken a year-long course in the Russian novel with René Wellek as an undergraduate. So, we had the basics.

At Madison I was able to pick the brains of a number of senior scholars ranging from Marshall Claggett, a specialist in medieval science, to Germain Brée, a scholar of modern French literature, and this was an enormous help to me. In the Humanities Center, Marshall Claggett, who was then Director of the Center, asked me if there were any books the Center could get that would help my studies. I gave him a list of some Loeb Classics—ancient Greek and Latin texts with facing English translations—and he mused on it for a while, finally saying that he thought the Center should have a complete set. A few weeks later I helped him unpack and shelve such a set, which was an great aid to my work, since I could find key passages quickly in the English texts and then study the Greek or Latin original more carefully, making my rusty Latin and rudimentary Greek functional in this way.

Well, I drafted my chapters, and Bob edited them, and then he drafted two (on the oral heritage of modern narrative and meaning in narrative) and I edited those. In this way the book got written, and ultimately published by Oxford. Nearly thirty-five years later Bob and I happened to sit opposite one another at a dinner, where we decided to see if our publisher was interested in a second edition. They were, and we planned it, but the work went slowly, and then Bob died. He was a fine scholar, a great human being, and a dear friend. His death meant the death of the edition as well as far as I was concerned, since I did not have the heart to go on alone. But time eases such pains, and our publisher was very patient, so, after a while, I began thinking about how the book might be revised.

Reading the book over again after so many years, I was impressed by how much those brash young men had read, remembered, and pondered. They knew things that I do not know now, and they had thought about them in ways no longer available to me. Situated firmly in its own time, the book seemed to resist revision to the point of impossibility. The *Nature of Narrative*, after all, had helped to create the field of narrative studies, and I had extended my own thinking on narrative in such other books as *The Fabulators, Structuralism in Literature, Structural Fabulation, Fabulation and Metafiction, Textual Power*, and *Paradox of Modernism*. Many other scholars had also entered this field, producing rich and powerful studies on both the theoretical side and the historical side—scholars like Bakhtin, Todorov, Genette, Barthes, and McKeon, to mention only a few of the most obvious. Yet *The Nature of Narrative* had remained in print and seemed still to offer a useful perspective on the history and theory of narrative. This place, however, was to some degree historical—a perspective from a particular point in time, the middle of the twentieth century.

Given all those considerations, I saw no way to re-write the book and produce a new edition. Gradually, however, I realized that it might be possible to republish the original text, making minor stylistic adjustments, and to invite some younger scholar to supplement that text with a section on developments in the study of narrative since the first edition. And that is what has happened. The author who has joined this project is not a brash young man, but he is younger than me, and in a better position to speak of what has happened to narrative studies in the past few decades than anyone else I know. James Phelan has been for many years the editor of the leading journal in the field of narrative studies, the official journal of the Society for the Study of Narrative, called simply *Narrative*. Without his collaboration, this second edition of *The Nature of Narrative* would not exist. And I think he has done an excellent job of covering what has happened to narrative studies in the forty years since this book first appeared.

Preface to the Second Edition
by James Phelan

I was first introduced to *The Nature of Narrative* in my own brash
youth: in 1969 in a required course for sophomore English majors
at Boston College taught by Robert E. Reiter. I then studied the
book more carefully in 1976 when I put it on the reading list for my
Ph.D. special field exam on "Theories of Narrative" supervised by
Sheldon Sacks at the University of Chicago. In the years since, I
have had occasion to consult it and recommend it to others, but I
was never expecting Bob Scholes's kind invitation to contribute "a
section on developments in the study of narrative" to a new edition.
Being asked to contribute to a book that has been part of one's forma-
tive experience is a surreal experience. If I were a novelist, I imagine
I'd feel the same way if, say, Henry James or Virginia Woolf invited
me to write a concluding chapter for a new edition of *The Ambassadors* or *Mrs. Dalloway*. Of course you feel flattered and say yes. Of
course you also feel terrified and inadequate. But then you go and
make some decisions about how to do the job and then, when they
turn to be obviously the wrong ones, you make some new ones, and
you keep going like that until you get something you can live with.

Of the many decisions I have made, there are three that I want to
highlight here. First, I retain Scholes and Kellogg's focus on literary
narrative because I believe that is the best way to underline the
continuity between their work and developments over the last forty

years. At the same time, I point out that narrative theory has expanded its scope to include nonliterary narratives of all kinds and that this expansion has consequences for work on literary narrative. Second, I hew closely to Scholes's request for a discussion of "developments in the study of narrative." What this means, in practical terms, is that rather than tracing the history of narrative since 1966 (post-modern experimentation, the emergence of digital narrative, the memoir boom, and so on), I offer a narrative about narrative theory, and I punctuate that narrative with examples from both pre-1966 and post-1966 literary narrative. Proceeding this way, I hope, will allow the reader to see more connections between the theoretical parts of Scholes and Kellogg's work and more recent advances and proposals, even as it gives me more space to present those developments.

Third, I steer a middle course between presenting the developments totally on their own terms and offering my version of a Grand Unified Field Theory of Narrative (GUFTON). To do the first would be to adopt a false and, I suspect, unsustainable pose of objectivity; to do the second would be to exhibit a misguided narrowness of vision about the field and of rhetorical purpose on this occasion. Contemporary narrative theory is too diverse for "a section on developments in the field" since 1966 to become the presentation of a GUFTON. But the very diversity of the field also means that any narrative of its evolution over the last forty years must involve a large degree of selection. That selection in turn must inevitably reflect the storyteller's view of the field, including how different aspects of it relate to each other. Consequently, while I have reached the point where I can live with my decisions and selections, I am acutely aware that my narrative is not the only plausible one that could be written, and I think it would be healthy for my readers to have a similar awareness.

I am grateful to David Herman, Brian McHale, Peter J. Rabinowitz, and Bob Scholes for their helpful comments on my narrative. I am also grateful to Elizabeth Marsch for her eagle-eyed copyediting and her diligent assistance with the Works Cited. Above all, I am deeply grateful to Bob Scholes for making the leap of faith that led him to invite me to contribute to his and Robert Kellogg's landmark book.

A few pages of my contribution have previously appeared in my entry on "Rhetorical Approaches to Narrative" in the *Routledge Encyclopedia of Narrative Theory* (pp. 500–504), edited by David Herman, Manfred Jahn, and Marie-Laure Ryan (London: Routledge, 2005) and in my entry on "Plot" in the *Encyclopedia of the Novel* (pp. 1008–1011), edited by Paul Schellinger (Chicago: Fitzroy Dearborn, 1998). I am grateful to both publishers for permission to reprint those pages.

The Nature of Narrative

1

The Narrative Tradition

For the past two centuries the dominant form of narrative literature in the West has been the novel. In writing about the Western narrative tradition we will in one sense, therefore, necessarily be describing the heritage of the novel. But it will not be our intention to view the novel as the final product of an ameliorative evolution, as the perfected form which earlier kinds of narrative — sacred myth, folktale, epic, romance, legend, allegory, confession, satire — were all striving, with varying degrees of success, to become. Instead, our intention will be almost the opposite. We hope to put the novel in its place, to view the nature of narrative and the Western narrative tradition whole, seeing the novel as only one of a number of narrative possibilities. In order to attempt this it has been necessary to take long views, to rush into literary areas where we can claim some interest and competence but not the deep knowledge of the specialist, and perhaps to generalize overmuch in proportion to the evidence we present. For these and other excesses and exuberances, we apologize, hoping only that the result will justify our temerity in having undertaken such an elaborate project.

The object of this study of narrative art is not to set a new vogue, in either literature or criticism, but to provide an antidote to all narrow views of literature, ancient or modern. In any age in which criticism flourishes, and ours is certainly such an age, a conflict between broad and narrow approaches to literary art is sure to arise. An age of criticism is a self-conscious age. Its tendency is to formulate rules, to attempt the reduction of art to science, to classify, to categorize, and finally to prescribe and proscribe. Theoretical criticism of this sort is usually based on the practice of certain authors, whose works become classics in the worst sense of the word: models of approved and proper literary performance. This kind of narrowing down of the literature of the past to a few "classic" models amounts to the construction of an artificial literary tradition. Our purpose in this work is to present an alternative to narrowly conceived views of one major kind of literature — which we have called narrative.

By narrative we mean all those literary works which are distinguished by two characteristics: the presence of a story and a story-teller. A drama is a story without a story-teller; in it characters act out directly what Aristotle called an "imitation" of such action as we find in life. A lyric, like a drama, is a direct presentation, in which a single actor, the poet or his surrogate, sings, or muses, or speaks for us to hear or overhear. Add a second speaker, as Robert Frost does in "The Death of the Hired Man," and we move toward drama. Let the speaker begin to tell of an event, as Frost does in "The Vanishing Red," and we move toward narrative. For writing to be narrative no more and no less than a teller and a tale are required.

There is a real tradition of narrative literature in the Western world. All art is traditional in that artists learn their craft from their predecessors to a great extent. They begin by conceiving of the possibilities open to them in terms of the achievements they are acquainted with. They may add to the tradition, opening up new possibilities for their successors, but they begin, inevitably, within a tradition. The more aware we are — as readers, critics, or artists — of the fullness and breadth of the narrative tradition, the freer and the sounder will be the critical or artistic choices we make. For mid-twentieth-century readers a specific problem must

be overcome before a balanced view of the narrative tradition becomes attainable. Something must be done about our veneration
of the novel as a literary form.

With Joyce, Proust, Mann, Lawrence, and Faulkner, the narrative literature of the twentieth century has begun the gradual
break with the narrative literature of the immediate past that
characterizes all living literary traditions. Specifically, twentieth-
century narrative has begun to break away from the aims, attitudes, and techniques of realism. The implications of this break
are still being explored, developed, and projected by many of the
most interesting living writers of narrative literature in Europe
and America. But, by and large, our reviewers are hostile to this
new literature and our critics are unprepared for it, for literary
criticism is also influenced by its conception of tradition.

Rather than pick out one or a dozen reviewers to exemplify the
hostility of contemporary criticism to much that is best in contemporary narrative art, we can take as an example a great scholar
and critic, whose views are now acknowledged to be among the
most influential in our graduate schools of literature (where the
teachers, critics, and even the reviewers of the future are being
developed) and whose attitude toward modern literature, for all
the learning and sensitivity with which he presents it, is surprisingly similar to that of the most philistine weekly reviews. This
scholar-critic is Erich Auerbach, whose book *Mimesis*, in its paperback, English language version, is one of the two or three most
widely read and currently influential books in its field. And its
field is a broad one: Western narrative literature. It is a great
book, but Auerbach's single-minded devotion to realistic principles leaves him unwilling or unable to come to terms with
twentieth-century fiction, and especially with such writers as Virginia Woolf, Proust, and Joyce. He finds *Ulysses* a "hodgepodge,"
characterized by "its blatant and painful cynicism, and its unin-
terpretable symbolism," and he asserts that along with it, "most
of the other novels which employ multiple reflection of consciousness also leave the reader with an impression of hopelessness.

There is often something confusing, something hazy about them, something hostile to the reality which they represent."

Auerbach's dissatisfaction with post-realistic fiction is echoed by the dissatisfactions of lesser men, which we meet on nearly every page of current literary reviews and journals, where much of the best contemporary writing is treated with hostility or indifference. And current attitudes toward contemporary literature also carry over into current attitudes toward the literature of the past. The tendency to apply the standards of nineteenth-century realism to all fiction naturally has disadvantages for our understanding of every other kind of narrative. Spenser, Chaucer, and Wolfram von Eschenbach suffer from the "novelistic" approach as much as Proust, Joyce, Durrell, and Beckett do. In order to provide a broader alternative to the novelistic approach to narrative, we must break down many of the chronological, linguistic, and narrowly conceived generic categories frequently employed in the discussion of narrative. We must consider the elements common to all narrative forms — oral and written, verse and prose, factual and fictional — as these forms actually developed in the Western world. While fairly rare, an undertaking of this sort is not without precedent.

Such, in fact, was the aim of the first book in English wholly devoted to the study of the narrative tradition, Clara Reeve's *The Progress of Romance through Times, Countries, and Manners,* which was published in 1785. Clara Reeve, confronted by the common eighteenth-century prejudice against romance, endeavored to provide a pedigree for the form, to show especially that "the ancients" employed it, and to distinguish it from its follower, the novel, without prejudice to either form. Her distinction, indeed, is the one preserved in our dictionaries today, and it is still employed by critics who make any pretensions to discriminating among narrative forms:

I will attempt this distinction, and I presume if it is properly done it will be followed, — if not, you are but where you were before. The Romance is an heroic fable, which treats of fabulous persons and things.

— The Novel is a picture of real life and manners, and of the times in which it is written. The Romance in lofty and elevated language, describes what never happened nor is likely to happen. — The Novel gives a familiar relation of such things, as pass every day before our eyes, such as may happen to our friend, or to ourselves; and the perfection of it, is to represent every scene, in so easy and natural a manner, and to make them appear so probable, as to deceive us into a persuasion (at least while we are reading) that all is real, until we are affected by the joys or distresses of the persons in the story, as if they were our own.

Along with this clear and useful formulation, Reeve made half-hearted attempts at some other categories: a miscellaneous group of "original or uncommon" stories, which included such "modern" works as *Gulliver's Travels, Robinson Crusoe, Tristram Shandy,* and *The Castle of Otranto*; and another class of "tales and fables," which included everything from fairy tales to *Rasselas*. She also struggled with the problem of separating the Epic from the Romance, tackling such formidable considerations as the Osianic question. (She hesitated, saying *Fingal* was "an Epic, but not a Poem" and finally located Ossian with the romances.) She made it clear throughout that a romance might be in either verse or prose, but felt that an epic must be poetical. She was also disposed to think of epic as a term of praise, so that a really fine poetic romance such as Chaucer's Knight's Tale (the example is hers) would deserve the title of epic.

For her time, and considering the limits of her education, Clara Reeve was astonishingly well informed and free from prejudice. Her veneration for "the ancients" and her moralistic approach to literary achievement were shared by greater minds than her own. Until quite recently, in fact, very few attempts to deal with narrative literature in her comprehensive way have been made; and her knowledge, balance, and good sense would benefit many a modern book reviewer, could he attain them. Still, the difficulties Clara Reeve encountered in 1785 may be instructive for us in the present. After novel and romance she had trouble reducing other narrative forms to order—and so have modern critics. But even more troublesome is her tendency to attach a value judgement to a descriptive term like "epic." One of the greatest difficulties arising in modern criticism stems from a tendency to confuse descriptive and evaluative terminology. "Tragic" and "realistic," for example, are normally applied to literary works as terms of praise. Such usage can be found in the book and theater review pages of nearly any of our periodicals. A serious drama can be damned for its failure to be "tragic." A narrative can be damned as "unrealistic." But the greatest obstacle to an understanding of narrative literature in our day is the way notions of value have clustered around the word "novel" itself. One reason Clara Reeve could see the progress of romance with such a relatively unprejudiced eye was the fact that she lived before the great century of the realistic novel, the nineteenth.

But now, in the middle of the twentieth century, our view of narrative literature is almost hopelessly novel-centered. The expectations which readers bring to narrative literary works are based on their experience with the novel. Their assumptions about what a narrative should be are derived from their understanding of the novel. The very word "novel" has become a term of praise when applied to earlier narratives. We are told on dust-jackets and paperback covers that such diverse works as Chaucer's *Troilus and Criseyde*, Geoffrey of Monmouth's *History of the Kings of Britain*, and Homer's *Odyssey* are "the first novel." But if we take these designations seriously, we are bound to be disappointed. Judged as a "novelist" even Homer must be found wanting.

The novel-centered view of narrative literature is an unfortunate one for two important reasons. First, it cuts us off from the narrative literature of the past and the culture of the past. Second, it cuts us off from the literature of the future and even from the advance guard of our own day. To recapture the past and to accept the future we must, literally, put the novel into its place. To do this we need not part with any of our appreciation of realistic fiction. When the novel is in its place the achievements of such as Balzac, Flaubert, Turgenev, Tolstoy, and George Eliot will not lose any of their luster. They may even shine more brightly.

The novel, let us remember, represents only a couple of centuries in the continuous narrative tradition of the Western world which can be traced back five thousand years. Two hundred years of considerable achievement, of course; modern Europe has nothing to be ashamed of where its production of narrative literature is concerned, whatever its failings in other spheres; but still, only two hundred years out of five thousand. The purpose of this study is to examine some of the lines of continuity in this five-thousand-year tradition by considering some of the varieties of narrative literature, by discerning patterns in the historical development of narrative forms, and by examining continuing or recurring elements in narrative art. Our task is incomparably easier than Clara Reeve's. Though the need for a broad approach to narrative art is as pressing now as it was in 1785, the intellectual developments of the intervening years have brought many more of the necessary tools to hand.

From various sources we have learned more in the last hundred years about the pre-history of literature and about pre-modern literature than was ever known before. Vital information that was simply not available to the literary historians and critics of the eighteenth and nineteenth centuries is now available to us. The anthropologists, beginning with Frazer in *The Golden Bough*, have given us priceless information about the relationship between literature and culture in primitive society, opening the way to such literary studies as Jessie Weston's *From Ritual to Romance*. The psychologists — Jung even more than Freud — have given us equally important insights into the ways in which literature is related to an individual's mental processes, making possible a new and fruitful school (despite some excesses) of literary studies — archetypal criticism. The students of oral literature, such as Parry and Lord, have enabled us for the first time to perceive how written and oral literatures are differentiated and what the oral heritage of written narrative actually is. Literary scholars like the classicists Murray and Cornford and the Hebraist Theodore Gaster have shown ways in which some of the new extra-literary knowledge can enhance our understanding of literature. Historians of art and literature, such as Erwin Panofsky and D. W. Robertson, Jr., have made the attitudes and world view of our cultural ancestors more intelligible to us than ever before. And such a brilliant critical synthesizer as Northrop Frye has shown us how it is possible to unite cultural and literary study in such a way as to approach closer to a complete theory of literature than ever before.

Deriving what we could from the example as well as from the techniques and discoveries of such scholars as these, we have attempted to formulate a theory which would, as clearly and economically as possible, account for the varieties of narrative form and the processes that produce them and govern their interrelationships. Faced with the facts of history, with the various kinds of narrative which have been recognized and classified — often according to different and conflicting systems — and with the "influences," affinities, and correspondences which have been observed, we have tried to do justice to both the intractabilities of fact and the mind's lust for system and order. Our results, with their full and proper range of illustrations and qualifications, are developed in the following chapters. In the remainder of this chapter, we offer a kind of "argument" or gloss for the more elaborate exposition to come. It is a minimal, stripped-down version of our view of the narrative tradition, representing not *a priori* convictions which have shaped our study but rather a pattern we found emerging in the course of it.

The evolution of forms within the narrative tradition is a process analogous in some ways to biological evolution. Human beings, considering themselves the end of an evolutionary process, naturally see evolution as a struggle toward perfection. The dinosaur, could he speak, might have another opinion. Similarly, a contemporary novelist can see himself as the culmination of an ameliorative evolution; but Homer, could he speak, might disagree. Yet the epic poem is as dead as the dinosaur. We can put together a synthetic epic with a superficial resemblance to the originals, just as we can fabricate a museum dinosaur; but the conditions which produced the originals have passed. Nature will never recover that lost innocence which she displayed in the creation of those beautiful monsters, nor will narrative artists ever again be able to combine so innocently materials drawn from myth and history, from experience and imagination.

Of course, the evolutionary analogy breaks down. The *Iliad* is as great a wonder as a live dinosaur would be. Individual literary works do not always die off, though their forms may cease to be viable. Nor is their reproduction a matter of natural selection. Literary evolution is in some ways more complex than biological evolution. It is a kind of cross between a biological and a dialectical process, in which different species sometimes combine to produce new hybrids, which can in turn combine with other old or new forms; and in which one type will beget its antitype, which in turn may combine with other forms or synthesize with its antitypical originator.

To find a satisfactory means of ordering and presenting the complex processes at work in the evolution of narrative forms is a difficult task. The solution here presented is a compromise between the chaotic and the schematic. It is not offered as a simulacrum of the actual conscious or unconscious mental processes of narrative artists but as a handy way of reducing such processes to manageable terms. Its main purpose is to reveal, by clarifying them, the principal relationships which do exist and have existed historically among the major forms of narrative literature.

Written narrative literature tends to make its appearance throughout the Western world under similar conditions. It emerges

from an oral tradition, maintaining many of the characteristics of
oral narrative for some time. It often takes that form of heroic,
poetic narrative which we call epic. Behind the epic lie a variety
of narrative forms, such as sacred myth, quasi-historical legend,
and fictional folktale, which have coalesced into a traditional narrative which is an amalgam of myth, history, and fiction. For us,
the most important aspect of early written narrative is the fact
of the tradition itself. The epic story-teller is telling a traditional
story. The primary impulse which moves him is not a historical
one, nor a creative one; it is *re*-creative. He is retelling a traditional story, and therefore his primary allegiance is not to fact,
not to truth, not to entertainment, but to the *mythos* itself — the
story as preserved in the tradition which the epic story-teller is
re-creating. The word *mythos* meant precisely this in ancient
Greece: a traditional story.

In the transmission of traditional narrative it is of necessity
the outline of events, the plot, which is transmitted. Plot is, in
every sense of the word, the articulation of the skeleton of narrative. A myth, then, is a traditional plot which can be transmitted. Aristotle saw plot (*mythos* is his word) as the soul of any
literary work that was an imitation of an action. Sacred myth, a
narrative form associated with religious ritual, is one kind of
mythic narrative; but legend and folktale are also mythic in the
sense of traditional, and so is the oral epic poem. One of the great
developmental processes that is unmistakable in the history of
written narrative has been the gradual movement away from narratives dominated by the mythic impulse to tell a story with a
traditional plot. In Western literature we can trace this movement twice: once in the classical languages and again in the vernacular languages. In the course of this evolutionary process narrative literature tends to develop in two antithetical directions. A
proper understanding of the growth of the two great branches of
narrative which emerge as the traditional impulse declines in
power is essential to a true appreciation of the evolution of narrative forms. To understand this development properly we must

take into account both the nature of the separation between the
two great branches of narrative and the interaction and recombi-
nation of the two.

The two antithetical types of narrative which emerge from the
epic synthesis may be labeled the *empirical* and the *fictional*. Both
can be seen as ways of avoiding the tyranny of the traditional in
story-telling. Empirical narrative replaces allegiance to the *mythos*
with allegiance to reality. We can subdivide the impulse toward
empirical narrative into two main components: the *historical* and
the *mimetic*. The historical component owes its allegiance specifically to truth of fact and to the actual past rather than to a traditional version of the past. It requires for its development means
of accurate measurement in time and space, and concepts of
causality referable to human and natural rather than to supernatural agencies. In the ancient world empirical narrative manifests itself first through its historical component as writers like
Herodotus and Thucydides carefully distinguish their work from
Homeric epic. The mimetic component owes its allegiance not to
truth of fact but to truth of sensation and environment, depending on observation of the present rather than investigation of the
past. It requires for its development sociological and psychological concepts of behavior and mental process, such as those which
inform the characterization of the Alexandrian Mime. Mimetic
forms are the slowest of narrative forms to develop. In the ancient
world we find the strongest mimetic elements in the Theophrastian Character (a narrative counterpart of the dramatic Mime),
in such a realistic "idyll" as Theocritus' *Adoniazusae* (No. 15),
and in such a passage as the Dinner at Trimalchio's in Petronius.
Mimetic narrative is the antithesis of mythic in that it tends toward plotlessness. Its ultimate form is the "slice of life." Biography
and autobiography are both empirical forms of narrative. In biography, which is developed first, the historical impulse dominates;
in autobiography, the mimetic.

The *fictional* branch of narrative replaces allegiance to the
mythos with allegiance to the ideal. We can subdivide the im-

pulse toward fictional narrative into two main components also: the *romantic* and the *didactic*. The writer of fiction is set free from the bonds of tradition and the bonds of empiricism as well. His eye is not on the external world but on the audience, which he hopes to delight or instruct, giving it either what it wants or what he thinks it needs. While empirical narrative aims at one or another kind of truth, fictional narrative aims at either beauty or goodness. The world of romance is the ideal world, in which poetic justice prevails and all the arts and adornments of language are used to embellish the narrative. Where mimetic narrative aims at a psychological reproduction of mental process, romantic narrative presents thought in the form of rhetoric. As the general titles of the two great branches of narrative imply (empirical and fictional) they represent, within the world of narrative literature, an opposition akin to the scientific and the artistic approaches to ultimate truth. In the ancient world, Greek romance, with its alliance between the rhetorical and the erotic, typifies romantic narrative. In the movement from the *Odyssey* to the *Argonautica* we can see the epic becoming more literary and fictional, moving toward such pure romance as the *Aethiopica*. In a modern language such a progression as the *Chanson de Roland*, Chrétien's *Perceval*, and the *Grand Cyrus* reveals the same pattern of evolution.

The didactic subdivision of fiction we may call *fable*, a form which is ruled by an intellectual and moral impulse as romance is ruled by an esthetic one. The human intellect being what it is, fable tends toward brevity in narrative, and is inclined to lean heavily on romance for narrative articulation if the narrative artist has anything like a sustained flight in mind. Aesop's fables are typical of the form, but in its usual combination with romance Xenophon's *Cyropaedia* and the narrative allegories of the Middle Ages and Renaissance are major examples. So-called Menippean satire is fable combined with anti-romance, Lucian's *True History* beginning as a parody of Odysseus' adventures. Literary epic moves from romantic to didactic narrative in Vergil, who did not become Dante's guide in the *Commedia* by accident. Didactic and romantic narrative seek one another out for mutual support and for justification in the face of attacks such as Plato's attack on poetry in the *Republic*. Sidney's *Defense* of literature is made from the fictional side of the great division we have been considering. He defends literature as presenting an ideal, or "golden," world and as instructing through delight. But Fielding's account of his practice in his Preface to *Joseph Andrews* and elsewhere is made from the empirical side of the line, on the basis of his work's truth to general human nature, though he certainly intended to provide delight and instruction as well.

We have been considering the breakdown of the epic synthesis into two antithetical components. We must now consider briefly the new synthesis in narrative which has been the main development in post-Renaissance narrative literature. This was a gradual process, beginning at least as early as Boccaccio, but it is most obviously discernible in Europe during the seventeenth and eighteenth centuries. The new synthesis can be seen clearly in a writer like Cervantes, whose great work is an attempt to reconcile powerful empirical and fictional impulses. From the synthesis he effected, the novel emerges as a literary form. The novel is not the opposite of romance, as is usually maintained, but a product of the reunion of the empirical and fictional elements in narrative literature. Mimesis (which tends to short forms like the Character and "slice of life") and history (which can become too scientific and cease to be literature) combine in the novel with romance and fable, even as primitive legend, folktale, and sacred myth originally combined in the epic, to produce a great and synthetic literary form. There are signs that in the twentieth century the grand dialectic is about to begin again, and that the novel must yield its place to new forms just as the epic did in ancient times, for it is an unstable compound, inclining always to break down into its constituent elements. The disintegration of the novel is much too complicated to consider here in detail, but we can note that it is reflected in the extreme measures

taken by such as Joyce and Proust to counteract it, in the return
to romance of Isak Dinesen and Lawrence Durrell, in the reduction of naturalism to absurdity by Samuel Beckett, in the rise of
science fiction and the nightmare novels of Céline and Hawkes,
and even in the best-seller list, which tends to fragment into sociological narrative and spy-adventure tales, Mary McCarthy and
Ian Fleming inevitably reminding us of fiction's ancient heritage
from Theophrastian Character and Greek romance.

In its instability the novel partakes of the general nature of narrative. Poised between the direct speaker or singer of lyric and
the direct presentation of action in drama; between allegiance
to reality and to the ideal; it is capable of greater extremes than
other forms of literary art, but pays the price for this capability
in its capacity for imperfection. The least formal of disciplines,
it offers a domain too broad for any single work to conquer, and
it continually provokes literary compromise and subterfuge. The
greatest narratives are inevitably those in which the most is attempted. Narrative literature provides, as William Faulkner observed, opportunities for cautious success or glorious failure. It
has been, historically, the most various and changeable of literary
disciplines, which means that it has been the most alive. For all
its imperfections it has been — from the epic to the novel — the
most popular and influential kind of literature, seeking the widest
audience in its culture and being more responsive to extraliterary
influences than other kinds of literature. It is this various, complex,
and often contradictory nature of narrative art which we shall be
exploring in the following chapters.

2

The Oral Heritage
of Written Narrative

No one knows how long man has had speech. Language is probably even older than man himself, having been invented by some "missing link," a creature in the phylogenetic chain somewhere between man and the gibbon. It may have been as many as a million years ago that man first repeated an utterance which had given pleasure to himself or to someone else and thereby invented literature. In a sense, that was the beginning of Western narrative art. But we shall avoid tracing our subject to its origins. None of the assumptions that one is trained to bring to the study of narrative since Homer would be relevant to the appreciation of primitive literature. Even if the language should be intelligible, the works themselves, often concerned with the doings of only vaguely anthropomorphic creatures, produce bafflement or disgust in the untrained audience. Inevitably the critic seeks to impose such familiar categories as myth, legend, and folktale on a body of texts which defies classification in such terms.

In the strict etymological sense of the word, literature does not occur without writing. It is by definition the art of letters. Our ancestors used to proceed on the assumption that the fortuitous distinction between "written verbal art" and "oral verbal art," which is implied by the word *literature*, resulted in a useful separation of civilized, and therefore intelligible, narrative from primitive, and therefore unintelligible, narrative. In recent years we have learned differently. Oral and written narrative are formally distinct, and profoundly so, but they are not culturally distinct in any meaningful way. Milman Parry, one of the greatest authorities on orally composed heroic poetry, wrote, "Literature falls into two great parts not so much because there are two kinds of culture, but because there are two kinds of *form: one part of literature is oral, the other written.*" It will be our concern in this chapter to consider the heritage of written narrative in the orally composed narrative of ancient Greece and Northern Europe, emphasizing particularly the influence of oral narrative poetry on subsequent forms of written narrative. We shall examine some of the formal distinctions between oral and written narrative, insisting at every opportunity that these are formal literary distinctions rather than criteria for distinguishing between primitive and civilized cultures. We shall therefore use the word *literature* in a broad sense, without regard to its etymology, to mean all verbal art, both oral and written.

In an age such as ours, when the ability to read and write is common and the illiterate are the culturally and economically deprived, experience would seem to confirm an association of illiteracy with cultural impoverishment. But to generalize solely from our modern experience, to imagine that all unlettered individuals have in every age been the culturally deprived, is illogical and untrue. Our peculiar modern form of nearly universal literacy, which accounts for the opprobrium attached to the word *illiterate* as well as a goodly share of misinformation about the nature of language, is a product of the cultural and technological revolution of the Renaissance. Literate, a human being needs neither priest nor teacher. Books and the ability to read are gateways through which oppressed generations have found their freedom. In an age of literacy such as ours, books become symbols of freedom and truth. To burn or ban a book is to commit a sacrilege against humanity. It is a gesture hostile not only, or even mainly, to property, but rather to a symbol of the human spirit.

But not every age has thus idealized the inked shapes of the scribe's and the compositor's craft. In the *Phaedrus,* Socrates tells a story about the Egyptian god Thoth, who invented writing. Desiring to share his invention with the people, Thoth went before the god Thamus, the ruler over all Egypt. When he showed his letters to the King, claiming that they would increase both the memory and the wisdom of the Egyptians, Thamus replied:

O most ingenious Thoth, one man has the ability to develop a new skill, but another to judge whether it will be a curse or a blessing to its users. Now you, the father of letters, through your affection see in them the opposite of their true power. For this invention will cause those who use it to lose the learning in their minds by neglecting their memories; since, through this reliance on letters which are external and alien to the mind, they will lose their ability to recall things within themselves. You have invented not a medicine to strengthen memory but an inferior substitute for it. You are providing your students with a way of seeming wise without true wisdom; for they will appear to have learned without instruction; they will seem to know a good deal while they are really ignorant of many things; and they will become public nuisances, these men who look wise but lack wisdom.

The sanctity of the printed word in our culture has at times allowed the worst of Socrates' fears to be realized. Words in their printed forms have become more real for us than either the sounds on the lips of living men or the concepts they represent. Books as mere physical objects sometimes surpass wisdom in the world's esteem. Any lie or outrage which takes on the dignity of print becomes a thousandfold more menacing. And forgetfulness within themselves has robbed literate people of the ability even to conceive of the production of great literature by unlettered poets and story-tellers. It is inconceivable to us that the ancient Greeks would have permitted a writing system such as the Minoan Linear B, found in the ruins of the royal palace at Knossos and at Pylos, to remain the monopoly of servants and bookkeepers, scorned by poets and teachers alike. But the evidence seems to indicate that Linear B, antedating the composition of the Homeric epics by at least five hundred years, played no part in the literary or educa-

tional life of the Mycenean Greeks, a fact which accounts in part
for its eventual abandonment by them. The introduction, again by
clerks, of the Phoenician alphabet onto the mainland of Greece is
usually dated in the eighth century. Although it had seemed inconceivable until it was conclusively demonstrated by Milman
Parry, we now know that the composition of the Homeric epics
occurred long before the widespread use of writing in Greece for
anything like its modern purposes.

Parry's demonstration of the oral composition of the *Iliad* and
Odyssey consisted of two parts, both confirming the hypothesis
that orally composed literature is distinguishable from written
literature on the basis of its form rather than its content. Starting
with the written texts of the Homeric poems as they have come
down to us, Parry noticed that the traditional epithets and locutions, which have to a minor extent always constituted an element
of the "epic style" in subsequent Western tradition, were invariably used by Homer in the same metrical and semantic situations.
These traditional elements of the Homeric diction, in quantity and
quality vastly richer than in the works of later poets, he called
formulas. He defined the formula as "a group of words which is
regularly employed under the same metrical conditions to express
a given essential idea." Such fixed epithets as "son of Atreus"
and "king of men" for Agamemnon, or "of the glancing helmet"
for Hector, or "wine-dark," "loudly resounding," and "echoing"
for the sea, have always been recognized as characteristic of
Homer's style, and their effect has been imitated by writers of
literary epics from Apollonius onward. However, not until Parry
discovered that the whole Homeric corpus, about 27,000 hex-
ameter lines, was entirely formulaic did critics realize that what
had all along appeared to be only a superficial stylistic feature was
in fact inescapable evidence that the *Iliad* and *Odyssey* were
orally composed. Ninety per cent of the first fifteen lines of the
Iliad, for example, is demonstrably formulaic; that is, investigators
have matched it with identical groups of words in the same metrical environments elsewhere in the Homeric corpus. As far as we
know, the percentage for any given passage of Homer will be

about the same. In the writings of no known literary poet is the percentage of verbatim repeats even in this vicinity. Quite the contrary: literary poets strive to make each line unique, reserving repeated phrases for very special rhetorical effects.

The second part of Parry's demonstration was in some ways even more fruitful than the first. In order to prove the converse of his first proposition, that a highly formulaic poetic diction is evidence of oral composition, he set about showing that oral poets do not compose except with formulas. They improvise, using the conventional formulas in their poetic tradition as a basis for forming metrically and semantically appropriate lines. In a study of present-day South Slavic oral epic in Yugoslavia, he found both Christian and Moslem singers who, to the accompaniment of a one-stringed musical instrument called the *gusle,* could compose epic poems approaching the *Iliad* and *Odyssey* in length, complexity, and literary interest. The singers themselves think that they are capable of repeating a whole epic verbatim, and take pride in their memory of what they must conceive to be a kind of fixed "oral text." When Parry took down the same song twice from the same singer, however, he discovered that exact correspondences between two performances were rare. Individual lines and episodes were composed differently in the two versions, but they both used the same formulas. On the level of line formation, the presence of traditional formulas, not line-for-line similarity between two texts, invariably identified an oral composition.

While Parry's discoveries do provide a much firmer basis for making educated guesses, they cannot give final answers to all of our questions about Homer. From his investigations in Yugoslavia and from reports of orally composed epic in other parts of the world we are able to reformulate the question of Homer's identity, for example, though we can still not answer it with certainty. The individual singers in a tradition of oral poetic narrative are as important as the individual poets in a tradition of written narrative, but the role of the singer is vastly different from that of the poet.

The singer is utterly dependent upon his tradition. The plots that he learns, the various episodes with which he elaborates them, and even the phrases out of which he constructs his lines are traditional, and in the broadest sense "formulaic." He neither composes nor memorizes a fixed text. Each performance is a separate act of creation. Until he actually sings a narrative, that song does not exist, except as a potential song among infinitely many others in the abstract apparatus of the singer's tradition. Conversely, when the song is over it has ceased to exist. Only to the extent that the singer himself or some member of his audience learns something new about the tradition during the course of a performance can that individual song affect the tradition and thereby take on a slight aspect of permanence in the memories of those who heard it.

Probably because they are manifestations of a tradition rather than the inventions of an individual brain, most of the orally composed narrative poems that have been preserved in written texts have not, even traditionally, been associated with the names of individual poets. The attribution of the *Iliad* and the *Odyssey* to Homer, or of the Old Icelandic *Poetic Edda* to Sæmundur the Wise, much as it must now be qualified by our knowledge of oral tradition, is exceptional. The runic signatures of Cynewulf, integrally worked into the texts of apparently oral Anglo-Saxon narratives, provide an especially knotty problem for scholars. They should probably be taken as the sign either of a scribe or of an oral poet who was familiar with both writing and the bookish attitudes toward authorship which come so naturally to literate men but which must be quite incomprehensible to oral poets. The fact remains that the Cynewulfian narratives, whatever the origin of the signatures may be, are as highly formulaic and traditional in their rhetoric as *Beowulf*. Whoever Cynewulf may have been, the poems associated with his name were composed out of the common Anglo-Saxon oral tradition and cannot represent the work of an individual poet in anything like the modern sense. Therefore, whether for convenience, as in the case of Homer and Cynewulf, or out of respect for tradition, as in the case of *Sæmundar*

Edda, we use the name of an individual poet to designate the authorship of an orally composed narrative, we should conceive of his role as singer or performer as coming closer than the modern concept of "authorship" to describing the man behind the poem.

The idea that a poetic narrative could have been "corrupted" in the process of oral transmission is based on a common misconception of the workings of oral tradition. If an orally composed poem such as the Old Icelandic *Völuspá* is obscure, the difficulty must be attributed either to an inferior performance or, what is more likely, to corruption in the process of manuscript transmission. An oral performance may be indifferent, but it will not be obscure or "textually corrupt." On the other hand, a great singer, one who has spent many years in perfecting his art, can surpass any performance he has ever heard. Even if he learns a story through an inferior performance, he can bring his mastery of the tradition to the singing of a song many times longer and more skillfully wrought than the one from which he learned the basic plot and the names of the characters. In this case, we should say that a poem had been "perfected" in the process of oral transmission if such a statement were not just as erroneous as the idea of textual corruption. It would imply that an entity, a song, had been transmitted, and such is not the case in an oral tradition. We can speak of the elements of the song — the plot, the episodes, the conception of character, the knowledge of historical events, the traditional motifs, the diction — as being transmitted, but we cannot speak of the oral transmission of the song itself.

We shall perhaps come closest to the usual conception of the identity of Homer, while doing the least violence to the facts of oral composition, if we think of him as being the greatest of many generations of Greek epic singers, a master of his art who in the nature of things could not surpass his tradition, but who created the best performances of which his tradition was capable. The greatness of Homer is the greatness of his tradition. The breadth of his knowledge and sympathy, the objectivity and accuracy of his representation of actual men and events, the sureness of both his piety and his satire are the achievements of an ancient Greek epic tradition named "Homer," not of a single poet limited to his own observation and memory. The oral poet's rapport with his literary culture is total. Opportunities for the kind of originality and individual expression sought in written literature are minimal. The oral singer illustrates the extremest form of the individual talent at the service of the tradition, also perhaps the extremest form of the tradition at the service of the individual talent. The two are simply aspects of the same entity. Without songs the tradition would die; without the tradition there would be no songs.

And yet, the tradition can change. It can accommodate itself — slowly, to be sure — to changes in the external cultural and physical world which its songs represent and even to changes in the linguistic forms of which its songs are made. The mixture of archaisms and regional dialect forms in the basically Ionic Homeric texts is a compromise between the most archaic Arcadian-Cypriot and Ionic forms, which the tradition could not completely dispense with in its movement to mainland Greece, and later Attic forms, which the tradition employed in an effort to remain contemporary and readily intelligible. A parallel linguistic mixture characterizes the text of *Beowulf*, an orally composed Old English epic whose tradition looks back to the cultural ascendency of Mercia, though the basic linguistic matrix of the poem is later West Saxon.

In addition to the gradual substitution, where it is possible, of new linguistic forms for older ones, an oral poetic tradition is also capable of generating new formulas by analogy with older ones. For example, an Anglo-Saxon half-line formula used to describe "the joy of noble retainers" is *eorla dream*. With the gradual accommodation to Christian themes and stories, the tradition could generate the new formula *engla dream*, "the joy of angels," on the pattern of the old one. In the somewhat technical language used by investigators of the diction of orally composed poetry, the two formulas *eorla dream* and *engla dream* are said to constitute a "formula pattern," or "formulaic system." Parry defined the formulaic system as "a group of phrases which are enough alike in thought and words to leave no doubt that the poet who used them knew them not only as single formulas, but also as formulas of a certain type." The existence of such abstract systems, or patterns, allows for a gradual evolution in the traditional diction. Even more significant is the role played by formula patterns in the individual singer's art. Albert B. Lord, whose book *The Singer of Tales* is a continuation and elaboration of Parry's work in Yugoslavia and his theory of the oral composition of Homeric epic, believes that

> the fundamental element in constructing lines is the basic formula pattern. There is some justification for saying that the particular formula itself is important to the singer only up to the time when it has planted in his mind its basic mold. When this point is reached, the singer depends less and less on learning formulas and more and more on the process of substituting other words in the formula patterns. . . . This will be the whole basis of his art.

On the level of line formation, then, the basic entities of an oral poetic tradition will not be the fixed formulas (on the basis of which, however, we can positively identify the poetry as orally composed). They will be instead the abstract patterns in accordance with which singers can produce new phrases. On this level the tradition is seen to consist rather of a "grammar" than of a set of fixed elements. It is a grammar superimposed on the normal grammar of the spoken language; but like that grammar it is learned below the level of consciousness and carries with it profound restrictions on both the apprehension and the conceptualization of the external world. Evolution of thought has to take place within the double set of restrictions imposed by linguistic structure as it is ordinarily conceived and by the "grammar" of the traditional wisdom. Eric A. Havelock has convincingly argued that Plato's assault on the poets in the *Republic* was a revolutionary attempt to free Greek thought, once and for all, from the tyranny of the "grammar" of the oral tradition.

Forming metrical and intelligible lines is not the oral poet's only challenge. He must also to a certain extent "make up" his story as he goes along. Less is known about the larger elements in the "morphology" of orally composed narrative poetry than about the abstract formula patterns. Parry and Lord have pointed out the existence of what they call traditional "themes" in the South Slavic and Greek oral epic. And similar analyses have been made of traditional thematic elements in Anglo-Saxon, Old Icelandic, Old French, and Finnish oral narrative poetry as well. Lord has defined the "themes" of oral poetry as "groups of ideas regularly used in telling a tale in the formulaic style of traditional song." The several stereotyped descriptions in the *Odyssey* of a visitor being welcomed by a hospitable host constitute an oral "theme" in Lord's sense of the term. Descriptions of the *eorla dream* in Germanic oral narrative, in which the band of noble retainers gathers about the king to feast and drink and boast, constitute such a "theme" in that tradition. The great practical difficulty with the term "theme" to denote a formal element in the stylistic apparatus of oral narrative poetry is that the same term is used in diverse and sometimes quite contradictory ways in general literary criticism.

As an alternative to this specialized use of the term "theme" in the analysis of orally composed poetry, we propose the word *topos,* a technical term from Greek rhetoric which has been given currency in literary scholarship by Ernst Robert Curtius in his *European Literature and the Latin Middle Ages.* We do not wish to imply that necessary historical connections exist between the actual *topoi* used by Greek rhetoricians and the elements in ancient Greek epic which are called "themes" by Parry and Lord, but rather that from a structural point of view the somewhat stereotyped rhetorical elements such as the *locus amoenus* (description of an ideal landscape) and *puer senex* (praising a young man by attributing an old man's wisdom to him) are similar enough to the stereotyped groups of ideas in orally composed narrative poetry to warrant the same descriptive term.

A *topos*, whether it occurs in an oral narrative or a written one, is a traditional image. It is not identifiable or even analyzable on the basis of either the formulas or the uniquely arranged words a poet might use to construct it, but rather on the basis of the image to which the words refer. We will postpone a complete discussion of the thematic analysis of narrative images until Chapter 4. Briefly, it may be said here that insofar as a *topos* refers to the external world its meaning is a *motif;* insofar as it refers to the world of disembodied ideas and concepts its meaning is a *theme*. Traditional *topoi* consist, then, of two elements: a traditional motif, such as the hero's descent into the underworld, which may be extremely durable historically; and a traditional theme, such as the search for wisdom or the harrowing of hell, which may be much more subject to gradual change or replacement in the course of time. The *topoi* of oral narratives are identifiable on the basis of their consistent association of a given motif with a given theme. In written narrative, on the other hand, the relationship of motif and theme, even in a conventional *topos,* is subject to the poet's manipulation. The thematic content of the *topoi* of ancient narrative is, of course, extremely difficult to analyze. The Homeric *topoi,* like those of the Germanic oral poetic tradition, were at one time closely associated with religious ritual, and their thematic content may therefore still be vaguely sacred, even though the narrative is remarkably free of direct references to cult.

The *topoi* of oral narrative poetry often occur in patterned sequences, one *topos* selecting another, or even a whole series of them selecting another whole series. As one example of such patterning in the *Odyssey,* Lord has shown that the testing of the Ithacans upon the return of Odysseus is represented by the repetition of a pattern of *topoi* whose motifs are "abuse," "rebuke," and "recognition." The theme underlying this pattern of motifs is "that the resurrected god in disguise is rejected by the unworthy, who cannot recognize him." The pattern begins in Book XVII when the *abuse* of Odysseus by Melanthius is followed by the *rebuke* by Eumaeus and the *recognition* by the dog Argus. Later, abuse is administered by Antinous, Eurymachus, and Ctesippus; rebukes are administered by the suitors and by Telemachus; and recognition takes place in the boxing match with Irus, the scene with Eurycleia, and the trial of the bow. Such patterns suggest that structural elements which are intermediate in size between single *topoi* and whole songs may govern the arrangements of individual *topoi*. We might use the term *myth* for such an articulated sequence of *topoi*. Like the *topos* on one hand and the whole song on the other, the myth consists of two basic aspects of narrative meaning: the *representation* of the external world (motif) and the *illustration* of what we can think of as ideas and concepts (theme).

The representational aspect of the myth is *plot;* its illustrative aspect, like that of the *topos* and whole song, is *theme*. The oral singer must develop simultaneously both aspects of the myths he incorporates into his song. When oral poetic narrative breaks down with the advent of literacy in the modern sense, or as a result of some other kind of radical cultural differentiation, the illustrative aspect of myth is developed in allegory and in discursive philosophical writing. The representational aspect of myth is then developed in history and other forms of empirical narrative.

The traditional nature of the union of plot and theme that characterizes oral narrative poetry is only one aspect of the epic synthesis. Epic also stands midway between sacred myth, a story whose events take place entirely outside of the profane world of historical men and events, and secular narrative, a story whose events take place entirely within the profane world of historical men and events, or within a fictional world whose operation is governed by the same laws as those that govern the actual world. Perhaps the easiest way to get some feeling for the complex synthesis achieved by the oral epic is to view it as the sole literary production of an undifferentiated culture. This is bound to be a great oversimplification, but such a view does justice to the role of oral epic in preserving a culture's most cherished religious, political, and ethical values, as well as preserving a traditional poetic "grammar," in terms of which new experiences will be apprehended and contemplated. Four hundred years after the gradual process of establishing a canonical Homeric text had begun, Plato recognized the monolithic structure of the Homeric *paideia* as the chief enemy to the advancement of thought. As long as Homer remained the only teacher of every subject, allegorical interpretation of his "hidden meaning" was the only avenue open to philosophical speculation.

We know next to nothing about the actual process through which the Homeric epic achieved the written form in which it has been transmitted to us. A great deal of evidence suggests that the Greek epic tradition contained most of the traditional stories that have survived from later ages in non-epic, mainly dramatic, form. Some non-Homeric epic performances even reached written form before dropping from sight. From the now lost *Chrestomathy* of Eutychius Proclus of Sicca, which has been summarized by Photius (c. 820–891) and others, we learn the names, approximate length (expressed in numbers of lines or books), and subject matter of the epics that were still available to the Alexandrian Greeks in written texts. None of these texts was so long as the *Iliad* or the *Odyssey*, a fact which seems to indicate special circumstances of both performance and transcription in the case of the Homeric texts.

The uses of writing in Greece during the eighth, seventh, and sixth centuries must have been vastly different from our present-day uses of it. The existence of engraved tablets and stones, whether in seventh-century Greece or in Northern Europe twelve hundred years later, does not of itself point to a system of education or a literary culture based on writing. Written documents, even telegrams, are mentioned often enough in the Yugoslav epics to demonstrate that an oral literary tradition can survive in close proximity to writing used for other purposes. If we are to imagine the transcription of even a crude ancestor of the traditional Homeric text from oral dictation, we must assume a familiarity with the use of letters and writing that could have taken centuries to achieve. The mere introduction of writing into one area of a culture does not result in anything approaching "literacy" in the modern sense. For that we need an established tradition of education based upon letters — an idea that would have struck even the seventh-century Greek mind as outrageous.

Lord's experience in Yugoslavia suggests that a number of alternatives are available for the transcription of oral narrative into writing, nearly all of which result in inferior representations of live oral performances. If the singer dictates to a scribe, or if he himself learns to write and dictates to himself, he must perform much more slowly than he normally does. Under such circumstances it is easy for him to lose both the beat and the chain of his thought. Only when the singer is willing to dictate slowly and patiently, to a scribe who is thoroughly familiar with the tradition, one who can stop and ask him to repeat a line that has gone wrong, will the written text be superior to an actual performance. Some special circumstance would have to motivate such an arduous effort on the parts of both singer and scribe, for the resulting text could be of no use to the singer. It would have to be made at the request of a collector. Some such method of production is what we are obliged to conceive as the source of the original Homeric written texts.

When an oral performance has been reduced to writing by its two "authors," the performer and the scribe, and has entered into a quasi-literary tradition, the genuine oral tradition continues unaffected. However, it may eventually be challenged by a spurious, pseudo-"oral tradition" arising out of the newly established textual tradition. A new kind of professional entertainer, one who merely memorizes written texts and goes about reciting them, can begin to compete with the genuine singer. When the term "oral tradition" is misapplied by literary scholars it usually refers to this kind of oral recitation of a fixed literary text which has been composed in the modern way with pen and paper. The method of composition, not the mode of presentation, distinguishes the genuine oral tradition from the written. In his experience in Yugoslavia, Lord had no difficulty in distinguishing genuine oral composition from mere oral recitation of a written text. One is formulaic, the other is not.

A "transitional text," one that represents a combination of oral and written composition, does not seem to be a possibility, much as some Homerists, medievalists, and others (including ourselves!) would like to believe in it. All the evidence of direct observation of living traditions points to the conclusion that even if the poet does his own writing, he will apparently compose in either the traditional oral-formulaic way (exhibiting all the hallmarks of oral composition) or in the literary way (exhibiting the originality of thought and phrase that characterizes literary composition). What does seem to be a distinct possibility, however, and constitutes the best guess about the transmission of the Homeric text, is that the transcription of genuine oral performances will combine with the oral recitation of the resulting written texts to develop gradually into a quasi-literary tradition. If this happens, the written texts may gain ascendancy over the genuine oral tradition, receiving the attention of the best minds, both of the scribes and the performers. In the face of spreading literacy and formal, academic instruction in the meaning of the authoritative text, the genuine oral tradition slowly drifts down the cultural scale. In the meantime, new, genuinely written, literary forms begin to emerge out of a combination of the old oral tradition with the new academic tradition.

Speculation about the process in which the Homeric epic achieved its traditional written form probably ought not to depend entirely upon our knowledge of analogous situations in present-day Yugoslavia or in Northern Europe during the Middle Ages. It is difficult to imagine that a foreign written tradition could have exercised anything like the terrific pressure and potential influence on Greek oral epic that written Christian culture brought to bear on native oral traditions elsewhere in Europe. The Greek transition must have been gradual, evolving from

within the dominant literary culture, one form in a sense volun-
tarily giving over to the other. Elsewhere in Europe, however,
oral traditions have either been quickly suppressed by a dominant
alien written tradition or have been driven underground, to the
sod huts and smoky chimney corners of an ignorant and impotent
peasantry. The cultural alternatives available to a Homeric singer
of seventh-century Greece on one hand, and to a Bosnian or
Karelian singer of the nineteenth century on the other, are hardly
comparable. The ancient Greek was singing-master to princes,
but the others performed before audiences of cultural illiterates,
in the full, terrible, modern sense of that word.

Old Testament texts bear many evidences of descent from oral
tradition, and we may perhaps imagine a gradual, centuries-long
transition from oral to written narrative among the ancient He-
brews analogous to the one we posit for the Greeks. But when
these two mighty cultural streams merged, they swept all in
Europe before them. They brought literacy and a reverence for
the authoritative text. Above all, in the case of the Hebrew strain,
it was an Authoritative Text that commanded absolute devotion.
Alcuin, an English scholar of the ninth century who was the out-
standing figure in the revival of classical letters in the court of
Charlemagne, succinctly expressed the attitude of the Church
toward pagan song. When he learned that the monks at the North-
umbrian abbey of Lindisfarne were entertaining themselves with
songs about the Germanic hero Ingeld he inquired sarcastically of
them, "What has Ingeld to do with Christ?" Alcuin's cry echoes
throughout the Christian Middle Ages.

More to our purpose is a slightly earlier account of the confrontation of the two cultures in Anglo-Saxon Northumbria. It is the
Venerable Bede's story in *The Ecclesiastical History of the English People* of the poet Cædmon, which F. P. Magoun, Jr. has
called "the case history of an Anglo-Saxon oral singer." Cædmon
is said to have composed many English narrative poems on the
basis of sacred doctrines and narratives expounded to him by the
monks of Whitby during the rule of the Abbess Hild (658–680).
The most striking feature of Bede's account of Cædmon is the

story of the miracle through which the simple, secular, middle-aged man received the gift of narrative song. Until an angel appeared to him in a dream, with the request that he sing the creation of the world, Cædmon had been unable to compose poetry in public. On the festive occasions when the harp passed from hand to hand, with everyone expected to take his turn singing, Cædmon went home. The miracle of the dream is one explanation for the remarkable ability of a man late in life to use thoroughly traditional oral formulas in songs which are devoted exclusively to Christian teaching. Of Cædmon's singing Bede says that he never composed "any sort of trivial or useless poem; but only those which concerned religion suited his pious tongue." Another explanation for Cædmon's use of traditional Anglo-Saxon formula patterns in his *Hymn* and in the surviving Anglo-Saxon paraphrases of Genesis and Exodus (if they really do represent his performances) is that he learned and practiced his art in private, postponing his public debut until he had found a way of devoting his song to the service of God.

Another story which tradition links with the miracle of Cædmon's dream is contained in a mysterious Latin *Praefatio* and *Versus* which modern scholarship associates with the Old Saxon poems *Heliand* and *Genesis*. Dating from about the tenth century, but surviving only in the second edition of Matthias Flacius' *Catalogus Testium Veritatis* (1562), these are brief and contradictory accounts (1) of the command of Charlemagne's son, the Frankish Emperor Louis the Pious (reigned 814–840), that "a certain man of the Saxon nation, who among his own people was thought to be a distinguished poet, undertake to make a poetic translation of the Old and New Testaments into the German language, so that the sacred lesson of the divine teachings might be accessible not only to the literate but to the illiterate as well"; and (2) "that the same poet, while he was still entirely unacquainted with that art, was urged in his sleep to adapt the precepts of the sacred law to a poem in the meter appropriate to his own [Saxon] language."

These stories have in common the references to a native tradi-

tion of oral narrative which is accommodated not only to a culture of books, but to a culture of the Book. For a singer like
Cædmon or the anonymous Saxon *vates* of the *Praefatio* the problem was not only one of dictating to scribes. It was mainly the
problem of using the traditional formulas and *topoi* to convey
utterly new plots and ideas. A more formulaic poem than *Heliand*
can hardly be imagined. Nearly every verse consists of formulas
or formula patterns found either elsewhere in the poem itself or in
the Anglo-Saxon poetic corpus. Its traditional character is not
restricted to formulaic composition. It employs many of the traditional motifs found in such secular poems as *Beowulf*. These motifs point unmistakably to the recent emergence of the Old Saxon
oral tradition from a heroic culture quite unlike that of the New
Testament narratives on which the plot of the *Heliand* is ultimately based. It is equally clear, however, that the Saxon singer
was closely in touch with medieval Christian culture. When due
allowance is made for traditional formulas and motifs, his narrative is a close paraphrase of such works as the pseudo-Tatian
harmony of the Gospels and the commentaries of Hrabanus Maurus on Matthew, Bede on Luke and Mark, and Alcuin on John.

Strong traces of both oral composition and a heroic culture
characterize the poems of the thirteenth-century Old Icelandic
Poetic Edda, the Old High German *Lay of Hildebrand*, such
Anglo-Saxon poems as *Waldere, Deor, Widsith*, and the *Finns-
burg Fragment*, and even the heroic ballads of the Faroe Islands,
which were not taken down in writing until the last century. But
for a reflection of the Germanic oral tradition as it must have
flourished before the coming of the Book, we can do little better
than to consider the Anglo-Saxon *Beowulf*. The poem exists in
only one manuscript, written by two scribes about the end of the
tenth century. Like all the other poems just mentioned, except
the Faroese ballads, *Beowulf* probably does not represent a transcription directly from an oral performance. Most scholars have
regarded its variant linguistic forms and spellings as evidence of
a textual tradition of up to two and a half centuries, thus placing

its composition in the early decades of the eighth century. Of the oral composition of *Beowulf* there can no longer be a reasonable doubt. Its diction is demonstrably formulaic, and its *topoi* are shared by similar poems in Old English and the other Germanic languages.

While it is abundantly clear that oral singers are capable of learning their stories and themes from books, at least through literate intermediaries, there is relatively little evidence of book learning in *Beowulf*. Its content as well as its style seems to reflect the existence of a highly developed oral epic in Germanic antiquity. We shall never know just how highly developed this tradition was or what might have become of it if left to its own devices. The invading Roman-Christian culture simply overwhelmed it. We must guard against the temptation to take for granted that an epic tradition is characteristic of a primitive people, for this is very far from being the truth. We have seen that in the case of the relatively unmolested Greeks the epic was the last stage before the advent of an essentially modern literary and philosophical culture. Evidence of other sorts, such as splendid weapons and ships and advanced political and legal institutions, shows the pagan Northern Europeans to have been approaching a cultural development analogous to that of the Greeks of the eighth century. When Christianity entered Northern Europe in the centuries between A.D. 400 and 1000, it encountered a literary culture that had achieved the epic synthesis of myth and mimesis and was at the point of the sort of differentiation which leads to separate collections of laws, genealogies, myths, religious rituals, and secular narrative fictions.

The *Beowulf* singer's concern for the larger social and political consequences of Danish relations with the Frisians and Heatho-Bards, or for the ethical requirements of a good king, are characteristic of his epic tradition. They are to be found in *The Wanderer*, *Widsith*, and *Deor*, as well as in poems from the Eddic anthology. Much later, in romances like *Sir Gawain and the Green Knight* and countless others dealing with the court of Arthur, we may find political and ethical themes, but with less bearing on the actualities of a particular time and place, less relevance to active political life. In the epic, the preservation of an ordered society is the highest good and the goal toward which the hero's physical and intellectual discipline is bent. And the epic society tends to be a particular one, whose remains can be sifted by present-day archaeologists. The elegiac tone of *Beowulf* is only partly a consequence of the hero's death in defending his society against the ravages of a supernatural enemy. It is due in larger measure to our knowledge that Beowulf's strength and wisdom have been spent in vain. They have not been perpetuated among the Danes and Geats. The societies he has saved will not rescue themselves from the purely social evils that are fated to destroy them.

Like Homer, the *Beowulf* poet describes an oral singer in action. The morning after Beowulf has defeated Grendel in Heorot, the Danes come to view the bloody arm and to visit the blood-stained mere into which Grendel has disappeared. As part of their joyous celebration, a singer, who knows many old songs, composes a new one about Beowulf's deed, "fluently knitting his words together." The singer goes on to tell of Sigemund the Dragon Slayer and of Heremod, a Danish king whose bad behavior was the opposite of Beowulf's and Sigemund's. This short passage (867b–915b) is instructive in showing both how the values preserved in the myths of an oral tradition may be summoned up as a guide for comprehending the present event and how the present event is thereby incorporated into the tradition. By associating the motif of Beowulf's defeat of Grendel with that of Sigemund's slaying the dragon, the singer is making a thematic statement about the significance of Beowulf's own encounter with a dragon at the end of the poem. The dragon fight can, at least in one sense, be understood as a recapitulation of the Grendel episode, with which Sigemund had already been cited as a parallel.

Again like the Homeric epics, *Beowulf* conveys through its traditional diction and its historical allusions the impression of itself being the kind of poem that would have been sung in the aristocratic society it describes. We feel, in other words, that a gathering of peasants or of pious monks, who would enjoy a saint's life or a ballad about their social and spiritual betters, would not be a fitting audience for *Beowulf*. It is anything but an example of the *cantilenae* or *carmina rustica* of which we hear so much from Latin writers describing Germanic culture. If our intuition is right, *Beowulf* represents instead the genuine oral tradition in its highest cultural role, the education of princes. This is a role that the tradition could not have played for many generations after the conversion of England to Christianity and the establishment of a book culture as the basis for aristocratic education. It argues for the early composition of the poem.

If he read it, or heard it recited, King Alfred could not have responded to *Beowulf* without some traces of the patronizing nostalgia we inevitably feel for the relics of a noble world long lost. Alfred's attitude toward literacy and books was entirely modern. It was in his estimation the great cultural scandal of his day that so few men could read, and he did not have in mind the cultivation of schools and libraries for the perpetuation of the likes of *Beowulf*. History, law, philosophy, and Holy Scripture were his curriculum. No matter how pleased he may have been to while away his idle hours in the company of singers, learning the rudiments of their art, Alfred's national policy was one that spelled the doom of oral literature. It is more for his courage in breaking with the ancient traditions than his effort to preserve them that Alfred deserves his epithet "the Great."

An Old French oral narrative art, represented most notably by the *Chanson de Roland*, seems to have been more congenial to books and acceptable to contemporary Christian culture than was the Anglo-Saxon. The *Roland* was composed at least three hundred years later than *Beowulf*, and yet we feel in its case too that it depicts approximately the kind of aristocratic and heroic culture that its own composition around the year 1100 was the product of. The persistent medieval tradition that a version of the *Chanson de Roland* was sung by the *jongleur* Taillefer to encourage

the Norman troops before the Battle of Hastings accords with
numerous similar accounts of the rhetorical function of heroic
poetry on the field of battle. That the Old French epic tradition
should have flourished so late, lasting well into the high Middle
Ages, which we ordinarily associate with the romance and the
literary revolution wrought by it and the Provençal lyric, attests
to the durability of a well-founded tradition and to its flexibility.
In an investigation of the formula patterns and *topoi* of several
Old French *chansons de geste*, S. G. Nichols, Jr., has concluded
that the text of the *Chanson de Roland* was formed in the convention of "oral, formulaic, and traditional diction."

Only the achievement of a cultural rapprochement more radical than seems to have been possible in the Germanic North is
sufficient to explain what Gaston Paris called an "esprit ger-
manique dans une forme romane" in the Old French epic tradition. Charlemagne (reigned 768–814), like his son Louis the
Pious, was, according to his biographer Einhard, active in bringing the fruits of Latin literary technology to his Germanic subjects. In the *Vita Caroli Magni*, Einhard records that Charlemagne
had the unwritten laws of the Saxons, Frisians, and Thuringians
compiled and reduced to writing. More significantly, he also "had
the old rude songs that celebrate the deeds and wars of the ancient kings written out for transmission to posterity." Above all, he
maintained the union in one fairly stable nation of the Germanic-
speaking Franks and Saxons on one side of the Rhine with the French-
speaking peoples on the other, thus encouraging the diffusion across
linguistic barriers of both thematic and formal elements from the
Germanic to the Romance oral epic tradition. While the Germanic
tradition was being put to the service of the Church and was being
recorded in writing for (a presumably literate) posterity, the Romance
epic tradition managed to survive and flourish in the new world
created by Charlemagne.

By the eleventh century, the Northmen who conquered England were speaking French. The old Germanic genius for military
and political organization was being revitalized in Romance-

speaking Europe under fourth- and fifth-generation Germanic leaders, a renewal of heroic activity in an alien land which was generating a renewal of heroic tradition in an alien tongue. Nothing can better reveal the ability of the Old French epic tradition to reflect the changing times than its treatment of the story of the death of Roland. Einhard's account of the Gascon attack in 778 on Charlemagne's rearguard high in the Pyrenees comes as a minor interlude between his descriptions of the operations against the Saxons in the North and the Italians in the South. There is no suggestion that the Basque-speaking Gascons were motivated by anything other than a fierce love of their own independence and resentment of the invasion of their territory by the Franks. After the engagement in which fell "Eggihard the King's steward, Anselm the Count Palatine, and Roland the Governor of the March of Brittany, with very many others," Einhard states explicitly that no punitive action could be undertaken against the Gascons. Lightly clad and operating on familiar ground, they dispersed under the cover of darkness with their rich spoil from the Frankish baggage train before the heavily armed Franks could maneuver.

In the interval between the eighth and eleventh centuries this episode took on the now familiar shape. The Basques and the Franks became the Saracens and the Christians. The two forces are engaged in a world war, with the survival of an essentially eleventh-century French nation and an eleventh-century Church Militant at stake. Thus the prosaic historical account is vastly expanded in its political and social implications to reflect the realities of the Europe of the First Crusade, a Europe in transition from a collection of eighth-century tribal communities to the Europe of modern times. Simultaneously, the historical account is contracted in scope as well. The ability of an epic tradition to reflect more or less accurately the major facts and values of a contemporary world will account for the expansion. The epic conception of heroic character requires the contraction. Roland is elevated from the least to the most important of the personages

named at the encounter, and the whole issue between the two
vast forces is focused directly on him.

Without very special precautions, however, it will be misleading simply to compare the historical accounts of the death of
Roland with the poetic one. Most investigators of medieval epic
understand the relevant entities in their researches to be texts —
texts of folktales, fertility myths, historical chronicles, patristic
theology, and so on. Admittedly such texts have in their favor as
evidence the excellent virtue of their palpable existence. But written texts cannot be granted a high degree of relevance in the
study of oral tradition. At least they cannot be relied upon in the
ordinary way. It is necessary to use both texts and our knowledge
of actual historical events (not just contemporary accounts of
them) to reconstruct as well as we can the nature of the oral
tradition. It was the Old French oral tradition which produced
the *Roland* (or a version of it that stands behind the Oxford text
in the manner outlined earlier in the instances of *Beowulf* and the
Homeric epics). If we should begin in the customary way, by
considering an historical account of an event, the epic treatment
of it will seem to involve the intrusion of imaginative distortion
and contamination with obviously non-historical myths and *topoi*.
If, on the other hand, we begin by reconstructing as clear a conception as possible of the oral tradition, we can see the historical
event as intruding upon the traditional stock of myths and *topoi*,
as requiring some sort of readjustment in the tradition to accommodate it, rather than the other way about. A prototype of Beowulf doubtless existed in the Anglo-Saxon epic tradition before
the events of sixth-century Denmark and Gotland were associated
with him. And the Old French epic tradition had prototypes of
Roland to whom the events of history were attracted in the process of evolving the *Chanson de Roland*.

The relevant question, therefore, in analyzing the relationship
of any oral poetic narrative to history is the extent to which traditional myths and *topoi* may have been replaced with the representation of unique events in time (insofar as we may be able to

reconstruct those events by archeological and literary inferences). If the replacement is thoroughgoing, the tradition cannot be called epic: it has moved instead toward metrical chronicle. If there is no recognizable replacement at all, the tradition will be either sacred myth or (if the *topoi* are apparently emptied of either ritual or allegorical content) romance. In addition to replacing some traditional myths and *topoi* with the representation of historical events, the oral epic replaces others with the representation of a more generalized hypothetical actuality. We find men of recognizable psychological and social types acting in accordance with the same natural laws as those governing the actions of real men.

It will not do, therefore, to analyze poems like *Beowulf* as though they resulted from an intrusion of folktale and fertility myth on psychology and history. Nor, when speaking of individual poems, can the history and psychology be regarded as intruders either. It is the oral tradition, not the individual poem, which takes them up. Any single oral performance or text is both generated by and restricted by the "grammar" of its tradition and will reflect only a selection from the infinite possibilities that are the tradition itself. When we do not posit pure myth or pure mimesis as the norm, it becomes just as natural that medieval traditional poetic narratives contained allusions to verifiable historical events as it is that their history was not such as Tacitus, Bede, or C. V. Wedgwood might have written. That Beowulf had traces of the corn god about him is just as normal as the fact that he is not another Osiris. We have called the oral epic tradition a synthesis, but it is not a conscious one. Nor does it begin in a pure state and then refine itself into another pure state. Only the synthesis, not any one of the pure states, can be called epic.

There is no name for the kind of poem which the Old French epic was in the process of becoming when it collided with the romances of Chrétien de Troyes and his followers. We see a pure example of the type, however, in Sir David Lindsay's little sixteenth-century masterpiece *Squire Meldrum*. The line of descent from *Roland* to *Squire Meldrum* would include the Spanish *Poema de mio Cid*, composed a little more than a generation after the death of its hero in 1099, as well as such written poems in English as Barbour's *Bruce* and Blind Harry's *Wallace*. Historically, the *Cid* is extremely accurate, and its oral style is clear, strong, and totally unadorned. Its middle-class hero is motivated almost as much by social ambition for himself and his daughters as he is by either Roland's kind of personal code of heroic honor or Charlemagne's vision of a unified Christian empire. The *Cid*, unlike *Squire Meldrum*, is still the story of a hero on the national stage. He is the destroyer of huge armies of Saracens and the savior of his people. Unlike *Roland*, and even more unlike *Beowulf* and the Eddic lays, the *Cid* is popular. Its audience was further removed socially, if not historically, from the grand actions it celebrates than were the audiences of the earlier epics. The oral tradition that produced the *Cid* was the stuff out of which ballads are made. It reflects the epic tradition, but above all the oral epic tradition, on its way down the cultural scale. The *Bruce* and *Wallace*, although the written compositions of individual authors, were both the continuation of a central core of the old epic tradition and the start of something new. Their newness for contemporary readers would have rested in the synthesis they attempted between the matter of a new empirical narrative and the style of the old fictional narrative. Works in this genre are sometimes called "chronicle poems," but "metrical biographies" would serve as well.

Taken together, the chronicle poem and what we may call the allegorical anatomy — another somewhat neglected genre, represented by such long and learned poems as *The Romance of the Rose* and *Piers Plowman* — accounted for a sizeable percentage of medieval vernacular narrative poetry. The two forms are not easily analyzed in modern critical terms. They seem in some respects to fit between the two extremes of the disintegrating epic tradition: the prose history and the metrical romance, both of which are easily recognizable in modern terms. The histories of

Snorri Sturlason and Jean de Joinville are in many respects comparable to historical writing in classical antiquity. Nor have the romances ever lacked admirers. But these two major genres do not exhaust the narrative possibilities. The allegorical anatomy mediates in a complex way, which we shall describe in a later chapter, between discursive philosophy and romance, while the metrical biography and chronicle poem fall between romance and history. It is this latter path, between romance and history, which leads the way from epic to the novel, and of all the medieval narrative forms that had begun down this path in oral tradition it was the Icelandic family saga which travelled farthest before being overtaken by Latin books and the Book.

Its apparent cultural isolation makes the narrative art of thirteenth-century Iceland seem almost miraculously precocious. It may owe debts to Irish prose narrative and to a common Germanic genius for prose style and secular history; but if so, no records of this heritage have survived. Exerting essentially no influence on subsequent European prose fiction, the family sagas nevertheless achieved a purity of form, subject matter, and style that justifies some interest in them for their own sake. They were not the product of a written saga tradition in which an essentially modern form of both authorship and literary borrowing were operative principles. The saga style is remarkably uniform and formulaic from saga to saga. The parallel passages that many critics cite as examples of literary borrowing by one saga author from another are more easily explained as elements common to an oral tradition. That the sagas were written down cannot be denied. That a single writer must be thought of as standing behind each of the individual saga texts is also reasonable. But that the writer depended upon either books or his own individual invention for the major elements of his story does not seem justified by the evidence. The sagas would not be as good as they are if they were individually created compositions in anything like the modern sense.

When writing came to Iceland, presumably about the year

1000, with the parliamentary adoption of Christianity as the state religion, at least three oral traditions were well developed. Our evidence for the first of these, the oral poetic tradition, the remains of which are preserved in the *Poetic Edda*, is primarily its resemblance in form and subject to the relics of other pagan Germanic narrative poetry, suggesting therefore a common origin in a demonstrably pre-literate culture. Secondary evidence is to be found in the formulas and *topoi* of the Eddic poems themselves. The second oral tradition was the law, one third of which was recited from memory at the Parliament on each of three years by an elected *lögsögumaðr* ("lawspeaker"). The third oral tradition was history. If we should posit the existence in Scandinavian culture of an all-embracing oral epic tradition, one which contained traces of secular history, law, myth, ritual, and the accumulated wisdom of the race, we must place it considerably earlier than the settlement of Iceland in 870. By the twelfth and thirteenth centuries, we have written evidence of a highly differentiated literary culture and circumstantial evidence of its relative antiquity. In other words, by the time they were introduced to writing, the Icelanders had progressed further toward an essentially modern array of narrative forms — both prose and poetic — than had the Greeks when the Homeric epics were written down. By virtue of their isolation, the Icelanders had, with radical innovations, carried forward the Germanic narrative traditions as they had flourished before the coming of the Book. They demonstrated that unlettered artists were able to achieve both a secular history and a realistic prose fiction with only minimal influence from books and writing. Because the development of a powerful art-prose and a secular history has been considered impossible without writing and individual authorship, the very quality of Icelandic narrative has until now been the best argument against the oral composition of the family sagas. With the Homeric epics as a model, however, the argument from quality is weakened, if not destroyed.

The family sagas, or "sagas of the Icelanders" (*Íslendinga sögur*), constitute but one of several important Icelandic prose genres. On one side of them stand the histories, *Sturlunga Saga* and *Heimskringla* — accounts of more or less contemporary events in Iceland and of the lives of the Norwegian kings, respectively — as well as dozens of lives of individual kings and bishops. On the other side of the family sagas are the so-called *fornaldar sögur* ("sagas of former times"), which are prose retellings of the heroic and mythological stories that had been the subject of the earlier oral poetic narrative tradition, specimens of which have been preserved in the *Poetic Edda*. The *Völsunga Saga* (whose story turns up almost simultaneously in Germany as the *Nibelungenlied*) and *Hrólfs Saga Kraka* (an analogue to *Beowulf*) are narratives of the *fornaldar-saga* type. And finally, the *fornaldar sögur* seem to have blended with numerous translations of French romances (*riddara sögur*) to produce a hybrid form called *lygi sögur* ("lying sagas"). The *lygi sögur* continued to be composed in modern times, alongside an extraordinarily rich folktale tradition and a popular form of ballad-like narrative poem called *rímur* ("rhymes").

We have permitted ourselves this brief technical survey of the richness of thirteenth-century narrative genres in Iceland in order to demonstrate the tremendous energy with which the fragmentation of an oral epic tradition can occur under the right circumstances, and the speed with which various narrative impulses can manifest themselves in separate kinds of narrative. Not only do we see in Iceland the repetition of the Greek pattern, in which the epic amalgam gives way to history and romance; we find in the family sagas a new synthesis of myth and mimesis as realistic narrative fiction. In the three hundred years (from 1000 to 1300) between the time that Eddic narrative may have ceased to engage the best literary talents and the time the last of the family sagas were composed, Iceland had witnessed a decay and development of narrative forms which in Europe proper took more than twice as long to be accomplished.

We are told by Snorri Sturlason in the preface to *Heimskringla* (so called because of the two opening words of the first section, which mean "the world's circle") that he has relied on the oral tradition of history. His principal sources were poems composed by court poets in praise of the kings whom they served, the historical writings of Ari the Wise (1067–1148), who seems to have depended almost entirely on oral tradition, and the information provided by learned men (presumably in conversation). Snorri is a conscious historian: he is after the truth. In his preface he develops a fairly sophisticated method for using his oral sources and determining the reliability of variants. The court poetry to which he refers must have played a complex role in the oral tradition of history. It was not the traditional Eddic poetry, but rather a verse much more complicated in rhyme and diction called skaldic poetry.

Heimskringla, like the family sagas, is shot through with skaldic verses, usually associated with the names of historical poets. The verses were probably not composed orally in the sense of drawing upon only the resources of a fixed oral "grammar" in the course of rapid composition before an audience; although they may have been composed, and were certainly transmitted, without the use of writing materials. They were short fixed texts which managed to survive many generations intact until they achieved definitive form in the written texts of the sagas. The verses often epitomize the high moments of a story and serve a structural as well as a thematic function. They should probably be regarded as an essential element in the oral tradition of historical prose.

In comparison with Herodotus, Snorri's habit of mind is distinctly less empirical than the Greek's, and his notion of historical form for narrative is not so sophisticated. He seeks the truth, but his standards are poetic rather than empirical. Despite his drastic rationalization of the story of the rise of Odin and in his treatment of mythological figures generally, he has none of Herodotus' suspicion of poets in general, as a lying breed, nor of his rational standards of probability. In terms of narrative form, Snorri is satisfied with the genealogical pattern, which allows him to expand his material on those rulers in whom he is most interested and whom he knows most about, such as St. Olaf. The Greek combination of a rationally tested narrative cast in a unified and limited form is not Snorri's. His narrative is poetically tested and presented in the loose form of genealogical narrative.

In one sense, *Sturlunga Saga* ("History of the Sturlung Family") represents an advance over *Heimskringla*. It is not so well unified, being a loose collection of historical narratives written by several authors rather than a single work. But the collection restricts its subject to events in Iceland from about 1120 to 1280, and the central core of the book, the *Íslendinga Saga* of Sturla Thórdarson, is utterly convincing as an account of the lives of powerful and imaginative men in a time of political turmoil and intrigue. Comparison with Thucydides leaves *Sturlunga Saga* a poor patchwork of anecdotes and densely contracted details perhaps; but the mythic element of the Greek historian has been refined out of the secular history of the Icelanders to such a degree that the impression of accurately (if not always artistically) related fact is all the stronger. In *Sturlunga Saga* and in the written records of Icelandic law we find the extremes of primitive Germanic rationalism. The law is, of course, a poor substitute for the fully developed tradition of rational thought out of which the Greek historians operated. Nothing remotely similar to Greek philosophical discourse developed out of pagan Germanic culture. Perhaps the purging of myth from historical narrative was for this reason all the more urgent. If Icelandic historical method remained oriented toward tradition rather than toward discursive thought, it was a tradition refined by the pragmatism of hard-headed lawyers. The lawspeakers and the historians were often enough the same men.

The family sagas share the genealogical ground plan typical of the history, but the focus is frequently much narrower. In *Njáls Saga*, for example, it is narrowed to three generations, with emphasis on the generation of Gunnar and Njal. The narrative articulation of *Njáls Saga*, like that of several of the individual histories in *Sturlunga Saga*, is provided by a motif directly from Icelandic

life, the perfect motif, in fact, to give unity and shape to a genealogical narrative pattern — the family feud. The intense cultivation of civil law in Iceland, at the expense of (or in lieu of) every
other area of public life, itself necessarily imposed an almost
artificial order on the lives of the Icelanders, presenting the saga-
men with ready-made materials for narrative presentation, and
producing inevitably a unique kind of narrative, tied closely to
history and to the actualities of contemporary life. In the hands of
a master the saga form was capable of power and perception of
an order unaspired to by the writers of romances. In Njál himself,
the man of law caught up in a lawless feud, we have that conflict
between the ideal and the real which is characteristic of the combination of fictional and empirical impulses, giving such narratives that problematic quality which makes them so different from
romance with its manageable narrative and poetic justice on the
one hand, and from the inevitability of history on the other.

How vital the oral poetic narrative tradition which is preserved
in the *Poetic Edda* may have been during the period in which the
family sagas were written down is impossible to say. The characters and events of the sagas doubtless owe something (and probably more than has generally been recognized) to the traditional
topoi of the Eddic narrative. Hallgerd, one of the few non-historical characters in *Njáls Saga,* bears an intriguing likeness to the
Brynhildr of *Sigurðarkviða in Skamma* ("The Short Lay of Si-
gurd"), one of the Eddic poems. And an adventure in which
Grettir descends into a pool to fight a preternatural monster in
Grettis Saga is strikingly similar to an episode in *Beowulf.* Even
the character of Gunnar in *Njáls Saga* is partly significant in terms
of older, epic conceptions of the hero. His involvement in the feud
that consumes him and the family of Njál is not merely an example of chaotic reality in contrast to the rational ideal of the law.
It exemplifies the mythic ideal of the hero in conflict with the
rational ideal of the law, a conflict which in history did lead to
the chaos of the Age of the Sturlungs, in which the saga was composed. In some respects, the family sagas are epic poems in prose,

with the mythic and fabulous element drastically curtailed and replaced by a strong emphasis on the historical and the mimetic. But this curtailment of myth and emphasis on mimesis is so nearly complete as to be at times more suggestive of the novel than the epic.

The real miracle of Icelandic narrative art, without which the family sagas could not have existed, was the history. It was starkly factual, overwhelming in its genealogical detail, and (in *Sturlunga Saga*) brutally candid in its portrayal of individuals. The family sagas are most conveniently understood as a blending of history and law with the traditional epic, the *topoi* and myths of the latter giving way at nearly every point to themes, plots, and motifs representative of a rational and secular actuality. The epic itself could hardly withstand the two-pronged attack of history and Christianity, being replaced *qua* poetry by the more "poetic" skaldic verse. Theories which postulate the short Eddic lays as a pre-epic stage of narrative development seem utterly without foundation. These highly condensed epitomes of heroic narrative reflect instead a general cultural movement away from rather than toward the epic. In much earlier times the Eddic tradition had doubtless been a *via media* between empirical and fictional narrative, but by the twelfth century the epic was no longer viable. The power of its myth was sapped by Christianity and the validity of its plot was challenged by history and law.

With no urban civilization, no tradition of philosophical thought, and no tradition of "slice-of-life" satire the novel may be a theoretical impossibility. The Icelandic family saga does represent, however, a re-synthesis of old epic with new empirical forms that exhibits at least some similarity to the re-synthesis for which the rest of Europe was to wait another three hundred years. As the European Middle Ages closed in on Iceland during the centuries that followed the Age of the Sturlungs, the purely fictional impulse of the old epic narrative continued to be satisfied by the intellectually vacuous *fornaldar sögur, riddara sögur,* and *lygi sögur,* but its empirical impulse had been spent on the brilliant histories and family sagas and was to leave no monument to life in those dark and terror-ridden centuries.

The term *saga*, which in Icelandic now means any prose narrative long or short, oral or written, is derived from the word *segja* ("tell" in Icelandic). When the Icelanders began writing down traditional stories that had existed for many generations as oral narratives they apparently applied the word *saga* not only to the story but occasionally to the written record of it as well. The terms used to distinguish among history (*saga*), family saga (*Íslendinga saga*), heroic saga (*fornaldar saga*), romance (*riddara saga*), and marvelous adventure (*lygi saga*) are modern. Although such distinctions are both logical and necessary for the specialist, it would be well for the general literary scholar if the word "saga" could have a narrower meaning than it does in Icelandic. In popular American usage it is an ameliorative term. Jaded readers for whom "epic" does not draw enough current may yet be enticed to read the *Iliad* if the poem is described as a stirring "saga" of the Trojan War, while both "saga" and "epic" are applied to cinema plays that might more accurately be called heroic romance. Properly used in literary criticism the word "saga," unqualified by more specific modifiers, should apply to the Icelandic family sagas and other realistic, novel-length, traditional prose narratives like them. The key word is "traditional," for otherwise the sagas might be indistinguishable from novels. By "traditional" is meant narrative which bears the formal and rhetorical stigmata of oral composition.

The formal characteristics of oral composition have already been described. They include above all else a "formulaic" diction; that is, their language is controlled by a traditional "grammar" which provides a limited number of patterns selected from the total language of the culture by which metrically (in the case of poetry), syntactically, and semantically appropriate utterances are formed. The mastery of this "grammar" permits the oral narrative artist to compose orally before an audience. It is the universal experience of mankind that the oral composition of prose sentences is more difficult than the oral composition of metrically perfect verse. Some critics believe that prose cannot develop orally because of the difficulty of controlling the logical and syntactic rhythm of the prose sentence. They have restricted illiterate man to the esthetic use of verse and to the non-esthetic use of what Northrop Frye has called the "associative rhythm" of normal speech. On the contrary, however, a detailed analysis of the famous "saga style" of the family sagas would in effect yield a description of the "grammar" of Icelandic oral narrative prose. The existence of such a "grammar" was the primary basis for the achievement of an oral prose in medieval Iceland. Orally composed prose will necessarily be highly stylized.

Another characteristic of oral narrative is consistency in the thematic significance of motifs and plots. Such meanings are made possible by traditional *topoi* and myths, conventional narrative elements which simultaneously govern a story's representation of actuality and its illustration of ideas. In order to discover the formulaic character of a narrative's diction or the conventional nature of its structure and theme, the critic must consult a body of narrative large enough to embody norms and to serve as at least a fragment of a "tradition." Fortunately, the Homeric corpus is ample. The Anglo-Saxon is barely sufficient. The Eddic is probably too small. Aside, however, from its purely "formal" characteristics, orally composed narrative is distinguished from the work of individual narrative artists in what might narrowly be termed its "rhetoric." In this respect, many traditional narratives seem to be at least provisionally identifiable as traditional without comparing them to a larger body of texts.

Oral narrative invariably employs an authoritative and reliable narrator. He is gifted, like Homer and the "Author" of the Old Testament, with the ability to observe an action from every side and to tell the secrets of men's hearts. We are accustomed to identifying this omniscient narrator with the author, and to saying that the author is everywhere present to interpret and evaluate the characters and events of his narrative for us. We are also accustomed to referring to this reliable, omniscient, omnipresent narrator as "objective." By this we mean that, again like Homer and the authors of Old Testament narrative, he does not talk about himself, but about the characters and actions of his story. Nor does he cultivate the intimacy of his audience at the expense of their sympathy with the story. Aristotle praised Homer for taking on the personalities of others, by which he apparently meant that Homer neither talked about himself nor detached himself from the interests of the story. Of course the omniscient narrator is very far from being "objective" in the other sense of adopting a point of view resembling that of a neutral human observer of exclusively external events. He is objective in the senses that he is not "subjective" and that there is no ironic distance between himself and the author or between his interests and those implicit in the story. We shall notice in a later chapter on point of view that the Homeric invocations of the muse are a movement in the direction of authorial self-consciousness, providing a very slight and a highly stereotyped exception to the general rule that traditional oral narrative is told by an "objective" and authoritative narrator.

Since there is no ironic distance between the author and the teller of a traditional story we are not in the habit of distinguishing between them. The audience shares the narrator's knowledge and values, depending upon him at every point for judgments about the characters and events in the story. The audience adopts the narrator's god-like view, which accounts for the only fictional irony of traditional narrative: that narrator and audience together know the characters of the story as they could not possibly know each other or even themselves. With the development of self-conscious tellers in non-traditional, written narratives, the ironies multiply. The disparity between the narrator's view of the characters and their views of themselves and each other, which is a constant in fiction, is augmented by a disparity between the narrator's view of his story and the audience's view of it. In any written narrative, therefore, there will be at least a potential, and usually an actual, ironic disparity between the knowledge and values of the author and those of his narrator. The traditional, oral narrative consists rhetorically of a teller, his story, and an implied audience. The non-traditional, written narrative consists rhetorically of the *imitation,* or *representation,* of a teller, his story, and an implied audience.

Rhetorically, the use of writing permits the individual, creating narrative artist to add an important level of complexity and of potential irony to his story. The new level has always appeared to result from the introduction of a self-conscious narrator and an opening of ironic distance between him on one side and the author and audience on the other. In the light, however, of our discussion of oral narrative we can see that what in fact made possible the revolutionary complexity of point of view in written narrative was the introduction, not of narrators, but of *authors.* Somewhat awkwardly, we have had to use the expression "author in the modern sense" throughout our discussion of oral narrative. We have asserted that the Homeric epics, the Old Testament, *Beowulf, The Song of Roland,* the family sagas, the *Kalevala,* the Faroese ballads, and other oral narratives were not composed by "authors in the modern sense." In the case of narrative poetry, which is usually sung, we can refer to the "singer of tales." In the case of orally composed prose narrative, we may speak of the "teller of tales." In neither case is he an author: he is the instrument through which the tradition takes on a tangible shape as a performance. He is the narrator. In the words of Stephen Dedalus in *A Portrait,* he places his story "in mediate relation to himself and to others."

Whatever interest Stephen's famous definitions of lyric, epic, and dramatic may have as criticism or as mystery, they do illustrate a modern impulse to get the author back out of narrative. The apparent ability of a Homer or a Shakespeare to remain, "like the God of the creation . . . within or behind or beyond or above his handiwork, invisible, refined out of existence, indifferent, paring his fingernails" had been praised by Romantic critics as the highest achievement of the "sympathetic imagination," a highly valued poetic faculty. Joyce's own approach to the problem of refining the author out of existence was in some sense dramatic, for he attempted so to fuse narrator and narrative that his imitation of the interaction among the three essential rhetorical elements — teller, tale, and implied audience — had the same relationship to himself as a play bears to the dramatist. But Joyce's narrative remains an imitation of a narrator telling a story, regardless of the ingenuity with which his narrators may be located in relation to their stories and their audiences. Permitting ourselves to enter for a moment into the mysteries of Stephen's esthetic, we might describe Joyce's technique as a "dramatic" representation of an "epical" form.

The rhetorical distinction between oral narrative and written narrative has been partly worked out by Northrop Frye. Without knowing about, or at least not using, the discovery of the oral composition of much traditional narrative in both verse and prose, Frye has been unable to attribute their true significance to the two "radicals of presentation" he uses in distinguishing between *epos* (in our terms, oral narrative) and fiction (written narrative). He defines *epos* as "the literary genre in which the radical of presentation is the author or minstrel as oral reciter, with a listening audience in front of him." And *fiction* is for Frye "literature in which the radical of presentation is the printed or written word, such as novels and essays." Despite its practical unworkability, this distinction is full of insight. Some oral narratives do indeed betray the fact that they are performances before an audience, so the second fact, that they are presented to *us* from the printed page, need not of itself destroy the usefulness of Frye's distinction. On the other hand, however, many highly original, nontraditional, written narratives offer themselves to us from the printed page *as if* they were oral performances before an audience. The novels of Conrad that are narrated by Marlow come to mind as a modern instance.

It is in the nature of things that the radical of presentation of a narrative is nowadays going to be the printed page. Those narratives which were not written by authors are in most cases distinguished from narratives composed by an author in writing by their failure to present a created narrator as a presence distinct from some higher creator. Medieval romance is a narrative genre which rhetorically qualifies for Frye's *epos* but which is disqualified from our "traditional oral narrative." The greatest of the medieval romances were not orally composed, although they depended heavily on traditional elements, some of which may even have been taken directly from oral tradition or from transcribed versions of oral narratives. The romances associated with the names Chrétien de Troyes, Wolfram von Eschenbach, and Gottfried von Strassburg are probably to be attributed to the creative geniuses of those individuals. Such works as the Knight's Tale and *Troilus and Criseyde* are written compositions in the full modern sense. And yet, in medieval romance we frequently meet with a narrator like Chaucer's and Wolfram's who is depicted as telling a story to an audience. Wolfram's narrator even admits to his audience that he doesn't know a single letter of the alphabet, thereby increasing the distance between himself and the author. The sudden acquisition by medieval narrative artists of the new role of authorship found them unprepared and somewhat ill at ease. Like all authors they attempted to "refine themselves out of existence." The most natural course was found to be a fairly straightforward imitation of a teller reciting his story to an audience. But even this emergency measure opened the Pandora's box of irony, giving such masters as Chaucer, Wolfram, and (in the Renaissance) Rabelais and Cervantes new fields to conquer.

The oral story teller "mediates," to use Stephen's word but not his idea, between his story and his audience. Not only is there no author with whom to set up an ironic relationship, but (which amounts to the same thing) there can be no ironic relationship with the story itself. The oral tradition is both the story and the author. For the performer to encourage the intimacy of the audience at the expense of the story would amount to setting himself up as an author who uses the tradition merely to advance his own individually conceived ends. Satire, if it is to exist in oral tradition, must be built right into the tradition itself. It will not be a function of ironic distance between an "author" and his created narrator, nor between the interests of the narrator and those of his story.

When an oral tradition is driven "underground" by a dominant written literature, it will naturally reflect the intellectual, esthetic, and social experience of those among whom it flourishes. In modern times, oral traditions have existed under such adverse cultural circumstances that the ballad and folktale have assumed the status of oral genres *par excellence*. Resistance to the theory of the oral composition of *Beowulf* or the *Poetic Edda* has with disappointing frequency been argued in terms of ballad and folktale. *Beowulf*, it has been affirmed, is no mere ballad, and must therefore be the product of an individual creating mind. We have not attempted in this discussion of longer narrative forms to treat the ballad or folktale as an element in the oral heritage of written literature. They were, at least until the Romantic Movement, in competition with, rather than influences upon, written narrative.

The formal characteristics of oral narrative are somewhat modified in both ballad and folktale. These genres have been sufficiently influenced by the idea of a written literature and by the conception of a fixed text that individual narratives are not actually composed anew with each performance. The texts doubtless evolved from genuine oral tradition, and they are not, properly speaking, "variants" of an original. But with only minimal use of writing itself they have attained a fixity that goes beyond the formulaic diction of real oral composition.

The same "sympathetic imagination," however, which refines both the author and the rhetorical irony out of existence in oral narrative controls the singing of ballads and the telling of folktales. Ironies of a quite different sort control a world in which rearguard scholars struggle to keep an author in *Beowulf* just when the telling of folktales and the singing of ballads are imitated by advance-guard narrative artists, for whom the refinement of the author out of existence is a consummation devoutly to be wished.

3

The Classical Heritage
of Modern Narrative

To understand the present we must possess the past. The literature of Greece and Rome is still of interest to us in the twentieth century because of its intrinsic merit, but for our special purposes in this investigation it has an even greater interest. The classical literatures provide us with prototypes of virtually all later narrative forms and with paradigms of the processes which govern their interaction and evolution. Of all the forms of full-length written narrative, only the novel failed to develop in classical times. And this non-event is probably the most important literary consequence of the fall of Rome. But we anticipate. Let us begin at the beginning.

The beginning, for us, is the moment when the epic passes from oral tradition into written and becomes the fountainhead of a new narrative literature. In Western literature Homer is at once the culmination of oral narrative art and the inauguration of written. As oral narrative, the Homeric poems are a powerful amalgam of various materials — religious, historical, social — shaped by a strong impulse toward artistic unity in narrative. We shall have more to say of this in our discussion of Plot (Chapter 6 below), but for the moment it is enough to note that this unity is built upon a certain naïveté about the nature of materials in the amalgam. Epic poems are made in cultures which do not distin-

guish between myth and history. As soon as the distinction begins
to be made — and this is a gradual process at first but gains mo-
mentum in time — it can be applied critically to the narratives
of the past and will become established in the esthetic and intellectual norms which influence current literary production. The
distinction between fact and fiction, once it is clearly established,
forces story-telling to choose the rubric under which it will function: truth or beauty. The result is a separation of narrative
streams into factual and fictional, producing forms we have
learned to call history and romance. In Western culture the two
streams both spring from the fountainhead of Homeric epic and
go their separate ways until they reunite in the novel. The novel's
combination of factual and fictional elements is not naïve and
instinctive but sophisticated and deliberate, made possible by the
development of a concept called realism, which provides a rationale for a marriage that rationalism had seemed to forbid. We can
see the breakdown of the epic amalgam in the development of
Greek historical narrative, just as we can see the realistic solution
to this breakdown beginning to be formulated by Cervantes,
Scarron and other post-Renaissance writers as they grope toward
realism. But now we must consider the breakdown of the Homeric amalgam itself. For our purposes it is the most important
aspect of Greek narrative.

The word ἱστορ (histor) was used by Homer in the sense of an
inquirer, but the concept of history in anything like its modern
sense did not exist for him. It is characteristic of primitive epic
narrative that it takes actual historical persons, places, or events,
and combines them with characters derived from myth in a fictional fusion which generates its own narrative devices and techniques. Thus, in *Beowulf*, in the *Chanson de Roland*, and in the
Nibelungenlied we find combinations of this order, in which a
more or less recognizable Hygelac, or Charlemagne, or Attila is
found side by side with a mytho-fictional Beowulf, Roland, or
Siegfried, in a narrative which is clearly more fictional than historical. In Greece the archaeologists have succeeded in finding

the golden Mycenae of Agamemnon and the sandy Pylos of Nestor, but Achilles and his Myrmidons have left no marks on the real world because they are not of it. These combinations of historical and nonhistorical elements are not, in all probability, deliberate. The composers of primitive epic poetry seem typically to handle traditional materials with no clear idea that some are historical and some not.

With the progress of civilization in a culture, an awareness of the difference between the factual and fictional orders is bound to arise. It is unfortunate that we do not have the two epics which Xenophanes (c. 500 B.C.) is said to have written. For Xenophanes, perhaps better than any other figure, represents the spirit of rational and empirical inquiry which ultimately inhibits naïve combinations of fact with fiction and promotes the rise of empirical narrative. Xenophanes specifically attacked the anthropomorphic conceptions of the deity which lie behind all primitive religious mythology, naming Hesiod and Homer as major offenders against credibility. One would give a good deal to see what sort of narrative such a rationalistic mind produced twenty-five hundred years ago. But very likely the loss of these epics is due to their inherent lack of interest, Xenophanes in all probability not having succeeded in finding a workable substitute for the Homeric amalgam which he repudiated.

The development of the two post-Homeric narrative forms which are the principal Greek contribution to the narrative tradition can be traced directly to the peculiarly Greek development of rational, sceptical, and empirical modes of thought on a scale and with an intensity unmatched until the seventeenth and eighteenth centuries in Europe. We can see the results of this intellectual pressure most clearly and dramatically if we single out for consideration the three great narrative writers of pre-Alexandrian Greece: Homer, Herodotus, and Thucydides. Homer was an *epopoios,* or maker of verse; Herodotus, a *logographos,* or writer of prose; but Herodotus wrote out his prose with oral delivery in mind. Thucydides' writing was designed (he tells us in his first chapter) not "to meet the taste of an immediate public, but was done to last forever." The *Iliad* is a redaction of an oral narrative; Herodotus' *Histories* were written out, but for oral delivery; Thucydides' *Peloponnesian War* was a book in something like the full sense of the word. Homer wrote of the far past, Herodotus of the recent past, Thucydides of contemporary events. Because he is in the middle of this line of development, the case of Herodotus is of especial interest.

His is an inquiring mind with a strong rational bent which is balanced by his desire to present a moving and orderly narrative of his own. He begins, not with an invocation to the muse but with his own name and a statement of his method and purpose:

Herodotus of Halicarnassus' discoveries [*Herodotou Halikarnesseos histories*] are set forth here so that the recollection of the past may not be blotted from men's memories by time; and so that the great and wonderful deeds performed by both Hellenes and Foreigners (and especially the reason why they fought one another) may not lack renown.

He disparages poetic narrative frequently, and remarks on one occasion that "the Greeks in general have a weakness for inventing stories with no basis in fact." He illustrates this with a story about Herakles in Egypt (an interesting parallel to the Biblical Samson story) concluding, "Besides, if Herakles was a mere man (as they say he was) and single-handed, how is it conceivable that he should have killed tens of thousands of people? And now I hope that both gods and heroes will forgive me for saying what I have said on these matters." His piety is as real as his scepticism. His desire for historical truth is balanced by his love for a dramatic scene: he will give us in direct discourse a conversation held in bed by Darius the King of Persia and his wife Atossa. His most recent translator has remarked that for him "the poetical word was the natural word." Though his rhythm was prose, his diction was poetic. In Herodotus we can see the rationalistic spirit at work. Naïve epic will be impossible for the Greeks after this. And hard on the heels of Herodotus comes the highly rationalistic Thucydides, who carries much farther the separation of matters historical from the mythic and fictional elements in the Homeric amalgam. He speaks (like Herodotus) disparagingly of the "poets [*poietai*] who exaggerate the importance of their themes," and he condemns also (probably with Herodotus in mind) "the prose chroniclers [*logographoi*], who are less interested in telling the truth than in catching the attention of their public." His boast is that his book will probably be less appealing than earlier narratives because he has eliminated the "fabulous [*mythodes*] element" from it.

Thucydides certainly represents a high water mark of rationalism in ancient historical writing. No later Greek or Roman historian could surpass or even equal the degree of empiricism he attained. He went, in fact, as far as anyone could go in the direction of rationalistic historiography without what F. M. Cornford has called "the indispensable aid of accumulated and systematic knowledge, and of the apparatus of scientific conceptions which the labour of subsequent centuries has refined, elaborated and distinguished." Historiography in the West may be said to have remained static at Thucydides' level until Hobbes's famous translation of the *Peloponnesian War* in the seventeenth century, at which point the new empiricism was able to begin providing the kind of scientific concepts and data which were necessary to continue the separation of fiction from history in historical narrative. Thucydides himself, as Cornford has shown in his *Thucydides Mythistoricus,* was much more influenced by extra-historical formulations (from tragedy and hence ultimately from myth) than the disclaimers in the first chapter of his narrative would lead us to believe. And in fact much of the power of Thucydidean narrative derives from the Aeschylean elements in it. Athens as a tragic hero, displaying hybris for which it is properly punished, is the dramatic and mythic formulation which provides a firmer narrative articulation than mere chronology ever could.

Another major non-empirical element in Thucydidean narrative is a rhetorical one. He acknowledges in his first chapter the fact that he has made up suitable speeches for situations which occurred both before and during the war. The decorum of rhetoric, which is essentially both anti-mimetic and anti-historic, requires effective presentation at the expense of actuality. But beyond this fictionalizing according to logical and rhetorical principles, which Thucydides readily admits, lies such an episode as the Melian dialogue of Book V, in which the set public speech pattern of rhetoric is abandoned and dramatic private dialogue is introduced so that Athenian hybris can most effectively and convincingly be displayed. In the Greek world historical narrative remained poised between the oral arts of drama and rhetoric. From this stage, historical narrative could progress only by moving away from art in the direction of science. The implications of the historical posture, with its emphasis on "inquiry" could be worked out only by continually intensifying the form's empirical bias. But Roman history did not develop in this direction. The empiricism of Thucydides was imitated as a literary convention by the Romans more than it was emulated as a spirit driving the historian in the direction of factual accuracy.

Though history in the hands of the Roman writers did not become more empirical than it had been for Thucydides, Roman historiography was not merely a repetition of Greek technique with Roman subject matter. For one thing, the nature of historical subject matter itself changed. Aristotle thought of history as being distinguished from poetry in that it dealt with what "had been" rather than with what "might be," and he preferred poetry because it was universal rather than limited to the particular events of history. But more interesting than this formulation is his notion that epic poetry deals with a single action while history deals with a single period. What is lacking from his formulation of the difference between history and poetry (*Poetics* 1451, 1459) is the notion that history may deal with *many* periods in such a way as to select out a thread of narrative which gives a historical work a unity similar to the epic unity of a single action centered on a single hero. Aristotle obviously thought of the subject matter of history as something like the Peloponnesian War or the Trojan

War. He thought in this way because he had never seen a history of the kind that Rome's great historian Livy wrote, and indeed it is almost fair to say that Livy's kind of history did not exist in Greek literature. Though one hears of a "universal" history of Greece written by "Ephorus," a contemporary of Aristotle's, this is acknowledged to be a unique event in Greek historiography. In fact, the Greek tendency to limit history to a single event or period was deplored by the later Greek historians Polybius and Posidonius (respectively of the second and first centuries B.C.).

The Romans, on the other hand, seem to have started early with attempts to see the whole of Roman history, Livy's great work coming as the culmination of a long tradition of universal histories which have been lost (as, indeed, most of Livy's own work has been lost). This long view is characteristically Roman in that it is patriotically oriented, with Rome as protagonist and the action being Rome's growth and development. This Roman difference of focus and emphasis resulted in a history much more concerned with social, economic, and political institutions than that of the early Greek historians. The institutional side of Greek life is present in Thucydides, but always peripheral to the main interest, which is the greatest war in the history of the world and its effect on its participants. The rationalism of Thucydides is expended on an epic subject matter. Thucydides, like Herodotus and Xenophon, is mainly a military historian. Livy, on the other hand, is preeminently a political and social historian, and he shares this quality even with those Roman annalists and chroniclers who did not adopt his sweeping view of events. For Livy himself, the evolution of social and political institutions was not only a major interest; it was a major organizational principle in his work. He thought of Rome under the kings as the subject of a section of his history, and of republican Rome as the beginning of a new subject and a new section. In his narrative, classes like the patricians and the people function almost as characters; they are units of force which help to shape events, as are political units like the Senate and the Assembly.

What we are observing here is a change in the form and subject matter of historical writing in the ancient world, which is *not* accompanied by any real progress in empirical attitudes. In this department, historical narrative undergoes a kind of retrogression in the late Hellenic and Roman world. The fabulous element which Thucydides prided himself on having pruned from his narrative is deliberately reintroduced by Livy and others for artistic effect. In the works on rhetoric (or literary theory) of Cicero and Quintilian history is seen as an art: an art which owes a debt to truthfulness and impartiality and also a debt to ornamentation and heightened emotional effect. The evolution of historical narrative as a literary form was deliberately arrested by Roman literary theory, just as the evolution of written Latin was arrested. The empirical impulse to satisfy truth of fact, before all else, was frozen; and historical writing stayed always at some distance from reality, just as the written language kept its distance from the spoken. Greek historical narrative was, in its early phase at any rate, evolving away from epic, finding the terms for its evolution in its rejection of epic conventions. Roman historical narrative was much freerer to determine its own narrative conventions, and progressed in the direction of a greater sensitivity to institutions and social movements, but deliberately halted this progress to retain elements of tragic drama and oratory, and pathetic effects like those of the pseudo-epics and the romances.

After Tacitus, Roman historical narrative as a literary form had almost nowhere to go. Annals could continue to be written because every year provided new material, but in fact Roman historical writing fell off in quantity as well as quality. In literary history, whenever a form is allowed to set, or is prevented from following its natural evolutionary course, it tends to wither and die off or put out only the weakest and palest of shoots. If Roman historiography had been freed from its rhetorical restrictions, and had Roman philosophy been able to take up empirical thought where Greek had abandoned it, something more like Machiavelli or Hobbes might have appeared in imperial Rome. And if history had become more empirical in the narrow, factual sense, its progress toward modern, scientific history might have caused those elements in ancient history which were more broadly empirical, more interested in truth of sensation than truth of fact, to seek a new formal vehicle; which would have meant a move toward something like the realistic novel as we know it. As it was, the most significant form to branch off from the historical narrative tradition in Roman times was biography, which deliberately moved away from the empirical in the direction of the didactic and rhetorical.

Classical biography can be represented for our purposes through the work of Plutarch. Plutarch, though he wrote in Greek, was a fairly typical figure in the Greco-Roman culture of the Roman Empire; and he will serve us here as a representative of the various writers of Lives. The Life as a form derives from eulogistic oratory, from memoirs such as Ptolemy's of Alexander, and from history. Plutarch defined the limitations of the form very precisely in his life of Alexander:

For I write not histories but lives: the showiest deeds do not always delineate virtue and vice, but often a trivial action, a quip or a prank, will reveal more of character than the fiercest slaughters, or greatest parades, or sieges of cities. Thus, just as portrait painters attempt to establish a likeness through the features or a look in the eyes (where character is revealed), taking far fewer pains with the rest, I must be allowed to devote myself mainly to the signs of the psyche, and through these to represent each individual life, leaving to others the great deeds and battles.

We can observe that the Life aims at the souls of men, where virtue and vice are to be found, and that it hopes to find character and inclination revealed through light and casual actions rather than through great and weighty ones. In this very freedom from the concerns of historical narrative, however, the Life was necessarily more sensitive to ethical and fictional formulations. It is just a step from Plutarch to the romance lives of Alexander, which actually spring from the work of his predecessor Cleitarchus. In general, we may say that the line between fact and fiction is more carelessly drawn in biography than it is in history. Cicero himself, in a letter to the historian Lucceius, urged the historian to write a separate sketch of Cicero's consulship, in which he could properly depart from the rules of historiography and produce a work which would be more moving and more instructive. Plutarchian biography is written in just this spirit.

This kind of biography is almost the perfect complement of realistic fiction. Its subject is real, a "historical" personage, but its substance is highly fictionalized in the interest of emotion and moral instruction; to move and to teach is its object. Realistic fiction habitually invents an "unhistorical" personage and then seeks to actualize the substance of the character's experience so as to convey a sense of reality, a representation of life. In an empirically oriented culture, biography will tend to develop in the direction of "scientific" accuracy of fact; but without continual pressure from empirical modes of thought, the Life quickly slides over into romance, as it did in the saint's-life formulations of the Middle Ages. After Roman times the potential of biographical form for factual or mimetic narrative remained largely undeveloped until the seventeenth and eighteenth centuries.

Having traced the stream of empirical narrative through classical times, we must now return to the other main derivative of epic narrative, the romance. As the *logographoi* of Greece were working toward the de-fabulization of their narratives, the *epopoioi* correspondingly were de-historicizing theirs. The *Telegony*, for example, a sixth century B.C. continuation of Homer's *Odyssey*, showed a marked tendency to fictionalize: in it Odysseus is killed by Telegonus (his son by Circe) who finally marries Penelope while Telemachus marries Circe. Invention, not tradition, is obviously directing the symmetrical plotting of this story. In the fifth century, written fictional narrative virtually disappeared in Greece, squeezed out by the development of the brilliant Greek drama and the great historical works. But in the fourth century we can see a new fictional spirit developing which was to be of considerable consequence. Xenophon, a historian with a rather clear idea of the difference between history and fiction, devised a new combination of the two. In his *Cyropedia* he deliberately fictionalized the life of a historical ruler, aiming, as Cicero later observed, *non ad historiae fidem, sed ad effigiem justii imperii* (not at the trustworthiness of history but at a model of just government). Utopian fiction begins here, as does the historical novel. And in the story of Abradates and Panthea, Xenophon has given us what classical scholars generally concede to be the first Western love story.

Another landmark in the development of ancient fictional narrative was the third-century *Argonautica* of the Alexandrian Apollonius Rhodius. Using traditional mythic materials, and borrowing techniques from the rhetoricians, the dramatists and the historians, Apollonius wrote a poetic narrative in four books which divided its interest between heroic deeds and individual psychology. There will be occasion to examine this work in more detail below, as a part of a consideration of characterization in narrative, but for the moment let its existence be noted mainly as one factor in the background of the rise of the principal form of Greek prose fiction — the romance. Romance, of course, is a term borrowed from later usage as a general label for narratives in the Romance vernaculars, whence it passed into general European usage (e.g. French *roman*) as a term for long prose fiction as opposed to short (e.g. French *nouvelle*), and into English usage as a term for non-realistic fiction as opposed to the realistic sort which acquired the name novel (as in Clara Reeve's formulation, quoted in Chapter 1 above).

Classical scholars are still debating the nature of the antecedents of Greek romance. The form probably owes something to New Comedy, something to the writers of mimes, something to the rhetoricians, something to Eastern literature, and something to the new emphasis on love seen in the *Cyropedia*, the *Argonautica*, and in the whole of Alexandrian literature. It seems to have arisen as early as the second or first century B.C. The fragmentary

Ninus Romance of this period indicates that the early forms of
the romance may have involved narrative episodes clustering
around a character based on an actual historical personage —
something like the *Cyropedia*, but with the philosophical interest
in presenting an *effigium justi imperii* supplanted by an interest
in an exciting and erotic story. Whatever its antecedents, Greek
romance became a vigorous and flourishing form, practiced widely
around the Mediterranean, working into medieval vernacular literatures via the *Gesta Romanorum* and similar collections (as,
for example, the story of Apollonius of Tyre was taken over by
Gower from the *Gesta Romanorum* for an episode in his *Confessio
Amantis*, whence Shakespeare borrowed it for his dramatic romance *Pericles*). These narratives were revived and translated
into the vernacular in the sixteenth century so as to leave their
mark on such Renaissance fictions as Sidney's *Arcadia*, and ultimately on the developing European novel. The plot of *Tom Jones*,
for example, is essentially a Greek-romance plot.

The principal surviving Greek romances, dating mostly from
the second century A.D., are Chariton's *Chaereas and Callirhoe*,
Xenophon of Ephesus' *Habrocomes and Anthia*, Heliodorus' *Theagenes and Chariclea* (also called the *Aethiopica* — the longest
and most carefully constructed of them all), Longus' *Daphnis and
Chloe* (which mixes Theocritan pastoral with standard romance
formulae), and Achilles Tatius' *Leucippe and Cleitophon*. The
plot elements of these romances are highly stylized. A young
couple fall in love, are prevented from consummating their love by
various catastrophes which place them in grave danger while separated from one another, but they emerge chaste and unscathed,
to marry at the end of the narrative. (There are some exceptions.
Daphnis, for example, does not remain perfectly chaste; but
Longus is toying with the romance form, which he takes less
seriously than most of the romancers.) The principal characters
in a typical romance are definitely human beings, but extraordinarily attractive ones, and usually virtuous and honorable despite extraordinary pressures. In the romances chastity becomes

the most significant of all the virtues. As a rule in these tales, strict poetic justice prevails, and the truly virtuous characters are indestructible though always threatened with destruction.

In these narratives the fictional element dominates. Though the mythic and fabulous are played down (except insofar as all marriage plots may have something to do with fertility ritual) there is no attempt at an illusion of historicity or at a presentation of ordinary contemporary life. These are made-up stories which admit to being made-up stories. The emphasis is on plot rather than on character, the strange rather than the familiar, and, though a *deus ex machina* may take a hand in the action, the focus remains on the human rather than the divine. Though these stories turn away from sacred myth, their interest in suspense and narrative complication prevents them from approaching empirical organization or characterization, and their insistence on poetic justice keeps them forever insulated from the real world. The writers of these narratives are as aware of the difference between history and fiction as the historians. Like the historians they purge overt myth from their narratives but retain, unconsciously perhaps, certain mythic elements in their narrative articulation. But in direct and conscious opposition to the historians they revel in the freedom offered by fiction to invent pleasing and surprising events and complications without regard for probability and without reference to the actual world.

Every age and culture has its characteristic narrative forms. Rome, characterized in part by its Hellenophilic spirit, developed an extensive literature modeled on Greek patterns such as the historical writings we have already glanced at. There is, moreover, even today, a tendency to think of Roman narrative primarily as being of this sort; perhaps because of the dominance of Vergil in our school curricula. But the Romans made an extraordinary and original contribution to the development of narrative forms, the extent and nature of which has seldom, if ever, been properly appreciated. Before we can turn to this, however, the achievements

of Roman writers in the derivative forms other than history must
be considered. These in themselves are far from minor achievements, though the nature of the present discussion of the evolution of narrative forms tends to throw an undue emphasis upon
those other writers who managed, in Ezra Pound's phrase, to
"make it new." This is regrettable but necessary, even though it
makes Vergil, for us, a relatively minor poet.

Vergil, of course, is the most obviously derivative of the Roman
narrative artists. Still, in imitating Homer as closely as he did and
as well as he did, he did what Homer had never done. He set the
seal on the written epic form. From a fixed point, which we may
consider Homer to be, it is possible to draw a straight line in any
direction. But, given a second point through which our line must
pass, only one direction is possible. Vergil provided in the Latin
language such a second point of reference. The *Aeneid* is a synthetic (or "literary") epic. In it Vergil imitated all of what we
might call the accidentals of Homer — many of which had been
in Homer the result of the exigencies of oral formulaic composition
(recurring epithets, "epic" similes, and the rhetoric of oral poetry
in general). After Vergil a narrative poem could aspire to the
name of epic only if it dutifully observed the epic conventions
which Vergil had fixed. If we are to think clearly about narrative
forms, we shall have to modify traditional terminology somewhat.
A true epic is an oral-formulaic narrative, amalgamating mythic,
mimetic, and historical materials in a fictional form. Where *Beowulf* is a true epic, the *Aeneid* is a synthetic epic, which is to say
a romance in epic's clothing. Vergil's emphasis on the piety of
Aeneas and on the importance of the fatherland are ethical considerations which replace to a considerable extent the Homeric
interest in character displayed through action. Aeneas is not the
man-god of epic narrative, but the king-hero of romance. Thus
the first six books of the poem can follow the *Odyssey* closely, but
the second six, closer to the *Iliad* in subject matter, have not the
rich and problematic characterizations of Homer's narrative. Vergil takes narrative in the direction of allegory: English narrative

poets as different as Spenser and Milton are both closer to Vergil than to Homer. The world of epic is a problematic world of questions about life for which there are no easy answers. The ways of God to man may be accepted in epic but they are not justified. They remain inscrutable and capricious. As the synthetic epic turns toward romance it begins to provide answers for the questions and problems which make for dramatic tension in the primitive form, substituting an intellectual and philosophical interest for the interest in character gripped by fate which is typical of the epic. The *Odyssey* itself, whether or not it was written by a man called Homer, has moved a long way in the romantic direction from the problematic world of the *Iliad*.

In Latin literature, Lucan, who aspired to match or outstrip Vergil's success as a narrative poet, still had to accept his predecessor's concept of epic form. He countered, in the *Pharsalia*, by taking a relatively modern historical subject, Caesar's civil wars, and emphasizing the paradoxical and shocking aspects of his material, and by exploiting the rhetorical and the epigrammatic resources of his medium. As Vergil had pushed synthetic epic toward romance and allegory, Lucan pushed it back toward history and toward tragedy of the Senecan variety. In the Middle Ages Lucan came to be considered a historian much as Homer had been so considered in pre-Herodotean Greece.

The most influential of all the Roman narrative artists who derived their form or their matter from the Greeks has yet to be considered. No classical writer had a more profound influence on later literature than Ovid. But his influence had almost nothing to do with the evolution of narrative form. Ovid's great narrative, the *Metamorphoses*, is derived from the Greek theogonic tradition and from such anthologies of myth as the *Ornithogonia* (stories of men who became birds) ascribed to a certain Boios. This peculiar hybrid form was such a close combination of form and matter that it simply could not be adapted for general use. Ovid's great influence on later literature, then, derives not from his form but from the quantity of mythic materials he assembled

in the *Metamorphoses* and made readily available; and, more significantly, from his interest in psychology, especially the psychology of love, which is apparent not only in the *Metamorphoses*
but in the *Amores*, the *Ars Amatoria*, and the *Heroides* as well.
(This aspect of Ovid's achievement will be considered below in
Chapter 5.) He also made a formal contribution to the tone and
rhetoric of the short tale, which would inevitably be considered in
any study of the tradition of short narrative forms, but must not
be allowed to draw us away from our present consideration of the
development of the longer forms.

The Roman works thus far considered have represented refinements on forms and materials originally developed by the Greeks.
The unique Roman contribution to the development of narrative
form remains to be considered. Quintilian was thinking along
these lines but in a more patriotic spirit when he observed that
satira quidem tota nostra est. We may revise this statement to
observe that not merely satire but all eye-witness narrative forms
(which include most early narrative satire) reached their first
significant development in Roman times. This is not to say that
first-person narrative never existed before, but that narrative forms
designed to exploit first-person presentation in one way or another
had not been developed before; so that a Xenophon, writing of
his own experiences in Asia Minor in the *Anabasis*, automatically
wrote of himself in the third person, just as Caesar later did in
De Bello Gallico, and as even Villehardouin was to do in his *De la
Conqueste de Constantinople*, written early in the thirteenth century. Such men chose this mode of narration not out of pride or
humility, but because they associated the third person with formal
narratives of the epic and historical kind, with which they associated their own works. To write in the first person is to be less
formal and more intimate, as is Villehardouin's successor in primitive French historical narrative, de Joinville in his *Mémoires, ou
Histoire et Chronique du très Chrétien roi Saint-Louis.* In early
literature the first person is generally associated with such loose
and personal forms as the epistle and the memoir, the forms of
the amateur rather than the professional author. We find occasion-

ally a sense of self-awareness in the authors of works which are essentially neither first-person in form nor autobiographical in spirit, as when Hesiod opens the *Theogony* with a reminiscence of the time when a delegation of Muses visited Hesiod (referring to himself in the third person) and persuaded him to enlighten the world with the true histories of the deathless gods; but we find almost no first-person narrative in early Greek literature, with the important exception of the story of his travels told by Odysseus to the Phaeacians, which is embedded in the larger narrative structure of Homer.

This portion of the *Odyssey* is of great interest. It is the most magical, fabulous, and romantic thing in Homer. It is a traveller's tale, a road or journey narrative, and it is told in the first person. The traveller's tale is a persistent oral form in all cultures. It is, in a sense, the amateur's answer to the professional rhapsodist, skald, or jongleur. Its form is the simple linear form of voyage by land or sea, and in it fiction, which in its highest sense involves ordering and shaping for an esthetic end, is reduced to its most humble form — the lie. Traveller's tales in all countries are notoriously untrustworthy, and untrustworthy in proportion to the distance of the travels from familiar territory, just as ancient maps become less and less reliable toward their edges. The prose writers of the Roman Empire developed the first-person journey narrative as an art form and also established the pattern of the inward journey, the autobiography, in its two usual forms — the apology and the confession. All of these developments can be illustrated from the works of four men who came from various parts of the Empire in the period from the first to the fourth centuries A.D.: Petronius, Apuleius, Lucian, and St. Augustine.

Petronius in the *Satiricon,* so far as can be determined from the brilliant fragments which have survived, wrote the first picaresque narrative. (Like the term romance, which we apply retroactively to the Greek romances, picaresque originally designated a kind of European vernacular fiction but is here applied to the classical prototype of vernacular picaresque.) In picaresque narrative a rogue tells the story of his own experiences in the con-

temporary world, usually involving his travels from place to place
and through a wide spectrum of society. The main interests of
picaresque fiction are social and satirical. Petronius himself may
have derived his form in part from the lost Menippean satires of
Varro. The etymology of the word satire is still a much-debated
question, but Varronian satires were apparently a mixed bag of
prose and verse, imitations, parody, and farce. The *Satiricon* contains a good deal of such material, including a miniature epic
poem and some purely nonsensical poetic materials. As it evolved,
picaresque form became more concerned with society and social
satire than with the literary and philosophical materials in the
Varronian and Petronian amalgam, moving, in fact, away from
satire and toward a more purely mimetic kind of narrative, as
the sequence *Lazarillo de Tormes, Gil Blas, Roderick Random,
Tono-Bungay,* and *A Time of Hope* will serve to illustrate. The
social satire in Petronius is derived not from Varro but from the
Milesian tales, which Petronius imitated and borrowed from. (We
shall have more to say of these in connection with Apuleius.) But
the *Satiricon* itself was more interested in capturing the quality
of contemporary life than any previous full-scale narrative had
been. In Alexandrian literature Theocritus reached a high point
of mimetic presentation in his description of women going to the
temple of Adonis (*Idyll* No. 15), and the Greek presenters of
mimes who were called biologists were called so because they took
their subjects from common life. (Longinus refers to such sketches
as *biologoumena.*) But Petronius was groping toward a form of
full-scale narrative which would be appropriate for such realistic
materials as his famous description of the banquet given by the
newly rich freedman, Trimalchio; and in doing so he seems to
have arrived at something very like Renaissance picaresque. Because of the fragmentary nature of the surviving *Satiricon* texts,
it is impossible to speculate profitably on the form of the whole.
But we do know that it was episodic and was based on the travels
of the first-person narrator, the rogue Encolpius, through the
contemporary Roman world.

Another major Roman progenitor of the European picaresque was the *Metamorphoses,* better known as the *Golden Ass,* of Apuleius. Like the *Satiricon,* the *Golden Ass* employed materials from that famous lost collection of earthy stories, the Milesian tales. These tales are to the romances of classical times what the fabliaux were later to the medieval romances, and no doubt some of the same stories figure in both categories. In the episodic form of picaresque narrative such tales could easily be introduced either as episodes or as interpolated narratives, the first-person narrator merely serving as a connection from one tale to the next. Thus picaresque narration develops in part as a means of connecting separate stories. In his Address to the Reader, Apuleius even refers to his work as a collection of tales in the Milesian manner. Both Petronius and Apuleius have given us stories of grave-watching which probably have a Milesian origin, and both writers delight in dealing comically with sex, in what is no doubt the Milesian manner. Sex and death, of course, were exploited by the Greek romances as much as by Petronius and Apuleius, but in a different way. Borrowing our terminology from Vivian Mercier's study of *The Irish Comic Tradition,* we can observe that these Roman narratives stress the grotesque (that which makes fun of sex) and the macabre (that which makes fun of death), while the Greek romances in general exploit these fundamental aspects of the human condition for the sake of suspense and terror rather than for comic purposes. The picaresque narrative is the comic antitype of the romance. It approaches the mimetic, but for comic and satiric purposes mainly. It sets the contemporary world and a first-person narrator up against the never-never world and impalpable narrator of romance, employing a loose and episodic structure indicative of its relative indifference to plot, relying on wit and variety rather than empathy and suspense to maintain the interest of its audience. And as there is more of Greek New Comedy in the romances, so there is more of Old Comedy in the picaresque.

Apuleius is less concerned with mimesis than Petronius was.

Though his setting is realistic enough, the action is essentially fantastic in that it turns on the narrator's transformation into an ass. This break with external probability serves to emphasize the internal growth of the central character, the narrator. The climax of the narrative involves the moral regeneration of the hero, who has learned as an ass what it means to be a man. We can see satire turning into allegory in the *Golden Ass*, as the roguish young man of the opening, the bad example, becomes the devoted priest of Isis, the good example, at the end. The story of Lucius is a confession in fictional form, and its essential plan is the same as the plan of St. Augustine's *Confessions*. The similarity in narrative stance between picaresque and confession enables the two to blend easily, making possible entirely fictional narratives which are more in the spirit of confession than picaresque, like *Moll Flanders* and *Great Expectations*, and narratives which are picaresque in spirit but employ actual materials from the author's life such as *Tono-Bungay*. By turning the direction of the narrative inward the author almost inevitably presents a central character who is an example of something. By turning the direction of the narrative outward the author almost inevitably exposes weaknesses in society. First-person narrative is thus a ready vehicle for ideas.

Apuleius was also the author of a purely autobiographical sketch, the *De Magica* or *Apologia*, in which he defended himself against charges of bewitching the widow whom he had married and against informal allegations that he had murdered his stepson. The *Golden Ass* with its magic and its prosecution of the innocent Lucius certainly has interesting echoes of Apuleius' own life. Though he refers to his work in the opening address to the reader as a "string of anecdotes in the popular Milesian style," the quasi-autobiographical string is of more importance to the history of narrative than the interesting beads which are strung on it. Even the lovely tale of Cupid and Psyche, loosely attached to the narrative as an overheard bedtime story, has less significance for us than the picaresque-autobiographical shape of the whole work.

For Apuleius went farther than Petronius in one direction. The narrator of the *Satiricon* is a fictional character named Encolpius. But the narrator of the *Golden Ass* is called Lucius Apuleius. To some later readers the *Golden Ass* was a true autobiographical record, even St. Augustine writing that "Apuleius either reported or invented his transformation into the shape of an ass." Apuleius, though he presents a recognizable contemporary milieu, turns the first-person narrative inward toward the psyche. As the *Satiricon* leads toward the socially oriented picaresque, the *Golden Ass* leads toward the psychologically oriented confession.

The eye-witness narrative took still another direction in Roman times in the hands of the much-traveled Lucian of Samosata. Though he wrote in Greek, like Plutarch, he was a product of the Roman Empire. He is reputed to be the author of an existing short version of the same "Ass" story which is told by Apuleius (minus the personal and religious elements) but the exact provenance of the story is unknown. It was doubtless circulating in many versions, and Lucian and Apuleius were contemporaries. But, like Apuleius, Lucian has given us some ostensibly autobiographical writings, such as "The Dream," a talk in which he explains how he adopted his vocation (Culture). He also dabbled in biography, with a polemical life of his contemporary enemy, Alexander — not the Great, but (in Paul Turner's phrase) a "theatrically-minded mystic." Still, Lucian's main contribution to the evolution of narrative forms is of another sort. Employing the first-person, peripatetic narrator in his *True History*, he developed the form of the mock journey designed for an intellectual and satiric purpose rather than a mimetic or fictional one. The narrator of the *True History* explains in his preface that his work is intended to be a parody of the many fanciful and fabulous accounts that have been presented as fact by previous story-tellers who posed as historians — beginning with Odysseus, "Who told Alcinous and his court an extremely tall story about bags full of wind, and one-eyed giants, and cannibals, and other unpleasant characters, not to speak of many-headed monsters and magic potions that turned

human beings into animals." Using his first-person, eye-witness
narrator, Lucian pushes the travel narrative into the realm of the
absurd, doing away with both character and plot in the conventional sense, in order to score intellectual points at the expense
of historians, romancers, epic poets, and philosophers. His narrator travels freely in space and time, to the moon and elsewhere
for conversations with gods and with the heroes and villains of
the past.

Though the *True History* is a straight narrative, the form Lucian most frequently employed in his writings was the dialogue.
But often his dialogues were excuses for eye-witness narration by
his favorite character, Menippus. Lucian borrowed the name
Menippus from the satirical works of Varro, who in turn had
borrowed it from the real Menippus, a Cynic philosopher of the
third century, B.C., who was one of the first writers to deal comically with philosophical themes. Fantastic satirical narratives in
the style of Lucian, featuring voyages in space or time, have come
to be called Menippean Satires, though Varro, who originated the
term, may have had in mind Menippus' (and his own) mixture of
prose and verse as the distinguishing characteristic of the form
(by which criterion the *Satiricon* could be designated a Menippean satire, though to our modern eyes the term picaresque seems
more appropriate to it). In Lucian's hands the Menippean narrative is always comic and usually parodic as well, reflecting the
spirit of its most ancient and obvious ancestor, the Old Comedy
of Aristophanes. In the hands of Lucian's followers the form sometimes lost much of its Aristophanic flavor, combining with idealizing political philosophy (derived from Plato's *Republic* and
Xenophon's answer to it, the *Cyropedia*) to produce narratives of
the Utopian kind, but in the hands of its greatest practitioners
— Rabelais, Swift, and Voltaire — the satiric spirit of Aristophanes and Lucian is preserved.

The ultimate development in Roman first-person narrative
form, which had certainly been hinted at by both Lucian and
Apuleius, was the achievement of St. Augustine, who first em-

ployed the form of the full-scale autobiography as confession. Augustine, very much aware of the achievement of his fellow North African Apuleius, and very anxious to demonstrate the way in which God works through man for his salvation, turned naturally and almost effortlessly to the autobiography as a literary form. Taking God as his auditor, the Saint sought to understand and to account for the factors which had shaped his life. Petronius had turned the first-person narrative into a vehicle for social observation and satire; Lucian had turned it into a vehicle for philosophical satire. Apuleius in a fanciful way had touched on the conversion of the sinner to a nobler existence. But Augustine was the first to probe deeply into the psyche, to substitute self-observation for observation of the world, and to feel that the story of the self alone was important enough to sustain a lengthy narrative. It need not be emphasized that this is an especially Christian attitude. Because God cares about the soul of the sinner, that soul, that self, any soul, any self, becomes of momentous importance. It is the Christian and especially the Augustinian approach to man and the universe which leads the way to psychology. Without an Augustine we would never have had a Freud. Such passages in the *Confessions* as those on jealousy in infants (I, 7), on the motivations of youthful theft (I, 19; II, 4), and on love and lust (*passim*) are astonishing in the extent to which they turn an essentially fresh and untrammeled eye upon the self. After Augustine new depths of characterization were accessible to narrative artists whenever they could find the forms to contain and exploit them. And just as he was presenting a new and mimetic way of dealing with the inner life, Augustine, in his discussions of the Old Testament as allegory in the *Confessions*, was preparing the way for a Christian literature of allegory. For the most part, the Middle Ages learned Augustine's lesson of allegory better than they learned his lesson of mimesis, but it is characteristic of the great narrative artists of the later Middle Ages and the Renaissance — such as Dante — that they learned both lessons and devised new ways of combining the two techniques.

It should be possible to pause now and consider as a whole the state of narrative development at the end of classical times. The epic amalgam of fiction and history, myth and mimesis, had gradually broken down through a process analogous to what T. S. Eliot has called — with reference to seventeenth-century Europe — the "dissociation of sensibility." The rise of rationalistic modes of thought had encouraged history to dissociate itself from fiction; and fiction, freed from historical and mimetic considerations, had developed the idealizing narratives of Greek romance. The pseudo-historical Alexander-romances (as distinguished from Greek romances like the *Aethiopica*) represented a new combination of fiction and history, but based on the weakest elements of both. The romances of the Alexander-romance variety took their simple, linear plots from history and biography; and their simple, idealizing characterizations from romance. We can see that one of the results of the Hellenistic dissociation of sensibility was a marked separation of plot and character in narrative literature. History and biography had the characters; romance had the "well-made" plotting. And the historians, retaining their affinities with the tragic dramatists, were able to present their striking characters in a form which exploited their potential. When the verse-romancers borrowed from tragedy, as in Apollonius Rhodius' characterization of Medea in the *Argonautica*, they could and did achieve memorable characterizations. Vergil's Dido was an adaptation of Apollonius' Medea. Ovid, the greatest character-monger among the classical verse narrative writers, drew his figures mainly from mythological tradition. Lucan drew his from history. But the "invented" character who commands the deep interest of the reader and becomes etched into his memory was practically non-existent in post-Homeric narrative.

In a social satire like the *Satiricon* such figures as Trimalchio and his wife are interesting and memorable ones — but they are so as types rather than individuals. In the early forms of first-person narrative the only character who could have true individuality was the narrator, because he was the one character whose point of view could be made available to the reader; he alone could be seen from the inside. But only in the confession form was the inside view of the narrator presented. Even the apology (or *apologia*) was essentially concerned with justifying the narrator's life and hence — human nature being what it is — tended to avoid the secret thoughts and springs of action. (Rousseau, of course, was to change all this by presenting his *Confessions* as an apology and challenging his audience to examine themselves and see if they were any better than he had been.)

Virtually all of what may be called the primary narrative forms (in the sense of primary colors) had been employed in Western narrative before the fall of Rome, though some, like the autobiography, had hardly begun to be exploited. The development of vernacular literature in Europe was to a considerable extent a repetition of the development of the classical literatures: it, also, can be seen as a movement from oral to written forms, and from mythic to empirical and fictional formulations. But there are some interesting variations within this repetition of the developmental pattern, which may be traced mainly to two particular causes. The European literatures all sooner or later were affected by Christian modes of thought, and most of them were subjected rather early in their development to influences from the more developed culture of classical times, which gradually increased as more of the classical material was recovered and made accessible by translation during the later Middle Ages and early Renaissance. Instead of attempting a survey of the vast field of medieval, Renaissance, and modern narrative on a chronological or linguistic plan, we shall, in the chapters that follow, discuss the major forms of post-classical narrative as they are appropriate to our consideration of such general and continuing aspects of narrative as meaning, character, plot, and point of view. In this way a consideration of Renaissance and medieval allegory will naturally dominate our discussion of controlled meaning in narrative, and a consideration of the modern novel will dominate our discussion of point of view. But we shall frequently find it necessary to refer back to the examples and developmental patterns presented in this discussion of Greek and Latin narrative forms.

4

Meaning in Narrative

Meaning, in a work of narrative art, is a function of the relationship between two worlds: the fictional world created by the
author and the "real" world, the apprehendable universe. When
we say we "understand" a narrative we mean that we have found
a satisfactory relationship or set of relationships between these
two worlds. In some narratives the author tries to control the
reader's response more fully than in others. The most extreme
attempts at this sort of control we recognize as allegory and satire,
and because of the special problems raised by them, we have
devoted the second part of this chapter to a discussion of the
nature and history of attempts to control meaning. But for the
moment we are concerned with more fundamental problems, the
first of which must be the relationship between the actual worlds
of the author and the reader.

In an oral culture this problem does not exist. Singer and lis-
teners share the same world and see it in the same way. Those
elements in a traditional tale which in the course of time might
become irrelevant or confusing to the singers and their audiences
are, in the course of time, eliminated or accommodated to the new
ways; and, conversely, the oral tales themselves act as a conserva-

tive element in a culture, tending to curb new ways of living or of perceiving the cosmos. In a culture of written letters, however, such as our Western civilization has become, a fixed text will tend to survive its native milieu and be forced to make its way in alien surroundings. Not only will its language become archaic and obsolete, but the assumptions about man and nature and about the proper way to tell a story, upon which the tale is built, will also recede farther and farther from the assumptions of living men.

To understand a literary work, then, we must first attempt to bring our own view of reality into as close an alignment as possible with the prevailing view in the time of the work's composition. Even a contemporary work, if it springs from a milieu or a mind quite alien to the reader's, must be approached by him with a special effort if he wants to understand its meaning rather than merely to see what he can make it mean. Thus, the approach of a modern reader to a work from an alien milieu, ancient or modern, must depend to some extent upon historical scholarship or what used to be called "learning." This learning should be used for the sake of the literary work — not the other way round — and it should be used imaginatively, in order to bring the world of the reader and the author into as close an alignment as possible before confronting that ultimate mediator between them — the literary work itself.

This problem of the alignment of "real" worlds can be solved by the imaginative use of learning. A much more complicated problem, however, and one less easily resolved, is the nature of the relationship between the author's fictional world and his real world. This is a creative problem for the author, and it is a critical problem for the reader. It is the very problem upon which much criticism of narrative literature founders. We can best approach it by schematizing the possible kinds of relationship between these two worlds in what may seem at first to be an overneat and oversimple way. To begin with, not all narrative works are seriously concerned with meaning at all. There are different, and

significant, ways in which this unconcern with meaning can manifest itself, but they are best understood after an attempt to confront those works which definitely do aspire not merely to "be"
but to "mean" as well. Works which aspire to meaning do not all
seek to create or convey their meanings in the same way. They
adopt a variety of ways which are intimately connected to the
varieties of narrative form themselves, and can be seen as presenting a similar spectrum of possibilities shading into one another. The connection between the fictional world and the real
can be either *representational* or *illustrative*. The images in a narrative may strike us at once as an attempt to create a replica of
actuality just as the images in certain paintings or works of sculpture may, or they may strike us as an attempt merely to remind us
of an aspect of reality rather than convey a total and convincing
impression of the real world to us, as certain kinds of visual art
also do. That kind of art, literary or plastic, which seeks to dupli-
cate reality we will designate by the word "represent" in its various forms. For that kind of art which seeks only to suggest an
aspect of reality we will use the word "illustrate." In art the illustrative is stylized and stipulative, highly dependent on artistic
tradition and convention, like much oriental painting and sculpture, while the representational seeks continually to reshape and
revitalize ways of apprehending the actual, subjecting convention
to an empirical review of its validity as a means of reproducing
reality. The illustrative is symbolic; the representational is mimetic. In the visual arts illustration ranges between almost pure
meaning — the ideogram or hieroglyph — and almost pure pleasure — the non-representational design. It is tied to ends, not
means. But the representational is tied to the means of reproduction and varies as new ways of seeing or new artistic techniques
of reproducing are discovered.

We can approach a painting in terms of its design and try to
see it in a purely esthetic way. When we do this we are deliberately removing it from the area of meaning, even though we may
recognize in the shapes on the canvas suggestions of actual shapes

and things. Literature can never become quite so "pure," but the highly patterned and virtually meaningless configurations of the romance of adventure are a near equivalent. We can also approach a painting in terms of its symbolic meaning, interpreting the forms according to a system of stipulated meanings from traditional or other sources. This is an iconographical way 'of "understanding," whether the iconography be Augustinian or Freudian. Interpretation of purely illustrative literary works must be analogous to the iconographical approach to works in the plastic arts. We can also approach a painting in terms of its mimetic meaning, attempting to read the character of persons depicted and to comprehend the milieu in which we find them — an approach we are most likely to employ with portraits or other historically oriented artworks. Here, we are on the verge of considering the painter as psychologist or sociologist, an approach considered at best unfashionable as a mode of art criticism today, but quite the way in which the young James Joyce approached the canvases of Munkácsy or the mature Tolstoy represented the visual artist in the Italian chapters of *Anna Karenina*.

Western painting and Western literature have both distinguished themselves from much of the world's art by the extent to which they have emphasized the mimetic or representational potential of their forms; and the high tide of realism in both arts seems to have been reached in the later nineteenth century and then begun to recede, the plastic arts since carrying the nonrepresentational to an extent which literature will hardly be likely to match. Realism has proved so powerful an agent in narrative art that its influence may never wholly disappear; literary artists may never recapture totally the innocence of pre-novelistic romance. It has even been possible for one of the most formidable and influential attempts to see Western narrative whole — Auerbach's *Mimesis* — to consider the subject purely in terms of the development of realism. Still, in our consideration of meaning in narrative literature, we must be prepared to come to grips with the illustrative way of meaning as well as the representational, and especially, we must be prepared to note the way in which these different kinds of meaning combine and interact with esthetic design in the greatest of our narrative works.

Representational narrative can carry specific meaning, referring to actual individuals and events. History, biography, and autobiography do just this. Illustrative reference can also be specific, as it is in the historical allegory of Book V of *The Faerie Queene* or Part I of *Gulliver's Travels*. But both history proper and historical allegory seek continually for higher and more generalized meanings. The diarist or chronicler may simply record specific data, but the autobiographer or historian seeks a pattern which drives him in the direction of generalization. His story will become generalized to the extent that he discovers a pattern in it, and he may, by direct commentary on the action he narrates, or through a device like Plutarch's parallel Lives, make his individual characters into types. The historical allegorizer has already generalized his subject in the establishment of an illustrative connection between fiction and reality, the link between fact and fiction being an aspect of general resemblance. Swift's Flimnap resembles the actual Walpole mainly through a generalized concept of political dexterity symbolized by the fictional character's capers on the tightrope. The specific reference of figures in historical allegory is invariably accompanied by a generalized reference as well.

In representational narrative the notion of specific connection between the "real" world and the world of the story seems to precede the notion of a more generalized mimetic connection. From diarist and historian the narrative artists learn to present a world of apparent specificity, the world of mimetic fiction. Robinson Crusoe is not a real individual but he is an attempt to present an individual whose most important attribute is that he may pass for real. This kind of specific though not factual mimetic presentation shades into a more generalized kind of mimesis dominated by the notion of the typical rather than the notion of the apparently factual. Robinson Crusoe is a type of the middle class man and may be seen as such, but he is not so typical a character as Fielding's Squire Western, for example, in whom potential individuality has been suppressed for the sake of the typical. Fielding, in fact, locates his justification of this new kind of historical or biographical fiction precisely in its function as a way of presenting generalized human types, thus asserting its superiority to so-called history and biography, which present specific lies rather than general truth. Fielding's preference for the general (which he shares with Aristotle) makes him an intellectualizer, a didactic writer. The didactic assumes importance in narrative art whenever that art seeks a generalized connection with the real world.

We have been considering the connection between real and fictional worlds as a spectrum dominated by three hues — the recording of specific fact, the representation of what resembles specific fact, and the representation of generalized types of actuality. With the fourth hue of this spectrum these shaded differences in degree become so marked as to require a difference in terminology. The differences in degree have become a difference in kind. The ways of linking the two worlds which we have just enumerated are all "empirical": they are three different ways of "representing" reality. Confronted with a character in one of these fictional worlds we are justified in asking questions about his motivation based on our knowledge of the ways in which real people are motivated. Though Squire Western is not "realistic" in the same sense that Robinson Crusoe is, or Clarissa Harlowe is, he derives his justification and his meaning from his "realness," his representative quality. When Dr. Johnson defended Shakespearian characterization against the accusation of impropriety, he observed that there is always an appeal open from art to life. In this, as in other formulations, Johnson is of great use to us because his observation marks an important watershed in critical assumptions about the relationship between the real and fictional worlds. It is of the essence of that century in which the novel came into its own that art should be seen as a representation rather than an illustration of life, that it should be seen empirically and judged so, that criticism should abandon the tottering edifice of rules and decorum and rush into marshy ground after the *ignis fatuus* we have learned to call "realism." In the twentieth century we should be able to avoid critical impetuosity and see the representational and the illustrative as simply two solutions to the essentially unsolvable problem of putting life into art, of reconciling truth and beauty.

Illustration differs from representation in narrative art in that it does not seek to reproduce actuality but to present selected aspects of the actual, essences referable for their meaning not to historical, psychological, or sociological truth but to ethical and metaphysical truth. Illustrative characters are concepts in anthropoid shape or fragments of the human psyche masquerading as whole human beings. Thus we are not called upon to understand their motivation as if they were whole human beings but to understand the principles they illustrate through their actions in a narrative framework. An example or two may help to reinforce the distinction: a Theophrastian characterization of a miserly man would be a highly generalized mimetic type; Molière's Miser a somewhat more specifically rendered human being; Balzac's Old Grandet a highly individualized personality. All three are "representational," intended as literary reproductions of a type of man which can (or could) be apprehended empirically in life and presented in literature according to psychological or sociological principles. But Spenser's Mammon in Book II of *The Faerie Queene* is the essence of acquisitiveness itself, given a temporary shape as a character in a narrative framework. He is illustrative. Milton's Mammon, on the other hand, though he shares many of the traditional illustrative qualities of Spenser's allegorical figure, especially as he is presented in Book I of *Paradise Lost*, emerges after his speech in the Great Consult of Book II as more representational than illustrative. His characteristics are derived, principally, from Milton's personal feeling about the nature of a mind dominated by things, rather than from literary or theological tradition, even though this Mammon is not placed in the sort of representational milieu which would enable us to recognize him immediately as a "realistic" figure. To understand properly what Milton is doing with a characterization such as Mammon we must be aware of the difference between illustrative and representational characterization, and to give Spenser his proper due as a narrative artist we must realize that he has something in mind very different from Milton's quite representational kind of characterization.

There are of course some narrative works which gain many of their effects precisely by straddling this precipitous border between the illustrative and the representational. The tales and romances of Hawthorne are a case in point. To some critics it seems evident that these stories should be read symbolically or allegorically; to others it seems equally clear that the meaning of Hawthorne's fiction lies in an understanding of the psychology which motivates his characters. Obviously, both critical approaches depend on an assumption about the nature of the work, an assumption which ought itself to be examined closely in the context of each narrative. It is highly likely that Hawthorne himself never settled consistently into a posture of either representation or illustration, and that the power and intellectual complexity of his fiction is derived from an intricate process of oscillation between these two ways of creating a simulacrum of the real world. A proper understanding of Hawthorne, then, must be based on a grasp of the way in which this oscillation operated in his performance of the creative task.

Much of the more interesting literary characterization can be seen as deriving from the instinct or desire of narrative artists to work on both sides of the gap we have postulated, to make their characters at once representative and illustrative. But this instinct or desire takes a different form in different writers, depending partly on the extent to which the writer is conscious of his technique. One suspects that Hawthorne may have operated more instinctively than deliberately, and one feels even more strongly that his method, instinctive or not, is to blur rather than to bridge, to fuse rather than to juxtapose, to present not a work that can be read on several levels but a work that must be read between two levels. A critic considering this aspect of Hawthorne might build a favorable value judgment into his criticism by referring this phenomenon to Hawthorne's "unified sensibility," or he might equally allow his terminology to masquerade as judgment by calling this a "fuzziness" of focus. We must avoid invidious distinctions arrived at through question-begging terminology, but it may help to clarify the way in which Hawthorne deals with the gap between the illustrative and the representational if we consider some other great narrative artists who have clearly confronted the problem of this gap in ways quite different from Hawthorne.

James Joyce grew up as a narrative artist in a tradition dominated by realistic and naturalistic theory and practice, in which the representation of slices of "real life" could be seen as the true end of narrative literature. His earliest narrative efforts, *Dubliners* and *Stephen Hero,* are clearly efforts in this tradition. Gradually he grew more and more impatient with the limitations of realism and shaped his art accordingly. We can even catch him in revisions of *Dubliners* actually "putting in symbols" so as to lift the stories from their flat naturalistic level, and we can see that the later stories in that collection become more and more concerned with symbolic richness. The very titles of his works, from *Dubliners* and *A Portrait* to *Ulysses* and *Finnegans Wake,* reveal a shift from the representational to the illustrative as the dominant mode of Joyce's thought. From the beginning Joyce was aware of the division between the realistic and the symbolic — it had been one of the great literary battlegrounds of the *fin de siècle* — and his determination as a narrative artist became more and more clearly to bridge the gap between these two modes of narrative with as wide a bridge as possible, hanging on to the naturalistic and representational with stark intensity but insisting on a scheme of correspondences that made the petty objects and creatures of his literary foreground illustrative of heroic and universal types and principles. We can take Molly Bloom as an example — a representational portrait, psychologically sound enough to astonish Jung with its validity and profoundness, but also clearly and deliberately connected to the nymph Calypso and the wife Penelope of literary tradition, and to the *gea tellus* of primitive myth and the general principles of earthiness and undiscriminating fecundity which Molly illustrates through her highly "realistic" stream of thoughts and sensations. The deliberate nature of Joyce's bridge between the illustrative and the representational, and the width of the gap he has chosen to span, is in sharp contrast with Hawthorne's instinctive blurring of this gap. Proceeding in this manner we could formulate quite explicitly the reasons why Joyce and Mann, for example, can be properly treated as members of one narrative school, while Hawthorne and Melville belong to another. But the uses of this distinction between the illustrative and the representational are not merely categorical. They should be critical, mainly, and should help us not only in understanding individual works but also in seeing the evolutionary character of the narrative tradition.

As soon as representational characterization began to exist as a literary possibility and impinge upon the minds of artists brought up on the illustrative, the problem and the potential of mixed kinds of meaning came into existence. In English letters Geoffrey Chaucer felt the beginning of that wave of representational characterization and meaning which seems to come full circle with Joyce. Just as Molly Bloom is a realistic creation invested with mythic significance, the Wife of Bath is a creature with roots in illustrative tradition modified by the first stirrings of the great wave of representationalism which culminated in the realistic European novel. To understand Chaucer we must see how he resembles Joyce superficially, and we must also sense how different it must have been to feel that nameless impulse we have learned to call realism driving one away from a traditional and illustrative characterization which had become a kind of unquestioned instinct. Chaucer's language is the least of the barriers we have to overcome in order to understand him. We must make an effort of historical imagination to get close to his meaning. To keep that effort clear and orderly we can employ the distinction between illustrative and representational as a way into Chaucer's mind and art, taking his characterization of the Wife of Bath as our point of departure.

Insofar as the image represents a type of actual woman, Chaucer's Wife of Bath is a traditional type. Psychologically and socially the "real" world of the fourteenth century was simpler than our own. Human nature tended to be for Chaucer, as it still is for those who believe the old saw, the same the world around. Both the events of history and the behavior of individual people were reducible to fewer types than modern man can easily imagine, and they were in general readily evaluated. The most immediate literary antecedent, and the source for much that we find in the characterization of the Wife of Bath, was La Vieille of *The Romance of the Rose*. Like the Wife, La Vieille delivers an ironic homily on the subject of a girl's duty to herself in dealings with wealthy lovers. In fact, the circumstances of La Vieille's sermon in *The Romance* are interesting enough to deserve a brief digression, for they may illuminate Chaucer's conception of the Wife.

Unlike the other characters whom the lover-narrator of *The Romance of the Rose* meets in the Garden of Pleasure, La Vieille is not an illustrative symbol. She is the type of woman who was once beautiful and has spent her youth on the pleasures of sex. Now that she is old and ugly she regrets only that she did not amass the fortune which could have been hers. While the "moral" she draws from the account of her own folly is obviously one intended for the edification of adolescent girls, she in fact addresses it to her sole auditor, a handsome youth by the name of Fair Welcome (*Bon Accueil*). The significance of Fair Welcome, however, is so remote from that of a representation of masculine youth — despite La Vieille's references to him as "my son" — that the inconsistency is hardly noticeable. The image of the fair young man is an illustrative symbol of feminine behavior, one which would be directly affected by La Vieille's advice. The direct and unabashed confrontation of two such different characters, one a type of actual woman and the other a symbol illustrating an abstract concept of feminine social behavior, is characteristic of *The Romance of the Rose*. The poem is far from being a consistent allegory. Even the famous portraits decorating the outside of the garden wall in the Guillaume de Lorris section of the poem become types of actual people — envious, sorrowful, villainous, penurious, elderly, and so on — rather than purely illustrative symbols of the abstract conception of such characteristics. Narratives such as *The Romance of the Rose* and *The Faerie Queene*, which we usually characterize as allegorical, are never purely so. The characters range from generalized types of the actual to stipulated symbols illustrative of abstract ideas. That the closest and most direct source of Chaucer's characterization of the Wife of Bath is to be found in such an allegorical setting is, however, clearly relevant. In fact, a case can be made for the Wife's being even more nearly an illustrative symbol than is La Vieille.

Most of our evidence for understanding the Wife of Bath comes from what she says about herself. She makes the analogy, for example, between herself and the Samaritan wife of John 4, whom Christ accused of not being married though she was living with her fifth husband. Her commentary on this scriptural passage, as well as on dozens of others cited in her Prologue, suggests that the Wife can be understood at least in part as an antithesis of the Bride of Christ. Unlike the Samaritan woman who was converted, taking Christ as her sixth husband and thus (to medieval commentators on the passage in John) becoming a type of the redeemed synagogue (i.e. the Church), the Wife is ironically in search of a sixth husband who will be a delight to her jolly body:

> Welcome the sixte, whan that evere he shal.
> For sothe, I wol nat kepe me chaast in al.

As a type of the carnal (in contrast to the spiritual) bride, the Wife might well have suggested to the medieval mind a type of woman in general, or even the abstract concept of femininity. The archetypal carnal wife is, of course, Eve. As Chaucer's Parson explains, the scriptural story of the fall of man can be understood as an allegory of the individual's fall:

There may ye seen that deedly synne hath, first, suggestion of the feend, as sheweth heere by the naddre; and afterward, delit of the flessh, as sheweth heere by Eve; and after that, the consentynge of resoun, as sheweth heere by Adam.

The Parson had already said that sin is a turning of the ordinance of God *up-so-doun:*

For it is sooth that God, and resoun, and sensualitee, and the body of man been so ordeyned that everich of thise foure thynges sholde have lordshipe over that oother; as thus: God shold have lordshipe over resoun, and resoun over sensualitee, and sensualitee over the body of man. But soothly, whan man synneth, al this ordre or ordinaunce is turned up-so-doun.

What, exactly, Chaucer means by "sensualitee" is not certain. He probably refers to the "sensible soul," the seat of the four humors and the emotions, in contrast to the reason and will, which make up the "rational soul."

Adam, as man's reason, caused the Fall by yielding his sovereignty to Eve, man's "sensuality," who had in turn yielded sovereignty to bodily pleasure at the prompting of Satan. Neither man's body nor his will was, strictly speaking, responsible for the Fall. It was man's reason that consented to turning the ordinance of God *up-so-doun,* simultaneously revolting from the lordship of God and abdicating its own lordship over the will and the senses. The Wife's argument for feminine sovereignty over the masculine is in its most general sense an argument for the *up-so-doun* ordinance of sin and the Fall. Seen thus, the Wife becomes an illustrative symbol of femininity, of the will's yielding to the demands of the senses and of its domination of the reason in turn. The "feminine" and "masculine," the *resoun* and *sensualitee,* are components of every human soul. As the sanctified soul, whether that of a man or a woman, was likened to the Bride of Christ, and

was foreshadowed by the bride of the Song of Songs in tropological interpretations of Scripture, so the sinful soul, whether that of
a man or woman, was one whose feminine aspect reigned over the
masculine.

The types of the henpecked or the uxorious husband represented not only a type of man; they were illustrative symbols of
consent to the *up-so-doun* ordinance of sin and the devil, in whatever sphere of human life it might prevail. This overturning of
the divine ordinance, reversing the order and hierarchy of the
golden chain of God's love, was the basis of much medieval
comedy. Inevitably satirical, the *up-so-doun* world of medieval
ironic comedy should be seen against the ordered world of ideal
(romantic) comedy: Augustine's City of Man seen against his
City of God. Satire and romance are the great medieval narrative
genres; they are both comic, for they are at bottom both versions
of the Divine Comedy.

The Parson's allegorical interpretation of the story of the Fall
explains a good deal of medieval "antifeminism." In the fabliaux,
like Chaucer's Miller's Tale or Merchant's Tale, the sexy young
wives escape all moral retribution. Implicit is the assumption
that a young wife is powerless to resist the advances of a fiery
suitor and that doing with him what comes naturally constitutes
no departure from universal feminine nature. The emphasis is on
the foolishness of the old husband and the ingenuity of the wife
and her lover — not on the wife's personality or moral nature as
an actual person. The inability of the "masculine" to control the
"feminine" and to live with it in a proper "marriage" is the allegorical theme of most such ribald and antifeminist narratives.
Chaucer's "Marriage Group" is less significant thematically as a
discussion of actual marriage than it is as a succession (except for
the Clerk's Tale) of satirical illustrations of the *up-so-doun* marriage of *resoun* and *sensualitee* in the City of Man.

If we can avoid the assumption that the Wife represents the
whole personality of a hypothetical person (especially a representation of the personality as it is understood by modern psychol-

ogy) we need no longer inquire into her "motives" in speaking so candidly of her youth or into her "sincerity" in propounding a philosophy of feminine sovereignty. Such questions become as irrelevant as the fact that in actuality only the two or three pilgrims who rode next to her on the way to Canterbury could even have heard her Prologue. We must guard against the possibility, however, that our new freedom in considering the multiple possibilities of the meaning of the Wife as a literary image might lead us as far astray as have the novelistic misreadings of the past. It does not *automatically* follow that, because the Wife cannot be the representation of an individual conceived in modern types, the image must *necessarily* be illustrative of abstract ideas, hence allegorical. Having escaped the triviality of a reading based on unhistorical assumptions about the "real" world of the fourteenth century, we must avoid the triviality of a reading based on unhistorical assumptions about the possible fictional worlds of the fourteenth century. The illustrative and the representational were so blended, if not in the same image at least in the same narrative, that pure allegory and pure realism were equally foreign to late medieval art.

The Wife of Bath's account of the celestial influences on her birth is a clear instance of the ambiguity of reference in Chaucer's image:

> Venus me yaf my lust, my likerousnesse,
> And Mars yaf me my sturdy hardynesse;
> Myn ascendent was Taur, and Mars therinne.
> Allas! allas! that evere love was synne!
> I folwed ay myn inclinacioun
> By vertu of my constellacioun;
> That made me I koude nought withdrawe
> My chambre of Venus from a good felawe.

The Wife was born during the hour or so that the sign of Taurus, which happened at the time to contain the planet Mars, rose above the eastern horizon. Taurus, being one of the two houses of Venus, produced a strong Venerian influence, which, added to the influence of Mars, would have wrought, according to medieval astrological lore, a "personality" much like the Wife's. As Mars in the chamber of Venus presided over her birth, she is in turn constrained to recapitulate the scene with every *good felawe*. If the image of the Wife is felt to represent a hypothetical "real" person, we ask such questions as, did the fourteenth-century audiences really believe the astrological lore? If not, does Chaucer want us to think that the audience would be moved by the Wife's apparent belief in it? Does, in other words, this character's view of herself as a predetermined product of planetary influence contribute substantially to the meaning of the image? Should any of the monumental irony of the apostrophe "Allas! allas! that evere love was synne!" be understood as the cry of an actual sinner, whose blind carnality prevents her from seeing that it is precisely love and marriage to Christ in the City of God that her sexuality so cruelly parodies?

Poised against the possibility of the Wife as representing a self-conscious individual is the possibility of her illustrating a life force, morally neither good nor evil in itself. In medieval moral allegory the images of Mars and Venus were symbols illustrative of the irascible and concupiscent powers of the "feminine" *sensualitee,* the chief agents in the body's attempt to control the will and the reason. Simultaneously the image is illustrative and representative, illustrative of forces that constantly challenge the ordinance of God and representative of the form in which the *up-so-doun* ordinance of sin might manifest itself in an actual personality. A full comprehension of the various illustrative and representational elements in a complex characterization such as the Wife should enable us to "understand" Chaucer better, to make the proper kind of connection between his fictional world and the real world. It should also enable us to appreciate more thoroughly the art with which this character was constructed. The appealing humanity of the man-hungry woman and the awesome power of the blind force of concupiscence, by their fusion in the same character remind us that vice and sin do not exist in the world save through the actions of vicious and sinful human beings, and, conversely, that the sin and the sinner are nonetheless separate enough for us to hate the sin and love the sinful human being. For the potential humanist in a thoroughly religious society, as men like Boccaccio and Chaucer clearly were, the only way that the theocratic and humanistic visions of the universe could be rendered and reconciled was in such a characterization as this, poised as it is between the earthly and heavenly perspectives. The esthetic problem of responding to new mimetic impulses in the framework of an essentially illustrative tradition, when solved as Chaucer solved it in this case, leads to a richness and power of meaning hardly attainable by continuing in the old tradition or giving way too completely to the new realism.

The interaction between illustration and representation in the fictional world is but one aspect of the complexity of meaning in narrative literature. We can see in the representational a further division between the psychological and the sociological. Most representational meaning in narrative lies in that area contested by the individual and society. Some novelists are more concerned with social portraiture, others with psychological, but representational values must be seen both psychologically and sociologically. They are the product of the novelist's concern for the identity of the individual and the welfare of society. Similarly, we can see the illustrative as varying radically depending on whether its symbols are orthodox and traditional or heterodox and personal. In Western narrative not only has the representational tended to displace or dominate the illustrative; the heterodox or personal symbol system has also tended to replace the orthodox. Even when traditional symbols are employed by a modern narrative artist, they are frequently employed in non-traditional and unorthodox ways. For a writer like James Joyce, symbolic reference to Freud, Frazer, de Sade, and Masoch is placed on a par with reference to Catholic liturgy or theology — the "Holy Office" is both a priestly function and a puberty rite. And for a writer like D. H. Lawrence it is quite natural to create a symbol system

drawn primarily from a combination of Freud and the Book of
Revelation, the relative dominance of the two being reflected in
the titles of his two main symbolic essays — *The Fantasia of the
Unconscious* and *The Apocalypse.*

Another significant aspect of meaning in narrative, which we
have barely considered thus far, depends upon a connection between the fictional and real worlds so tenuous as to be almost a
denial of connection. In some fictions the apparent humanity of
the characters and the apparent reference of some of the events
to possible human events are not meaningful in any sense, they
merely exist so as to engage the interest of the reader in fictional
happenings. In pure romance the characters do not represent real
individuals or types, nor do they illustrate essences or concepts.
They merely borrow human shapes or human characteristics because these have become in most Western fiction a necessary minimum of narrative equipment. This kind of fiction is as close as
literature can come to the non-representational in art. Such
"meaningless" narratives employ "esthetic" types which short-
circuit meaning by keeping its referential potential within the
context of the narrative. Villains, heroes, heroines: these are
esthetic types which operate strongly on the reader's emotions
but with virtually no meaningful impact. In *Tom Jones* Mr. Blifil
(the villain) and Sophia Western (the heroine) are virtually pure
esthetic types.

The intellectual vacuity of pure romance makes it a ready vehicle for illustrative or allegorical narrative, but when esthetic
types are merged with illustrative types, and purely emotional
situations or events are combined with allegorical situations or
events, the tension between ethical and esthetic impulses can
become complex, working modifications in both story and meaning. In a narrative by Hawthorne it is quite conceivable that some
elements take the shape they do because of their illustrative content and some because of their representational quality (as we
have already suggested), and that some are shaped by the purely

esthetic exigencies which require the tale to adopt a form capable of satisfying the reader's purely emotional expectations.

We can observe with some clarity the ways in which these different kinds of connection between the real and fictional worlds manifest themselves in narrative works, if we consider for a moment some of the varieties of characterization employed by Fielding in *Tom Jones*. In this novel the tutors, Thwackum and Square, are primarily illustrative or allegorical characters. They do not mainly represent sociological or psychological types, but illustrate philosophical and theological positions which are always in perfect opposition. And in the same novel Squire Western is a representative or mimetic character, representing a psychological type or humour — the choleric man, perhaps — and a sociological type for which his name provides the label — a Tory squire from the West of England. Because Western is both a permanent type of human nature — choleric — and a specifically localized sociological type — eighteenth-century country squire — Fielding was able to assert that the basis for this kind of characterization was truth to general human nature, regardless of time and space; while Sir Walter Scott was able to praise this particular characterization, Fielding's own view notwithstanding, for its unmistakable specialness, remarking the accuracy of the portrayal and observing that no other time and place had produced anything exactly like the eighteenth-century Tory squire of England. For us, it seems easy to reconcile these views by noting that the effectiveness of the characterization stems from the fact that it indeed does just what both Fielding and Scott say about it. It is representative of both general and specific human qualities.

In this sort of discussion a certain amount of oversimplification is inevitable, but we may be able to guard against an excess of it by looking a bit harder at the ways in which illustrative, representational, and esthetic elements are combined in Fielding's characterization. Thwackum and Square, on the one hand, and Western, on the other, though different in the ways we have just been considering, are also united by a number of characteristics.

Though Western is essentially a mimetic type, he is too typical to be quintessentially mimetic. Fielding's contemporary, Richardson, presents much more highly individualized characters, whose inner lives are far more complex. In a very real sense the psychological is more mimetic than the sociological. Characterization by sociological situation involves an inevitable generalizing process; it opens the way to illustrative characterization and allegory; whereas, characterization by presentation of thought process does not inevitably include reference to systems of psychological classification. The psychological impulse tends toward the presentation of highly individualized figures who resist abstraction and generalization, and whose motivation is not susceptible to rigid ethical interpretation. When Tom Jones acts, the question of whether he is "right" or "wrong" is always important to the story and to its meaning. The question or rightness or wrongness cannot be put so easily to the actions of Leopold Bloom, or even to the actions of Clarissa Harlowe. The inner lives of Richardson's characters are much more thoroughly realized and much more complex than those of Fielding's. In fact, Fielding's inability to understand Richardson is mainly the result of his inability to understand Richardsonian complexity of characterization. For Fielding, Pamela was a scheming hypocrite and Clarissa an angel — and he was equally wrong in both judgments because he could not "see," simply could not perceive the Richardsonian tangle of motivation. This difference between the two men was what Dr. Johnson had in mind when he distinguished Richardson from Fielding as one who could see into the mechanism of a clock while the other merely knew how to tell the time. Johnson's metaphor is unfair to Fielding but it perfectly describes the difference between the two kinds of characterization. The strong influence of Fielding on English fiction for the past two hundred years accounts in part for the tendency of the English novel to resist realism and maintain a persistent hospitality toward the typical and the allegorical.

In responding to Richardsonian characterization, the reader does not make a connection between the fictional character and an actual type or concept; he makes a connection between the character's psyche and his own. Richardson's characterizations are much more personal — drawn more deeply from the author's own being — than Fielding's, and the reader's response is also much more personal. The Richardsonian kind of characterization tends to take the character out of the area of "meaning." We can see Clarissa as a type of the bourgeoise and Lovelace as a type of the aristocrat, and we can read the rape of Clarissa as a symbol of the class struggle; but we do considerable violence to the individuality of the characters by considering them too seriously in this way. Still, by raising the possibility we can see that we do less violence to Lovelace than to his victim by seeing him as a type. His characterization is less personal than Clarissa's, and much of his character is composed of standard elements of Restoration Rake. But Lovelace is not the character we hold up as being typically Richardsonian. Pamela and Clarissa are creatures of true Richardsonian complexity, and this is illustrated perfectly by the injustice Richardson does his own creation when he insists on an exemplary interpretation of Pamela as a figure illustrative of Virtue Rewarded. Richardson's intellectual grasp of his own achievement is a slender one. He was a genius of the psyche but in all other things a rather ordinary individual, with an intellect far inferior to Fielding's.

In addition to being something of a social type — Restoration Rake — Lovelace is something of an esthetic type — the Villain — also, without whom Richardson's finely wrought timepiece would lack a mainspring. But Lovelace is too deeply and complexly motivated himself to be a pure esthetic type. He has too rich a personality. Normally we do not empathize at all with the esthetic villain, nor do we criticize the esthetic heroine. We are not interested in connections between the psyches of Mr. Blifil or Sophia Western and our own, nor do they suggest interesting correspondences to the types and concepts through which we apprehend the real world. They are of the story, serving mainly to polarize the reader's emotions and to assist in generating that raw desire for the consummation of the plot which hurries us so precipitously through the last part of Fielding's novel. Such esthetic types have great emotional value within the fictional world but no intellectual connection with reality; therefore, we can say that they have little to do with "meaning" as we have been using that term. In a quite different way the most mimetic characterizations seem also to exist largely outside the area of meaning. The highly individualized character draws the reader into a very intimate connection with the fictional world and makes that world assume something like the solidity of reality. By awakening complex correspondences between the psyches of character and reader, such characterization provides a rich and intense "experience" for the reader — an experience which may not only move him but also exercise his perception and sensibility, ultimately assisting him to perceive and comprehend the world of reality more sharply and more sensitively than he otherwise might. This is obviously a worthy function and it is on this basis that "realism" in fiction has quite properly sought its justification. But a narrative work, if such could exist, which presented only this kind of relationship between its fictional world and the real world would not be "meaningful" as we are using the term here. This is not to say that such a work could not be of great power and beauty, or even of great ethical value. We are deliberately narrowing the scope of that word "meaning" at this point, so as to include only those narrative works which project some generalized and therefore intellectual connection between the specific characters, action, and background of their fictional worlds and the general types and concepts which order our perception and comprehension of actuality. The meaning of esthetic types is more a matter of plot than of understanding, and the meaning of highly individualized characters with developed inner lives belongs primarily to a discussion of characterization. In considering character as meaning, then, we will be mainly concerned with those two varieties of character whose qualities do awaken generalized correspondences with the real world: with Thwackum and with

Western, with their ancestors and their descendants in the family tree of narrative.

We have begun a chapter on meaning with a consideration of characters and their ways of meaning because characters are the primary vehicles for meaning in narrative. Objects and actions can also have illustrative or representative significance and can be presented symbolically or mimetically or in both fashions. But objects cannot act without becoming characters in a sense, and without character there can be no action. Insofar as a narrative work is a structure of meaning, either representative or illustrative, it will in some ways resemble the structure of non-narrative discourse. The characters can be seen as units, like the sentence and the paragraph. Up to now, in considering characterization as meaning, we have been treating these units primarily as if they were static, with fixed meanings. But they are not. As characters move in a narrative plot their meanings change, just as the meanings of words change in different grammatical situations and in different contexts. An illustrative character like Fielding's Square becomes representational when Jones discovers him behind the arras in Molly Seagrim's room. The character created to illustrate a philosophical position has become involved in a situation quite at variance with that position. He is referable here to general human types of hypocrisy and sensuality which he represents. Indeed, much of the interest of his characterization can be traced to the tension between his illustrative and representational qualities. Much of Fielding's art and most of his meaning rests on the differences between theory and practice which he demonstrates by putting the illustrative character into a representational situation. Similarly, when Square repents on his death bed and writes a letter clearing part of Tom's reputation, he is neither illustrative nor representational, mainly, but a piece of plot machinery, aiding in the restoration of Tom to his rightful position. Still, his characterization remains representational enough for us to be interested in his motivation here, and to see that the humanity which led him to Molly Seagrim's bed is not inconsistent with the humaneness of his last action. And this action carries an illustrative meaning in its suggestion of the superiority of this sort of natural humaneness to any sort of philosophical principle.

We have found Fielding useful in exemplifying the ways in which meaning is conveyed through characterization because he has managed to balance and reconcile a variety of meaningful elements, including a strong mimetic element in which social and ethical rather than psychological representation is emphasized, a discernible illustrative element frequently tempered by the dominant social mimesis, and a strong esthetic or romance element which shapes both the mimetic and the allegorical for its own ends and stretches them into new complications of meaning. But *Tom Jones* is limited in its usefulness precisely because of its extraordinary reconciliation of historical, mimetic, didactic, and esthetic impulses. To deal more thoroughly with the problem of meaning in narrative literature we must turn to a historical consideration of the union of the didactic and narrative impulses, with emphasis on the two principal kinds of didactic narrative: satire and allegory.

PART 2.   THE PROBLEM OF CONTROL:
ALLEGORY AND SATIRE

The problem of controlled meaning in narrative is most conveniently approached by reviewing some of the categories our discussion has generated thus far. The forms of narrative such as history, biography, and autobiography which are specifically related to the real world we have called *empirical*. We have said that as narrative becomes less specifically related to the real world, replacing its allegiance to specific facts and experiences with an allegiance to a more generalized ideal, it becomes more *fictional*. This fictional generalization of reality is governed by two opposing impulses: the esthetic and the intellectual, the desire for beauty and the desire for truth. An extreme form of esthetically controlled fiction, which minimizes both specific relationship to reality and intellectual content, is *romance*. Extreme forms of intellectually controlled fiction, whether more or less specifically related to the real world, we have called *didactic*. It is with the didactic forms, primarily allegory and satire, that an investigation of controlled meaning in narrative will have to concern itself.

Two persistent problems in definition tend to inhibit all discussions of fictional works in which intellectual considerations influence narrative structure. These two problems are related. One is the tendency to use the word "didactic" in a pejorative as well as in a purely descriptive sense. We are likely to think of a "didactic" narrative as one in which a feeble attempt is made to clothe ethical chestnuts in fictional form, resulting at best in a spoiled story. When the term is used in this sense it effectively begs all questions of judgment and appreciation. Our criticism may be improved if we can strip the word of the unfortunate connotations it has acquired and allow "didactic" simply to refer to a work which emphasizes the intellectual and instructional potential of narrative, including all such works from the simple fable which points an obvious moral to the great intellectual romance which seeks to justify the ways of God to man or to present the psychological laws which govern man's behavior in society. A didactic work may illustrate complacently a moral truism, or put to the most strenuous kind of examination the most problematic and profound ethical and metaphysical questions. Aesop is a didactic author, and so are Dante, Milton, Swift, George Eliot, Lawrence, and Proust.

The other problem of definition which must be dealt with here is that of the frequently invoked distinction between allegory and symbolism. Forcefully established in English letters by Blake and Yeats, this invidious distinction sees symbolism as being organic, non-intellectual, pointing to some mystical connection between the mind of the poet and that unreal world which is the shaping mind or soul behind actuality, wearing what we call the "real" world as its vestment. In this essentially romantic view allegory is contrasted with symbolism as being overtly intellectual and excessively didactic, reflecting the real world in a mechanical and superficial way. But in the practice of *narrative* art (we must insist here on its separation from lyric) this distinction, whatever its absolute validity, is hardly tenable. In criticism of lyric art it is possible to make and hold a useful distinction between the symbol and the conceit as distinct kinds of metaphorical process which generate quite different kinds of meaning (though we would resist any attempt to assign higher esthetic value to either kind). But in narrative any recurring symbol, whether it is an object, a gesture, or a character, becomes defined and limited by its contexts. Narrative requires an irreducible minimum of rationality which inevitably tames and limits the meaning of the vaguest of images. The kind of non-intellectual and anti-rational evocation practiced by the symbolist poet is incompatible with the laws of narrative, which are as inexorable as the laws of physics, though less precisely ascertainable. Rather than divide narrative artists into symbolists and allegorists, we must come to grips in the work of each artist with the kind of interaction between illustrative, representational, and esthetic impulses characteristic of his mind and art. Thus, in the following discussion of didactic narrative we shall use the word "symbol" merely to refer to any illustrative image, "symbolic" to the illustrative aspect of any image, and "allegory" to the kind of didactic narrative which emphasizes the illustrative meaning of its characters, setting, and action. Though À *la recherche du temps perdu* and *The Faerie Queene* are both didactic, Spenser emphasizes illustrative meaning; Proust, representational. Spenser is an allegorist, Proust is not. Joyce is much more allegorical than Proust but, paradoxically, much less didactic, allegory having become almost purely esthetic for him, the delight in correspondences having taken precedence over their meaningful aspects. Leopold Bloom's Odyssean qualities contribute more to the fun of *Ulysses* than to its meaning. Joyce shows us how it is possible on rare occasions to be an allegorist without being a moralist.

Allegory and satire, the two extremest forms of didactic narrative, are not limited to a generalized relationship with the real world, as is romance, because (in terms of our analysis of narrative imagery) these forms may involve the stipulation of an "other" (Greek *allos,* hence *allegoria*) meaning to traditionally quite representational images. Nor, as we have noticed in the case of Joyce, need allegory always be used for didactic purposes. It is true that, in general, allegory tends to result from an exertion of intellectual control over esthetic forms like romance and folktale, while satire tends to result from an exertion of intellectual control over such empirical forms as history, travel narrative, and novella; but allegory is capable of carrying specific topical and historical reference in its stipulated "other" meaning, and satire is capable of using "mock" fictional forms (mock epic, anti-romance) to make quite general intellectual statements. Allegories and satires as we find them in nature, rather than in the critic's anatomy theater, are mixed forms. We have noticed that Fielding's great power as a novelist derives in part from his ability to hold the representational, illustrative, and esthetic aspects of his narrative in a fluid and homogeneous suspension. So the great allegories and satires result from subtle shifts in relative weight among the three aspects of their images rather than from a refinement of any one element into a pristine state.

Spenser and Dante are among the few narrative poets really to master allegorical composition. From them we can get some idea of what the essence of allegory is like, and what qualities are indispensable to allegorists. They have in common extraordinary literary learning and linguistic ability; ease and control in writing vernacular verse, based on enormous natural gifts and an arduous apprenticeship in versification; a deep commitment to ideas, balanced by an esthetic commitment to the art of narrative. Their great allegorical poems have in common an exploitation of the allegorical mixture of representational, illustrative, and purely esthetic qualities. In the *Commedia,* for example, the fictional character Dante grows to love his guide Vergil as a man, and poet, and friend. When they must part in Purgatory the illustrative

meaning of the separation of the hero from reason's guidance
hardly occurs to the reader who has been affected by the separation of the fictional men. But when the realization does come, it
comes with all the emotional power of the fiction. We realize how
frightening is the mystic's leaving reason behind in contemplating
the Heavenly Kingdom. This realization in turn reinforces the
emotion felt at the literal separation of the men. Similarly, Guyon's
invasion of the Bower of Bliss in *The Faerie Queene* is described
in such sensuously beautiful poetry that the seductiveness of the
place is thoroughly convincing. Reluctantly recalling the allegory,
however, we are suddenly and powerfully aware of the enormity
of the evil that so cunningly masks itself. Spenser here makes the
tension between representation and illustration so great that some
critics have condemned him for painting vice too attractively,
while others have condemned him for Guyon's destruction of
the Bower. The allegorical meaning here must come with great
power or be missed altogether.

Allegory is distinguished from other forms of fictional narrative
by the illustrative character of its imagery. The illustrative may
be combined with the representational, as in Dante and Joyce,
or with the esthetic, as in Spenser. But only rarely does it dominate the other two aspects of fiction altogether. Though allegory
demands a fairly consistent symbolism, which would seem to make
it inevitably guilty of mere mechanism in its presentation of ideas,
allegorical narrative in practice has often been anything but mechanical and simple-minded. Allegorical narrative is a mode of
thought and a mode of story-telling, and there is inevitably a
healthy tension between these two modes. One of the main qualities which differentiates narrative thought from other, "purer,"
modes of thought is the inevitable interplay among the various
attributes of a narrative work. The esthetic exigencies driving the
author toward the provision of a satisfying shape for his tale will
operate so as to modify and possibly enrich its intellectual content.
Just as the requirements of a strict form in verse may lead a poet
to meanings hitherto unconsidered and unattained, the esthetic

and representational qualities of narrative serve to subject ideas to a kind of tempering they cannot be subjected to in a merely discursive or philosophical mode of thought.

In some allegories, especially primitive attempts at allegorical narrative, the esthetic and mimetic elements do seem to be ignored or sacrificed to plainness of meaning. In Prudentius' *Psychomachia*, for example, one of the earliest extended allegories, the characters are female soldiers. Each fighter bears the name of a virtue or a vice. In unrealistic and esthetically unsatisfying cavalry charges and single combats, the armies of the virtues and the vices fight it out. Ultimately the virtues triumph. Our interest in the *Psychomachia* is centered entirely on the poem's illustrative significance. It is difficult to imagine that its representational or esthetic qualities could ever have been received as a sugar coating for the bitter pill of its moral instruction. Only from their allegorical significance do the sudden reversals in the fortunes of the two armies or the choices of particular characters to encounter others in specific passages at arms derive any logic, appropriateness, or truth. The allegorical significance makes sense out of the literal story — not the other way about. As story alone the poem neither delights nor instructs. The intellectual so dominates that the potential of the form for testing, qualifying, and enriching ideas by subjecting them to mimetic or esthetic complications is never developed. Even so, the usefulness of narrative as a mode of thought is apparent in this work.

Though at this remove in time it may be idle to speculate about the intentions of late classical and medieval philosopher-poets like Prudentius in constructing their primitive allegories, we can safely reject as an oversimplification the notion that the poems were composed as pleasant vehicles for the instructive load of their allegorical meaning. It may, we suspect, be nearer the truth to suppose that allegorical narrative was felt by the poets to be a genuine instrument of philosophical discovery. Not only the audience, but the poet as well, could trace out further the multiple ramifications of a philosophical proposition if it were put in the

symbolic language of allegory than if it were stated in the inadequate vocabulary of early medieval philosophy. Even primitive
allegory was a congenial mode of thought, not simply an effective
rhetorical device. The development of allegory as a narrative form
depended on the artist's discovery of the potentialities of those
antithetical impulses so largely ignored by Prudentius.

While Spenser's allegorization of heroic romance in *The Faerie
Queene* is more like Prudentius than is Joyce's allegorization of
mimetic fiction in *Ulysses*, the Renaissance and the modern allegorizer seem to move away from the primitive allegory of the
Psychomachia in opposite directions. Spenser stipulates philosophical, theological, and political meanings for esthetic images which
he took from a rich heritage of ancient and medieval heroic narrative; whereas Joyce stipulates esthetic meanings for the representational images of his empirical fiction. The Homeric apparatus in *Ulysses* is an illustrative "other" meaning which is stipulated
for the mimetically represented events of June 16, 1904. The epic
apparatus in *The Faerie Queene*, on the other hand, is the main
representational vehicle for the illustrative "other" meaning of
Spenser's highly intellectualized allegory. Thus, the determining
characteristic of allegory is not the nature of its meaning but
rather the heavily illustrative quality of its imagery. Historically,
however, allegory developed as a mode of thought and a mode of
story-telling that were ideally suited to the purposes of narrative
artists who conceived their obligation to instruct to be at least
as binding as their obligation to delight. This usual didactic function allegory holds in common with satire, to which we will briefly
turn before concerning ourselves with the historical development
of illustrative narrative.

Satire and allegory are not mutually exclusive modes. Whereas
the defining characteristic of allegory is its symbolic imagery
rather than its meaning, satire is most conveniently defined in
terms of its meaning. We shall have occasion a little later to discuss examples of allegory put to satirical purposes; first let us consider the cultural context in which satire is found. Historically,

satire appears as a precursor of realism. Almost of the essence in the satire of Augustan Rome and Augustan England is the ironical juxtaposition of a highly representational fictional world against the suggestion of an ideal world whose values are daily denied in practice. With this juxtaposition it is to the representational rather than the ideal that our attention is drawn. The epic conceptions of heroic wisdom and fortitude provide at best but an indistinct backdrop before which Trimalchio and Encolpius go through their outrageous antics in Petronius' *Satiricon*. Satire depends on notions of the ideal proper to epic, romance, and sacred myth, namely that the ideal world is good and the real world is bad; hence satire naturally flourishes when the world is in transition from an ideally oriented moral scheme of the cosmos to an empirically oriented non-moral scheme. But the validity of satire depends on its ability to convince the reader, at least temporarily, that the social and moral types of the real world are being represented more truly as caricatures than they had been in the idealizing art and thought to which the satire offers itself for comparison. The force of this superiority of satire over epic, romance, and sacred myth as a representation of the real world is double-edged. It strikes out against a particular society for having fallen away from conformity to an ideal past and against the ideals of the past for having so little relevance to the real world. The values of the satirist himself are therefore notoriously difficult to locate.

Frequently, in the course of a long narrative, they shift, especially when the author cannot resist the esthetic and mimetic potentials of his plot. The natural tendency is for satire to drift toward mimesis proper, the characters losing their status as generalized types and taking on the problematic qualities we associate with the novel. This movement is apparent in *Don Quixote*, for example, where we do not have character development in the novelistic sense so much as we have a development of Cervantes' interest in his hero as the representation of a whole man caught up in the conflicting demands of two worlds. A somewhat similar movement is found in both Grimmelshausen's *Simplicissimus* and Swift's *Gulliver's Travels*. Dickens is unable to resist this temptation in *Hard Times*. What starts as satire ends as mimetic fiction if the developing esthetic aspects of the narrative weaken our purely intellectual interest in the dichotomy between the real and ideal worlds. We become absorbed into the fictional world and experience a resultant emotional concern for the well-being of the hero. Such a drift into mimesis proper is thematically satisfying when, as in the case of Swift and Dickens, man's common sense and spontaneous emotion are seen as more reliable instruments than his reason for resolving the contrary claims of the real and the ideal.

Because of its strongly representational character, Roman satire was naturally drawn to empirical forms. The autobiography (Apuleius) and "true history" (Lucian) provided the best narrative vehicles to develop the essentially static satire of the caricature, dialogue, and Mime. The traveling, recording observer within a picaresque frame advanced the technique of mimetic fiction in general by offering a maximum of narrative articulation in exchange for only a minimum of esthetic distraction. But long narrative satire seems almost in the nature of things to be an unstable compound. It is continually threatened both by the esthetic impulse to tell an interesting story and by the representational and illustrative tendencies to focus attention on either the real or the ideal world. The esthetic impulse in *The Golden Ass*, for example, is satisfied by the marvelous metamorphosis of the hero, by the interpolated "Cupid and Psyche" story, and by the triumph of the ideal over the real in Lucius' conversion to the cult of Isis; at which point, however, the work ceases to be a satire. A frankly fantastic journey, following the voyage-visit-expulsion-return pattern of *Gulliver's Travels* and of Varronian satire generally, would seem to provide the most satisfying combination of representational, illustrative, and esthetic elements with which to explore the relationship between a particular society and its inherited social and moral ideals. When satire does turn to the marvelous journey and the other devices of romance for its narrative imagery

it becomes allegorical. Its intellectual preoccupations invest the
esthetic images of pure romance with illustrative meaning. And
the esthetic preoccupations of the narrative invest the representational images of satire with an emotional significance characteristic
of mimetic fiction.

Attempts are often made to connect *Gulliver's Travels* with
satirical anti-romances and Utopian literature, whether narrative
or not, but its affinities with allegorical romance and realistic narrative are often ignored. In the "Voyage to Lilliput" the political
allegory operates much like the political allegory in Book V of
The Faerie Queene. And at the same time the whole tenor of the
narrative is set by that delight in verisimilitude for its own sake
which unites Swift with his contemporary, Defoe. It is fairly easy,
in fact, when reading *Gulliver,* to separate passages with allegorical significance from passages which are given over to the pure
amusement of presenting unreal events with excruciatingly realistic details. The superiority of Part IV of *Gulliver* to the early
voyages is partly the result of Swift's growing ability to blend the
illustrative, representational, and esthetic elements in his tale.
The reader reacts to the Yahoos, for example, as illustrations of
certain aspects of human nature carried to extremes because of
the absence of rational or other restraints — gluttony, lust, avarice,
rage, jealousy. But the Yahoos are also shown to be images of human flesh in a highly representational way, in considerable
physical and psychological detail. They also contribute to the
culmination of the story itself, since the fear that Gulliver may
lead them in outlawry is a motivating factor in the Houyhnhnms'
decision to exile him. And Gulliver himself is not only a kind of
Everyman, illustrating the norm of humanity in contrast with
the Yahoos, who illustrate degenerated human nature, and the
Houyhnhnms, who illustrate a superhuman and unfallen reason-
ableness; Gulliver is also a representative individual with a complex personality. When he responds to the decree of exile with the
reflection that "I thought it might consist with reason to have
been less rigorous," our reaction is a complex one. We empathize

with the individual confronted with this problem, tending to agree with Gulliver and resent the rigor of the Houyhnhnms' rationality. But we also perceive how this situation illustrates the limitations of reason in dealing with human problems. Reason is good, and the Houyhnhnms are admirable creatures, employed by Swift to illustrate some of the ways in which human life might be improved by a subordination of irrationality (Yahooism) to rationality (Houyhnhnmism). But pure reason cannot be a guide for a fallen and degenerate human race. In dealing with other humans the wisdom, generosity, and humaneness of the Portugese captain who rescues Gulliver must temper the rigor of pure reason. Swift allows Gulliver to become highly unrealistic and absurd when confronted by Captain Mendoza (as he does on many other occasions as well) to illustrate the way simple-minded humanity can take even a positive good like reason and render it absurd by excessive veneration. Much of the critical confusion in the interpretation of Part IV of *Gulliver's Travels* stems from assumptions by critics that Gulliver himself must be regarded either as a "real" and developing character or as a mere tool of the allegorical satire. But Swift actually achieves his finest effects and subtlest meaning by refusing to allow Gulliver to be either pure representation of reality or pure illustration of idea. This part of *Gulliver's Travels* is the powerful and complex work of art it is because of Swift's ability to modulate and alter the mode of the narrative so easily and gracefully, but even more so it is because he can make such a near fusion of the two kinds of fictional image of reality. What began in Part I as a kind of allegorical game, with some episodes having "significance" and others merely toying with the representational possibilities inherent in the combination of big people and little people, has come in Part IV to be a very earnest and problematic palimpsest of the kinds of meaning available to the narrative artist and thinker.

The Houyhnhnms and Yahoos of *Gulliver's Travels* illustrate in part the sort of ironical contrast which is essential to satire: the Houyhnhnms are better than mankind and the Yahoos are worse.

The purpose of most satire is to examine the proposition that Yahooism is a more characteristic human state than Houyhnhnm-ism. With the breakdown or threatened breakdown of an ideally oriented moral cosmos this proposition seems to have enough validity to merit consideration, for it takes a sophisticated moral sense to rest content with the conception of mankind and human society as a combination of the two, containing the potentialities for good and for evil of them both. The Yahoo is in some measure an esthetic image. It arouses disgust and fear quite apart from any stipulated illustrative meaning and considerably in excess of the emotions aroused at the sight of actual humans or animals. As esthetic fiction appeals to our sense of beauty with its heroines and ideal landscapes it also appeals to our sense of the ugly with its villains, monsters, and dungeons. And as didactic fiction appeals to our sense of the rational it also appeals to our sense of the absurd. When satire becomes illustrative, therefore, it is frequently characterized by images of the ugly and the absurd, which are understood to illustrate aspects of the real world and to function in at least an implied contrast to aspects of an ideal world whose validity is being tested. But the images of the ugly and the absurd in satire are easily distinguished from similar images in the illustrative romance which provides the basis of much medieval and Renaissance allegory.

The female Yahoo who tries to rape Gulliver is a vividly representational image, the illustrative meaning of which is nearly identical to its powerful esthetic effect. Duessa in *The Faerie Queene*, on the other hand, is not only a type of the witch of romance, the hideousness of whose nether parts the poet cannot bring himself to describe; she is also an illustrative symbol of the corrupt Roman church, of the Whore of Babylon, of Mary Queen of Scots, and of a cosmic principle of duplicity. When the intellectual concerns of satire give illustrative meaning to its imagery, the symbolism is fairly simple and obvious. It rarely detracts from the preponderantly representational effect common to all satire. The illustrative image of allegory, however, carries such a complex and multivalent relationship to reality that its esthetic and representational aspects are often easy to overlook. Except for the illustrative images of primitive allegory, which define themselves in context, the imagery of medieval and Renaissance allegory requires some experience to interpret. It was the product of a literary and philosophical culture which for many centuries had interpreted the images of its epics, romances, and sacred myths *as if* they were illustrative narrative. We turn now to a consideration of this rich allegorizing tradition, sketching in the outlines of two of its principal sources: Greek philosophical allegoresis and Judeo-Christian scriptural exegesis. Neither strand of this interpretive tradition produced models of medieval allegorical narrative. Rather they provisioned a vast storehouse of symbols out of which allegorical narratives could be fashioned.

If the Muse of the Homeric singers had vouchsafed her sons a vision of the future as clear as their memory of the past, Plato's expulsion of them from his ideal state would likely have surprised them less than would some of the apologies that had come to be offered on their behalf. In drawing his indictment against them, Socrates alluded to these defensive arguments, only to dismiss them as irrelevant:

But Hera's being tied up by her son and Hephaestus' being thrown out by his father for trying to help his mother when she was being beaten, and the rest of the Homeric battles among the gods cannot be tolerated in the state whether or not they are supposed to be allegories. For the young cannot judge if a thing is allegorical or not, and notions accepted in youth are likely to become ineradicable and unalterable. It is therefore most important that the first poetic things encountered should be those best designed to inculcate virtue.

Theagenes of Rhegium (*c.* 525 B.C.) is generally credited with having been the first to resort to an allegorical interpretation of a supposed "undermeaning" (*hyponoia*) in explaining such offensive passages in Homer as the battles of the gods. Beneath the literal meaning (*logos*), the battles of the gods were held by Theagenes to be descriptions either of the conflicting elements — Hephaestus, Hera, and Poseidon representing fire, air, and water — or of moral conflicts. Anaximander, Heraclitus, Anaxagoras, and lesser pre-Socratic philosophers likewise recognized a *hyponoia* in the Homeric texts. Metrodorus of Lampsacus, the disciple of Anaxagoras, was the most thoroughgoing of the early allegorical interpreters. He assigned "physical" meanings to both the human and the divine personages: Agamemnon was ether, Achilles the sun, Helen the earth, Paris the air, Demeter the liver, Dionysus the spleen, and Apollo the gall. This tradition of Homeric allegoresis was well established at the time of Plato's birth, and it constituted, by the time he came to write the *Republic*, an important element in Greek philosophical speculation. It is this development which would have amazed the singers.

A plausible explanation for the growth of Greek philosophical allegoresis may lie in the fact that the ancient epic tradition had contained everything the Greeks knew of history, geography, cosmology, ethics, politics, physiology, and a host of subjects upon which later generations began to speculate. At the dawn of Greek rationalism only one text, the Homeric epics, could bring the accumulated wisdom of the past to bear on the mysteries of actuality as they presented themselves to the senses. The exalted position held by the epics prompted philosophers to search, with such dubious tools as etymology, for an adumbration of their own rationally produced doctrines within the *hyponoia* of the divinely inspired Homeric text.

The so-called epics of Hesiod, the *Theogony* and the *Works and Days*, represent the earliest surviving attempt to rationalize the mythical elements of the epic tradition and to bring them into closer correspondence with the data of actual existence. Poetry and philosophy had not yet become in practice, as they were not in Plato's thought to become even in theory, separate arts. Although the evidence seems to point to their having arisen simultaneously, by the fifth century B.C. the allegorical interpretation of the Homeric epics and the discursive representation of speculative thought were distinct, if still closely related, activities. This close relationship between poetical philosophy and philosophical interpretation of poetry, occasionally misunderstood by literary historians, is nevertheless of great historical interest. It is repeated in the period from the twelfth to the seventeenth centuries, the really great age of allegorical literature in the West, when a strong rationalizing impulse once again characterized the greatest imaginations. And the Greek experience will be helpful, if correctly understood, in understanding the medieval.

From Plato's point of view, that of prescribing the ideal *paideia*, the fictions of the poets, though beautiful lies, could nevertheless serve a useful purpose in education. Plato's imagery suggests that he thought of the student as receiving an impression from the "mold" (*typos*) of a story, the *typos* being in turn an expression of the story's "principle" (*nomos*). And in the course of the story a certain amount of mere "opinion" (*doxa*) would be expressed. Since the Homeric epics represent the gods as the authors of evil and as subject to discord, false principles both, they would impress the student wrongly with their false *typos* and corrupt him with their wicked or foolish *doxa*. As an educator Plato could not approve of fictions that not only lied in their representation of actuality (all fictions do that), but also lied in their doctrine. It is thus clear that Plato recognized a level of meaning on which fictions could be true (*typos, nomos,* and *doxa*) even though on their literal level (*logos*) they were false. Presumably fictions that satisfied Plato's requirements would be such things as moral fables and *exempla*, the chief ingredients then as now of the childish literary diet. Such didactic narratives are, of course, not necessarily allegorical. In the *Republic* Plato does not pass judgment on the supposed *hyponoia* of the philosophers. Whether it is there or not, he contends, it will not fix its impression on the youthful character.

The apparent effects of Plato's criticism of the poets in the *Republic* and of the allegorical interpreters in the *Ion* were two: the older, "philosophical," allegoresis waned and a newer, "rhetorical," allegoresis waxed. Arguing primarily from a sense of elegance, Plato convinced philosophers that reason was a better instrument than allegoresis for discovering truth. He convinced the rhetoricians that if the morality, and hence the cultural centrality, of the Homeric epics could not be defended on the basis of their representation of reality it would have to be defended on the basis of an allegorical (illustrative) meaning. In the hands of many of the Stoics and certain of the Neoplatonists, philosophical and rhetorical allegoresis remained a single tightly-woven strand. Similarly, both "physical" and "moral" interpretations of the myths remained inextricably commingled. The point remains, however, that with the defense of Homer against the attacks of Plato, we do not find the beginning of Greek allegoresis. We find instead a shift in emphasis from the fairly widespread allegoresis of the philosophers, who dignified the new cosmologies by finding them hidden in the Homeric *hyponoia*, to the allegoresis of the rhetoricians, who sought out in the *hyponoia* an ethical or religious doctrine that could be used to defend the ancient epics against the attacks both of the rationalists who complained of beautiful lies and of the moralists who complained of harmful lies. It is this tradition of defensive allegoresis, merging with the newly rediscovered *Poetics* of Aristotle, that we see operating in Sidney's *Defense of Poesy* and its Renaissance Italian progenitors.

In the *Poetics* Aristotle does not introduce the distinction between the allegorical and the representational level of meaning. The reason is not far to seek. Truly allegorical fictions would not satisfy his conception of poetry as the imitation of an action. Like Plato, Aristotle is concerned with literature as *mimesis*. The difference in the Platonic and Aristotelian evaluation of art results not from differing views of the function of art but from differing views of reality. Aristotle was at some pains to distinguish poetry from history. The superiority of poetry over history was its ability to represent not actuality itself but the typical. Whereas history was limited to describing events as they actually happened, poetry could present hypothetical events as they might well happen,

The agents in a poetic action were universal in that they said and did the things one would expect from men of certain types. Their actions were consistent in that they followed the laws of probability and necessity. Its consistency, its universality, and its representation not of actuality directly but of the laws governing actuality constituted the superiority of poetry over reporting. Since for Plato actuality was only an imitation of reality, poetry was for him only the imitation of an imitation. It was moving *away from* the real. In generalizing and universalizing, it was for Aristotle moving *toward* the real.

Plato's dissatisfaction with Greek poetry may have resulted from its failure to achieve an allegorical mode. Beginning as he did with a philosophy of ideals, which he insisted upon finding illustrated in the types of mimetic fictions, he was bound to be dissatisfied with an art which produced instead a universalized representation of actuality. If Socrates had not existed, Plato the artist would have to have invented him: only in the Platonic dialogue was it possible to merge the representation of both ideas and actuality in a form that did violence to neither. The few allegories that survive from either archaic or Attic Greek literature, such as Plato's allegory of the cave in Book VII of the *Republic* or Prodicus' allegory of "The Choice of Heracles" in Xenophon's *Memorabilia,* are the work of philosophers rather than poets. Their meanings are stipulated in the contexts in which they occur. Like the personifications in Homer, such as Panic, Flight, Terror, and Strife, the allegories of the philosophers do not develop beyond rather extended rhetorical figures. While the personifications may be evidence of a rationalizing tendency in religious cults, and hence a rationalizing tendency in epic and drama, the allegories are a poetizing element in philosophical discourse. The products of both tendencies contributed, along with the large number of stipulated allegorical meanings in the Stoic and Neoplatonic traditions of Homeric allegoresis, to a vast and consciously controlled body of allegorically significant images at the end of the classical period.

Rationalist attacks on the truth and morality of biblical texts were similar enough to those levelled against Homer that the interpretation with which Jewish and Christian apologists responded can easily be mistaken for a continuity into late antiquity of the methods of pre-Socratic Homeric allegoresis. Plato and his predecessors understood the Homeric texts to have been divinely inspired. Whatever of truth they might contain was to be found either in the *nomos* exemplified representationally or in the *hyponoia* hidden beneath the surface fiction. The literal meaning was (aside from the exceptions made by Plato) a beautiful lie. Plato's exceptions were ugly lies. While regarding the Bible as having been divinely inspired, traditional Hebrew exegesis differed from Greek allegoresis in accepting the scriptural writings as literally and historically true. The Eastern notion of vast, repetitive historical cycles, which characterizes Greek historical thought, may also at first have contributed to the Hebrew habit of interpreting scriptural texts on the basis of their literal accuracy and of the prophecy contained in the objective reality they recorded. Even when Philo, Origen, and others introduced Greek allegoresis into the Hebrew and Christian tradition of scriptural interpretation, the primacy and absolute literal accuracy of the historical meaning of the text was not seriously challenged.

For St. Augustine, who will have to serve as a representative example of what in fact is an extremely diverse and dynamic tradition of scriptural exegesis, the Bible was literally true. The first duty of the exegete, as Augustine outlined those duties in *De Doctrina Christiana*, was to understand the historical personages, utterances, and events which the letters, words, and figures of speech in the scriptural text signify. God was the author of the Bible. Through the inspiration of the Holy Spirit earthly authors became mere amanuenses. As an author, God was an allegorist. He frequently hid His meaning in the historical events recorded in the Old Testament. Only on the basis of a clearly understood historical meaning could the exegete proceed to an analysis of the meanings God had hidden in the events recorded by the Old and New Testaments.

The Hebrew and Christian emphasis on the objective reality recorded in Scripture did not provide an atmosphere hospitable to Greek allegoresis with its destruction of the literal meaning in the process of setting forth the *hyponoia*. And yet, of course, the Platonic dualism of idea and form did strongly influence St. Paul and Christian theology in general. It was the "realism" of traditional exegesis which prevented the "idealism" of Greek thought from producing in orthodox theology the split between the worlds of matter and of spirit that reduced imaginative literature to an imitation of an imitation in Platonic thought and that continued to constitute the principal heretical tendency in almost every Christian age. The synthesis between Hebrew realism and Hellenic idealism resulted in seeing the Bible, as a whole and in its parts, as the record and prophecy of a gradual evolution in time from body to spirit. The letter of the Old Law was seen as containing or foreshadowing the spirit of the New. The heroes of the Old Testament were in a process of becoming, whereas the heroes of Greek narrative were in a state of being. Process in Greek narrative was confined to the action of a plot. And even so, the action exemplified unchanging, universal laws; while the agents of the action, the characters, became as the plot unfolded only more and more consistent ethical types. Abraham, Jacob, David, and Samson, on the other hand, are men whose personal development is the focus of interest. For Christian readers, they become types, not of ethical men, but of Christ, and this by virtue of their personal development.

An historical event such as the sacrifice of Isaac was seen in biblical exegesis first as a type of the crucifixion and secondly as a type of the individual Christian's willingness to die with respect to sin and to the vanity of this world. As well, therefore, as being the foreshadowing of the events of the New Testament, the "typological" meaning of the Old Testament is Christian doctrine, which can be thought of as the teaching that Christ's redemption of fallen mankind was conditional upon the individual man's spiritual re-enactment not only of Adam's Fall (an all but inevitable consequence of the Fall itself) but also of Christ's life and death. In Christ the Word was made Flesh. Scriptural foreshadowings of the Flesh are foreshadowings of the Word. The typological exegesis of Old Testament history involves the twofold process of identifying the event in the life of Christ (the antitype) to which a historical event (the type) refers, and then referring this Christological meaning to a doctrinal and moral meaning applicable to the individual. Typological significance precedes, therefore, moral (or "tropological") significance.

A third way in which the events of the Old and New Testaments were meaningful to the exegetes depends on their being taken for foreshadowings in more concrete imagery of the ultimate union in time, or at the end of time, of the resurrected Church with God, a spiritual union already implied by seeing the individual moral life within the Church as mystically synonymous with the events in the life of Christ. This third significance, the "anagogical" meaning of scriptural history, did not always form a separate level of scriptural exegesis, for although the actual events upon which it was based had not yet taken place, the union which they would bring about was already recognized in the sacramental relationship between Christ and the individual Christian.

The "plot" of the Bible might be visualized as not merely a horizontal line from the beginning to the end of historical time, but also, just above such a line, a gradually rising one leading in time from mankind's expulsion from the earthly paradise to his reunion with God in the celestial one. The horizontal plot line would describe the progress of St. Augustine's City of Man; the inclined plot line the course of the City of God. The lives of the biblical heroes conform to the direction of the rising line, although they constitute but a tiny segment of it. The life of Christ also conforms to this movement and mystically comprehends it all. While it is true that the City of God begins, with the generation following man's expulsion from paradise, in matter and physical form, it ends in spirit. Later events are implied and foreshadowed in the earlier, but darkly. Paul's famous admonition that "the letter killeth but the spirit giveth life" is not a warning that the letter of the Old Testament or the Old Law is a beautiful lie. It is an admonition to read the letter (i.e. the personages, utterances, and events of the Old Testament) spiritually, as a foreshadowing of both the Flesh and the Word of the New Testament.

The Hebrew and early Christian search for significance in the events of history was "realistic" in its analysis of particular men and events. Augustine exhorted his pupils to study the "things" in Scripture, so that they might proceed from an understanding of physical nature to the mysteries hidden there. The scriptural *hyponoia* was contained in the concrete reality of Old Testament history and, since we are still in history, in the concrete reality presently about us. Unlike Greek cyclical theories of history, in which the consistent and universal laws of human nature were exemplified in particular individuals and events, the Christian theory of history clearly envisioned an evolutionary process from a beginning in time to an end, which gave unique significance to each individual event. Not only did each personage participate mystically with the events in the life of Christ; his personal evolution also moved the whole plot one step closer to its eventual fulfillment. While Greek criticism saw its narrative literature as an abstraction from the actual of the types which exemplified natural laws, Christian exegesis saw the Bible as a record of the actual in which could be read the story of the gradual spiritual perfection of man.

Augustine records in his *Confessions* that he first saw the error of the Manichean philosophers in their science. His own progress from that dark heresy to faith in the Christian God led through the objective contemplation of God's creation, thence through the Greek love of philosophy and the Greek rhetorical allegoresis, through Ambrose's method of scriptural exegesis, and finally to his own exegetical method and the doctrine of charity. As narrative, the *Confessions* is a realistic account of a spiritual progress. The only sense in which it occasionally suggests allegory is its implication that the character Augustine is a type of the prodigal son, of the young David, or of St. Paul — a type of the persons whose lives existed at individual stages of history and who yet partook simultaneously of the general perfection of the City of God by their gradual conformation to the image of Christ. While Augustine is much concerned to record the emotions and ideas accompanying each stage of his own development, his method cannot be fairly labelled "psychological" in anything like the modern sense of the word. We do not have a strong sense of the character Augustine's "personality" at the various stages of his development, and we see little of the social influences on it that we expect in modern psychological novels. Above all, Augustine's psychological detail is not offered as an end in itself. Unlike Rousseau, he has no desire to set forth the intimate record of his emotional and intellectual life for the sake of its intensity and uniqueness. As a character, Augustine is a "type": not a type of human nature, as are the types in classical history and biography, but a spiritual type — something like a Platonic idea — that manifests itself in history as a foreshadowing of, and in life as a conformity to, the life of Christ.

The stages in the spiritual perfection of mankind are for Augustine recapitulated in the individual process of perfection. The individual passes upward toward conformity with the plot line of the City of God until at his spiritual resurrection he becomes a member of the Church and is united with God. The important historical events recorded in Scripture become, through their spiritual interpretation, important events in the individual life. The individual spiritual resurrection itself foreshadows the final physical resurrection of the whole Christian community and is therefore "anagogical" in meaning. The historical past, the present and future of mankind, and of the individual, all united in Christ, manifest the same potential for perfection from matter to spirit. After the first tragic fall from grace, the Christian "plot" is comic in its tendency toward eventual resurrection and reunion.

The alternative to this rising, cosmic action of resurrection and reunion is not tragedy but irony. The double vision implicit in the distinction between the City of Man and City of God almost inevitably threatens a representation of worldly human behavior, no matter how idealized, with becoming satirical because of the failure of the actual to conform to the spiritual ideal. Only in those rare instances—we find them in Dante for example—in which narrative artists were able to sustain a love'of the sinner while hating his sin did medieval narrative even approach Greek or Renaissance tragedy. The usual attitude was one of ridiculing the sinner's folly in rejecting God, his only true good, in favor of the transitory gifts of Fortune. Only a confirmed worldling like Chaucer's Monk, whose attitude as narrator Chaucer ridicules, would conceive of man as condemned to endure the fate of the angel Lucifer, the subject of the Monk's first "tragedy." A tragic "fall" from high to low felicity in the City of Man was for the medieval Christian but an ironical reversal of one's potential for spiritual elevation to the City of God, a potential given to all mankind through Christ's sacrifice.

In the *Confessions,* the evolution in the spiritual condition of the character Augustine is made abundantly clear in the alternative representations of actual mental and emotional experience and expositions of Christian doctrine. The tensions between the discursive representation of pure idea and the narrative representation of pure actuality are therefore extreme. The narrative rarely merges actuality and idea. Augustine's representation of actuality adumbrates the *Bildungsroman* of modern tradition and his representation of idea looks forward to the treatises of medieval mystics. The *Confessions* are both more and less mimetic than classical narrative. In Augustine's theory of history, and in his vision of the individual's recapitulation and prophecy of the perfection of the Christian community in the process of his own spiritual perfection, Augustine provided both the theme and the method of later Christian allegory. He was, like Plato, unfitted in both temperament and his conception of truth to provide the model as well.

The transference of Augustine's method of scriptural exegesis

to the reading of imaginative narrative was one of the most momentous developments in the history of Western art. The mechanics of the process are far from being well understood. The
Greek allegoresis had reached a stage of development by Augustine's time that made a synthesis of the two traditions possible.
Early Christian iconographical reinterpretation of the images of
pagan art, the philosophical analysis of the personifications in
pagan mythology, and the strong Platonic element in late classical
and Christian metaphysics were other forces working toward a
peculiarly Christian allegoresis of imaginative narrative. Greek
and Christian methods met in the commentaries on Vergil. Augustine was familiar with Vergil's prophecy of the ideal city and was
profoundly influenced by it in the conception of his own *City of
God*. Crucial to a Christian interpretation of the *Aeneid* was a
willingness to see the poem as a prophecy analogous to the prophecy contained in Scripture and in contemporary events. Stoic and
Neoplatonic allegoresis already had read the *Aeneid* as an account
of the gradual ethical perfection of its hero. A thoroughly Christian allegoresis, however, involved reading Aeneas' journey from
the Old Troy of physical matter to the New Troy of the spirit in
such a way that the hero conforms gradually to the likeness of
Christ. For only as a reflection of the divine image does his
ethical perfection take on true moral significance. The fictional
hero, like the actual man of the *Confessions*, recapitulates the
stages in scriptural history through his similarity to scriptural
types of Christ. Similarly, the ideal city is a type both of the
Church and of the celestial paradise.

Neither the fathers of the Church nor later theologians particularly encouraged reading pagan imaginative literature as if it
were Holy Scripture. Although in the special case of Vergil it was
widely held that God had spoken through a pagan poet — especially in the messianic Fourth Eclogue, but in the *Aeneid* as
well — the inventions of the pagan poets were, in the early Middle
Ages at least, recommended largely for their Latin style. In the
hands of responsible theologians, the methods of scriptural exege-

sis could be applied only to the Bible because it, unlike imaginative narratives, was true. Meanings were hidden not in literary images but in the actual things those images represented. Yet by the fourteenth century, a slowly accumulating body of conventional Christian interpretations of classical mythology had supplied secular poets with images from ancient literature as charged with significance as were the biblical images from the works of the great exegetes that had filtered down to them through sermons and the liturgy.

Such fourteenth century compendia as the anonymous French *Ovide moralisé*, Pierre Bersuire's *De Fabulis Poetarum,* and Boccaccio's *De Genealogia Deorum* are only the end products of a mythographic tradition stretching back in time to the earliest allegoresis of Homer. We would not need to regard the medieval interpretation of pagan mythology as anything more than a continuation into Christian times of essentially Greek methods were it not for the development of poetic and exegetical conventions in which such pagan heroes as Hercules and Aeneas became types of Christ. In fact, the main relevance of both the exegetical tradition and the Greek philosophical allegoresis was not so much the establishment of literary models upon which medieval narrative poets based their own art, as it was the gradual accumulation of a body of conventional biblical and classical images with culturally stipulated symbolic meanings. Such images, together with the theories of literary interpretation that had given them their significance, provided a more or less coherent literary method by which narrative artists could consciously control the philosophical meaning of the traditional stories they retold.

A third tradition, one about which we have so little evidence as to leave even its existence a matter of speculation, involved the Christian reinterpretation of images from the mythic and heroic traditions of Celtic and Germanic antiquity. In the case of a fourteenth-century humanist version of a classical story, such as Boccaccio's *Teseide,* the author's own commentary may be conclusive evidence that the mythological figures in the poem as well as such characters as Teseo and Ipolita represent the culturally stipulated meanings they had acquired during thirteen Christian centuries. The wisdom of Theseus was such a fixed feature of the image that he had become a conventional type of the Christian king — as he was to appear again in Chaucer's Knight's Tale. Evidence of this sort is much harder to come by in interpreting the innumerable romances of the Arthurian cycle, the *Nibelungenlied*, *Beowulf*, the prose sagas of Iceland, and other works whose formal organization demonstrates their recent emergence from oral tradition.

In the orally composed Karelian songs about the mythical Kaleva District, which were not collected until Elias Lönnrot published them as the *Kalevala* in the 'twenties, 'thirties, and 'forties of the nineteenth century, essentially no trace is to be found of Christian interpretation of traditional myth. Only in the last song of Lönnrot's collection is the Christian story alluded to, and then for the purpose of dramatizing in completely traditional fashion the confrontation of the great Väinämöinen with the new infant hero who was to drive him from Finland. One concludes that the god-like magicians of the *Kalevala* tradition were felt to be utterly incompatible with Christian culture, despite centuries during which the singers had themselves been Christians. The Karelian oral tradition preserves, in its conception of heroes who defeat their enemies through superior magical songs, a far less "heroic" mythical tradition than Homer's. Almost everything about it suggests the tradition's having survived from extreme antiquity — at least in Northern European terms. Because it was necessarily transmitted by peasants, its mimetic elements are a reflection of folk life. We can surmise that had the tradition been allowed to follow its own course in a more aristocratic and rationalistic culture it would have developed its ancillary commentary and exegetical tradition as did the Hellenic and Hebraic mythical narrative. Its traditional images would then come to be explained with reference to conceptions of actuality, as in the case of Greek allegoresis, or with reference to a religious doctrine, as in the case of scriptural exegesis. At this point it would be ripe for a genuine synthesis with another cultural tradition, such as the synthesis in late antiquity between the significant images of Hellenic and Hebraic narrative traditions.

Do we have any evidence that such a synthesis was indeed possible in the case of Celtic and Germanic traditional narrative? Erwin Panofsky has shown that in the history of Western art certain stages characterized the Christian reinterpretation of classical images. The image of Hercules dragging Cerberus from the underworld, which to a painter in antiquity would have been iconographically significant in terms of Greek myth, would have no such significance for a Christian painter ignorant of the myth. For him, the image, emptied of its iconographical content, would be simply a *motif*. The motif of a man dragging another creature up from beneath the ground might, however, suggest to him Christ's dragging Adam up from hell. If he then used the classical motif to set forth the Christian *theme*, he would, in Panofsky's terminology, thereby create a new *image*.

Conversely, classical themes, such as the story of Dido and Aeneas, were by the later Middle Ages set forth in motifs representative of scenes from everyday medieval life: in the case of at least one Dido and Aeneas, a lady and gentleman engaged in a game of chess. The achievement of the Italian Renaissance was the realignment of classical motifs with classical themes. Even then, the reinterpretation was influenced by centuries of allegoresis. A Renaissance audience might understand Veronese's "Mars and Venus" as a life-like representation of personages in ancient mythology, but the painting would also be significant in terms of its illustration of the proper relationship between the concupiscent and irascible forces of the human personality, a significance assigned to the myth itself in the period during which classical motifs and themes had been out of alignment.

A roughly analogous process may take place in the meeting of two literary cultures. In addition to the apparently quite traditional epic exemplified by *Beowulf*, Germanic oral narrative was also hospitable to explicitly Christian themes. The whole formal apparatus of the Old English narrative tradition, for example, was put at the service of fairly close biblical paraphrases and stories of the saints and apostles. The literary images with which the Germanic singers represented Christ and the apostles were the same images that had only a generation or so earlier represented the traditional folk heroes. A striking example is to be found, among many others, in the Old Saxon *Heliand*. Twice we are given a full version of what might be called the *topos* of the royal banquet, a conventionalized description of the banquet at which in pagan times the comitatus and the king experienced their most precious moments of community. Such literary images must certainly have represented authentic ritual meetings during which the social and religious roles of both the king and his community were most ardently affirmed. The *topos* contains key words wherever it occurs in Old English and Old Saxon: "high hall," "bench," "floor," "joy," "pour out," "bright wine," "noblemen." In addition, the scenes in *Beowulf* and *Heliand* include the figure of an aristocratic lady, who goes among the warriors as they drink. Whatever actual religious and social types the *topos* of the royal banquet may have represented in pagan antiquity, it was taken over by Christian singers for new, and at times quite contrary purposes. The two banquet scenes in *Heliand* — nearly identical in form — represent, first, the feast of Herod at which Salome danced before the warriors, and, second, the wedding at Cana, where the aristocratic lady is the Virgin Mary, moving among the guests to discover that the "bright wine" had been consumed.

The analogy between the conventional images of an oral narrative tradition and the motifs of classical art is, of course, imperfect. A thousand years might intervene between the composition of the pagan Hercules and the formally identical Christ harrowing hell. In an oral tradition, however, the reinterpretation of narrative images must at least begin within a single generation. The old *topoi* cannot just lie about waiting to be copied in a new context as they might if they had been recorded in literary documents. Two questions arise concerning the reinterpretation of traditional Celtic and Germanic narrative images: To what extent did the pagan meanings continue to inform such *topoi* as the royal banquet, even when employed in an explicitly Christian narrative? To what extent was it possible for Christian audiences to reinterpret the images of an apparent pagan narrative?

With the example of such early medieval mythographers as Servius, Fulgentius, and Martianus Capella, as well as the later encyclopedias of Bede, Isodore of Seville, and Hrabanus Maurus, all presumably available to a cultivated Englishman of the ninth century, the ingenuity involved in reading Beowulf as a type of Christ would not be extraordinary. The singer in an oral tradition has no "intention" as far as controlling the "meaning" of his narrative is concerned. His intention is to sing the tale. When we ask, therefore, what meanings might have been stipulated by Christian Anglo-Saxon culture for the images in *Beowulf* we are asking a question about the audience of the poem that cannot be answered simply. As for the poem itself, nowhere is Christ mentioned. Nor is any clear conception of anything approaching Christian salvation expressed. The ethical values are high, but they do not transcend the "natural" morality exemplified in the heroes of classical antiquity. If *Beowulf* is a Christian narrative—and scholars are almost unanimous in affirming it—then it is so in the same sense in which Hercules dragging Cerberus from the underworld is a Christian image: emptied by its learned audience of pagan significance, the narrative is a concentration of narrative motifs which can, without altering their formal characteristics, be reinterpreted as Christian images, i.e. illustrative symbols.

The reinterpretation of relatively fixed narrative motifs by successive generations of Northern Europeans is best illustrated with the Christianization of those Celtic myths that subsequently contributed to the Matter of Britain in European romance. Such memorable images as the *Minnegrotte* in Gottfried von Strassburg's *Tristan und Isolt*, Percival's confrontation of the Fisher King in Chrétien's *Conte du graal*, and the half-expected but nonethelesss startling advent at Arthur's court of Galahad in the *Queste del Saint Graal* and in Malory, or of the Green Knight in *Sir Gawain and the Green Knight*, are all motifs which can be said to look backward in time to an origin in pre-Christian myth. As images in sacred myth, they would have referred simultaneously to the actuality of ritual and to the most ideal form of cosmic control.

For ancient man the significant elements of actuality and the archetypes of sacred myth were one and the same thing. Ancient man could not conceive of history in the modern sense. His significant (i.e. ritual) actions, by virtue of their identification with mythical events, took place outside of ordinary chronological time. The unique, nameless, humdrum, "sinful" events that occur in profane time, the succession of which constitutes "history" in the modern sense, were annually destroyed in ritual death, purification, and rebirth. The actual and historical world was destroyed and reborn anew each year. Sacred and profane time were annually synchronized. The cycles of Great Years found in more sophisticated ancient theology, even the Augustinian concept of the two cities, preserves the essential religious principle by which the participant in sacred ritual is taken out of historical time to become a participant in mythic events, transcending both historical time and the empirical world of which it is a function. The Augustinian formulation would have been difficult for pagan Northern Europeans, however, for it recognized both the reality and the uniqueness of the profane world. Needless to say, the present-day concept of a single, linear, non-sacred, evolutionary history, co-extensive with that of the physical cosmos, was unavailable to medieval pagans and Christians alike.

Inevitably, a culture's concepts of history and of reality will be closely allied. Without a sacred time, eternal and beyond the power of history, there can be no reality beyond the actual. The function of ritual is to interrupt historical time and to synchronize it with sacred time. It is related to empirical actuality and to historical time insofar as it is the vehicle through which human actions are felt to acquire significance, transcending history by identification of the human and actual with the divine and mythical. Man's strongest impulse is not to destroy the empirical world; rather it is to transform it into the mythical world, to regain Eden in this life, and to synchronize, once and for all, mythical and empirical reality.

Even as the mythic Beowulf had already found a place at the historical court of King Hygelac in Geatland well before the Germanic epic entered a process of Christian reinterpretation, so the Irish myths had in pre-Christian times begun the inevitable euhemeristic transformation of ritually significant personages into legendary kings and heroes occupying a vaguely historical setting. Specifically, the association of Celtic myth with the possibly historical Arthur was the accomplishment of medieval Welsh narrative artists, whose Continental kinsmen in Brittany were in turn responsible for introducing the legends into the mainstream of European art.

The mechanics of integrating myth with history and reinterpreting pagan images as Christian must have been somewhat haphazard. In *Beowulf*, the historically authentic Danish court is given a mythic origin as the place of settlement of Norse grain gods, while Grendel, the demonic foe of the Danes, is given a biblical genealogy. Roger Sherman Loomis has demonstrated how, in the case of the grail legends, the happy ambiguity of Old French *cors*, which could mean both "horn" and "body," might have prompted the reinterpretation of the *sains graaus*, for which *cors benoiz* was a frequent epithet, from the "blessed horn" of plenty in Celtic myth to the "blessed body" of Christ in the sacramental imagery of the twelfth- and thirteenth-century romances.

The medieval church would have confronted both the Celtic and Germanic myths in the form of heroic narratives rather than as undisplaced solar and fertility myths. Direct and intimate contact between the two cultures came earlier in France and Ireland than in England and Scandinavia, but even so we have little reason to suppose that the historical elements in the heroic narratives of any European culture were due solely to the hasty rationalization of sacred myth under the reproachful gaze of impatient missionaries.

The failure of the Karelian oral narrative to combine its myth with history may be related to its failure to reinterpret its images as Christian symbols. In sacred myth the images look both toward the cosmic forces, of which they are the embodiment, and toward the actual practice of ritual, of which they are the idealization. The gradual abandonment of ritual requires a gradual turning either to other elements of daily sensory experience or to the facts of history as a new basis in actuality for esthetic imitation. Whether an awareness of the reality of historical time precedes or follows its representation in narrative art, or (which is most likely) develops simultaneously with it, the presence or absence of an historical setting says something about the nature of the reality a particular narrative represents. Although the songs of the *Kalevala* have incorporated considerable detail from Finnish peasant life, it is ritualistic in nature. The hundred-odd charms, for example, and the descriptions of agricultural and mechanical techniques have not been sufficiently emptied of magico-religious significance to convey an impression of imitation solely for imitation's sake. The central characters exist not only out of historical time. They are superhuman personages whose power is belied by their peasant dress. The amount of mimetic detail in the *Kalevala* suggests the beginnings of a rationalizing process, but both its ritualistic traces and its non-historical context strongly imply that its images are still fairly powerful religious symbols, powerful enough to resist being understood solely as representative of actuality or being reinterpreted as illustrative Christian symbols.

The illustrative reinterpretation of traditional narrative motifs will apparently take place only when narrative artists have begun to understand their images as imitations of an empirical actuality distinct from the mythically significant actuality of ritual. Should this empirical tendency continue unimpeded in the direction of historical and mimetic narrative, the images will become simply traditional representational types. The Icelandic family sagas exemplify the product of such a development in Northern Europe. If, however, the empirical tendency is arrested at the point where a ritually symbolic actuality is still faintly apprehended, the narrative motifs may be nearly emptied of sacred reference before they have been altered enough to acquire reference to a distinctly profane actuality. Such is the case with folktale, ballad, and romance traditions that have, in the face of spreading literacy and the high culture of Western Christendom, passed to successively lower cultural strata, resisting the rationalizing tendency either to mimesis or to illustrative reinterpretation. Their heroes and heroines may remain preternaturally brave and beautiful, or their plots remain fantastically improbable, without referring either to empirical actuality or to ideas of which they are the consciously stipulated illustration. The images in such narratives represent types of the god-like or the demonic more powerfully than types of the actual. They are esthetic images with a minimum representational or illustrative significance.

Such esthetic fiction, historically the unrationalized plots and motifs of sacred myth, is always a fruitful source of narrative structure, even in highly rational narrative traditions. Mythic archetypes, being the products, after all, of the human imagination, appeal powerfully to even the most empirically oriented audiences through their manifestation of universal psychic patterns. Depending on his point of view, a narrative artist might rationalize an esthetic plot in several ways: he might understand esthetic images to be significant as shadowy prefigurations of Christian archetypes; he might use them as illustrative symbols for consciously stipulated and controlled ideas (most medieval and Renaissance allegory combines these two methods); he might understand esthetic images as historical personages and events, as representational images of the real world (the usual case in mimetic fiction); or he might understand them as archetypes of the unconscious, projected in slightly different guises by different cultures, but manifesting the same human reality from culture to culture (as Joyce did in *Finnegans Wake*). Only allegorical narrative, which uses esthetic images as illustrative symbols of ideas, rationalizes myth without necessarily making it more representational. The other uses of myth tend to stress the actual, either as a symbol standing for some higher reality (scriptural exegesis and modern literary "symbolism") or as reality itself. In the remainder of this chapter, we shall examine the historical shift away from rationalizing myth as allegory to rationalizing it as mimetic fiction, a shift which coincided with the development of European rationalism away from the abstract intellectualizing of medieval thought to the empiricism of modern science.

Everyday medieval ideas about narrative seemed to take into rough account the two ways in which stories can be meaningful: as representations of the world of experience and as illustrations of the world of ideas. Such a distinction is implicit even in the crude epistemology of the Wife of Bath, who begins her Prologue in *The Canterbury Tales* by alluding to two sources of knowledge:

> Experience, though noon auctoritee
> Were in this world, is right ynogh for me
> To speke of wo that is in marriage.

The *auctoritee,* whose guidance she could do without if she had to, is the "authority" of the old authors, the doctrine and teaching which, together with experience, leads the way to wisdom. "Authority" and experience are everywhere in Chaucer's poetry poised as potential rivals. Chaucer's comic narrator himself frequently expresses an attitude almost directly opposed to the Wife's in the matter of experience and "authority." Some special occasion, he tells us in the Prologue to *The Legend of Good Women,* must arise before he can be prodded away from his books to confront the world directly for himself:

> And as for me, though that I konne but lyte,
> On bokes for to rede I me delyte,
> And to hem yive I feyth and ful credence,
> And in myn herte have hem in reverence
> So hertely, that ther is game noon
> That fro my brokes maketh me to goon,
> But yt be seldom on the holyday . . . .

His books are not, of course, all summas and sermons. The narrator does read

> Olde appreved stories
> Of holynesse, of regnes, of victories,
> Of love, of hate, of other sondry thinges.

But he reads in preference to direct experience, and he reads in hope of learning the truth. If the modern reader is correct in suspecting that Chaucer ironically characterizes his narrator as too eagerly giving "feyth and ful credence" to his books, it is because Chaucer's interest in the validity of experience is modern. The narrator's trust in authority is truer to that hypothetical entity we call the "medieval mind" than is the Wife's reliance on personal experience.

The Parson of the Canterbury pilgrimage, unlike the narrator, apparently enjoys no form of imaginative literature at all. When his turn comes, he refuses to tell a proper story:

> Thou getest fable noon ytoold of me . . .
> Why sholde I sowen draf out of my fest,
> When I may sowen whete, if that me lest?

From the Parson's point of view — the desire to instruct his audience in the readiest path to heaven — no other literary form could be so effective as the sermon. An ordinary narrative would require the Parson to sow "draff" as well as "wheat." "Draff," which elsewhere in medieval discussions of meaning in narrative was called the "chaff" or "husk" or "cortex," consisted of a story minus its doctrinal content. The doctrine, the ancient authority, was conveyed in the "fruit" or "kernel" or "nucleus" of a narrative, the Parson's "wheat." And it was for this kernel that Chaucer's narrator read the "olde appreved stories."

The dichotomy of wheat and draff in the medieval criticism of narrative art was not always viewed so puritanically as it is in the Parson's Prologue. Chaucer frequently designated it with the more classical terms *sentence* (meaning) and *solas* (delight). Nor was there anything heretical about believing, with Harry Bailly, the Host of the Canterbury pilgrimage, that a good story ought to delight at the same time that it instructs. The Host laid it down as a term of the story-telling competition that the free supper would go to the teller of "tales of best sentence and most solas." In preferring the sermon to the story, the Parson spoke as teacher, not as artist. As for medieval narrative artists, whether they thought of the esthetic and representational elements of their stories as being mere *draf* or as potential *solas,* they confronted the challenge of combining the best teaching with the greatest delight. They were consciously didactic, but they were also conscious that the *whete* made only half a story. And most of them took pains to convert their *draf* into the most *solas.* The distinction between instruction and delight tended to focus critical attention on an author's philosophical ideas and his rhetoric, that is, on the inner "kernel" and the outward "husk" of his narrative. In fact, this distinction was itself a product of a critical tradition, descending from Horace and lasting well into the Renaissance, which viewed poetry as a branch of rhetoric. We find, therefore, that while most medieval narrative is consciously didactic it is just as consciously rhetorical.

When poetry is subsumed under rhetoric the effect is to reduce the roles of literary art as mimesis and as an expression of private feelings and values. Its validity is derived instead from the soundness of its doctrine and from the effectiveness of its language in persuading an audience to accept that doctrine as the truth. The view of narrative art as rhetorical and philosophical came naturally to the learned culture of the Middle Ages, trusting as it generally did in the reality of universals and the superiority of authority over experience. The primitive allegories of Prudentius, Martianus Capella, and Alain de Lille were popular with clerics who had been brought up on the natural philosophy expounded in such works as Macrobius' *Somnium Scipionis,* where they might have learned, for example, that the gestation period in man is seven months. For such audiences, the *Psychomachia,* the *De Nuptiis Philologiae et Mercurii,* and the *Anticlaudianus* were confrontations with reality, not reality as it might be dimly perceived through the confusion of sensory experience, but reality as it had been clarified by the reason and refined by philosophical tradition. The modern reader must strain his historical imagination to understand that the essential action of primitive allegories is almost purely intellectual and that the patterned movement of ideas can be both beautiful and exciting without bearing any relationship to the empirical data of sensory experience whatsoever.

The area in which his rhetorically controlled fiction met and fused with a philosophically controlled meaning was the true domain of the medieval narrative artist. This infinitely complex relationship between the husk and the kernel of a narrative was not the subject matter of any of the *artes.* The rhetorical tradition provided the husks and philosophical doctrine provided the kernels, but the artist had to decide on the best ways of fitting his particular kernels into his particular husks. To some extent, of course, this "fit" was stipulated by literary tradition. The vast body of theologically significant narrative *topoi* and images which resulted from scriptural exegesis and Hellenistic allegoresis provided illustrative symbols with a conventionally understood "fit" between kernel and husk. Likewise, decorum would suggest, for example, that an elevated rhetorical style was appropriate not only to heroic romance but to the ideal ethical values most often set forth in allegorical romance. A similar decorum would associate the lower rhetoric and more mimetic setting of the fabliau and beast epic with satire. But the particular meaning of a particular image was in the last analysis the responsibility of the artist. In recognition of the fact that traditional illustrative symbols varied in meaning from context to context, even in Scripture, the exegetes discovered "good" and "bad" meanings of many of them. The lion *in sensu malo* could stand for Satan; in another context the same image might be understood *in sensu bono* as meaning Christ, "the lion of Judah." The habit of construing symbols either *in bono* or *in malo* is essential in reading medieval allegory. But the mere illustration of philosophical meaning was not the sole function of allegorical symbols, even though it may seem so to the modern reader eager to "understand" an allegorical narrative.

The strong rhetorical bias of medieval and Renaissance allegory assured a degree of loving attention to narrative husks far in excess of the requirements of narrative kernels. Given the three oratories in Theseus' stadium in the Knight's Tale, for example, we get the point of Chaucer's figures of Mars, Venus, and Diana long before the descriptions of them have come to an end. Or once we understand that the three sisters Fidelia, Speranza, and Charissa in the House of Holiness in *The Faerie Queene* represent faith, hope, and charity, we hardly need such additional iconographical detail as Fidelia's cup with its terrible serpent, Speranza's anchor, and Charissa's brood of nursing babes. In instances such as these the allegorical kernel seems to generate appropriate images almost for their own sake, as the seed of a lyric conceit sometimes expands and flowers in sheer joyous amplitude. A great part of the pleasure of allegory is doubtless to be accounted for by the ingenuity of an artist who can actually sustain both a fiction and a complex idea. But a different pleasure is derived from those quiet moments when the intellectual and fictional actions come to a temporary halt and the poet amuses himself by amplifying and refining the implications of them both through the application of essentially static detail. In the two instances mentioned above the detail is illustrative, each element of the description fitting appropriately into a rich constellation of symbolic meaning. But as medieval artists began to take notice of the particularities of time and place which present themselves to the senses, they found new images in the world of experience with which to amplify and adorn their illustrations of the world of authority.

Late medieval and Renaissance artists obviously enjoyed representing the social and psychological types of which they were becoming empirically aware and at the same time illustrating through these representational images the essences and universals of abstract ethical and theological thought. Hilda, the puritanical young American artist in Hawthorne's *Marble Faun,* was discomfited by her suspicion that early Renaissance painters used their mistresses and peasant girls from the fields as models for frankly female Virgins. These charmingly nubile Mothers of God are emblems not only of Hawthorne's own experiments with the tension between art as illustration and art as representation. They are emblems as well of the impulse which moved such narrative artists as Dante, Chaucer, and even Langland to test and illustrate the truths of authority through the particular facts of thirteenth-century Florentine and fourteenth-century English experience. The "quiet moments" in the narrative movement of Dante's *Commedia* allow him to exercise prodigious gifts of mimetic characterization, reminiscent of the Roman biographers and historians. The tendency in post-Romantic criticism to stress the representational element and the function of personal experience in the narrative art of Dante and Chaucer has made it difficult for the modern reader to discern the underlying element of doctrine and authority in their work. As a result, we have in general failed to appreciate the role of medieval and Renaissance representational art in giving significance to the actuality of which it is the representation. It was able to do this not solely because the world of experience had by itself become meaningful in new ways, but also because artists gradually discovered that traditional illustrative symbols might be found, in a somewhat disguised form, beneath the detail of the world of experience. The Augustinian concept of the two cities, the City of God and the City of Man, for example, could be illustrated in Dante's Florence or Langland's England in terms of actual political, social, and religious institutions.

Philosophically and temperamentally Dante and Langland were more nearly akin than at first glance their poems would seem to indicate. The mathematical precision of Dante's narrative structure and the stupendous breadth of his learning are, of course, lacking in *Piers Plowman*. But both poets found fit instruments for their invective in a vigorous vernacular language that conveyed a satirist's indignation at the degree to which their particular Cities of Man had fallen away from, or had failed to achieve, a conformity to the City of God. Before the development of what might be called "Renaissance empiricism" as a habitual mode of thought, representational characterization and setting had been mainly the province of comic satirists, whose fabliaux and novelle seldom aspired to the serious or problematic. Serious narrative artists had relied mainly on traditional esthetic and illustrative imagery, the most seriously and philosophically oriented coming to the point of carefully controlled allegory. But in *The Divine Comedy* the grand design of the allegory infuses the representational images with its own high seriousness. Although in *Piers Plowman* Langland's references to the actual are more covert than Dante's, the failure of the various orders of Englishmen to fulfill the obligations of simple social and political justice is given grave and apocalyptic significance. Rather than name and describe real people, Langland describes types, most of which have at least a dual reference. His king is both the king of England and all kings. His field full of folk is both England and the whole human community. In his description of social types Langland looks forward to the satire of the fifteenth, sixteenth, and seventeenth centuries, when the allegorical "other" meaning of illustrative symbols became more and more firmly anchored in the actual world, the general philosophical and theological references gradually weakening into vague overtones. Gay's *Trivia*, for example, has much in common with sections of *Piers Plowman;* but in Gay the general overtones are vaguely ethical and classical, while in *Piers Plowman* an urgently apocalyptic theology is being illustrated through the representation of social and political types. Dante and Langland considered fallen man capable of regaining something like Paradise in the actual world. Their satire may, therefore, have measured the actual against an impossibly high ideal. The height of this ideal and the desperately serious concern they felt for the whole community of living men led them to seek out representations of the actual with which to amplify and illustrate their conception of the ideal. Langland did not know, or at any rate could make no use of, the narrative literature of classical antiquity. He knew the Bible by heart and had read widely in theology; but in contrast to Dante, Boccaccio, and Chaucer he had tasted none of the fruits of the humanistic revival of secular learning in the thirteenth and fourteenth centuries. He does not, for this reason, immediately strike us as a typical English poet. We suspect that if, like Shakespeare, he had had a Golding's Ovid or a North's Plutarch to plunder he might still have preferred his own characteristic brand of learned ignorance.

Spenser, despite his own deep affinity to Langland and the author of *Sir Gawain and the Green Knight,* believed that the father of English poetry was Chaucer. Chaucer had taught his sons to read the ancient classics and the works of their French and Italian contemporaries, a lesson which from Spenser's time onward they have rarely failed in. From Chaucer, from Ovid, from Ariosto and Tasso, Spenser learned the art of story-telling in verse as neither Langland nor Dante could have taught it to him. Langland, as well as using the traditional symbols of the exegetes, had fit his allegorical kerneis into the generalized representational husks of the satirist. Dante had, at many points, fit his allegory into the specifically representational husks of the biographer and historian. But Spenser's allegory finds its most characteristic images not in the world of experience, but in the Faeryland of myth and romance. Nor does Spenser exploit in *The Faerie Queene* the representational authority of a narrative persona, which had given the effect of personal experience to the narratives of Dante, Langland, Chaucer, and Boccaccio. Instead, his narrator adopts merely the Vergilian singer's ethos of learning, piety, humility, and veneration for the past, intruding from outside the story only to invoke the Muses, to dedicate his efforts to the glory of Elizabeth, and to comment on the progress and meaning of the narrative — never to offer an eye-witness account of the events being told. But *The Faerie Queene* looks back to the literary epic of Vergil and forward to that of Milton in more respects than what might be called its esthetic (in contrast to representational) narrator. If we feel more at home with Spenser than with Langland it is because both his thought and his fictional world are less firmly rooted than Langland's in the intellectual and social facts of a particular time and place. With its roots diffusely spread through classical antiquity and medieval romance, Spenser's narrative art is still of a piece with the narrative tradition as it has thus far survived the freaks of time.

Spenser's characters, setting, and action — much of his narrative "husk" — tend to be esthetic images taken from myth, heroic legend, and romance, while his doctrine is based on a broadly humanistic Christian ethic and theology. Thus, both in his imagery and his ideas Spenser makes fewer specific references to the world of actual experience than did Langland and Dante. He devotes greater attention to the purely esthetic qualities of the narrative, illustrating philosophical essences through traditional esthetic images rather than through a representation of historical and social particulars. But his epic and romance apparatus is not devoted exclusively to the purposes of allegory. A good deal of the ethical significance of the poem is conveyed through a generalized representation of human types in the manner of Vergil and Milton. His heroes, although illustrative of specific virtues, are nonetheless types of men, not symbols of pure intellectual abstractions. In this respect they differ from many of the minor characters that they meet in the course of their adventures. In Book II, for example, Sir Guyon encounters allegorical illustrations of emotions which are conducive to, or inimical to, the virtue of temperance. One of these allegorical figures, Shamefastness, is interpreted for him by Alma, who guides the hero through an allegorical castle of the well-tempered body. A blushing damsel who refuses to respond to Guyon's questioning, she baffles the hero until Alma explains:

> "Why wonder ye,
> Fair sir, at that which ye so much embrace?
> She is the fountain of your modesty;
> You shamefast are, but Shamefastness itself is she."

Guyon may possess and illustrate the qualities of a temperate man, but he is not a symbol standing for Temperance itself.

A somewhat similar complication of meaning is found in all allegorical narratives. Some images are significant as representations of actual types and others as stipulated illustrative symbols. In a representational narrative, such as Sinclair Lewis's *Babbitt*, the masterpiece of characterization is an empirically universalized type, in terms of which we can henceforth *apprehend* actuality. It is new, it is surprising, but it is typical. In allegorical narrative, the masterpiece of characterization, such as Spenser's Despair, is an illustrative symbol, in terms of whose stipulated meaning we can henceforth *contemplate* actuality. But even characters like Spenser's Despair do not always remain consistent illustrations of the abstract ideas denoted by their names. It is true that, in contrast to Red Cross and Guyon, Spenser's allegorical figures are only faintly representative of typical human beings, nor do their encounters with the heroes result in actions typically experienced by knights in armor. In a mimetic narrative we would have to be shown a man almost overcome by despair; in an allegorical narrative we are shown a man almost argued into killing himself by an old hermit whose name is Despair. In actuality someone cannot be reasoned into despair. A mimetic narrative must represent a man's falling into despair; an allegorical narrative illustrates it stipulatively. Presumably Red Cross did not yield utterly to despair in Book I of *The Faerie Queene*, for if he had he should have killed himself. He did, however, come close enough to it to exemplify the condition, if not the actual psychological process by which it is arrived at, and to this extent he is a representational character. When at the last moment Red Cross is saved from suicide by Una's reminder that he is among the elect, Despair himself despairs, and attempts to hang himself. Allegorically this may be meaningful; certainly the failure of his attempt is. But the action is more meaningful in mimetic than in allegorical terms. In his desperate act Despair also momentarily represents a despairing man. His lonely hermitage and the narrator's information that Despair had many times before attempted suicide confirm this view. Yet his immortality, his omniscience, and his passionate interest in Red Cross's sinfulness identify him at the same time as the illustration of an idea rather than the representation of a man. This interplay in the same character between the representation of ethical and psychological states and the illustration of ethical and psychological absolutes is further enriched in *The Faerie Queene* by the strong emotional pull of the characters as simple esthetic types — heroes, heroines, villains, and enchantresses. Of course the illustrative and the esthetic seem nowadays to dominate Spenser's narrative, but like almost any allegory, its images are partly significant simply as a representation of the real world.

If the representational aspects of *The Faerie Queene* have not in general been analyzed (because they have been taken so much for granted) by critics whose norms of narrative art are the epic and the novel, the same is even more true of Milton's *Paradise Lost*. Milton might have retold the myth of the fall of man in purely allegorical terms, as had been done so often in the Middle Ages. Instead, the poem endows the old story with a new kind of power and meaning precisely through the representational characterization of its major figures. His humanity is what makes Milton's Satan so formidable a literary construct. And their humanity is what makes Adam and Eve such poignant figures. They are, of course, our first parents, and their expulsion from Eden is the cause and the type of all our woe. The story, in other words, is

still sacred myth. But it is not allegorical; Milton's Adam and Eve
are the representation of a human couple, a whole man and a
whole woman. Unlike the stories of Chaucer's "Marriage Group,"
Paradise Lost cannot be read in such a way that its theme applies
indifferently to man or to woman. Eve is a woman, not the "feminine" nature of mankind. Adam is a man, not the "masculine"
rational soul. What Eve does in the poem is typical of women;
what Adam does is typical of men. They are each hypothetical
individuals whose situations are, to use Auerbach's term, problematic. Of course Milton agrees with the medieval notion that
the rational soul is more powerful in men than in women; but it is
likewise clear that the old allegorical interpretation of the Fall is
only a backdrop against which is played the story of a man's falling from grace "through vehemence of love" for his wife. Milton's
terrible paradox is modern. It reflects both a modern reading of
Scripture and a modern conception of character. It may, in private moments, have tormented Chaucer and Dante, but neither
poet suggests that mankind in general has ever had to face a decision as agonizing as that of Milton's Adam. The Middle Ages
were spared because for them the Eve of the story was a part of
man and the Adam was another part. Insofar as our first parents
were a man and a woman they fell together, simultaneously with
the consenting of reason, not one whole human soul first, and
then another for the first one's sake.

Paradise Lost is, of course, not the most representational narrative in the English Renaissance. In the line of long poetical narratives which we have been considering — *The Divine Comedy*,
The Canterbury Tales, *Piers Plowman*, and *The Faerie Queene*
— Milton's poem achieved, however, an amalgam of myth and
mimesis, illustration and representation, which makes it more
truly epic than the others and which does show signs of the new
realism that in both the theory and practice of narrative art was
to sweep all before it. *Paradise Lost* is mimetic enough that criticizing it by the standards of essentially novelistic realism has not
seemed absurd, even to the best critics. Dr. Johnson, for example,

objected that Adam and Eve "are in a state which no other man or woman can ever know." They are not, therefore, typical of humankind generally. While the story of the Fall cannot fail to interest us, Johnson observed that we have known of the relevance of this sacred myth to our own lives all along:

These truths are too important to be new; they have been taught us in our infancy; they have mingled with our solitary thoughts and familiar conversation, and are habitually interwoven with the whole texture of life. Being therefore not new, they raise no unaccustomed emotion in the mind: what we knew before, we cannot learn; what is not unexpected, cannot surprise.

Nothing less than a revolution in the criticism of narrative is implied by these remarks, a revolution whose assumptions have for all time made any but the most trivial reading of earlier narrative dependent upon a well-focused historical perspective. Both the philosophical and the rhetorical orientation of medieval narrative theory, with its dichotomy between "kernel" and "husk" and its tension between the illustration of authority and the representation of experience, are critical concepts that must now be learned; they no longer come to us naturally. From classical epic Milton had learned the necessity of conveying his meaning through a life-like representation of gods and heroes, and from empirical fictions of the Renaissance he had learned how to improve on Homer and Vergil in the accommodation of subtle psychological representation to the esthetic demands of the epic conventions. Mixing allegory (to which, of course, Johnson likewise objected) with the representational and mythical, Milton supplied by the canons of his art a great plenty of "unaccustomed emotion in the mind." When it was elevated by Johnson and subsequent theorists of realism to an essential principle of narrative art, however, the demand for the new, the surprising, *and* the typical was a mine that exploded for all time the foundations of medieval narrative poetry.

The revolution adumbrated in Dr. Johnson's criticism of *Paradise Lost* demands of its narrative artists both originality and fidelity to probability, which comes to mean the literary representation of heretofore unrecognized types of actuality. The literary culture of the Middle Ages and of that side of the Renaissance which is reflected in the great epics demanded both originality (but less strongly than do we) and fidelity to philosophical truth, which tended to mean the unique literary illustration of commonplace ideas, "truths too important to be new." The newness of a medieval or Renaissance narrative was apprehended in the "fit" between its rhetorical surface and its underlying philosophical doctrine; the newness of a realistic novel is found in the "fit" between the fictional world it represents and its underlying perception of a new actuality. The remainder of our discussion of meaning in narrative will be devoted to a few remarks on the most recent attempts of narrative artists to exploit empirical and fictional forms that bring them ever newer, more surprising, and more universal perceptions of actuality.

One effect of modern empiricism has been to blur the distinction between the pure historical and mimetic forms of narrative on one hand and the novel on the other. After the final, powerful impact of the autobiography, for example, on the novels of Proust, Joyce, Lawrence, Wolfe, and Fitzgerald — to mention only a few obvious instances — a clear distinction between the confession and the novel can no longer be sustained. The convergence of the novel with the history, biography, and autobiography has resulted not so much from impatience with the story-teller's fantasy as from a modern skepticism of knowing anything about human affairs in an entirely objective (non-fictional) way. Science seems to have demonstrated that Aristotle's distinction between history and fiction was one of degree, not of kind. All knowing and all telling are subject to the conventions of art. Because we apprehend reality through culturally determined types, we can report the most particular event only in the form of a representational fiction, assigning motives, causes, and effects according to our best lights rather than according to absolute truth.

The more complex our view of the world becomes, the more we view even the most particular human facts as typical. Our knowledge of psychology, comparative religion, and community behavior has rationalized the heretofore irrational. Human beings are organisms whose actions are determined by a confluence of the laws governing their own inner nature with those which control a mechanical universe outside of them. If a particular person is well adjusted socially and emotionally, her happy circumstances are the result of a series of mechanical causes and effects. Human happiness no longer depends, as it did for Aristotle, upon the consciously directed ethical and social virtues of temperance, fortitude, prudence, and justice. If we are lucky we are virtuous. If we despair we are powerless to find the good. Only in part is this view an ironic reaction of the optimism of science. It follows logically from both the assumptions and the findings of science itself. In a mechanical universe the ethical hero of Aristotle and of heroic narrative is just another type of person. Together with the obsessed, the perverted, the weak, and the foolish, the hero is a mere passive product of heredity and environment. Like the other types, however, the hero still refuses to admit that he has no control, no hand in the shaping of his own character and his circumstances. But in his case the pretense makes him insufferable in the eyes of the others. Unlike them, he bears no burden of guilt, of shame, or despair. To the unthinking, his quick wit, his beautiful body, his physical courage, and his poise still merit praise, as though he made them himself. He is unsympathetic to the dark, inarticulate, passionate underside of human nature, for he does not experience it himself and he cannot believe that it is ever beyond one's ability to control.

The human types described in the notebooks of the psychologist and the social caseworker correspond to only the most ironical character types of classical and medieval narrative. In part, no doubt, this is because the older audiences enjoyed and demanded stories of what might be rather than what actually was. Both consciously and unconsciously, even the writers of representational narrative idealized the actual as far as their notions of probability would permit. But also in part, our conception of what constitutes an ironical or an idealized type of actuality has changed. Human beings simply are less noble creatures, less rational and self-controlled, than they were thought to be until the advent of detailed and systematic observation and description of human behavior. But this darker view of human character is not restricted to empirical fictions. In fact, images of the ugly and the absurd, which may historically have been inspired by the empirical impulse of the Renaissance and the Enlightenment, have now come to predominate in much contemporary esthetic narrative. The empirical elements of Grimmelshausen's *Simplicissimus*, Defoe's *Journal of the Plague Year*, or Voltaire's *Candide* now inspire the more purely esthetic anti-romance elements of Cabell's *Jurgen* or Barth's *Sot-Weed Factor*. We are given in Lewis Carroll's *Through the Looking-glass* a convenient metaphor to describe the tendency of modern esthetic narrative, whether didactic or not, to reverse the images of epic and romance, reflecting a fictional world as ugly and absurd as the world of romance had been beautiful and coherent. A more or less impotent child becomes the illustrative symbol of Everyman. Alice discovers that the most sympathetic and human figure in her mirror-image romance is a knight who cannot stay on his horse. As Victorian prudery receded before a more exact description of social and psychological types, the questing child of Carroll and Dickens has in the twentieth century become the Negro, the Jew, the homosexual, the prostitute, and other types of what Leslie Fiedler calls the "psychologically exploited." Such works as Burroughs's *Naked Lunch* are thus in one sense mirror-images of pure romance. As in romance, the esthetic utterly dominates the representational and the illustrative. But unlike romance, the fictional generalization of the actual world is governed by an impulse to set forth the ugly in as pure a form as possible. Since the esthetic aspects of such pure anti-romance, as of pure romance, are free of rational control, manifesting the absurd as purely as they do the ugly, the form might be called anti-allegory as well. Esthetic fiction which is governed by an impulse to embody pure Yahooism seeks its rational and empirical justification — or rather critics seek to justify it — as a kind of cosmic satire. Implicit in such a justification are the paradoxical assumptions implicit in all satire: a particular society is being ridiculed for having fallen away from a golden ideal, but the possibility exists that the ideal itself was only an absurdly inverted version of the true reality. When, however, neither the society nor the ideal from which it may be thought to have fallen is particularized sufficiently to be recognizable, we ought surely to admit that we are in the area of the purely ironic and meaningless, where the artist's sole concern is for the pain of his audience.

Traditional canons of the historian's or biographer's art provide ample latitude for describing character types that strain a modern conception of the probable. In fact, a Renaissance confession like Benvenuto Cellini's strikes us as being closer to Renaissance fiction than it is to modern autobiography. It lacks the sense of personal development, of historical awareness, of self-scrutiny that characterizes the hero of both the modern novel and the modern confession. Cellini's *Autobiography* seems to demonstrate that even a candid view of one's own life will be recorded in terms of the representational types that have been invented by narrative artists, that all knowing and all telling are subject to art. Even if we do not doubt that the things Cellini reports actually happened, we admire them more for their improbability than for their significance or, even, for their representational interest. Cellini records his indignation at an unfriendly critic's suggestion that a particular allegorical work of his did not have a controlled meaning. All art, Cellini observes to the reader, must mean something beneath the beautiful outward surface. It would be trivial otherwise. The naïveté of the record of his life suggests not only that Cellini was dependent upon the narrative types of Renaissance prose fiction in writing his *Autobiography*, but that he was unaware of this dependence and even of the fact that he was himself creating a work of narrative art.

Cellini no doubt considered the art of his *Autobiography* to reside in the life rather than in the telling of it. He was a passionate, impulsive, and irrational man. But he was a deliberate, conventional, and rational artist, who was at peace with himself and the world only at his workbench. We have no reason to doubt his claim of utter devotion to his art and to the defense of the dignity it bestowed upon him as a master. Indeed this is the meaning of the *Autobiography*. He conceived of it as a factual account of his complete devotion to art, without reflecting that the principles which govern the construction of an allegorical design in metal might also govern the construction of a confession. From our modern viewpoint, the *Autobiography* is a realistic narrative, which does not differ in kind from, say, Thomas Wolfe's *Look Homeward, Angel*. It is, however, less convincing as a life than Wolfe's novel. This is not because truth is stranger than fiction. It is because, while Cellini records the effects in his outward behavior of the inarticulate, dark underside of his nature, he neither understands nor describes it from within. Wolfe, in giving expression to and analyzing the intimate passions and experiences of his awakening artist, creates for the modern mind a truer and more universal type, precisely because of the richness of particular detail. Typically, life is particular and it is inarticulate and irrational.

Unlike Cellini, Wolfe probably saw the meaning of *Look Homeward, Angel* in the telling rather than in the life. Indeed Wolfe, like Joyce, considered all fiction to be autobiographical to an important degree. Conscious of being criticized for writing only thinly disguised autobiography, he contended that a more autobiographical book than *Gulliver's Travels* could not be found. Nor can the reader of Stephen Dedalus' theory of the autobiographical element in *Hamlet* lightly disregard its significance after contemplating the respective roles of the brothers Shem (James) and Shaun (John Stanislaus) in *Finnegans Wake*. Ever since Dr. Johnson's call for the new *and* the typical in narrative, the most important contributions have come from those writers who have turned within themselves for the reality out of which to forge new types. The raw material of human existence remains ever the same, the molds by which it is given significance and recognizable shape are forever being re-created by the writers of empirical narrative and drama. The new in empirical narrative depends upon an originality of vision, a creation of new types of actuality, and not upon a flight of the imagination away from the actual. If any distinction can be said to exist between the autobiography and the autobiographical novel it resides not in their respective fidelity to facts but rather in their respective originality in perceiving and telling the facts. It is in the knowing and in the telling, and not in the facts, that the art is to be found.

The critical habit of which T. S. Eliot complained in his influential essay "Tradition and the Individual Talent," that of studying the poet rather than the poem, can perhaps be traced to the Romantic artist's turning within himself for the new vision of reality that has become the dominant principle of his art. As he stated it, however, Eliot's objection was as anachronistic when it discouraged the study of the modern artist's life as the "biographical fallacy" itself is when applied to the works of Chaucer and Spenser. The anachronism resulted from Eliot's believing too literally the Romantic claim, enunciated in its most memorable form in Keats' "Negative Capability" letter, that the artist annihilates his own personality through his sympathetic imaginative identification with his subject. The Romantic poet, of course, was not annihilated in the contemplation of the actuality he sought to imitate. The two were at every point blended and merged. The one took on the coloration of the other. It is through the consultation of his own nature that the romantic and realistic artist arrives at his new vision of the actuality outside of himself. Actuality is the antitype of which his private world is the type. To imitate himself is to imitate the universal. One cannot choose but study Rousseau, Stendhal, Dickens, Flaubert, Tolstoy, Joyce, Proust, Mann, Wolfe, Hemingway, when he studies their art. Eliot's distinction exists when applied to Benvenuto's saltcellar. It ceases to exist when applied to his *Autobiography*, to Augustine's *Confessions*, or to any realistic fiction since Rousseau's *Confessions*.

The modes of knowing and of telling are almost two aspects of the same thing in empirical narrative. The "fit" between the representation and the actuality to which it refers is tight in the novel. It is looser in the epic. Ideally, the two become identical in the history, biography, and autobiography. Anything significantly new in a realistic narrative must correspond to something significantly new in actuality. And this can be achieved only through a new way of looking at life. Technically, the requirement of a new vision throws heavy emphasis on narrative point of view — perhaps, more accurately, on the relationships among point of view, subject, and audience.

In the confession, the subject and the narrator are literally the same person. One of the many lessons that Rousseau taught subsequent novelists was that even with the literal identity of subject and narrator, the mere span of time separating the two provides sufficient distance to allow for all the potentially ironical divergence in point of view between character and narrator that a novelist could require. Time became a significant dimension in the conception of character. It wrought all the changes necessary for a genuine multiplicity of points of view toward the same facts and underlined the importance of defining the knower in order to interpret his telling. Reality was in the eye of the beholder, and the beholder's eye changed with the passage of time.

Another lesson to be learned from Rousseau was his distrust of language. Time and again it is the task of the old narrator of the *Confessions* — as it was to be of the narrators of *Le Rouge et le Noir*, *À la recherche du temps perdu*, and *Aaron's Rod* — to say what had been in the heart of his young hero that lay too deep for him to know with his head and formulate into speech. It is the old narrator's task because if the young man could have spoken, it would not have been an experience worth recording. Almost by definition, the significant experiences are the ones which find no articulate, outward expression. When the young Jean-Jacques played the hero and brilliantly harangued the Senate at Berne for over an hour, the words poured forth in rhetorical splendor because he was acting a part. Had he had something important to tell the senators he could only have stood there in dumb and blushing confusion.

Not only is the anti-hero, an inarticulate and sickly youth, brought onto the stage of Western narrative, the narrator's attempts to articulate his inner experiences for him result in the creation of new types of actuality. New *and* typical, particular *and* universal. What before had been vaguely ironical is suddenly transformed under the pressure of Rousseau's vision into the new ideal. To be a heroic hero is now to be an ass. To indulge oneself in the exploration of his passions, his sickness, and his imagination is now to be a hero. It is the definition of this new (and in terms of the traditional ethical types, ironic) hero that provides the meaning of Rousseau's *Confessions*. It is a search for identity and for self-justification that ends in a new vision. Rousseau bequeathed to the realistic novel both the quest for a vision and the radically ironic nature of his own.

Two alternatives (not mutually exclusive) lie before the narrative artist who accepts Rousseau's pessimistic distrust of language and of the classical virtues. Either the new and the typical can be sought at deeper and deeper levels of man's inarticulate nature, with a consequently greater and greater strain on the ability of language to serve as a vehicle for communicating the vision, or language itself may become the ultimate material of art, with all human experience contained in some form or another of existing linguistic structure. The new cannot become the typical until it finds some formulation, some mold. Either the new will extend beyond the power of language to formulate it, or the new will already have been anticipated in existing grammatical elements and words.

In a brilliantly suggestive essay on "Art in a Closed Field," Hugh Kenner has said that for the narrative artist the limitations of language provide a "closed field" in which a large but finite number of elements are susceptible to infinite combinations and permutations. He suggests that a preoccupation with the finiteness of the elements, the "closedness" of the field, characterizes modern narrative. If Kenner's formulation is sound, we might make the further suggestion that again two alternatives, this time of essential philosophical attitude, face the narrative artist. He can accept his position with good humor and optimism and go ahead combining and permuting as brilliantly and meaningfully as it lies within his power to do, or he can combine and permute resentfully, demonstrating as he does so the hopelessness and meaninglessness of narrative art. Joyce exemplifies the former attitude and Beckett the latter.

The patient organization of rhetorical detail in *Finnegans Wake* is medieval in its devotion to brilliant outward design. Even more striking, however, is the medieval quality of the way in which the work is meaningful. Rather than referring to new types of actuality, its images carry allegorical meanings. When the allegorical significance is not culturally stipulated, that is, not traditional, it is a private significance attached by Joyce himself. To study *Finnegans Wake* is to study all the books Joyce read, or by some even less legitimate method stole from, as well as all the meaningful elements in his private life. Not even the ideal reader with the ideal insomnia will penetrate to the heart of *Finnegans Wake* without studying the poet. For at the heart of the *Wake* is the inarticulate underside of the poet himself, casting up out of the deepest recesses of his being, on a south-north trajectory, all the images ever dreamed by man. All the types of all the actualities are for Joyce but the symbols of an otherwise inarticulate allegory.

5

Character in Narrative

> What is character but the determination of incident? What is incident but the illustration of character? What is either a picture or a novel that is *not* of character? What else do we seek in it and find in it? It is an incident for a woman to stand up with her hand resting on a table and look out at you in a certain way; or if it be not an incident I think it will be hard to say what it is.

Thus Henry James in "The Art of Fiction." James, in that essay, displays little sympathy for the "queer predicaments" of critics and for their "clumsy separations," such as the "celebrated distinction between the novel and the romance." (This attitude, however, did not prevent James from making his own elegant "separations" when he chose. Still, we begin this discussion of character with James's statement not to convict the master of inconsistency but to illustrate something about conceptions of character in general.) James, consciously or unconsciously, refers all judgments of fiction to the novels written by himself or by those authors most like himself. The very incident he selects to illustrate the interdependence of character and incident is a Jamesian incident. The woman is a Jamesian character. She could easily be Isabel Archer, or Milly Theale, or Fleda Vetch; and the incident could be expanded in the hands of the master to a full chapter's worth of consideration. What might that look signify? What volumes of meaning are expressed in the position of that hand? And so on.

All readers of literature carry around with them notions about character and incident, in the form of unconsciously consulted touchstones which shape their evaluations of literary works. And, like Matthew Arnold, each one of us tends to select touchstones of a fairly narrow and limited sort. All Arnold's touchstones can be referred to his preference for high seriousness in art. Few of us, of course, make our touchstones or our critical assumptions as public as Arnold did his. But Henry James, though he has not presumed to give us touchstones, has spelled out in detail his conception of novelistic excellence. He insists that "the air of reality (solidity of specification) seems to me to be the supreme virtue of a novel — the merit on which all its other merits . . . helplessly and submissively depend." Art, he adds, "is essentially a selection, but it is a selection whose main care is to be typical, to be inclusive." And so, we may agree, things are or should be — in the novel. James's view — informed, sensitive and balanced as it is — is hopelessly novel-centered. His Isabel Archer is a character constructed on realistic principles such as those he advances. But is Vergil's Dido? James has his own doubts even about Don Quixote and Mr. Micawber as characters. Their reality is "a reality so coloured by the author's vision that, vivid as it may be, one would hesitate to propose it as a model." This is a crucial admission. Torn between his taste and his principles, James virtually admits the existence of various orders of reality in characterization, and in doing so leaves an opening for such "clumsy separations" as that dividing the romance from the novel. Don Quixote is not a character as Isabel Archer is, or as George Eliot's Dr. Lydgate is. He is alive but he is not real. There is more of myth and of fiction in Don Quixote than in Isabel Archer. There is more of mimesis in her. She may be quixotic, but he is Quixote. She may be typical, but he is archetypical. Yet, in their different ways, they both live. To suggest that one order of characterization is better than another is folly. To recognize that differences exist is the beginning of wisdom.

Homer's Achilles, for example, is a masterly characterization which is neither typical nor probable, neither inclusive nor detailed. Achilles is presented to us almost exclusively in terms of one facet of life — the emotion of anger. From the invocation, when the poet asks the muse to sing of the anger of Achilles

(Anger, *Menin*, is actually the first word of the poem), to the final moment when the funeral of Hector takes place through the forbearance and generosity of Achilles, his character is presented perpetually through the waxing and waning of his anger and through the qualitative gradations which anger assumes in him under various provocations. We can appreciate Homer's characterization more fully if we examine in some detail a particular passage. In Book XXI, after his comrade Patroclus has been killed, Achilles finally turns his anger, now wrought to the highest pitch, upon the Trojans. In battle he captures Priam's son Lycaon, who begs for his life to be spared. Achilles answers his plea:

Boy, do not offer me ransom nor a pretty speech. Before Patroclus met his fatal day, then I was happy to spare the Trojans and I took many alive and sold them abroad, but now of all the Trojans that God puts in my hands before the walls of Ilios — and especially of Priam's sons — there is not one that will escape death. So, my friend, you too must die. Why moan so much about it? Even Patroclus died, a much better man than you. And do you not see what kind of man I am, handsome and powerful — my father a great man and the mother that bore me a goddess — even upon me will fall stern destiny and death.

This is surely one of the great moments of literature; and it is a great moment of character. The action pauses. The battle seems to stop, in a most "unrealistic" way, if one could spare any attention to consider it. But of course we cannot. We are transfixed, watching the confrontation of two men. Achilles speaks. Patroclus is dead and Achilles' anger no longer rests upon a mere point of honor. As he rages for revenge, his anger is worthy of him and he of it. It is a monumental anger. And it is not only for Patroclus; it is also for himself. Patroclus is dead. He himself must die. What right has anyone to live? This speech is the speech of the man-god wrestling with his personal problem — why he, a superman with a divine parent, must bow to fate and death.

In the narrow sense of the word, the scene is unrealistic. Erich Auerbach would not consider it truly mimetic because it centers on a hero, Achilles, rather than an ordinary human being. But in some very important aspects the scene *is* mimetic. Death is common to all men. Its inevitability makes Achilles a man as well as a hero. The scene is mimetic also in its "rightness." These words come from Achilles with an overwhelming inevitability. They are not merely appropriate. They express the essence of the character in a way that is possible only because the character is simply conceived. The character of Achilles has none of those labyrinthine aspects which involve us so deeply in the characters of Dostoievsky, none of the multiplicity of facets which intrigue us in the characters of Proust. This is another order of characterization, monolithic and stark, but as impressive in its way as the Druid stones of Wessex. In the passage quoted here we can see the elements of the epic amalgam at work. History is present. The allusions to Troy and the Trojan War lend an air of historicity to Achilles' words, as does his mention of selling prisoners as slaves. But it is fiction which has arranged for this meeting, which has, in effect, held up the action to present to us with the clarity of the cinematic close-up a confrontation of two individuals. This conversation has no effect on the outcome of the battle or the war. It has been arranged by fiction solely to display Achilles and his anger in this powerful manner, by way of preparation for the death of Hector and for the final confrontation of Priam and Achilles. Myth is present in Achilles' reference to his divine birth and even more in his reference to his fated death. He has chosen to live gloriously and die young rather than enjoy a long and peaceful life. Fate and the gods will see to it that both parts of the bargain are kept. Along with this mythic and quite anti-mimetic conception, we have the words of Achilles, which are unmistakably the words of a living, breathing man. The blend of contempt and pity, of hostility and sympathy, which finds expression in this short speech is a very human blend, and Achilles' turn of thought — from Lycaon to Patroclus to himself, all united by their mortality — is a very human turn of thought, mimetic in the convincingness of its humanity; as mimetic in its way as the cry of Jesus on the cross: "My God, my God, why hast thou forsaken me?"

The power of characterization which Homer manifests in this

close-up of Achilles and throughout the *Iliad* and the *Odyssey* is, then, a very real power despite its difference from the manner of James, or Proust, or Dostoievsky. It is a power derived partly from its simplicity. Homer and other composers of primitive heroic narrative do not aspire to certain complexities of characterization which we find in later narratives and which we sometimes think of as essential elements in the creation of characterizations of interest. Characters in primitive stories are invariably "flat," "static," and quite "opaque." The very recurring epithets of formulaic narrative are signs of flatness in characterization. Odysseus is the man never at a loss — always, whenever we see him. In incident after incident, among gods, men, and monsters, he demonstrates this quality to us. Whatever the situation requires — strength, guile, politeness, generosity — he does the right thing. As Joyce observed, we see almost no other literary figure in so many postures. He is husband to Penelope, lover to Calypso, father to Telemachus, son to Laertes, warrior, explorer, storyteller, athlete, sufferer, triumpher, suppliant, and king. And in every one of these situations he does the proper thing to enable him not merely to endure but to prevail. He does not change, he does not age, except to play a role and fool his enemies. He is never tongue-tied, or clumsy, or even ordinary. Like Achilles, he is a monolith, though perhaps a less massive one. We scarcely notice this, however, because Homer is such a skilled manipulator of the monolithic.

This very quality of changelessness in Odysseus is exploited for the sake of contrast by James Joyce in his version of the Odysseus story, *Ulysses*. So little seems to have changed in Ithaca during Odysseus' twenty-year absence; so much happens in number 7 Eccles Street in only twenty hours. When Leopold Bloom, sitting in Davey Byrne's pub, watches two flies stuck buzzing on the window pane and takes a sip of Burgundy, his mind by a Proustian process of association is drawn back years into the past: "Seems to a secret touch telling me memory. Touched his sense moistened remembered." And he thinks back to his first taste of love with Molly on the hill of Howth, when he took a piece of seedcake from her mouth as they lay in one another's arms: "Kissed, she kissed me," he remembers. And then thinks, "Me. And me now." And the narrator tells us, "Stuck, the flies buzzed." Molly and Leopold, stuck for twenty years as the flies are for an instant, have changed so much that Joyce can bring a tremendous pressure of pathos to a focal point in that tiny phrase, "Me. And me now." But Bloom is not a "better" characterization than his Homeric prototype. Only a different kind.

The concept of the developing character who changes inwardly is quite a late arrival in narrative. True, we have such primitive motifs as the "unpromising hero," the awkward or diffident young man who turns suddenly into a heroic figure. We can find this, for example, in Moses, in Beowulf, and there are traces of it in non-Homeric stories about Achilles. This essentially mythic pattern often becomes attached to historical figures, as in the Chronicle Histories of Henry V, whence Shakespeare's characterization of Prince Hal. But the character whose inward development is of crucial importance is primarily a Christian element in our narrative literature. Most pre-Christian heroic narratives of the epic kind are based on notions of immortality through heroic actions which will live in the memory of the race. Achilles' intense concern over the slight he receives from Menelaus derives from just this concept. He has chosen a short glorious life in preference to a long but obscure one. If he is to be publicly humiliated, to have his posthumous reputation tarnished by this painful episode, then truly, what price glory? As long as a culture emphasizes heroic action and posthumous reputation (as in the old Teutonic European culture) its literature will remain concerned with such external attributes of man. When the private and personal relationship of the individual soul with God supplants this public concept of heroic excellence, then a culture will tend to develop a literature which deals with this private relationship and ultimately with other aspects of the inward life. When Jesus revises the Commandments in this way —

Ye have heard that it was said of them of old time, Thou shalt not commit adultery: But I say unto you, That whosoever looketh on a woman to lust after hath committed adultery with her already in his heart.

When He does this, then He is forcing His culture to take more cognizance of the inward life and less of the external actions of men. In older Hebrew literature we had had stories of men who change, seen in terms of sin and repentance. The story of David's sin in having Bathsheba's husband killed so that she could become his wife is a story of sin and repentance. But it is seen resolutely from outside the hero:

And it came to pass in an eveningtide, that David arose from off his bed, and walked upon the roof of the King's house: and from the roof he saw a woman washing herself; and the woman was very beautiful to look upon.

As the narrative continues, situation after situation develops in which individuals must be experiencing the intensest emotions, but the narrative proceeds on its serene, untroubled way, without apparent awareness of this inward violence. Even in the verse quoted above, Bathsheba's beauty is presented impersonally, as a fact, and not from David's point of view or in terms of his reaction to seeing her. The inward life is assumed but not presented in primitive narrative literature, whether Hebraic or Hellenic. This inscrutability of characters, their opaqueness, is neither a defect nor a limitation. It is simply a characteristic. Much of the power of the David story is generated by the matter-of-factness of this narration of such violent and emotional events. Such opaqueness in characterization functions for the modern reader as a kind of understatement, producing an ironic tension between the cool narrative tone and the violence which the reader imagines within the minds of the characters. The conscious employment of such irony we call litotes, and recognize it as a fundamental characteristic of Germanic narratives such as *Beowulf*. But the conscious employment of understated irony is nothing more than a realization on the part of the narrators of the fundamental understatedness of primitive narrative. Critics whose judgments are emotionally oriented tend to attach a special value to such understatement and talk about it rather nostalgically as "classic restraint" but there is no restraint involved in not doing something which it does not occur to one to do. The narrative posture of understatement, associated as it is with the opaque and static character, is simply a successful narrative formula, well suited to primitive narration, which develops in all cultures as the inevitable style in which heroic narrative is treated.

The inwardness of Christianity, as represented by Jesus' statement on adultery in the heart, opens up one way for the consideration of the inner life. Other ways seem to have been developing naturally from narrative experimentation and from the influence of non-narrative literature on narrative, especially Greek tragedy and the oratorical rhetoric of the Second Sophistic. The Christian way leads through St. Augustine to allegorical and autobiographical representation of the inward life of developing characters. The dramatic and rhetorical way leads through Ovid to the omniscient dramatization of the crucial moments in the inward lives of characters in difficult situations. Modern psychological narrative can usually be related to both the Ovidian and Augustinian traditions.

The developing character begins in fictional Western narrative when Christian concepts are blended with the late Celtic romances. The Perceval or Parzival story, which reached a very high point of development in the hands of both Chrétien de Troyes and Wolfram von Eschenbach in the twelfth century is an excellent example of just this kind of combination. The translators of the new English version of Wolfram's *Parzival* refer to it as the first story in Western European literature which shows "the inner development of the hero." In its drift toward Christian allegory, this narrative underwent many changes, including the invention of a specifically Christian background for the Grail, and the gradual displacement of Gawain by Perceval as the hero. But the most significant development — a feature of both Chrétien's and Wolfram's treatments — is the presentation of Parzival as a developing hero. In Book V of Wolfram, Parzival says of one of the clownish actions of his youth, "May I suffer shame and scorn forever in this life and the next if this lady did do anything amiss when I snatched her brooch from her and took her golden ring as well. I was a fool then, not a man, and not yet grown to wisdom." A speech of this sort represents a revolution in romance characterization. From Parzival to Spenser's Redcross Knight is just a step. This is not to say that the dynamic character automatically makes a romance better than narratives in which the characters are static. Wolfram's rival Gottfried von Strassburg produced his great version of *Tristan* almost simultaneously with Wolfram's *Parzival*, without a hint of developmental characterization. Christianity was more of a hindrance than a help to Gottfried. His characters were essentially pagan, though overlaid with a veneer of medieval Christianity. The traditional story called for no growth or change of character. It was, and is, simply not that kind of story.

We should note that it is possible to treat a character in the developmental manner without presenting his inward life in much detail. Even a character like Parzival is relatively flat and opaque. The developmental formulation itself is primarily a plot formulation rather than a character formulation. It involves seeing the character at long range, with limited detail, so that his change against a particular background may be readily apparent. Spenser, by breaking down the human psyche into component parts, is able to filter out irrelevancies and show development along different lines in the knights of Holiness and Temperance, St. George and Sir Guyon, of Books I and II of *The Faerie Queene*. The narrative of development in a particular direction tends toward the exemplum and the allegory. But the character who merely changes through age and experience, without developing along ethically schematized lines, does not seem to generate a limiting plot pattern the way a purely developmental character does. Change is an aspect of a mimetic approach to characterization. Development is really a moral motif which functions much like mythic pattern or any traditional story line as a factor which limits the extent to which character can be explored for its own sake. Though Parzival develops, we know much less about him, even, than we know about Achilles or Odysseus who remain essentially static. Parzival's characterization is limited by his developmental motif, his progress in Christian knighthood. Achilles' characterization is limited by Homer's thematic interest in the phenomenon of anger. But Homer, whose commitment to mimesis is greater than Wolfram's, presents the character of Achilles more thoroughly in terms of anger than Wolfram presents Parzival in terms of Christian development. Even St. Augustine himself, whose psychological insights are without question profound, is using his own character in an exemplary fashion, for a moral purpose, and selects — perhaps even modifies and distorts — the events of his past life so as to serve the religious purpose that was his dominant motive in turning to the form of confessional narrative in the first place.

We can, then, distinguish between two kinds of dynamic characterization: the *developmental,* in which the character's personal traits are attenuated so as to clarify his progress along a plot line which has an ethical basis (as in *Parzival, The Faerie Queene* Bk. I, *Pilgrim's Progress, Great Expectations,* and *The Power and the Glory*); and the *chronological,* in which the character's personal traits are ramified so as to make more significant the gradual shifts worked in the character during a plot which has a temporal basis. This latter kind of plotting and characterizing is highly mimetic and is perhaps the principal distinguishing characteristic of such realistic fictions as the novel, which does not emerge as a literary form until Western culture develops a time-consciousness sophisticated enough to make the kind of temporal discrimination which this sort of characterization requires. E. M. Forster summed up this situation neatly when he contrasted ancient and modern narrative as "life by values" and "life by time." The emphasis placed on time by critics of modern fiction is not merely a ploy designed to show off the ingenuity of the critics; it is the inevitable response of readers seriously interested in coming to terms with literary works in which time is a major structural element — works of the eighteenth century and after.

Modern narrative artists have available both the traditional and the new ways of focusing a narrative on a significant character. One of the major reasons for the apparent differences in the character of Stephen Dedalus in *A Portrait* and in *Ulysses* stems from Joyce's having emphasized a different kind of characterization in the two works. In *A Portrait* Stephen's character is attenuated so as to show his development along esthetic lines as an artist who combines the religious functions of priest-teacher and sinner-scapegoat. But in *Ulysses* he is seen in a temporal rather than a developmental manner, as frozen for a day in time, rather than progressing swiftly through it toward an evolutionary goal, and his character is presented in a much broader and less attenuated manner. Even in *A Portrait,* however, Joyce has availed himself of the modern prerogative of enriching and complicating his presentation of the developing character, making Stephen more highly specialized both as individual and as type than, for example, the Pip of Dickens's *Great Expectations.* Pip is neither so special nor so symbolic. He is typical rather than archetypal, and his story has the concentrated power of the moral exemplum which draws strong support from the consensus ethos of its time, while Stephen's story dwindles deliberately toward an ambiguity and anti-climax which are more mimetic than exemplary.

If we can distinguish at all between character and incident — to return at this point to the problem posed by James with which we began this consideration of character — we must do so in terms of the inward life. The incident James used for an illustration, the woman looking out with her hand on a table, would hardly be an incident in a play (one is tempted to allude here to James's failure as a playwright), would be much more likely in a movie, and would be most likely in a novel. The reason for this progression of likelihood is that the essence of such an incident must lie in the psyche of the character. In a play, only speech or action can reveal character. In a movie the close-up provides a way of revealing more of the psyche than can be managed on the stage through mere expression and gesture. But in narrative only is the inward life of the characters really accessible. Again, as Forster has remarked, "the novelist has a real pull here." The most essential element in characterization is this inward life. The less of it we have, the more other narrative elements such as plot, commentary, description, allusion, and rhetoric must contribute to the work. A successful narrative need not emphasize the inward life and present it in detail; but it must be prepared to compensate with other elements if it is to remain an object of interest to men. The Greek romances compensated with involved plotting, vivid description, and ornate rhetoric, and so did their English and French imitators of the sixteenth and seventeenth centuries. Poetry in narrative can also compensate. When Milton describes Satan in *Paradise Lost,* a single poetic phrase of potency, such as "and care/Sat on his faded cheek," does away with the need for elaborate analysis of character or elaborate dramatization of the inward life. There are many ways in which a narrative artist can project the psyches of his characters. Without any claim or hope of exhausting the possibilities, we shall examine here some of the more important methods.

The simplest way of presenting the inward life in narration is that of direct narrative statement. When the narrator of *Njál's Saga* says of Hallgerd that she is impetuous and willful, he is giving us simply and directly the keys to her character. All her later actions are derived from these two principles of impetuosity and willfulness plus her tendency to dishonesty which is also presented simply and directly through a character named Hrut (who is, we are told, "always reliable in matters of importance"). Hrut remarks in the opening passage of the saga that Hallgerd has "thief's eyes." These attributes, together with a crucial physical detail — her long, blond hair — are all we need for apprehending her character completely. Saga characterization is an almost pure and perfect example of the external approach to character. Nearly every character is formally introduced in saga with a sentence or two of attributes. Even the most complex character in *Njál's Saga*, Njál himself, is introduced in this way. All his subsequent actions are implicit in his introductory description. First we are given his genealogy. Then we are told:

He was wealthy and handsome, but he was marked by the fact that he could not grow a beard. He was such a good lawyer that no one could equal him. He was wise and could see clearly into the future. He gave sound advice and was kind; everything he advised people to do turned out well for them. He had a gentle, noble mind, with both foresight and an excellent memory. He resolved the difficulties of anyone who consulted him.

His wife was named Bergthora. She was Skarphedin's daughter, a great and noble woman but somewhat harsh natured.

The sagas are very interested in character. Their vocabulary of descriptive terminology applied to characterization is rich and flexible. By combining a few attributes a saga narrator constructs a character much as a molecule is made from a combination of atoms. But the sagas never attempt to penetrate inside the character. Only words and actions are described; thoughts are never analyzed. Still, the great moments are often moments of character. When Hallgerd, that willful and impetuous woman described above, gets married, she causes trouble. She marries three times, always provokes her husband at least once to strike her, and either deliberately or accidentally causes the death of each of them. When her third husband, the great warrior Gunnar, is besieged by his enemies, he defends himself successfully until his bow-string breaks. Then he turns to his wife:

He said to Hallgerd, "give me two locks of your hair and you and my mother twist them together into a bow-string for me."

"Does anything depend on it?" she asked.

"My life depends on it," he said, "because they will never get the better of me as long as I can use my bow."

"Then I will remind you now," she said, "of the time you struck me. I do not care whether you defend yourself for a long time or a short one."

"Everyone should do something for his fame to rest on," said Gunnar. "I won't keep on asking you."

The saga tells us that he held them at bay a long time with his halberd alone, "But in the end they killed him." Though we cannot see into her mind, Hallgerd's behavior here is of interest because of that mind. The incident expresses perfectly that "willful and impetuous" temperament. The characterization is doubly right—right in relation to the narrative presentation of the woman's qualities, and right in relation to human nature in general. A simply conceived character, in a narrative calculated so as to project the qualities of that character starkly and vividly, can achieve profundity of meaning and impact without complexity or richness. Like Achilles, Hallgerd is a monolithic characterization, all the more impressive in that she has been rendered with the fewest possible strokes of the sculptor's hammer. As in the epic, character in the saga is conceived in terms of plot. In this perfectly self-contained narrative world, the characters are not endowed with any attributes extraneous to the action being presented. This economy of presentation, in which every aspect of character is giving expression in action, is a major factor in the power of the great characterizations of epic and saga.

This kind of representation of the inner life through direct narrative statement is found in other primitive literatures, but nowhere so vigorously developed as in Iceland. The especially distinguishing characteristic of family sagas, which sets them apart from all other literatures of the Middle Ages, is their interest in what we could call manners. The individual attributes, which function as atoms in the molecular construction of saga characters, are very frequently social attributes. They are not merely physical characteristics or attributes referrable to ethical absolutes, but are expressed in terms of observable and agreed-upon standards of social judgment. Take the description of Gunnar Hammundarson, for example, who seems in many respects a typical physical-force hero out of the really primitive heroic tradition. We are told how tall and strong he is, and what a good swimmer. In these respects there is not much to distinguish him from such a hero as Beowulf. But there is more to him:

> He was handsome and light-complexioned, with a straight nose that was somewhat turned up at the end. He had sharp blue eyes, red cheeks, and a full head of fine blond hair. He was extremely well-bred, robust, generous, even-tempered, and loyal to his few well-chosen friends. He was prosperous.

This physical description is more detailed than comparable descriptions in epic poetry. But that is not the main point to be made. Such terms as well-bred [*kurteiss*] and prosperous [*auðigr at fé*] have a reference primarily to manners and social position. Lionel Trilling has said that all characters in fiction, even Priam and Achilles, exist by reason of their observed manners. This may be so, but Achilles is not presented in a context of manners to the same extent that Gunnar and Njál are. Northrop Frye has arranged a schematic anatomy of characterization which locates characters according to their control over their environment. But Gunnar and Njál have just about as much control over their environment as Achilles and Beowulf. Yet the characterization of the two Icelanders is more mimetic in the sense that it is more concerned with the characters' relation to a social environment. It would make no sense to say that Achilles was well- or ill-bred, or that he was prosperous. These considerations are irrelevant in his case. They would be descriptions of manners in a world in which manners are not really significant. But in the world of saga they are significant because the saga-man chooses or the saga tradition requires that they be so.

The technique of characterization in saga stands midway between the heroic epic and the novel of manners. Even such an unphysical novelist as Jane Austen employs techniques for introducing characters reminiscent of the direct description of the sagas. The introduction of Emma Woodhouse, for one, is similar to saga introduction of characters, and there are many such formal introductions scattered throughout the pages of Jane Austen. Of course, she relies much more on nuance than the saga narrators, and her irony is much more delicate, but the technique is amazingly similar. In Jane Austen, of course, we also get analytical passages dealing with the psyches of her protagonists, but most of her lesser characters are seen from the outside only, and are introduced with brief passages descriptive of their minds, morals, and manners. If a gigantic figure such as Hallgerd could be reduced to the proportions of the drawing room, she could take her place easily and naturally among Jane Austen's females.

The notion of peering directly into the mind and dramatizing or analyzing thoughts instead of words and deeds seems to arise quite late in most literatures. The sagas avoid it so carefully that one almost senses a taboo against it, yet it may be that the technique of such presentation was simply not available to primitive narrators, just as perspective was unavailable to painters before the Renaissance. In the past, narrative artists have frequently employed supernatural machinery (*dei ex machina*, if you will) to open up the minds of their characters. When Achilles reaches the peak of his anger with Agamemnon during their quarrel, Homer tells us that

Now bitter pain came to the son of Peleus, as within his hairy chest his heart hesitated between two choices: either to draw his sharp sword from next to his thigh and lay about him, seeking to kill the son of Atreus, or to stifle his rage and restrain his spirit.

Then, rather than narrate Achilles' internal conflict, he dramatizes it by introducing Athena who is seen by Achilles alone and who convinces him to vent his anger in words rather than deeds at this moment. What, in a modern fiction, would be referred to some internal psychological process, presented perhaps as an interior monologue or an analytical narrative, is referred by Homer to divine intervention and to the external processes of fate and the will of the gods. One of Athena's main lines of argument here is that the gods will treble Achilles' rewards in glory if he will refrain from violence at this moment. Primitive narrative often turns to myth rather than mimesis at just such psychological moments. It is God, in the Book of Exodus, who hardens Pharaoh's heart in his dealings with Moses. And even Joseph observes, in the Book of Genesis, when he is forgiving his brothers, "Now therefore be not grieved, nor angry with yourselves, that ye sold me hither: for God did send me before you to preserve life. . . . So now it was not you that sent me hither, but God: and he hath made me a father to Pharaoh, and lord of this house, and a ruler throughout all the land of Egypt." This sort of treatment of mental process is essentially mythic rather than mimetic, but some of its effects strike the modern eye as peculiarly realistic. A character in saga, who always operates according to the attributes he is given on his first appearance in the story, tends to behave mechanically according to those attributes. But a character whose mental processes and the actions deriving from them are subject to sudden supernatural influences inevitably displays some of those irregularities of behavior which seem to twentieth-century eyes quintessentially human because they are irrational.

The use of supernatural machinery to reveal mental process and provide motivation is a device which persists in synthetic epic forms, both pagan and Christian. Aeneas' motivation in leaving Dido is presented in terms of a dream sent to him by the gods to remind him of his destiny. Dreams are frequently used in early narrative for such purposes, and are wonderfully suited to characterization which is poised between the mythic and the mimetic. Dreams can be referred to the divinities which shape our ends, or to the mental processes of human beings. Joseph's brethren assume his dreams are merely a reflection of his ambitions, and there is considerable hostility and fear in their cry, "Behold, this dreamer cometh"; but events prove the dreams divinely inspired and not merely reflections of Joseph's overweening pride.

In Christian synthetic epic the devil figures prominently as a *deus ex machina* who assists in the dramatizing of motivation and the revelation of character. In *Gerusalemme Liberata*, when Tasso wishes to motivate Gernando to perform a foolhardy and contentious action, he introduces "The hidden devil that lies in close await / To win the fort of unbelieving man." This devil "whisp'reth in his ear" for four stanzas, after which "the kindled fire began / To ev'ry vein its poison'd heat to reach, / It swell'd his scornful heart, and forth it ran / At his proud looks, and too audacious speech." Thus Tasso, in Edward Fairfax's sixteenth-century English rendition: and Milton's Satan owes something to Tasso's. Even in mock epic, as in *The Rape of the Lock*, the machinery is employed partly as mock motivation for the characters.

Another technique for presenting the inward life, which has an ancient and honorable history, is that of the "interior monologue." Because this term is often applied indiscriminately to modern fiction and sometimes used interchangeably with "stream of consciousness," we must do a bit of defining and clarifying before employing either term. "Stream of consciousness" is properly a psychological term rather than a literary one. It describes a mode of mental process. "Interior monologue" is a literary term, synonymous with unspoken soliloquy. Hence, in this study, the term "stream of consciousness" will be used to designate any presentation in literature of the illogical, ungrammatical, mainly associative patterns of human thought. Such thoughts may be spoken or unspoken. As a literary phenomenon, stream of consciousness is of fairly late development, with its most obvious roots in Lockean theory of the workings of the mind and Sterne's adaptation of Locke in *Tristam Shandy*. Interior monologue is another order of phenomenon. It is, in narrative literature, a direct, immediate presentation of the unspoken thoughts of a character without any intervening narrator. Like direct discourse or dialogue it is a dramatic element in narrative literature, but it can be present only in narrative literature because only in narrative can a soliloquy remain unspoken and yet be understood by an audience. This is an observation somewhat less banal than it may seem at first. Since in the drama soliloquy must be spoken aloud in order for the audience to apprehend it, the character who speaks must be of a soliloquizing nature. Hamlet is Shakespeare's Great Soliloquizer because he is, as a character, well designed for soliloquies; whereas Othello, for example, is not. But in narrative literature any character's mind can be opened up and his inner thoughts revealed, no matter how unlikely he might be to vocalize them in a soliloquy. The mind of the average sensual man — a Leopold Bloom, perhaps — can be revealed only with great difficulty in drama, but the novelist can expose any kind of mind directly to the reader. One of the major developments in the history of narrative characterization is the tendency in modern literature for interior monologues to be employed widely and without specific occasion, while in ancient times they were used sparingly and in fairly well specified situations. As a narrative device, interior monologue has a history much more ancient than stream of consciousness, but because we find the two devices combined in modern writers like Joyce and Virginia Woolf we often fail to distinguish between them, and hence remain unaware of their quite separate and different histories.

Interior monologue in classical narrative artists exhibits a number of interesting characteristics, some of which serve to distinguish it from later manifestations of the device, but many of which seem to have remained characteristic of it in its modern forms also. Some authors who developed and exploited the monologue in the ancient world are Homer, Apollonius Rhodius, Vergil, Ovid, Longus, and Xenophon of Ephesus. Even these men, however, who employed the device with considerable skill and power, used it sparingly. Its use was not a widespread practice in antiquity.

Homer's use of the interior monologue is especially interesting. His practice is a combination of formulaic behavior and complete ease and flexibility. By way of contrast, in such vernacular primitive epics as have survived we do not find the interior monologue

employed. There is not a hint of such a thing in *Beowulf*, for example. We cannot tell whether Homer invented this technique
or simply was employing a common device of Greek oral narrative, because we have almost no record of his predecessors' work.
But we can see that he had a concept which made the interior
monologue a likely device for him — a concept which is in fact
necessary if the interior monologue is to come into being in any
literature. In half of the interior monologues in the *Iliad*, one entire line recurs at a crucial point: *alla ti e moi tauta philos dielexato
thymos* (but why does my own heart [*thymos*] dispute with me
thus?). Odysseus uses the phrase in his monologue expressing fear
(*Iliad*, XI, line 402). Menelaus uses it in his monologue expressing
fear (XVII, 97). Agenor uses it in his monologue expressing fear
(XXI, 562). And Hector uses it in his monologue expressing fear
(XXII, 122). Achilles, who never has to struggle with fear, does
not employ this line in a monologue, but it occurs, in his speech to
his comrades after Hector's death, at the precise moment when his
thoughts turn from the war and the Trojans to the dead body of
Patroclus, which has not been given a proper funeral (XXII, 385).
In every case, including this one, the identical line occurs at a
pivotal point in the monologue, as the direction of thought turns
from unworthy or unsuitable considerations or feelings to worthy
or suitable ones. In the case of the four interior monologues expressing fear of battle, the line introduces the shift from fearful
to courageous thoughts.

Having observed this phenomenon, we can learn a number of
things from it. We can see how Homer is able to invoke a formula
so as to make important and vivid for the occasion a character as
minor as Agenor, who has only a moment on stage in the whole
Iliad. The formula vivifies, but it does not individualize the characters. In fact, insofar as it is formulaic, it tends to unite through
the typical rather than to individualize. Yet Homer works into the
formula, when he wants to, individualizing touches. Hector's monologue is three times the length of Agenor's because of the specific
thoughts he expresses which are peculiar to him and his situation.

But the most important thing we can learn from this recurring line in Homeric interior monologue is the assumption that must have lain behind it in the mind of the author about the nature of the human psyche. The *thymos,* which can mean something like heart or something like mind, is seen as disputing (*dielexato*) with the will of the individual. The psyche has been divided into two parts which dispute for mastery, often in a manner hinting at a concept of the ego, which cares for its own preservation, and a superego, which drives the individual toward acceptable action. Some such concept of the divided psyche seems essential for the development of the interior monologue technique, and it is just this concept which was seized on and exploited by Homer's followers in narrative art. The prevailing concept of thought in ancient times is undoubtedly the one presented by Plato, who described thought as "the talk which the soul [*psyche* has replaced *thymos* as the internal speaker] has with itself about any subject which it considers" ("Theaetetus," 189, E; "Sophist," 263, E). This is an accurate description of what must have been Homer's concept also. And we can see in Homer a little dramatic formula, in which a character seems to be giving way to the promptings of his *thymos* but pulls himself together in the formulaic line we have been considering and proceeds to do the right thing.

The fact that this formulaic line was employed by Homer in Achilles' spoken discourse, as well as in the unspoken thoughts of other characters, exemplifies the ancient tendency to think of thought simply as speech minus the sound. This concept of thought as a sort of internal dialogue, taking the same linguistic form as oral speech, remained the prevailing assumption about the nature of thought until a few centuries ago. The prevalence of this notion is crucial to the representation of thought in literature; because if thought is simply unspoken speech, it can be represented exactly as speech would be represented, and the arts used to organize and enhance speech, the arts of rhetoric, may be properly applied to unspoken speech as well as to words actually pronounced aloud. Thus characterization through thought amounts, as long as this assumption prevails, to characterization through rhetoric. The notion that thought may not be merely unspoken speech but another order of verbalization altogether does not begin to develop until the seventeenth century in Europe and does not begin to affect narrative literature until the eighteenth. When it does, it helps to work a revolution in narrative characterization, preparing the way for the stream of consciousness, a method of narration in which action is reduced to impression and thought, and the language of thought is organized on psychological principles rather than rhetorical ones. But in the ancient world thought and rhetoric remain hard to separate. Most of the classical monologues we are about to consider here are not *necessarily* interior in the sense of unspoken. The poets often use the words for spoken discourse to present what they may or may not have considered as uttered aloud. This problem is discussed in more detail in the Appendix.

Homer, of course, was more interested in action than thought. In all of the Homeric monologues we have been considering, one right course of action is open to the character and is ultimately resolved upon. But, as any psychologist who has invented an unsolvable rat-maze can testify, the really interesting mental processes begin when the mind is confronted by unsolvable problems. The refinement and development of the technique of the interior monologue in narrative literature really begins when the narrative artist chooses to focus on a mind tormented by a dilemma. As far as we know, the credit for this development in narrative must go to Apollonius of Rhodes — a narrative artist who has had nothing like his due acclaim — though he undoubtedly learned something from the Greek tragic dramatists. Vergil learned the technique from Apollonius, Ovid probably from both of them, as the examples in the Appendix will indicate. With refinement, of course, comes stylization, and we shall see that as the technique of the interior monologue developed it was used less flexibly than it had been in Homer's hands. Homer is formulaic in his rhetoric, but quite flexible in his employment of the device. In the *Odyssey* most of the monologues come, naturally, when Odysseus is alone, en route from the hospitality of Calypso to that of the Phaeacians. Several of these monologues are introduced by the identical line: *oxthesas d'ara eipe pros hon megaletora thymon* (and deeply moved he spoke to his own mighty heart). They generally open with an identical phrase also: *O moi ego* (O woe is me). But when and where the device will be employed seems to be dictated only by the logic of the narrative and not by a tradition which calls for a special kind of monologue in a highly specialized situation. With Apollonius commences a tradition of building a narrative toward a highly specialized situation which will require a very special kind of monologue. This is a different kind of thing from Homer's simple employment of monologues in parts of the *Iliad* to present characters struggling with their fear. It tends to thrust the monologue itself into a central position, emphasizing characterization through thought rather than action, and ultimately resulting in the stylization of the monologue itself. This tradition of stylization begins with Apollonius.

The sole interior monologue of any size in the *Argonautica* occurs at a crucial moment in the third book. Jason and his Argonauts, strangers in a strange land, have been assigned an impossible task by King Aeetes. The task can be performed only with the aid of Aeetes' daughter Medea, who is skilled in magic. The gods, who are helping Jason, arrange for Medea to be wounded by one of Eros' arrows, so that she falls in love with the handsome stranger. Medea, smitten by the arrow, is torn between her newly acquired passion and her loyalty to her father. There is no one to whom she can confide all her thoughts. She attempts to resolve her dilemma in a debate with herself. Apollonius treats her inner struggle at length, combining narrative analysis with a long passage of interior monologue. (See text and translation in the Appendix.) We can separate the characteristics of the passage into a number of items to be compared with other uses of this technique: 1) the monologuist is a woman (all Homer's were men), 2) she is in love, 3) the moment is a moment of crisis, 4) she is torn between what is "right" and what she is driven to do, in this case between loyalty and passion, 5) her situation is such that she can confide in no one, 6) she considers suicide as a possibility.

Vergil, of course, borrowed enormously from Apollonius for his presentation of Dido in the *Aeneid*. He provided Dido with a sister Anna, who usually acts as her confidante (as Chalciope did for Medea) during the course of her difficult love affair with Aeneas. But Dido too reaches a point when she can no longer confide in anyone. At night, in her bed (like Medea) she weighs the conflicting demands of love and honor, deciding finally on suicide as the only way out. (See text and translation in the Appendix.) Jason and Aeneas are given no comparable interior monologues, though Vergil used the monologue skillfully to present Aeneas' temptation to kill Helen during the destruction of Troy. Because it is the women who fall uncontrollably in love in these poems, the most interesting and significant monologues inevitably fall to them. From early times sex and psychology have inevitably sought one another out. Had Apollonius or Vergil retold the story of the *Odyssey* instead of merely imitating it, it is very likely that we would penetrate into the psyches of Calypso, Circe, Nausicaa, or Penelope in ways that Homer would not have considered. (The closest we come to such a thing in Homer is Penelope's prayer to Artemis in Book XX, which is not an interior monologue, but nonetheless a precursor to Apollonius' presentation of Medea's prayer and thoughts.) The inner life of the female of the species contemplating her erotic situation has been a focal point of narrative concern with the psyche from Medea and Dido to Anna Karenina and Molly Bloom. The emphasis on the feminine psyche in ancient times was due, no doubt, to the prevailing view that women were more passionate than men, summed up neatly for us by Ovid, in his account of the dispute between Jove and Juno over whether the male or the female finds love most pleasurable. As Ovid tells it, the King and Queen of Heaven consult the hermaphroditic Tiresias to settle their dispute, and the seer earns the enmity of Juno by asserting that the female gets more pleasure than the male.

In Ovid's *Metamorphoses*, gods and men seem to fall victim to

the arrows of love as often as women, but the males simply translate their urges into action and attempt to prevail over the desired female by force or guile. It is the women in love who provide the occasions for extended dramatic monologues. We find
that Ovid, however, seizes on the technique and exploits it with
far less restraint than Apollonius and Vergil. He retells the story
of Jason and Medea in a very brief compass, but gives Medea
an interior monologue fully as long as the comparable one in
Apollonius, seizing unerringly on the most interesting part of the
Argonautica for extended treatment. This tale, in Book VII of the
Metamorphoses, is followed soon in Book VIII by the similar story
of the unhappy Scylla who, like Medea, betrays her father to his
handsome enemy — in this case Minos — and Scylla's moment
of debate and decision is the occasion for a similar monologue.
This story is soon followed in Books IX and X by three related
tales about the unfortunate love affairs of ill-starred females, all
of which provide occasions for interior monologues in the pattern
already established: Byblis, who loves her twin brother; Iphis,
who loves another girl; and Myrrha, who loves her father. All
the extended interior monologues in the *Metamorphoses* are thus
accounted for in these four books. Moreover, except that suicide
is not contemplated in all of them, they retain all of the characteristics of the monologue of Medea in the *Argonautica.* The mon-
ologuists are women — in love — in a moment of crisis — torn
between passion and right action — and they can confide in
no one.

In the ancient literary epics the major interior monologues,
then, tend to take a very specialized form. In each of the cases
cited, the situation is a dilemma, and the monologue takes the
shape of an argument, reaching, in Ovid especially, who really
worked on the technique, a very sophisticated pattern of reasoning in some cases. (See, for example, a portion of the interior debate of Myrrha, in the Appendix.) The germ of this pattern of
interior debate was certainly present in the formula for the fear-
monologue used by Homer in the *Iliad,* but in Homer there is none

of the elaborate argument and heightened rhetoric which the monologue acquired in its Alexandrian and Roman manifestations. In the Ovidian monologues the artist's interest in character itself is about to be lost, so deeply does it become submerged in the intellectual process of debate. It is not unlikely that debates of this kind were part of the standard training of a rhetorician. We know that the famous debate of Ajax and Ulysses over the shield of Achilles, which is also recounted by Ovid, was used in the schools of rhetoric as a drill. In the ancient world, at the point of most intense penetration into the inner life, in the monologues we have been considering, we find not psychology but rhetoric, and it is rhetoric which dominates the monologue of characterization in all Western literature, from the Greeks to the Renaissance, not excluding the great monologues in Chaucerian narrative and Shakespearean drama. By rhetoric in the monologue we mean language in its formal dress — words artfully deployed so as to move the reader or audience by focusing on him and his responses. By psychology we mean a real attempt to reproduce mental verbal process — words deployed in patterns referrable not to verbal artistry but to actual thought, focusing not on the audience but on the character. The stream of consciousness insists on psychologically oriented patterns. The interior monologue has traditionally invited rhetorical display. Though the two are often combined in modern narrative, we can see how Joyce, for example, in *Ulysses* leans always toward stream of consciousness and psychology, while Faulkner, in *The Sound and the Fury*, leans toward the rhetorical monologue.

In the ancient writers the monologue became a set piece, an opportunity for display of verbal virtuosity. It was natural, then, that it should have been incorporated into the highly stylized patterns of the prose Greek romances. In the *Ephesian Tale* (*Habrocomes and Anthia*) and in *Daphnis and Chloe* we find monologues employed, again at crucial moments. The romances differ from the literary epics which preceded them in a number of obvious ways which have some bearing on the treatment of interior monologue in them. They are in prose; they are not concerned with traditionally recorded events of a historico-legendary character; and their main subject matter is love — shared equally by a man and a woman. As the heroic male figure of the epic is replaced by a more erotically oriented character in the romances, we begin to get male love-monologues to go along with the customary female ones. In the romances, the standard place for such a monologue becomes the moment of falling in love. In Xenophon's *Ephesian Tale* both Habrocomes and Anthia indulge in similar soliloquies at that crucial moment. (See texts and translations in the Appendix.) These soliloquies resemble the monologues in Ovid and the earlier writers, but they are much shorter and simpler. There is a disposition in Xenophon to spread them around in the form of laments and prayers uttered aloud rather than in truly interior monologues. In Longus' *Daphnis and Chloe* the new formula for a monologue celebrating (or lamenting) the birth of love is carefully observed in the cases of both lovers. We can see from the examples (in the Appendix) that the formula here is much like that used by Xenophon, but handled more subtly and delicately. There is even an attempt in Daphnis' monologue, to suggest the disturbed mind hopping from one object to another associatively, though the individual thoughts are still rendered more rhetorically than psychologically.

Thought, in the narratives of the ancient world, continued to be presented as unspoken speech. And speech, to a considerable extent, was presented in literature as unwritten writing. In both Latin and Greek, literary languages, based on established standards, came into being; and the literary languages gradually became further and further separated from common speech, making the representation of ordinary speech a virtual impossibility in narrative, and keeping the representation of anything like ordinary thought in the realm of the inconceivable. Writing in Latin, a daring innovator like Petronius could introduce apparently vulgar locutions into his narrative; but to be literate in Greek meant to write imitation Attic Greek, which made it impossible to be literate and mimetic at the same time. As the gulf widened between literate and vulgar Latin, the Roman writers also remained cut off from the possibility of representing thought realistically. When narrative literature began to achieve written status in the vernacular languages of Western Europe, the possibility for realistic representation of thought patterns in narrative opened up once again. But the new literatures had to work through a whole series of primitive epics and *chansons de geste,* in which action rather than thought was emphasized, before the interior monologue was developed again as a significant literary device. We can quite properly pick up the history of the interior monologue with Chaucer's employment of it in *Troilus and Criseyde,* which is hardly different from Xenophon's in the *Ephesian Tale.* The traditional erotic narrative required monologues in hero and heroine upon the birth of love in their hearts, and that is just what Chaucer gives us. (See the Appendix for texts.) Chaucer, in fact, feels the pressure of the ancient formula so strongly that he makes a significant departure from his source. Much of the *Troilus* is a direct translation from Boccaccio's *Filostrato.* But the *Filostrato* has only the newly stricken Troilo's prayer to Love; it lacks the traditional lover's monologue of anguish. Chaucer supplied the deficiency by taking Boccaccio's hint that Troilo in love gave himself over to singing. The English poet rummaged around until he found a Petrarch sonnet which seemed appropriate for this situation, which he then translated as the "Song of Troilus." It is as rhetorical as can be, and contrasts markedly with Criseyde's monologue of Book II, which is also a departure from the source. In Criseyde's monologue Chaucer departs from Boccaccio not merely to find a substitute source but in order to elaborate himself on the character of his heroine. This difference in his treatment of the two monologues points up Chaucer's pivotal position in the development of narrative art. His Criseyde displays a character more complex than Boccaccio's Criseida and a train of thought more psychologically oriented than anything yet presented in narrative monologue. We see rhetoric fading into psychology in this monologue. The women of the Greek romances and that other widow, Dido, all stand behind Chaucer's characterization here, but Chaucer is projecting his character into new realms of psychological and social considerations, both of which are beautifully reflected in that pivotal line of the monologue, "I am myne owene womman, wel at ese." Chaucer's rich widow is at this moment mainly a woman of the waning Middle Ages, for all her Trojan trappings. Her words would not be unsuitable to the Wife of Bath, and her characterization, like those of the Canterbury Pilgrims, leads in English literature toward that great surge of characterization which is the glory of Elizabethan drama. It may well be that the way they hover between the rhetorical and the psychological in characterization has a good deal to do with the brilliant success of both Chaucer and Shakespeare in this department of literature.

Insofar as narrative literature is concerned, we can observe that the monologues tend to be rhetorical in what we call romance, and psychological in what we call realistic narrative. This distinction is, in fact, as crucial and basic as any which can be made to distinguish the two forms. It is more important than a work's time and place of origin or its fictional location, more important than any mere question of subject matter. The enormous seventeenth-century romance *Artamène, ou le Grand Cyrus* bristles with monologues and soliloquies of the rhetorical type, and is frankly derived from the *Cyropedia* of Xenophon and the *Aethiopica* of Heliodorus. Though it dates from almost three hundred years after Chaucer's *Troilus*, it is more rhetorical and less psychological. It is, in fact, virtually the last gasp of the pure romance form before the onslaught of realism. It is not without its virtues, but they are the virtues of a rococo excess, not those of balance and reconciliation. In narrative literature the great watershed which divides the major streams is the seventeenth century. After the rise of empiricism and the subsequent inevitable development of a science of psychology, a movement from rhetorical to psychological characterization in narrative was also an inevitability. For modern writers, as the science of psychology has grown in vigor and influence, a great problem has been to employ the developing knowledge of the human psyche without losing all those literary effects which rhetoric alone can achieve. The problem has been the achievement of new, workable combinations of psychology and rhetoric, and the great narrative artists have solved it in various ways. Dickens, it is almost fair to say, was preserved by his innocence; Flaubert by his knowledge. Great instincts or great pains can produce great works, but they will be works of a very different kind.

Of course, not all attempts to reconcile the psychological and the rhetorical in characterization waited for the seventeenth century or for the birth of a formal discipline called psychology. One of the first European writers to struggle with this problem was Boccaccio, who, three hundred years before the purely rhetorical flourishes of the *Grand Cyrus,* did much to liberate the interior monologue from its traditional employment as a set piece to be indulged in primarily to render the pangs of awakening love or the inward debate of a conflict between desire and duty. He employed the interior monologue, together with extended passages of narrative analysis of his characters' thoughts, frequently and on a variety of occasions in many of his hundred tales. In general, Boccaccio's interest in character exceeds that of other continental practitioners of the novella. The *Gesta Romanorum,* which is the main link between the tales and romances of the ancient world and the short narratives of the vernacular tongue, is concerned mainly with bare narrative bones suitable for use as exempla in sermons; and even Boccaccio's followers and imitators in the Renaissance usually manifest more interest in plot and less in character than Boccaccio. This interest is apparent throughout the *Decameron* but nowhere more strikingly than in a tale which seems to require it least: the seventh tale of the eighth day, which is basically a fabliau centering on a practical joke. It is of the same order as Chaucer's Miller's Tale and might share with that story some such descriptive title as The Scholar's Revenge, but in

Boccaccio's hands it becomes quite a different thing indeed from
the standard fabliau, almost losing all resemblance to the rest of
the tribe. The plot is simple. A scholar in love with a lady is tricked
by her into spending the night in a freezing courtyard. He takes
his revenge by tricking her into spending all day naked in the
broiling sun. To this simple narrative skeleton, which includes
none of the opportunities for high jinks afforded by the Miller's
Tale, Boccaccio brings an attention to detail and a devotion to
the feelings and mental states of his characters virtually unparal-
leled before this in European literature. The tale, for all its simple
plot, is one of the longest in the collection, running three times
the length of the average story in the *Decameron*. One is tempted
to ask why such resources of art were lavished on this unpromising
tale, why the characterization was so important, why the pain of
cold and heat and the other bodily and mental anguish of these
two characters required such detailed presentation; and especially
why the traditional reconciliation of the two main characters,
which is a feature of most of the stories considered as analogues
and possible sources of Boccaccio's tale, and which would be quite
in keeping with the fictional orientation of most of the *Decameron*
tales, is not employed in this instance. One answer to these various "whys" lies in Boccaccio's desire to render the lady's suffer-
ing, in particular, as palpably anguished as possible, while at the
same time preserving our sympathies for the scholar who is visiting this anguish upon her. A careful analysis of the use of interior
monologue and narrative analysis of mental process in this story
will reveal that it is designed in large part to preserve our sympathy for the revenger without diminishing our sense of the pain-
fulness of the revenge. This has the effect of making the story
more interesting than some others for the modern reader, who is
especially interested in and responsive to intensity of feeling, but
this does not explain why Boccaccio should have chosen just this
story in which to make this effect, which is a singular one, even
for him. One possible answer, that suggested by Luigi Groto, "the
blind man of Adria," and by Sansovino and others, is that the tale
is in some respect autobiographical.

This, if true, would account better than anything else for the intensity and the psychological orientation of the characterizations in the tale. This tendency to put the narrator's self into the narrative (an autobiographical *attitude* which is not necessarily connected with autobiographical *form*) we think of usually as a "romantic" tendency. Perhaps we might do' better to think of it as a realistic tendency. Whether or not it spoils the neat divisions of our literary histories, realism is bound up in a very complicated way with that European phenomenon we call "romanticism," though we think of it quite properly as representing an attitude opposed to the romantic. This realistic tendency toward the adoption of an autobiographical attitude in narrative is in fact one of the main distinctions between novelistic characterization and the kinds of characterization presented in all earlier narrative, and is intimately connected with the distinction between the rhetorical and the psychological ways of presenting character. It is the novelists who tend to put themselves into their characters, and, conversely, to find in themselves an extraordinary range of dramatic possibilities, made up of aspirations, suppressed desires, masks and anti-masks, nobility and depravity. Why does *La Princesse de Clèves* seem such an advance in characterization over its romance ancestors of just a generation before? Partly, no doubt, because of its more specific historical setting but mainly, we would suggest, because Mme. de La Fayette has projected her own sensibility into the psyches of her unhappy triangle of characters. The *personal* quality which enters French literature with Montaigne flowers a century later in the letters of Mme. de Sévigné and the novel of her friend Mme. de La Fayette. Even in less civilized, less sensitive England, is there not much of Defoe not only in Robinson Crusoe but in Moll Flanders and Roxana as well? And is not Richardson's greatness derived largely from his ability to fuse his own sensibility with those of his letter-writers, and especially with his heroines? Fielding and Thackeray project their own personalities mainly into their narrative personae, but Richardson and Sterne make characters of their narrators and project their own psyches into all their characters. Jane Austen projects herself to a greater or lesser extent into all her heroines, but treats her other characters more in the manner of Fielding, which accounts in part for that sense we have of her art as being poised somewhere between that of Fielding and Richardson.

Of all the giants of the age of the novel can we not say that the principal thing which unites them is a special care for characterization which is inextricably bound up with the creation of character from the facets of the artist's own psyche? Is not this the main thing which unites such diverse figures as Joyce, Lawrence, Proust, Dostoievsky, Tolstoy, Flaubert, Balzac, and Stendhal? The autobiographical urge reveals itself in England with a great surge simultaneously with the rise of the novel. Pepys, Evelyn, Cibber, Gibbon, and Boswell manifest this spirit in recognizably autobiographical form. But Rousseau in France sets the tone of the narrative age to come, developing both the novel as autobiography and the autobiography as novel.

Lawrence Sterne in England provided the emerging novelistic narrative with the epistemological device that in the hands of twentieth-century novelists was to provide a major structural alternative or supplement to organization by mythic or fictional plot patterns, or by the chronological patterns of saga and history. By demonstrating that fiction could be articulated by means of Lockean patterns of association, Sterne showed the novelists of the future how character could, in effect, make plot. William James's term, the "stream of consciousness," is in itself derived from the thinking of that line of empirical philosophers which goes back to Hume and Locke. And it was Sterne who first made the stream of consciousness an organizational element in fiction. We should note here how intimately the epistemological thinking of Locke and Hume is related to what we have been calling the autobiographical spirit. Locke's theories derive from observation of his own mental processes. In fact, until experimental psychology was developed in our own century, most thinking about mental process was based on self-analysis, including some of Freud's earliest and most dramatic psychological breakthroughs.

Thus, the development of novelistic methods of characterization, and the shift from rhetorical to psychological presentation of the inner life, is closely connected with the whole movement of mind we call romanticism, and especially with the rise of the autobiographical spirit, which can trace its roots back to such Renaissance autobiographers as Montaigne and Cellini, and ultimately to such Christian figures as St. Theresa and St. Augustine.

In narrative literature after the eighteenth century the two principal devices for presenting the inner life are the same two that had been employed by Apollonius and all his followers: 1) narrative analysis in which the character's thoughts are filtered through the mind of the narrator with more or less interpretive commentary, and 2) the more direct and dramatic interior monologue. In nineteenth-century fiction as in Boccaccio, the two techniques are often employed together throughout a narrative, but some novelists indicate an obvious preference for one method or the other. George Eliot, in *Middlemarch,* prefers to narrate and comment. Stendhal, in *The Red and the Black,* though he will often comment, dramatizes with interior monologues to an extraordinary extent. Until near the end of the nineteenth century the interior monologue seems not to have developed any special syntactical patterns of its own. The elaborate rhetoric of the romancers is gone, but the disjointed meanderings of the stream of consciousness have not yet been mastered and reduced to a new and peculiarly modern variety of rhetoric. The unspoken thoughts of Julien Sorel, for example, appear in a prose very much like the prose of his spoken discourse. The un-proselike syntax of modern stream of consciousness seems to have established itself as a literary technique as a by-product of the interest of the nineteenth century in abnormal mental processes. Just as psychology itself took its real impetus from the study of abnormal cases, psychological prose in the monologue owes much to the interest in the disordered psyche manifested by a writer as vigorous and influential as Dostoievsky. The abnormal individual and the normal individual under abnormal stress, as in the ancient monologues, offered the writers of the nineteenth century opportunities for striking effects in characterization, which were reflected not only in the narrative works of the time but in the vogue of the verse dramatic monologue as well.

One of the first places where the truly modern note is sounded in monologue — the sustained stream of consciousness with its associative patterns of language — is toward the end of Tolstoy's *Anna Karenina*. It is highly likely that James Joyce learned as much from this as he did from encountering Dujardin's *Les Lauriers sont coupées*, though he chose to give the little-known Frenchman the credit. The last four chapters of Part Seven of *Anna Karenina*, and particularly Chapters 27–29, are devoted to Anna's interior monologue in the period just prior to her suicide. Her mind is disordered, her thoughts a jumble of immediate sensory impressions, recollected ideas, and faltering attempts at analysis of her own situation. To present her state of mind dramatically — and it is always his habit to dramatize mental process with interior monologue — Tolstoy abandons the more or less logical and coherent syntactical patterns he normally uses in the interior monologue, and employs the associative patterns of stream of consciousness. In Anna's mind the two artistic devices fuse in so powerful a fashion that the effects have been felt from County Dublin to Yoknapatawpha County. Anna is the forsaken female, torn between love and loyalty, contemplating suicide; and the shades of her literary ancestors, Dido and Medea and the unhappy lovers of Ovid, loom behind her in her pathetic final moments; but the philosophers of the English Enlightenment and the ribald parson's cock-and-bull story also participate in this powerful and terrible scene.

The notion of employing stream of consciousness thought pattern in a continuous interior monologue may be credited to Dujardin, but Joyce, it should be observed, does not himself employ this technique. In *Ulysses* he may tune in on his characters' mental processes at any moment, but he lavishes his greatest effort on the three set pieces: Stephen in "Proteus," Bloom in "Nausicaa," and Molly in "Penelope." And even here, though Joyce is as original in technique as any writer ever has been, Bloom meditating on his love is of the fellowship of Troilus — pathetic and betrayed, and Daphnis — comic and unfaithful; while Molly resembles Criseyde and Chloe not only because she is "wel at ese" as Criseyde was, but because she is both faithless as Criseyde and faithful as Chloe; all three — Longus, Chaucer, and Joyce — have used interior monologue to display and dramatize mental process. Moreover, although Molly's culminating monologue in *Ulysses* is essentially comic, its technical affinities with Anna Karenina's culminating monologue are uncanny. That knowledge of feminine psychology which Jung praised in Joyce owes much to Joyce's sensitivity and to his marriage, no doubt, but also owes something to Tolstoy and the narrative tradition going back through Stendhal, Chaucer, Boccaccio, Ovid, and Vergil, to Apollonius of Rhodes.

In the attempt of post-Lockean interior monologues to dramatize mental process mimetically and psychologically rather than rhetorically, a problem ultimately arises. If we are to do away with that heightening of expression which is the prerogative of rhetoric, and if the dominant mimetic impulse pushes us toward ordinary characters in recognizable situations, how are banality and triviality to be avoided? In a slightly different connection Flaubert raised this very question in *Madame Bovary*. Speaking of Rodolphe the narrator observes,

He could not tell — this man of many affairs — a distinctive feeling hidden in common words. Because whores or women of easy virtue had murmured these same expressions in his ears, he could not really believe that they were genuine this time. This is degrading, he thought; such exaggerated expressions hide indifferent emotions. As if an overflowing heart does not sometimes pour out in the most empty phrases, since none of us can ever spell out perfectly our desires or our ideas or our unhappiness, and human speech is like a cracked kettle on which we beat out tunes to make bears dance, when all the while we want to move the stars.

Flaubert is talking about speech, here, but what he says applies also to any attempt to represent thought processes in purely ver-

bal form. In *Madame Bovary,* Flaubert himself uses interior monologue sparingly, sometimes employing narrative analysis and
sometimes what we might call physical correlatives to symbolize
mental states. In his narrative analysis he indulges in commentary
and direct manipulating of the reader's response rather more than
is usually recognized. He is especially careful to preserve sympathy for Emma in her affair with Rodolphe by telling us directly
of *her* sincerity and exposing *his* insincerity and shallowness as in
the passage just quoted. This technique, of course, is not new.
Boccaccio, for one, used it frequently. It is mentioned here mainly
because Flaubert is widely supposed to have done away with
narrative commentary and kept the author out of his fiction. What
he actually did, however, was to place no emphasis on the personality of his narrator in order to lend such commentary as he makes
(which is sparingly made but highly significant) the authority of
impersonality and impartiality, though in actuality it is neither
impersonal nor impartial; it is a refined and restrained projection
of the sensibility and intellect of Gustave Flaubert, and, in that
limited sense, is autobiographical.

Flaubert's other method for revealing the inner life is more significant, in that it stems from his recognition of the inadequacy
of speech as a conveyor of emotions. His use of physical correlatives for Emma's thought processes solves for him the problem
of presenting Emma realistically without heightening the language of her thoughts and consequently violating his conception
of her character, which is based on coupling her extraordinary
capacity for emotion with a profoundly ordinary intellect. By
using her dog, her bridal bouquet, Binet's lathe, and other physical objects to symbolize Emma's mental states, Flaubert is able
to project the desired image of her psyche without relying heavily on narrative analysis and impeding the limpid flow of the
narrative, and without heightening and distorting the language of
her thoughts.

A narrative artist with gifts very different from Flaubert —
George Eliot — prefers to solve the problem in the less oblique

manner and rest the principal weight of her characterizations directly on narrative analysis, paying the inevitable price in the resulting sluggishness in the flow of narrative, just as Proust pays the same price — as any analytic narrative artist does, however great his genius. Thus *Middlemarch* bristles with passages of analysis, and the story advances to a ruminative rhythm, grinding slowly but exceeding fine, with the narrator moving continually in the analytical passages from specific consideration of the characters to careful and delicate moral generalizations, couched in the first and second persons plural. Much of the strength and beauty of *Middlemarch* lies in such passages as this one:

Nor can I suppose that when Mrs. Casaubon is discovered in a fit of weeping six weeks after her wedding the situation will be regarded as tragic. Some discouragement, some faintness of heart at the new real future which replaces the imaginary, is not unusual, and we do not expect people to be deeply moved by what is not unusual. That element of tragedy which lies in the very fact of frequency, has not yet wrought itself into the coarse emotion of mankind; and perhaps our frames could hardly bear much of it. If we had a keen vision and feeling of all ordinary life, it would be like hearing the grass grow and the squirrel's heart beat, and we should die of that roar which lies on the other side of silence. As it is, the quickest of us walk about well wadded with stupidity.

How "un-Flaubertian" and yet how fine. Her rhetoric, with its carefully chosen metaphors, perfectly adapted to the astonishing range of her intellect and vigorous enough to keep her compassionate prose well this side of sentimentality, is always controlled, artful, and impressive. Even the brief passage quoted here begins to illustrate this, but it should be seen in its context in Chapter 20 of *Middlemarch* for its art to be fully appreciated. And since no character in the novel can be granted a mind impressive enough to make the kind of moral generalization George Eliot wants made repeatedly in this work, the narrator must perform the task. This kind of "intrusion" by the narrator is not really as "un-Flaubertian" as many modern critics would have us believe. Looking back at the passage from *Madame Bovary* quoted above, we can see that the mind of Flaubert's narrator moves in a pattern similar to that of the narrator of *Middlemarch:* from the specifics of character and situation in the novel to a generalization about mankind, couched in the first person plural.

Still, though they are not necessarily as dissimilar as has often been supposed, Flaubert and George Eliot can represent for us the two principal ways of reacting to the problem of representing in an interesting and affecting manner the psyches of ordinary human beings, whose verbal patterns in speech and thought are inadequate in themselves to generate the kind of interest and emotion that the authors seek on their behalf. George Eliot relies mainly on narrative analysis, Flaubert on the symbolic use of physical correlatives. George Eliot's greatest disciple in English fiction, D. H. Lawrence, is in a sense a disciple of Flaubert as well. There is a very revealing passage in one of his lesser novels, *Aaron's Rod,* which strikes a note of dissatisfaction with words similar to that in the passage from Flaubert above:

> In his own powerful but subconscious fashion Aaron realized this. He was a musician. And hence even his deepest *ideas* were not word-ideas, his very thoughts were not composed of words and ideal concepts. They too, his thoughts and ideas, were dark and invisible, as electric vibrations are invisible no matter how many words they may purport. If I, as a word-user, must translate his deep conscious vibrations into finite words, that is my own business. I do but make a translation of the man. He would speak in music. I speak with words.
>
> The inaudible music of his conscious soul conveyed his meaning in him quite as clearly as I convey it in words: probably much more clearly. But in his own mode only: and it was in his own mode only he realized what I must put into words. These words are my own affair. His mind was music.
>
> Don't grumble at me then, gentle reader, and swear at me that this damned fellow wasn't half clever enough to think all these smart things, and realize all these fine-drawn-out subtleties. You are quite right, he wasn't, yet it all resolved itself in him as I say, and it is now for you to prove that it didn't.   [Chapter 13]

Flaubert would no doubt throw up his hands (or perhaps his dinner) at such a passage, at such an admission of defeat by the word-user, but it is clearly an outgrowth of that dissatisfaction with words as conveyors of feeling which Flaubert himself was one of the first narrative artists to formulate, and which is typical of much modern fiction. In Lawrence's case his turn to symbolism in much of his better fiction is designed mainly to provide a vehicle for communication to the reader of the essence of characters who are themselves more or less inarticulate. In narrative analysis Lawrence often seems to take sides for and against his characters so violently that he runs the risk of driving the reader to react in precisely the opposite way to that in which the narration is supposed to move him. The symbol, for Lawrence, is often a more effective vehicle than analysis just because he cannot maintain that calm, narrative compassion which George Eliot relies on so heavily and effectively. Lawrence's "The Ladybird," "The Fox," and "The Captain's Doll" are all short novels built around the symbols named in their titles, which are symbols of character in every case — designed to perform some of the work of characterization which would otherwise require more in the way of narrative analysis or interior monologue. And these three novellas are certainly among Lawrence's most successful narrative performances.

The great modern practitioners of stream of consciousness characterization have, of course, faced the problem posed by Flaubert and Lawrence of the limitation of verbal patterns as conveyors of thought and characterization through thought. They solve the problem in a number of ways. If the character is intelligent and sensitive enough, then he can be allowed to articulate his own mental processes. Stephen Dedalus or Quentin Compson can be as articulate and sensitive as Joyce and Faulkner care to make them, without offending anyone's sense of probability. If, on the other hand, the character is subnormal, other possibilities emerge. Septimus Smith and Benjy Compson are in this category. Some psychologist has proved that Benjy is not a true psychotic but a literary construct. This being so, it is fortunate that Benjy is in a book, where he belongs. Actually Faulkner and Virginia Woolf are using the supposed mental limitations of these two characters as a means of getting away from routine rhetoric and introducing a more poetical verbal pattern into the monologue. What results is a kind of super stream of consciousness in which the character's limited mind accounts for an excessive distortion of normal thought patterns, which communicates all the more effectively on a level well above anything the character himself may be supposed capable of achieving. This is a powerful device in the hands of a master, as Benjy's monologue indicates. It is also the beginning of a retreat from a purely mimetic concept of characterization. The step from *The Sound and the Fury* to *As I Lay Dying* is only a short one; and in *As I Lay Dying* Faulkner, simply as a matter of narrative convention, heightens nearly all the characters' verbal patterns in monologue with his own rhetoric — the sane as well as the insane. Once realistic tenets are abandoned as the primary laws of narrative, the problem disappears.

Joyce, in *Dubliners,* hewed close to the Flaubertian line, even exploiting for pathetic effect inarticulate expression of sincere emotion, as in the elegy for Parnell read in "Ivy Day in the Committee Room." In *Ulysses,* however, the interior monologues of Leopold Bloom — as brilliant a compromise between psychology, rhetoric and poetry as they are — did not satisfy him as a total expression of Bloom's character. Lawrence observed in *Lady Chatterley's Lover* that the psyche is divided into what he called an "upper consciousness" and an "under-consciousness." There is a level below that level of "admitted consciousness" at which "inner intuitive knowledge" becomes verbalized. He is carefully avoiding the Freudian term here, but he is obviously referring to the subconscious. The problem he poses is how to realize in fiction that non-verbal, under-level of consciousness. George Eliot, with no assistance from Freud, had been aware that even in prayer there is often a level of the psyche hidden by a person from himself. This awareness is one of the major disunctions between the modern and the ancient conceptions of character. Prayer, in particular, was designed in ancient narrative to reveal thought and character with unquestionable validity, and this attitude persists right up through Shakespeare, whose characters' self-revelations in prayer and in soliloquy are intended to have absolute validity for the audience. A modern writer concerned for characterization, as George Eliot was, finds it necessary to be, in Flaubert's phrase, a triple thinker, which means among other things that he must be concerned with that area of thought which the individual's upper consciousness will not allow to be put into words. For George Eliot, the solution was simply to let the God-like narrator step in and verbalize this hidden level. For Joyce, a number of solutions seemed effective.

Consider the following passage from Stephen's interior monologue in "Proteus." He is asking himself whether he could save a man from drowning as Buck Mulligan has done:

Would you do what he did? A boat would be near, a lifebuoy. *Natur-lich*, put there for you. Would you or would you not? The man that was drowned nine days ago off Maiden's rock. They are waiting for him now. The truth, spit it out. I would want to. I would try. I am not a strong swimmer. Water cold soft. When I put my face into it in the basin at Clongowes. Can't see! Who's behind me? Out quickly, quickly! Do you see the tide flowing quickly in on all sides, sheeting the lows of sands quickly, shell-cocoacoloured? If I had land under my feet. I want his life still to be his, mine to be mine. A drowning man. His human eyes scream to me out of horror of his death. I . . . With him together down . . . I could not save her. Waters: bitter death: lost.

The Freudian slip in the last line — I could not save *her* instead of *him* — is Joyce's fitting way of showing the subconscious at work, as the repressed recollection of his mother short-circuits its way into Stephen's line of thought when that line of thought comes close enough for the associative leap to be made from one level to the other.

This is certainly an effective solution to the problem of revealing the subconscious in the interior monologue, but it is only a partial solution in that it still is capable of dealing only with those thoughts which evade the censor and leap into the verbalized stream of what Lawrence called the "upper consciousness." Joyce uses similar slips to reveal Bloom's inner thoughts as when "the wife's admirers" pops out in speech instead of "the wife's advisors," but again this leaves too much hidden to satisfy Joyce, who was not a man for half measures or partial solutions. The "Circe" chapter is his principal solution to the problem of dramatizing the subconscious. He simply employs a surrealistic or expressionistic dramatization which enables Bloom, especially, to act out a revelatory Freudian phantasy which provides a more thorough picture of his under-consciousness than any interior monologue could hope to achieve. Commentators often refer to this as a "dream sequence" or something of the sort, and try to locate the action in the drunken consciousness of one or both of the protagonists. Such attempts inevitably break down because Joyce has given up realistic solutions to the problem of characterization here (as he does elsewhere in the "Cyclops," "Oxen of the Sun," and "Ithaca" chapters). Recognizing that the subconscious is not itself bound by the physical laws of the actual world any more than it abides by the moral codes of society, Joyce turns to surrealistic phantasy as the appropriate mode for its dramatization. What we can see in both Joyce and Faulkner is that mimetic characterization, if pushed far enough, leads to its own destruction. When the narrative artist finally penetrates the labyrinth of the psyche, he finds there not a mechanical marvel but a world of myth and monsters. Thanks to Freud and Jung, in the heart of the labyrinth the Minotaur lives on. Perhaps it was in the human subconscious that Yeats discerned that rough beast slouching toward what Joyce would have called its "re-arrival."

Thus the mimetic impulse toward the presentation of character through the dramatization of the inner life in a stream of consciousness monologue dissolves inevitably into mythic and expressionistic patterns upon reaching the citadel of the psyche. The impulse toward narrative analysis, on the other hand, reaches its dissolution in a different way. Joyce's characterization of Leopold Bloom is rooted in the belief that Bloom has a character which can be rendered exhaustively, producing a complex but coherent image of the true Bloom, a valid and consistent portrait of the whole man in his complete psychological and sociological being. But suppose one were to lose faith in the existence of the self as a material whole, and say with Lawrence, "The bulk of people haven't got any central selves. They're all bits," or with Proust, "None of us can be said to constitute a material whole, which is identical for everyone."? Lawrence and Proust are talking about different things in these passages — Lawrence means that people have no souls, whereas Proust means that existence depends on a multiplicity of apprehensions of ourselves by ourselves and by others, which makes our existence a matter of relativity — but they are both really grappling with an especially modern problem which is having a profound effect on modern literature. One of the major trends in twentieth-century characterization is away from the attempt to penetrate the individual psyche and toward a focus on the apprehension of "impressions" which claim no absolute validity as facts. This is the dominant technique of characterization in such narrator-dominated novels as *Lord Jim, The Good Soldier, À la recherche du temps perdu, Absalom, Absalom!* and the *Alexandria Quartet*. This technique was described by Erich Auerbach as "a method which dissolves reality into multiple and multivalent reflections of consciousness," and Auerbach spoke out strongly against the novels which employ it, sensing (rightly) in them "something hostile to the reality which they represent." The interior monologues and narrative analyses on which characterization rested in the great realistic fictions of the nineteenth century have been largely abandoned in the twentieth because, on the one hand, writers find them inadequate to deal with the important but sub-verbal world of the under-consciousness and, on the other, because writers have lost faith in the realness of realism. Much modern narrative is characterized by consciousness of a gap between the apprehendable and the true which makes realistic presentation of character far less necessary than it had seemed in the previous century. The characterizations of Beckett and Durrell, though vastly different from one another, are also vastly different from the characterizations of Tolstoy and George Eliot.

In considering the ways in which narrative artists have attempted to present individual characters and explore their individual lives, we have neglected, thus far, any consideration of the techniques and purposes of so-called type characters. One reason for this apparent neglect is our belief that insofar as a character is a type, he is less a character. Though the word "type" itself opens the door to some confusion, and is often used loosely enough, we understand that in all its significations it refers to something outside the character himself. A type may be referable to the most general sort of idea, as Everyman is a type of general humanity; or to a specific non-human entity, as Vergil's Fama represents rumor; or to a mental state, as in Spenser's Despair. We have religious types (Christ-figures, Madonnas, etc.), psychological types (whether referable to Aristotelian or Freudian psychology), physiological types (whether referable to Jonsonian humours or such concepts as ecto- and endomorphism), intellectual types (Thwackum, Square, Dr. Pangloss), social types, and geographical types — to name only those that come readily to mind. Many of these concepts go back to ancient times. Thought of this kind is generalizing thought. It looks for the common, unifying elements in disparate things. It always tends toward the dehumanization of character, whether we find it in the Characters of Theophrastus, in Greek New Comedy, or in narrative allegory. In every case, whenever we consider a character as a type, we are moving away from considering him as an individual character and moving toward considering him as part of some larger framework. This framework may be moral, theological, referable to some essentially extra-literary scheme; or it may be referable to a part of the narrative situation itself. When we consider characters as villains, ingénues, *ficelles*, choral characters, *nuntii*, and so on, we are thinking of them not as characters in themselves but as elements which contribute to the whole, as parts of the plot or meaning of a work.

The same character, of course, can be considered in terms of his individual characteristics or as a part of some larger scheme. An "archetypal" character, even, is simply a character of a certain type. A scapegoat figure has something in common with all other scapegoat figures, and even as an individual character his quality will be partly determined by reverberations from the various types whose echoes he awakes in the memories of his audience. Mr. Pickwick and Sam Weller are highly individualized characters, but they share many attributes with such predecessors as Tom Jones and Partridge, Roderick Random and Strap, Don Quixote and Sancho Panza; and with such successors as Huck Finn and Jim, and even Sherlock Holmes and Dr. Watson. In a highly individualized characterization such overtones are intellectual and emotional bonuses for the literate reader. Conversely, characterizations which are primarily "typical" may be invested with enough individuality to extend their appeal downward from the literate elite at whom they were aimed to a less literate class of readers. Teachers who advise their students to read *The Faerie Queene* "for the story" do more damage to Spenser's art than they would to Fielding's if they were to offer the same advice in connection with *Tom Jones.* Yet Spenser's characters do have elements of individuality which function within their "typical" limits, and Spenser does indeed manipulate these characters in the form of a "story." He can be read as a story-teller. But he cannot receive his due recognition as a narrative artist from this kind of reading. His characters dance to an intellectual music, and if we choose not to hear the music the dance must inevitably seem crude and trivial. With Fielding, story comes before meaning, and a character like Squire Western can be given an individuality beyond anything in Spenser. But to encompass all of Squire Western we must think of him in both his individual and typical aspects. Fielding thought of his characters as representing types of general humanity, untrammelled by limitations of time and space. Scott praised Squire Western as a characterization, however, because he was so unmistakably the product of a particular time and place. We moderns are most likely to couch our own praise of this

brilliant characterization in terms of its uniqueness and originality — they don't make 'em like that no more. But no matter how
thoroughly individualized a character may be, for the literate
reader he will be the richer through the various modes of family
resemblance which connect him to the world of ideas, the social
world, and the literary past. Anna Karenina gains from our recognition that she is of the sisterhood of Madame Bovary and Dido.
Dorothea Brooke gains from our recognition that she is of the
sisterhood of both Emma Woodhouse and St. Theresa. Isabel
Archer gains because we can see in her a resemblance not only to
Dorothea Brooke and to Scott's Diana Vernon, but to the Roman
goddess Diana (the virgin with the bow) whose memory she
awakes as surely as does Meredith's Diana of the Crossways,
though the clue in the name of James's heroine is the more subtle
one. The ideal readers of narratives—ancient or modern—must
be prepared to respond to the emphasis of the narrative with respect to character, placing individuality or "typical" connection fore-
most to the extent which the narrative itself calls for such priority;
but above all such readers must bring to their consideration of character a versatility of response commensurate with the infinite
variety of narrative characterization. We may not need great
audiences in order that great narratives be produced, but we
surely need great audiences in order that narratives be understood and appreciated greatly.

6

Plot in Narrative

Plot can be defined as the dynamic, sequential element in narrative literature. Insofar as character, or any other element in narrative, becomes dynamic, it is a part of the plot. Spatial art, which presents its materials simultaneously, or in a random order, has no plot; but a succession of similar pictures which can be arranged in a meaningful order (like Hogarth's "Rake's Progress") begins to have a plot because it begins to have a dynamic sequential existence. The images on a strip of motion-picture film are an extreme development of this plot-potential in spatial form. Aristotle, who had the tragic drama mainly in mind, said that plot was the soul of mimetic literary works. In discussing the novel, E. M. Forster quarreled politely with Aristotle and gave character priority over plot. The reasons for this we shall consider when we turn to the characteristic plots of realistic fiction. They are not unlike the reasons which moved Henry James to try to blur the distinction between plot and character in the passage quoted at the beginning of Chapter 5 above. But Aristotle was thinking in absolute terms. He could conceive of a tragedy without much character study (*ethos*) but not of one without action (*praxis*). Though narrative art differs from dramatic in many ways, including some that Aristotle did not know, he was certainly right to insist that in a temporal art form the dynamic and sequential

element is the primary one. And this, which he calls *praxis* sometimes and *mythos* sometimes, we refer to as plot. Distinctions have
been made from time to time between story, plot, and action.
Here we make only the simple one between story as a general
term for character and action in narrative form and plot as a more
specific term intended to refer to action alone, with the minimum
possible reference to character.

Primitive epic narrative is poised between the world of ritual
and legend, on the one hand, and the world of history and fiction
on the other. As such its plots are in a transitional stage between
the artless plotting of folk tradition and the consciously artful or
consciously empirical plotting of romance and history. These plots
are episodic, and present the deeds (or *gestes*) of a hero in some
chronological sequence, possibly beginning with his birth, probably ending with his death. In the *Epic of Gilgamesh,* which is
the earliest Western epic preserved in writing and also one of the
most primitive, the whole sequence is present. In *Beowulf,* much
later but only somewhat less primitive, the episodes are reduced
to two major ones, the latter including the hero's death. In the
Iliad, we are down to a single episode developed at length, with
neither the hero's birth nor death included in the time-span of the
action. In these three works (which represent three sequential
stages of the evolutionary process though they were not composed
in chronological sequence) we can trace a major development in
narrative plotting. Epic begins as a kind of anthology of heroic
deeds in chronological order. Its unity is the simple unity provided by its protagonist, who connects the events chronologically
by moving in time from one to the other, and thematically by the
continuous elements in his character and the similar situations
which they inevitably precipitate. Epic, becoming romanticized,
can evolve into an endless proliferation of heroic deeds, as in the
Middle Ages the Arthurian and Carolingian cycles did. From the
Chanson de Roland to *Orlando Furioso* we can trace an evolution
of this sort, the simple linear plot of the epic being supplanted by

the multifoliate plot of the romance. Or epic can evolve into a tightly constructed narrative centering on a single deed. The Arthurian Cycle leads to the exquisite *Sir Gawain and the Green Knight* and also to such a relatively loose anthology as Malory's *Morte d'Arthur*. Both *Orlando Furioso* and *Sir Gawain and the Green Knight* are manifestations of the romantic impulse to make a beautiful story, but Ariosto's beauty is beauty of adornment and elegant variation, while the *Gawain* poet's beauty is that of balance and restraint.

The linear simplicity of primitive epic — the chronicle of the deeds of the hero — provides the ground plan for the unheroic picaresque narrative. Picaresque presents us with the deeds of an unhero, a rogue, seen through his own eyes and thus located in the actual world; but the picaresque narrative in its plotting is very similar to the epic song of deeds, unified by its single protagonist, but not poised between his birth and death since the picaresque figure normally tells his own life story and is in no position to employ his own birth and death as neat boundaries for his tale. The picaresque episodic plot is the most primitive form of plot employed in the novel, but it has retained its vitality and still flourishes today. The novel, having no form of its own, has borrowed from all its predecessors, and we shall try to keep this in mind as we consider the plot characteristic of the earlier narrative forms, returning now to the epic itself.

The epic plot is to a certain extent bespoken by epic characterization. The plot is inherent in the concept of the protagonist, but that concept is not realized in the narrative until this character is expressed through action. We can see in Homer a movement away from the traditional epic narration of the deeds of the hero. Though Achilles' problem as man-god is a part of his characterization and influences his behavior, Homer is not presenting us with so mythic a narrative as the poets of *Gilgamesh* or *Beowulf*. The notion of starting a story with a plunge *in medias res,* which came to be thought of as a typical "epic" device in Western literature, does not merely mean to Homer — nor to Horace who pointed out the device — starting in the middle and then filling in both ends of the hero's life. Insofar as Achilles' life is the "thing" in question, this narrative — unlike *Gilgamesh*, or *Beowulf*, or the *Chanson de Roland*, or *El Cid* — ends in the middle even as it began there. The deeds of Achilles, or the life of Achilles, or even the death of Achilles are not the subject of this narrative. The plot of the *Iliad* focuses on one episode in the hero's life, just as his characterization focuses on one element of his psyche; and the subject is the same in both — anger. The plot of the *Iliad* is the story of Achilles getting angry — the how and the why of it — and of the appeasement of his anger — the how and why of that. The narrative ends with the funeral of Hector, not with the death of Achilles nor with the fall of Troy; because that funeral represents the triumph of Achilles over his greatest antagonist, himself. It represents the final purgation of his accumulated rage. It glorifies his lesser antagonist Hector, but because it does so through his sufferance alone, it glorifies Achilles more. With the help of the gods he has become himself again; the narrative has reached equilibrium. The voice of the singer of tales ceases its singing.

Great efforts have been made by critics to establish the "unity" of *Beowulf*, by which is meant the artfulness of its narrative. But its unity as a narrative has been forever fixed by its very conception. It has many of the obvious kinds of unity that any heroic narrative about a single protagonist must have. Such unity as we find in the *Iliad*, however, is beyond the *Beowulf* poet's aspirations. His tradition had not progressed to the point where such an essentially fictional conception was available to him. And this is the main point to be made about the plot of the *Iliad*. In it, fiction has played a considerable part, perhaps as strong a part as it could play without projecting the whole narrative into the area of romance. In the great epics as in the great novels, the balance among the various extremes of narrative is a precarious one.

As the traditional epic form breaks down into its empirical and fictional elements, kinds of plotting suitable to these elements tend to be refined and developed. Historical forms emerge quite easily, since they are very close to the forms of primitive heroic narrative. Plot in historical narrative is a chronological affair, covering whatever span of time its subject requires. The simplest forms of historical narrative, appearing in a culture that has writing and a linear concept of time but lacks a developed theory of historiography — as in the European Middle Ages — are chronicles and annals. The chronicle usually begins at whatever point the chronicler believes life to have begun, or his civilization to have been founded, and works its way toward the continuous present, at which point it merges with the annals, which are simply a yearly record of events. This kind of historical writing is to true narrative history as a diary or journal is to true narrative biography or autobiography. In records of this kind we usually feel the lack of two elements essential to narrative art: selectivity and movement. The two are interrelated. In chronicle, annals, and diary the lack of selectivity impedes movement and inhibits the growth of anything like a plot. But the artful diarist who senses a kind of plot in his life will be selecting appropriate materials half unconsciously, as Pepys and Boswell do. And so will the artful annalist or chronicler.

Plot requires (as Aristotle, who was not afraid to utter a necessary banality, observed) a beginning, a middle, and an end. In historical narrative this means that a subject must be discerned in the past and cut off from the irrelevant matters with which it has only a temporal connection: the conflict between Persia and Greece, the Peloponnesian War, the March Up Country of the ten thousand, the Jewish War, or something similar. Such subjects provide ready-made beginnings, middles, and ends for narrative plots. And so does the life of a single man provide a neat formula for plotting. What more perfect beginning than birth or more perfect ending than death? This is simply the old epic formula pushed well into the domain of empirical narrative. This kind of plot can also be idealized and adapted to the uses of fictional narrative as in Xenophon's *Cyropedia*, which is a didactic romance organized along biographical lines, as are most of the Alexander romances and Saints' Lives which descend from Xenophon's seminal combination of biographical form with didactic and romance matter.

The old epic tendency was to present the life of a hero in terms of his most heroic achievements, but the biographer looks for those episodes which are most revealing of the character of his subject. In narratives which are fictional in plotting as well as in spirit the tendency is either to focus on a single episode in the hero's life (the *Iliad, Sir Gawain and the Green Knight*) or a single sequence of episodes, such as the interminable interruptions which separate lover from beloved in Greek romance, all of which are interpolated between the moment of falling in love, at which the story proper commences, and the consummation of this love in marriage, where the story inevitably ends. All plots depend on tension and resolution. In narrative the most common plots are the biographical (birth to death) and the romantic (desire to consummation), because these are the most obvious correlatives for the tension and resolution which plot demands. One of the reasons stories have appealed to man for so long a time lies in their neatness. The reader of a narrative can expect to finish his reading having achieved a state of equilibrium — something approaching calm of mind, all passion spent. Insofar as the reader is left with this feeling by any narrative, that narrative can be said to have a plot.

In the ancient world, narrative literature's constant tendency to fragmentation is illustrated thoroughly by the way the empirical narratives concentrate on characterization and the fictional concentrate on adventures. As modern historiography developed in the eighteenth and nineteenth centuries, a further fragmentation became noticeable between the "scientific" and the "artistic" historians. The "artistic" historian insists on retaining plot and character in his work, thus maintaining its place in narrative art. The "scientific" historian subordinates these narrative qualities to impersonal considerations of social and economic forces. Carlyle's

French Revolution can serve as an example of a consciously artistic history. The rise of scientific history is paralleled by the rise of the novel as a form. The artful historical narrative stands between the hyper-empiricism of scientific history and the romanticized empiricism of the novel, and has had to defend itself from encroachment on both sides. It can be argued that Carlyle's book is at least as fine a work of narrative art as Dickens's novel, *A Tale of Two Cities*, which was admittedly derived from a reading of Carlyle; and that it is in the main a historically accurate work. Yet the serious modern student who must concentrate on the facts has no time for Carlyle, and the less serious or younger student is handed Dickens because the historical pill has a thicker coating of fiction in the novel. *A Tale of Two Cities* is still a staple of the high school curriculum, while the *French Revolution* is hardly read at all.

At this point our study of literary form takes us close to certain practical problems in education, reminding us that the literary tradition and the educational tradition are interdependent. The standardized curricula of modern colleges, and the widespread influence of these curricula in establishing the prejudices of the "general" reader, determine to a considerable extent which works from the past and which kinds of work remain part of our living literary tradition. For good or ill, the academic mind now influences the transmission of literature to posterity more powerfully than it has since the days of Alexandria. Very few works are likely to survive for long if they are excluded from college curricula. And the curricula themselves are more and more designed for neatness and ease of handling rather than to display their subject matter to best advantage. Most efficient utilization of plant, not most effective presentation of literature, is what drives academic institutions to such devices as the quarter system. More and more we find courses chopped into neat historical segments or squeezed into narrow generic categories. Woe to that work of literature which is neither novel nor drama, neither romantic nor Victorian. A great deficiency in our teaching of narrative literature in par-

ticular stems from our emphasis on the novel at the expense of all
other narrative forms. Because we concentrate so on the novel,
we miss great achievements in other forms of narrative. Because
other forms do not fit into our streamlined curricula, generations
of students matriculate and are graduated without ever becoming
aware that these forms are worthy of notice. Achievements as
brilliant as the short prose tales of Yeats and the *Autobiography*
of Sean O'Casey languish virtually without readers or critics,
while the lyrics of Yeats and the dramas of O'Casey are taught
and read everywhere. We need to know more thoroughly than we
know now, and the knowledge needs to be spread more widely,
that the novel, though it may be the greatest of narrative forms
yet evolved, is still only one form among many, ancient and modern, which deserve our attention and our sympathetic understanding, both in their own right and because of what they can
reveal to us about the nature of the novel itself.

The main plot forms of empirical narrative which we have considered so far are (a) the historical form, based on an event from
the past with its causes and consequences, torn from its irrelevant
and casual surroundings and isolated in the form of a narrative, or
based on a related sequence of events treated in this manner; and
(b) the biographical form, taking its shape from the birth, life,
and death of an actual individual. Up to a point the autobiographical form is the same as the biographical form in terms of plot, the
most obvious difference between the two being a matter of point
of view. But the difference in point of view is inevitably linked
with a difference in plot. The resolution of an autobiographical
form cannot come from the protagonist's death. This easiest of
equilibria to achieve in narrative art is barred to the writer of
autobiography. He must find another kind of stasis on which to
rest his narrative, or leave it hanging unresolved, "to be continued." This means that some other order of resolution needs to
be found for an autobiographical narrative to conclude its plot
line with an esthetically satisfying end. In practice this has not

often been done. Most autobiographers continue beyond their natural concluding points, aiming toward that unattainable stasis of the narrator's death. But to the extent that the autobiography is a story of the author's inward life, its natural concluding point is not his death but the point at which the author comes to terms with himself, realizes his nature, assumes his vocation. St. Augustine's narrative proper ends with his conversion at the close of Book VIII of the *Confessions,* though the fruits of that conversion in the form of theological discussion and Biblical commentary fill up several more books. Rousseau's narrative also reaches its climax and resolution in its eighth book when he beholds the notice in the *Mercure de France* of the prize offered by the Dijon Academy. He tells us, "The moment I read this I beheld another universe and became another man." And later adds, "All the rest of my life and my misfortunes followed inevitably as a result of that moment's madness." The second part of the *Confessions* continues through a twelfth book, and Rousseau planned a third part which he did not write. Inevitably, once an autobiography continues beyond the moment in which the author comes to terms with his vocation, its interest turns outward and its form becomes openended. Cellini's autobiography ends with his departure for Pisa in 1562. Joyce's *A Portrait* (which is autobiographical in plot and content though not in point of view) ends with Stephen's departure for Paris in 1902. Yet how different are these two departures in terms of plot. Cellini is sixty-two years old. His narrative has been open-ended since his vision of God's approval of him and his work, which took place midway in his story. But Joyce's narrative ends after Stephen has accepted his vocation and is accepting the voluntary exile which it entails.

To observe this characteristic of autobiographies is one thing; to wish them all cut short at the most esthetically satisfying place is another. At this point the difference between the reader's attitude toward a work he knows to be fictional and a work he knows to be factual operates so as to bring different esthetic principles into action. When Joyce presents his autobiography in fictional form, calling his central character Dedalus, he serves notice on us that he may take some poetic liberties with the facts of his life. He also contracts to resolve his narrative at an esthetically satisfying and meaningful point. When Wordsworth subtitles his autobiographical narrative "the growth of a poet's mind" he is also contracting to present a shaped and ordered narrative. But a writer of factual autobiography is not under quite the same obligation to shape his story. Sean O'Casey gives us a brilliant portrait of himself growing toward his vocation in the first two volumes of what is now a six-volume work. After that his narrative becomes more memoir than autobiography. His interest turns outward and he fills his pages with brilliant portraits of such figures as Yeats, Lady Gregory, and AE. The first two volumes are an exercise in rather tight, controlled, autobiographical form. After young Sean's vocation is assured and assumed the form loosens and opens up. But it is still narrative and still art. It is art not merely because his portraits of figures like Lady Gregory and AE verge on caricature, but because of his selectivity of detail, because of the way he shapes his chapters toward a crisp conclusion reminiscent of a stage curtain, and because of his prose style, which varies from gutter slang to purple passages but is always artful. And it is narrative because of the chronological ground plan which inevitably provides a loose framework of episodes — crises and resolutions — to stiffen with narrative articulation the loose and journalistic elements of the work. The plotting in that part of O'Casey's narrative which is typical of full-scale autobiography, is the simple chronological plotting of the historical kind of empirical narrative. But the plotting of the early part of this autobiography is based on a traditional pattern which provides it with a much firmer narrative articulation. The Christian story of redemption and atonement, which St. Augustine saw as the pattern reflected in his own history, has been secularized to give shape to the story of the artist or writer. This pattern had been adumbrated in Lucian's brief autobiographical account of how he became a man of letters, but Augustine's demonstration of how pattern and insight could be combined in a full-scale narrative really established the form. A writer like Joyce, aware of the nature of the autobiographical tradition, was in a position to exploit the various facets of this tradition more thoroughly than is usually the case. By making Stephen's true vocation that of "priest of the eternal imagination" he exploits all the tradition of Christian allegory with which Augustine and St. Theresa had invested the form, and all the tradition of the artist's coming of age, which has its equally venerable antecedents in Lucian and Cellini. Thus Joyce can present a narrative that has the appearance of a loosely chronological collection of episodes but is actually as formal and patterned as the Catholic liturgy. In *Ulysses* and *Finnegans Wake* Joyce moved on to new patterns and great narrative experiments. In *A Portrait* he was content to accomplish more in a traditional framework than had ever been accomplished before.

The relationship between patterned and merely chronological narrative we have been considering as an aspect of autobiographical plotting is illustrative of the general situation of historical narrative. Scientific history tends to move away from artistic narrative patterns. So does scientific biography. The impossibility of autobiography becoming scientific combines with the nonavailability of death as a satisfactory form of resolution to keep autobiography within the realm of narrative art. Those histories and biographies which aspire to artistic status tend to move away from merely chronological narrative toward more esthetically satisfying patterns. This means, in effect, that historical narrative will borrow mythical or fictional means of articulation to the extent that it is willing to sacrifice science to art. The artistically minded historian or biographer, even before he writes a word, is looking for esthetically satisfying patterns in the people and events he considers as potential subjects for his work. And every historian or biographer who hopes to reach an audience beyond his fellow professionals is to some extent artistically minded. In the ancient world such a general audience was the only one available, and all historical and biographical narratives were artful. With

the rise of professional and academic captive audiences, the need
to captivate diminished, allowing the textbook to grow and Carlyle's despised enemy Dryasdust to come into his own. The historian who succeeds in marrying science and art with the fewest
sacrifices on either side is no doubt the one with whom Clio, Muse
of history, is best pleased. But, like its younger relative the novel,
historical narrative is an unstable compound, always threatening
to give way too much to one or the other of the opposed fictional
and empirical pressures which continually beset it.

Just as historical plotting tends to be less artful than the plotting
of traditional epic, fictional plotting tends to be more artful. But
the line between fictional and traditional or mythic plotting is not
always easy to draw; and, because narrative art never wholly
loses its traditional characteristics, fictional plots have a way of
establishing themselves as myths just as myths have a way of becoming fictionalized. Though we have touched on the question
before, it will probably be well to clarify here what we mean by
myth. We can begin to do this by pointing out the ways in which
our employment of the term differs from Northrop Frye's influential definition in the *Anatomy of Criticism*. "In terms of narrative,"
Frye tells us, "myth is the imitation of actions near or at the conceivable limits of human desire." The characters in myth are gods
who "enjoy beautiful women, fight one another with prodigious
strength, comfort and assist man, or else watch his miseries from
the height of their immortal freedom" (p. 136). This definition of
myth makes for a certain neatness in discussion, but it does a certain amount of violence to the facts of narrative history. The gods
of Ovid's *Metamorphoses* answer to this description, but what of
the gods of more primitive mythological narrative? The destruction of Ásgard hangs heavy over the gods of Norse mythology.
Like men, they must accept their fate. Such myths as those of
Attis, Adonis, Osiris, and Tammuz, which figure so prominently
in the *Golden Bough*, do not present the gods as involved in actions "at or near the conceivable limits of human desire." These
myths are not solely projections of human aspirations. They are

projections of human fear as well. The pseudo-myth, like Apuleius' tale of Cupid and Psyche, is closer to Frye's definition than many actually mythic narratives.

Unlike Frye's definition, which emphasizes the supernatural qualities of myth, the definition we have been employing emphasizes its traditional qualities. We have been using the terms "myth" and "traditional narrative" synonymously, because *mythos* in Greek carried this meaning precisely. It is possible, however, to refine our meaning further and to distinguish quite clearly at least three distinct kinds of primitive traditional narrative, which arise in most cultures, out of which what we know as epic poetry sometimes evolves. Bronislaw Malinowski in his study of contemporary primitive society in New Guinea, found that the natives themselves distinguished among three such kinds of tale: the *ku-kwanebu,* or imaginative folktale, designed to amuse an audience; the *libwogo* or legend, a quasi-historical tale of ordinary or fantastic events, regarded as true history by the audience; and the *liliu* or sacred myth, which is an expression of and justification for primitive theology, manners, and morality. We can see the ways in which epic narrative represents an amalgamation of primitive modes of narration such as these, and we can see how the distinction between the legend, regarded as truth, and the folktale, regarded as amusement, anticipates the tendency of post-epic narrative to separate into fictional and empirical branches. In this primitive culture, however, all three of these kinds of literature are traditional; the stories are passed from one recognized "owner" to his heir. In such a culture newly invented stories must be only somewhat less rare than accurate historical narrative. The most tradition-bound of all forms of narrative in any culture, of course, is the sacred myth; and in such myths we find the most profound revelations of cultural conditions and ancient human attitudes and beliefs.

At first, sacred myth makes its way unchallenged by rational or empirical modes of accounting for natural phenomena. It is preoccupied with the supernatural, and, because of its sacred character, it is especially rigid and traditional. As an embodiment of religious truth it is not to be tampered with or embroidered upon. Confronted with rationalistic criticism, as it was in Greece, myth tends to lose the special character given it by rigidity and preoccupation with the supernatural. Its supernatural elements wither away or present themselves as consciously fictional or allegorical. Its traditional and rigidly preserved stories lend themselves to alteration or adaptation; they become rationalized and humanized or fancifully exaggerated. Once a culture loses its innocence with respect to myth, it can never recapture it. But myth, in yielding up its special characteristics, dies only to be reborn. Because mythic narrative is the expression in story form of deep-seated human concerns, fears, and aspirations, the plots of mythic tales are a storehouse of narrative correlatives — keys to the human psyche in story form — guaranteed to reach an audience and move them deeply. Though rationalistic attacks on myth as falsehood tend to invalidate it historically, they are powerless against its psychological potency.

Though the facts are shrouded in the mists of pre-history, we can speculate that sacred myth is the most ancient form of narrative. Before story-telling reached a pitch of sophistication sufficient for it to take amusement or historical recording as its province, it must have been at the service of primitive theology. The sacred myths are rooted in ritual celebration of the most vital concerns of the human race. The function of myth, as Theodore H. Gaster has cogently hypothesized, is to project "the procedures of ritual to the plane of ideal situations, which they are then taken to objectify and reproduce." Sacred myth is a link between magic and religion. It is not an "explanation" of natural phenomena but a gloss on rituals which themselves evolved out of the worship of natural phenomena. These rituals developed as imitative enactments of the cyclical processes of nature, designed to provide magical encouragement to those processes. Though there are many kinds of sacred myth, the most important kind is that associated with rituals celebrating the annual cycle of vegetative life.

So important is this kind of ritual to the concept of plot in narrative that we must pause a moment and consider it. Our knowledge of these matters is a fairly recent development in literary study, and our understanding of them is far from complete; but Sir James Frazer and the anthropologists and literary scholars who have continued his work have given us a very clear and powerful idea of the nature of such ritual and the kind of role it plays in the articulation of literary materials. Fertility ritual is based on a cyclical concept of time rather than a linear or progressive one. In primitive societies time is seen primarily as a way of dividing the individual year rather than as an accumulation of successive years. The year is divided by the equinoxes and solstices which mark the sun's annual progress through the heavens and serve as indicators of seasonal variations in rainfall, temperature, and other natural phenomena associated with the cycle of vegetative life. In different parts of the world these astronomically designated points in the annual cycle may refer to varying conditions of climate, but they inevitably come to be seen as marking stages in the yearly combat between the forces of fertility and sterility, of life and death, and ultimately of good and evil. The rituals associated with this conflict take a variety of forms. But virtually all the forms of ritual are designed to express one or more of the four major elements in the Seasonal Pattern. The elements are, in Gaster's terminology, rites of "mortification, purgation, invigoration, and jubilation." Such rites frequently find expression in sacred myths which present part or all of this pattern in the form of cosmic narrative, translating the annual magical ritual into a timeless and transcendental shape.

For our consideration of plot in narrative literature two aspects of fertility ritual and the sacred myths associated with it are of crucial importance. Both have to do with developmental processes which affect myth. One concerns the change myth undergoes as the concept of time current in a culture shifts from a primitive, cyclical view to a more sophisticated linear concept. The other concerns the changes myth undergoes when cut off from ritual and subject to merely literary exigencies. Both these changes should be seen against what we may call the primary formal pattern of fertility ritual. In this progression — mortification, purgation, invigoration, and jubilation — we have a cyclical process. Jubilation can be taken as the top of the circle, which is reached when fertility is assured, but inevitably leads to mortification as concern shifts from the accomplished year to the next, in which fertility is not assured. But the cycle is one which can be broken at any point. Ritual tends to be associated with one or two of these four elements in the seasonal pattern, but myth may deal with one, two, or the whole cycle. Both myth in narrative form and mythic drama emerge from such rituals as these. But because of the inherent literary differences between narrative and drama, the sacred materials come to be treated differently in the two forms. Both are subject to a certain amount of what we may call (without pejorative implications) contamination from other literary forms.

Narrative myth, similar to narrative folktale and legend in form, and quite cut off from ritual which is itself dramatic in form, is necessarily more susceptible to this sort of "contamination"; and narrative literature thus achieves its grandest development in ancient literature in the form of epic, which is, as we have insisted, an amalgam of myth, legend, and folktale. But drama is very close in form to ritual and has tended always to emerge as a form under theological auspices, whether in ancient Greece or medieval Europe. Thus drama has inevitably retained more of the ritualistic pattern than has narrative. The rituals which seem to have had the most profound influence on Greek drama, and hence on Western culture, are four types singled out by F. M. Cornford in *The Origins of Attic Comedy*: 1) The Carrying Out of Death, 2) The Battle of Summer and Winter, 3) The Young and the Old King, 4) Death and Resurrection. Gilbert Murray and Cornford have traced both the tragic and comic drama in Greece to these same ritual types. The difference between tragic and comic drama begins as a difference in attitude toward the sacred materials, associated with a difference in emphasis. As the evolution from ritual brings drama further and further into the realm of esthetic considerations, the esthetic impulse toward neatness of form (which in drama dominates the impulse to adorn and elaborate) reinforces the original tendency of tragic and comic drama to concentrate on the opposite aspects of the cycle inherited from ritual. Tragedy tends to specialize in mortification and purgation, while comedy tends to specialize in invigoration and jubilation. Aeschylean tragedy often took the form of cyclical trilogies which comprehended much of the full seasonal pattern, but the later dramatists tended to move away from tragic cycles to individual dramas which concentrated on the fearful side of the seasonal pattern, developing a typical plot design based on a sequence of events leading to death or expulsion from society. In comedy the joyful side of the seasonal pattern is emphasized, its typical plots leading to marriage, celebration, and reunion or reconciliation with society. These formulations, originally dramatic, inevitably influenced narrative literature in a variety of ways: tragedy directly affecting plotting in narrative history; comedy directly affecting plotting in romance; and the novel ultimately drawing upon both tragic and comic formulations, often simultaneously.

This evolution and separation of comic and tragic plots is the most significant change undergone by mythic materials when cut off from ritual theology. The other change in mythic materials which is of great importance for narrative literature has to do with the shift from myth seen in the context of a cyclical concept of time, to myth seen against a linear or progressive concept. This change in the human conception of time is an aspect of that universal movement toward a rational understanding of the cosmos which tends to make itself felt in most cultures but is virtually the identifying characteristic of our Western culture. The crucial point which must be made in discussing the relationship of this temporal concept to myth and literature is made by Gaster in discussing the significance of the struggle between Baal and Yam in the Canaanite seasonal myth. In this struggle Baal represents the forces which must triumph if the annual cycle is to be renewed and the fertility of nature assured for another year. The relation of this conflict to developing concepts of time is made so clearly by Gaster that we can do no better than quote it here directly.

The fight of god [Baal] and dragon [Yam] — a counterpart of that enacted in ritual in order to bring in the new lease of life — is a constant theme of seasonal myths throughout the world. Moreover as the concept of time develops from the cyclic to the progressive, this fight comes to be projected both *backward* into cosmogony and *forward* into eschatology; for that which was regarded in more primitive thought as the necessary preliminary to each successive lease of life comes now to be regarded as the necessary preliminary to the entire series and likewise to the establishment of the new dispensation at the end of the present order. In the familiar language of Judeo-Christian cosmogony and apocalypse, the God who engaged and vanquished Leviathan at the beginning of days will perforce do so again at the end of them in order to usher in the New Age.

The whole journey of man in Judeo-Christian sacred myth falls between Genesis and Apocalypse, the first and last books of the Bible: between birth and that death which constitutes rebirth; between the deathless life of perfection in the Garden of Eden followed by expulsion and subjection to death, and the deliverance from death in the City of God, the New Jerusalem. The annual cycle of fertility ritual becomes, with the progressive concept of time which informs Jewish and Christian sacred myth, a linear spiral with a beginning and an end: the death-which-is-birth at the end of the spiral being the counterpart of the birth-which-is-death that begins it.

The full narrative pattern of sacred myth we have been considering involves both the descent from perfection, which corresponds to mortification and purgation in ritual, and the ascent to the new ideal state, which corresponds to the invigoration and jubilation of ritual. The pattern of descent, or fall, corresponds to the tragic pattern in drama; the pattern of ascent, or rise, corresponds to the comic pattern in drama. But we can distinguish to some extent between the forms of tragedy and comedy as they

evolved in Greek drama and the broad falling-rising pattern of
narrative myth. Both comedy and tragedy in Greece evolved
away from sacred mythology toward a kind of literary perfection
of their forms. This evolution involved a displacement of the
ritualistic pattern by other kinds of pattern, as the frame of reference became less cosmic and more human. As tragedy and comedy
moved toward their esthetic fulfillment, tragedy found its area of
concern located in past time, an earlier and more heroic age, and
it found its specific story materials crystalized in narrative literature such as Homeric epic, which itself included in the epic amalgam elements of displaced sacred myth. That the tragic dramatist
should single out the most mythic material in his narrative sources
is not a coincidence but an inevitability. Tragedy came to be
dominated in Greece by a fairly narrow range of plot possibilities.
As Cornford has pointed out, "the tragedian had to take some
traditional story ('myth') with its quasi-historic characters, and,
although he might modify details and even invent new characters,
he could not alter the most important incidents." As comedy
evolved in Greek drama it came to concentrate on contemporary
rather than past materials, ordering these thematically on the
loose structure inherited from ritual. Where tragedy has a *mythos,*
comedy has a *logos* or informing idea. The domination of inherited
plot in tragedy forced the tragic dramatists to exceptional exercises in creative characterization. Since plot remained much the
same and was the dominating "soul" of tragic drama, the tragic
dramatists were forced to create individual characters of extraordinary intensity to provide the motivation which the plot demanded but did not necessarily furnish. Comic dramatists, on the
other hand, turned to quasi-realistic characterization based on
figures copied from contemporary life. Cornford discerns in the
progress of comedy "a steady drift from Mystery to Mime," in
which characterization tends to shift from professional types (the
Swaggering Soldier and the Learned Doctor) to character types
based on an elaborate classification according to age, sex, and disposition. The "perfection" of comic form consists in the combina-

tion of generalized characters typical of contemporary life with a flexible plot formula based on intrigue and leading to marriage. This is the shape assumed by New Comedy in Greece and all its descendants. The "perfection" of tragic form consists in the discovery or adaptation of specific characters and plots to the quite rigid pattern of pride, flaw, downfall, and recognition which Aristotle discerned and established as the ideal tragic pattern.

Romance, with its desire to please an audience, takes over the joyful pattern of comic drama, gives it the expanded, cinemascope production so easily achieved in narrative, and substitutes rich rhetoric and lush description for the tomfoolery of comic drama. The romantic desire to adorn, to beautify, and to induce pleasurable suspense, results in the suppression of the purely funny elements in comedy, which are not really in the plotting but in the treatment of the plotting. In *Tom Jones* we can see Fielding putting the funny elements back into the romance plot, where they naturally fit very well. And we can discern in Fielding's literary ancestor Longus, a similar disposition, though not carried nearly so far, to bring romance back to the comic earth from which it originally sprang.

If in pure romance we can see a refined and displaced aspect of fertility ritual, we can find in didactic fiction or fable a reaching back toward the materials of sacred myth. The Biblical pattern of fall and rise, expulsion from Eden and ascent to the New Jerusalem, death and resurrection, is in itself, as we have suggested, a projection into a progressive time scheme of the old seasonal cycle. Didactic narrative in the West has been primarily a Christian preserve, reaching its greatest development in the late Middle Ages and the Renaissance. Such allegorists as Dante and Spenser deliberately construct their narratives on the Biblical plan, and even St. Augustine presents the story of his own life in the form of the great Christian archetype. The Bible, as the great and inviolable compendium of Christian sacred myth, is a storehouse for narrative artists who wish to reinforce their stories with traditionally meaningful materials, or who wish to borrow patterns for the articulation of their narratives.

The concepts of the Garden of Eden and the New Jerusalem influence Western literature in ways more subtle than patterns of plotting. The concept of the Fall, the view of man as inferior to his ancestors who lived in a Golden Age, has influenced the tone of narratives from Ovid's *Metamorphoses* to Willa Cather's *O Pioneers!* And similarly, the concept of the New Jerusalem, the view of man as progressing toward the City of God, has had an enormous influence, especially in the secularized form of the Utopian narrative. The possibility of mankind achieving the ideal society on earth is pre-Christian, reaching an elaborate embodiment in Plato's *Republic;* but in the Christian world it inevitably either conflicts with or merges with the Christian City of God. To conceive of the ideal city as possibly realizable on earth, of the New Jerusalem built, as Blake put it, "in England's green and pleasant land," smacks of heresy, but it is nonetheless fundamental to all liberal and progressive thinking. A different view on this crucial question is one of the great causes of the hostility between the Church and Marxism. In didactic narrative those fictions we now call Utopian accept this progressive possibility (B. F. Skinner's *Walden Two* for instance) while those fictions we now call anti-Utopian (Orwell's *1984*) reject it. The whole idea of projecting a narrative into the future is a terribly daring one, and is one of the latest narrative possibilities to be discovered and exploited in Western literature. The journey in space, however fantastic, has a pedigree going back to Lucian at least; but the journey forward in time is really a development of the nineteenth century. The possibility has been there ever since the progressive concept of time evolved and the New Jerusalem was established as the future boundary of human existence, to go with the past boundary of the creation. But not until very recently has narrative literature been able to do much with this future. The great proliferation of science fiction narrative in our time is due to the opening of this virgin territory; and the scramble for its occupation has involved writers mainly concerned with fictional romance as well as those concerned with didactic fiction. At last these forms have found their true and natural territory. Just as myth and history belong to the past and mimesis to the present, pure romance really belongs to the future, which is absolutely cut off from any possible reference to truth of fact or truth of sensation. This fragment of narrative evolution, so recently achieved, should give us some sense of the great, continuing, and inexorable process in which narrative art is involved. The schools and the professional men of letters have been slow to come to terms with the concept of futuristic fiction, but, inevitably, they will adjust. The romance of the future is very much our own literature and we must begin to understand it. Its plots can be derived from the old Greek romance plots of separation, danger, and reunion; or from the simple and ancient plan of travel — the road or journey narrative; or from the various Utopian and anti-Utopian formulas already devised. But its possibilities for variation of adventures and expression of ideas are limited only by the limitations of the human mind to conceive them. To criticism, however, the future is closed, and we must return here to consider one of the plot patterns most frequently employed in romance.

The journey to a distant goal (as in the *Aeneid*), and the return home (as in the *Odyssey*), and the quest, which involves voyage out, achievement, and return (as in the *Argonautica*) are typical plots of that heroic romance which lies between primitive epic and erotic romance. The traditional romantic narratives of the Renaissance, from *Orlando Furioso* at the beginning to the *Grand Cyrus* at the end, tend to combine the heroic and erotic materials in a more equal balance than either Greek romance, which emphasizes the erotic, or ancient literary epic, which emphasizes the heroic. But from Apollonius Rhodius on, the combination of quest and love in narrative had been established and was available. The chivalric ideal and the ideal of courtly love, both so important to the later Middle Ages, offered the perfect intellectual foundation for the combination of heroic and erotic romance. Combined with Christian sacred myth, with its spiritualizing tendencies, this sort of intellectual milieu produced such humanistic romances as Tasso's *Gerusalemme Liberata* and Spenser's *Faerie Queene*.

We have discussed historical, mythic, and fictional plot forms. It remains now to consider the plot forms usually adopted by mimetic narrative. With respect to plot the mimetic is the antithesis of the mythic. We can see this clearly in the ancient drama, which developed the Mime, a form of dramatic representation quite different from both tragedy and New Comedy in its plotting. Cornford describes it this way: "As practised by the Alexandrian writers, the Mime has no action at all; it represents characters in a situation which does not change. The interest is entirely focussed on the study of character, and no preoccupation with larger issues stands in the way of extreme realism." The ancient Mime, of course, like the Theophrastian Character, was interested in general character types, not in unique individuals. The main lesson of Auerbach's *Mimesis* — the most unshakable and valuable part of that excellent work — is that the great realistic narratives combine the tragic concern for the individual with the comic concern for society to produce a representation of reality which is a just reflection of actual conditions and at the same time displays a tragic and problematic concern for the individual, regardless of his place in the social hierarchy. The typical figure of the Theophrastian Character is not an individual but a representative of a social deformity, and thus is properly presented comically and held up to a ridicule based upon social norms. The problematic quality which marks the great serious novels is to a considerable extent the result of the novelists' insistence on inserting individualized characters into typical situations, or — stated another way — tragic characters in comic situations. We can see this happening in the drama before it happens in the novel. One of Shakespeare's great gifts as a creator of character is his ability to fill the mold of type with individuality. Like the great novelists, who learned so much from him, Shakespeare is one of those writers who projects himself into his characters, seeing things from their point of view. Rhymer's criticism of him is based on his failure to construct in the old rhetorical way, from the outside, according to type. We all know that Rhymer was wrong in his judgment of Shakespearean characterization, but we are less aware that the observation on which he based this judgment was a shrewd one. Shakespeare does not create his characters according to type, in the old rhetorical way. The character Shylock in the *Merchant of Venice* is an instance of a social type (the grasping, Jewish usurer) individualized beyond the point appropriate for comic treatment. The poetry of some of Shylock's lines ("Hath not a Jew eyes?") tends to thrust this character out of the comic realm into the problematic, if not the tragic. Similarly, in the *Misanthrope* Molière presented a social type with more individuality than a stock figure, the "misanthropic man" of a Mime or Character, should properly possess. Rousseau could take Alceste in Molière's play seriously —too seriously no doubt; and Shylock, in the nineteenth century could be played as a tragic figure — another excess; but these excesses were possible only because of the problematic quality derived from the presence of individual or tragic "toads" in social or comic "gardens." What are Julien Sorel, Raskolnikov, Emma Bovary, and Anna Karenina but individuals in a mimetic world acting out the pattern of their mythic destinies?

The novelists who created these characters were not only borrowing the old tragic pattern for the articulation of their plots; they often achieved rich and complex ironic effects because of the incongruity of the mythic pattern in the world of the nineteenth century. George Eliot's complaint that no life so heroic as St. Theresa's existed for Dorothea Brooke is a milder echo of Stendhal's complaint about the banality of the nineteenth century and Flaubert's hatred of the bourgeoisie who seemed to typify his age. The decorum of separate tragic and comic formulations had given way by the nineteenth century to a powerful new impulse to find a common vehicle which would unite the

neoclassical realism of social type and the romantic realism of
unique individuality. The novel's great virtue lay in finding a way
to combine the tragic concern for the individual with the comic
concern for society. That the novelists called this impulse "realism" and felt that they had arrived at the ultimate way of representing "reality" must not deceive us. Theirs was simply a new
decorum, more easily achieved in narrative than drama, and itself
subject to alteration as new ways of conceiving of the individual
and society became available. The new sciences of psychology
and sociology had their inevitable effect on the artistic representation of the individual and society, providing new schemes of meaning and new kinds of plotting for the use of narrative artists; but
they also disputed with art for the control of the representation
of actuality, driving both narrative and dramatic art ultimately
away from essentially mimetic or realistic formulations. Before
the rise of these latest branches of science, literature controlled
the present; just as before the rise of scientific historiography it
controlled the past. History was so clearly an art in the ancient
world because historiography had not become quite scientific
enough for scientific history to dispute with artistic history. Just
so in the nineteenth century did the novel control the field of
present social and psychological reality, while the sciences of society and the psyche were slowly and painfully being born. Now,
however, these sciences are strong and active, forcing narrative
artists either to embrace them and write fiction which accommodates the scientific truth of psychology and sociology in order to
be "realists," or give over "realism" entirely, as Proust and Joyce
discerned, in order to find a new dispensation under which narrative art may prosper. But we anticipate. The rise of realistic fiction begins with the recognition of social, intellectual, and emotional types, and their presentation for comic and satiric purposes.

The revival of Theophrastian Characters in the seventeenth century is a prelude, perhaps an indispensable one, to the rise of
novelists like Fielding who are primarily concerned with the representation of general character types. Fielding could employ such

generalized characters in his plot-dominated kind of fiction with
enormous success, but the ultimate in mimetic characterization
requires a greater freedom from plot than Fielding allowed himself in *Tom Jones*. The ultimate form of mimetic plot is the "slice
of life," virtually an "unplot." The naturalistic novelists often
aimed at this kind of form, but its achievement really carries narrative into the domain of the sociologist, who, with his tape recorder can produce a book like *The Children of Sanchez* —
powerful, vivid, and truer to the facts of life than any made-up
narrative can hope to be. All the narrative forms, if pushed to
their ultimate capabilities and purged of "impurities," disappear
into the outer fringes of the world of art or of the actual world.
Historical narrative becomes scientific and bloodless. Mimetic
narrative becomes sociological or psychological, turning into the
case history. Didactic narrative becomes hortatory or metaphysical. Romance, the only narrative form which is ineluctably artistic, since it is the product of the story-telling impulse at its purest,
diminishes in interest as its perfection carries it too far from the
world of ideas or from the actual world. A pure story, without
ideas or imitation of actuality to tie it to human concerns and
experiences, would be, if such a possibility were realizable, totally
uninteresting to adult readers. In some children's stories this in-
finitude of inanity is approached. But, in general, narrative artists
have sensed the dangers of purity in their art and shied away from
it, consciously or not. The narratives which people have admired
most are those which have combined most powerfully and copi-
ously the various strands of narrative: the epic and the novel.
The epic, dominated by its mythic and traditional heritage, nevertheless included fictional, historical, and mimetic materials in its
powerful amalgam. The novel, dominated by its growing realistic
conception of the individual in an actual society, nevertheless has
drawn upon mythic, historical, and romantic patterns for its narrative articulation. The great historical narratives and the great
allegorical romances also have combined many of the strands of
narrative in their rich fabrics. Romance turns to didactic allegory

or mimetic characterization in order to enrich itself. History turns to mythic plotting or romantic adventure in order to captivate and move its audience. Myth, mimesis, history, romance, and fable all function so as to enhance one another and reward the narrative artist whose mind and art are so powerful that he can contain and control the richest combination of narrative possibilities.

The possibilities for the future of narrative literature lie in the new combinations which may be worked out between the novel, now clearly emerged as a form, and such older forms as romance and history. As Henri Focillon pointed out in *The Life of Forms in Art,* artistic forms all tend to follow a cyclical pattern which can be described in four stages: primitive, classical, mannered, and baroque. The novel reached its classical form in the period from Stendhal to Tolstoy; it moved toward mannerism in the Edwardians, as writers like Galsworthy, Bennett, and Proust stretched the form in the direction of sequence novels like those now being written by Snow and Powell or the endless narratives of comic strip and soap opera; it moved toward the baroque in Joyce, Faulkner, and Beckett, who twisted and strained the realistic norm to the breaking point. After the baroque, according to Focillon, comes a return to primitivism, which we might find in the contemporary return to picaresque narration. But literary forms are not precisely the same as forms in the plastic arts such as Focillon had in mind, and the novel's turn toward the baroque means a re-turn toward narrative romance as well as a renewed interest in primitive myth.

The novel, a form dominated by the mimetic impulse, has always borrowed its plot materials from other forms. We can see a gradual shift in the sources for novel plots from the beginnings of the form in the seventeenth century to the present time. *Don Quixote,* the great progenitor of the form, is, in its plot, a compromise between the romantic quest pattern and the life-to-death pattern of historical biography. *Lazarillo de Tormes,* the lesser, earlier, but no less influential progenitor of the novel, exhibits in its picaresque form the elements of simple road or journey narrative and the chronological pattern of historical autobiography. These two combinations (biography-quest and autobiography-journey) dominate the rise of the novel. *Gil Blas* and its imitators represent the autobiography-journey pattern; *Tom Jones* and its successors, the biography-quest pattern. Of course, the two flow together. Smollett in *Roderick Random*, for example, casually grafts a romantic love-quest plot onto his essentially picaresque pattern. But, in general, eighteenth-century novels stick to picaresque, historico-biographical, and erotic plot formulations. What they avoid, and what the realistic novelists of the nineteenth century frequently turn to in their greatest works, is the tragic plot formula leading to violent death and/or expulsion from society. Approaches toward this in the eighteenth century, such as Richardson's *Clarissa* and the Abbé Prévost's *Manon Lescaut* stand out by virtue of their singularity. But the novels we think of as representative of the great period of realistic fiction on the European continent—*The Red and the Black, Madame Bovary, Crime and Punishment, Anna Karenina, Fathers and Sons* — generally reflect a careful adherence (deliberate or not) to the ancient tragic formula. These great realistic novels generate their power by the tension they exploit between their mimetic and mythic characteristics. The characters are highly individualized versions of recognizable social types, and the patterns through which they move are woven out of the *mythos* of the tragic drama. The actions are heroic, but the characters themselves are more intimately revealed to us than the monolithic creatures we associate with heroic narratives; they are more penetrable than even the carefully sculptured characters of Euripidean drama.

As, in the novel, mimetic narrative tends to expand and develop its treatment of characters' inner lives, the most tragic character becomes the one capable of the most intense feelings. Modern tragedy is always tragedy of intensity. As tragedy of intensity came to be understood as the mimetic alternative to the old mythic pattern which required violence of catastrophe, the realistic novelists began to make a theoretical case for what they felt to be a new and more realistic kind of tragedy. The old formulations seemed too mythic, too much of the theater perhaps, and the novelists worked toward a kind of plotting appropriate to the new, realistic concept of tragedy. In the passage from *Middlemarch* quoted on page 197, George Eliot is redefining tragedy in a more mimetic way. Arnold Bennett in *The Old Wives' Tale* followed her lead in an attempt to define tragedy so as to make it the province of mimetic narrative. The naturalists found in Darwin's natural selection the deterministic qualities they needed for a new fatalistic element in literature to take the place of the Erinyes which ruled men's lives under the old mythic dispensation. We can see in such a typically Edwardian novelist as Arnold Bennett an attempt to present the new kind of ordinary tragedy in a plot structure which was itself more ordinary. In getting away from the tragic formula leading to violent catastrophe, Bennett turned back to a historical pattern based on chronology, as the old affinities between myth and history reasserted themselves. Bennett's actuarial view of humanity reintroduces through sheer chronological perspective a deterministic aspect into narrative art, with time, rather than fate, managing the catastrophe. Bennett attempts to generate tragic and comic responses to the lives of Sophia and Constance based not on the mythic patterns of tragedy and comedy but on a chronological plan which leads the reader through pale replicas of invigoration and mortification.

With the coming of the twentieth century, plotting in narrative became dominated by time as it never had been before. First the old chronological formulas of the various kinds of historical narrative were given their most thorough employment yet in nonhistorical narrative; then plots began to be developed which were based on rearranging time so that the resolution became not so much a stasis of concluded action as a stasis of illumination, when the missing pieces of the temporal jigsaw puzzle were all finally in place and the picture therefore complete. In the *Forsyte Saga* Galsworthy revived the old chronological plan of the Icelandic

family saga, continuing the story of the Forsytes for several generations. This kind of narrative tends toward open-endedness. It
need not ever be resolved but may be continued indefinitely like
the lives of characters in comic strips or soap operas. D. H. Lawrence used something like this plan in *The Rainbow* and *Women
in Love,* and its elements still appear in sequence novels like C. P.
Snow's *Strangers and Brothers* and Anthony Powell's *Music of
Time.* The movement toward the chronological plot in modern
narrative is part of the general movement to emphasize character
in narrative. The loose chronological plot frees characterization
from dramatic exigencies and allows it to be developed without
being cramped by the necessary preparations for a mythic end.
Such a simple and relatively primitive form of the novel as the
picaresque has retained its vitality precisely because its episodic
pattern allows for free and full character development without in-
terference from the requirements of a tightly-knit plot. E. M.
Forster's assertion that despite Aristotle character must take precedence over plot is very much the assertion of a modern, mimetically oriented novelist.

The rise of modern psychology, itself a phenomenon of the later
nineteenth century, marks the zenith of mimetic narrative. It also
provides some new variations for the old, autobiographical plot
pattern of discovery of true vocation. Joyce's *A Portrait* is in the
old pattern of Lucian and St. Augustine, but Lawrence's autobiographical novel, *Sons and Lovers,* is not. There is a bit of family
saga in the plotting of *Sons and Lovers,* but the novel's real plot
is the story of Paul Morel's attempt to solve the problems generated by his special relationship with his mother. A plot summary
of this novel could be couched in the standard terms of clinical
psychology without doing much violence to the story. After
Freud's theories became widely available, the new psychological
plot became almost as much a formula as the old Greek romance
plot. The discovery of the self, the recovery from the trauma or
wound in the psyche, offered narrative artists a new kind of comic
formulation referable to psychology rather than to myth. Destruc-

tion of the individual due to trauma rather than *hamartia* offered a new scheme for tragedy. The ritualistic-romantic quest for the Grail is metamorphosed in modern fiction into the psychological search for identity. Some of the problems posed by the new interest in psychological characterization have been considered in Chapter 5 above. But its general effect has been to drive the old romantic formulations out of serious fiction and into the realm Graham Greene has called "entertainment." Such a division between novels and entertainments is characteristic of the current tendency of the novel to fragment.

Character and plot, once again, are tending to separate. Serious works, in which the empirical is emphasized get the characters; adventure stories get the plots. Novelists from Fielding to Tolstoy have resisted this tendency, but modern novelists are finding it increasingly hard to resist. In *Ulysses* Joyce's narrative hangs loosely on its borrowed Homeric framework, but its concern is really with character, not plot. It is more of a portrait than *A Portrait of the Artist* — more static, less dynamic; more mimetic, less mythic. Proust's great narrative also nods at the conventional with its autobiographical plot of self-discovery and assumption of vocation, but it too is more interested in character than plot. To provide some kind of tension and resolution for narratives which compromise so little with traditional plot forms, the modern novelist has sought to borrow techniques of organization from painting and music. To call a narrative work "a portrait" is to warn the reader at once not to expect much action, to look for resolution in the completion of an artistic pattern rather than in a stasis achieved in the lives of the characters. In his precocious first draft of *A Portrait* Joyce defined a literary portrait as an attempt to present the past not in "its iron memorial aspect" but as a "fluid succession of presents." Thus a portrait should be "not an identificative paper but rather the curve of an emotion."

The older novelists used to like to wind up a narrative by telling us what happened to everybody "afterwards." We can find this in Balzac and George Eliot as well as in Dickens. A modern writer like Lawrence Durrell, however, can end his *Alexandria Quartet* with "workpoints" which indicate ways in which the narrative could be extended backward and forward in time, indicating just how artificial is the equilibrium we seem to have reached at the end of the fourth volume. Music, like painting, has been pressed into service by narrative artists seeking new varieties of tension and resolution to supplant the traditional culminations of stories. E. M. Forster has singled out the recurring musical phrase in Proust as an example of "rhythm" in fiction, just as he cited the hourglass shape of James's *The Ambassadors* as an example of "pattern." But in a larger sense Proust's novel is rhythmic and musical in the way situations are repeated as variations on a theme, in the way characters group, separate, and regroup themselves as in a dance to what Anthony Powell has called *The Music of Time*. Proust's, Powell's, and Durrell's major works all nod at traditional plotting of the autobiographical and chronological kind, but they combine this with more serious attention to themes and variations. Where Galsworthy and Bennett gave most of their allegiance to time, these writers give theirs to music, having found in that art an esthetic principle which enables them to deal with time more creatively, as time is dealt with in music, and achieve beauty of form without sacrificing characterization to the resolution of a traditional plot.

On the whole, however, of all the aspects of narrative, plot seems to be not only the most essential but also the least variable, insofar as its general outlines are concerned. We demand variety of incident more than we demand variety of plot in our fiction. When we pick up a modern picaresque tale, whether it is narrated by Felix Krull or Augie March, we know in a general way what to expect. We know our destination though we do not know specifically what scenes we shall pass by the way. The specifics of incident admit of as much variation as the specifics of characterization, and it is in this area that we expect an author to exercise his originality in plotting. Plot, in the large sense, will always be *mythos* and always be traditional. For an author like

Jane Austen one plot, in this large sense, can suffice for all her novels. But there are some smaller senses of the word "plot" which we have not yet considered, that must at least be mentioned before we can conclude.

Every separable element in a narrative can be said to have its own plot, its own little system of tension and resolution which contributes its bit to the general system. Not only every episode or incident but every paragraph and every sentence has its beginning, middle, and end. It is in these small areas rather than in the large ones we have been considering that individual achievement may be properly assessed. Here, we may distinguish the master from the hack or journeyman. Here every work becomes a thing in itself rather than a part of some complex generic tradition. In a plot-summary we often cannot tell a great work from a feeble one. What we respond to in the greatest narratives is the quality of mind transmitted to us through the language of characterization, motivation, description, and commentary — the intelligence and sensitivity with which the fictional events are related to the perceivable world or the world of ideas: the accuracy and insight of the artist's picture of the brazen world in which we live, or the beauty and idealism of the golden world created in the fiction. Quality of mind (as expressed in the language of characterization, motivation, description, and commentary) not plot, is the soul of narrative. Plot is only the indispensable skeleton which, fleshed out with character and incident, provides the necessary clay into which life may be breathed.

7

Point of View in Narrative

The problem of point of view is narrative art's own problem, one that it does not share with lyric or dramatic literature. By definition narrative art requires a story and a story-teller. In the relationship between the teller and the tale, and that other relationship between the teller and the audience, lies the essence of narrative art. The narrative situation is thus ineluctably ironical. The quality of irony is built into the narrative form as it is into no other form of literature. What the dramatist can achieve only with considerable effort, and what is utterly alien to the lyricist, is the natural basis of narrative art.

Irony is always the result of a disparity of understanding. In any situation in which one person knows or perceives more — or less — than another, irony must be either actually or potentially present. In any example of narrative art there are, broadly speaking, three points of view — those of the characters, the narrator, and the audience. As narrative becomes more sophisticated, a fourth point of view is added by the development of a clear distinction between the narrator and the author. Narrative irony is a function of disparity among these three or four viewpoints. And narrative artists have always been ready to employ this disparity to make effects of various kinds.

If we push far enough the question of why irony makes the

effects it does, we shall end up in the largely unexplored territory of how and why stories play a part in the life of man. Without attempting to penetrate too far into this forbidding country, we can hazard the notion that stories appeal primarily because they offer a simulacrum of life which enables an audience to participate in events without being involved in the consequences which events in the actual world inevitably carry with them. Our pleasure in narrative literature itself, then, can be seen as a function of disparity of viewpoint or irony. Because we are not involved in the action represented, we always enjoy a certain superiority over the characters who are. Simple irony in narrative is often just the exploitation of this superiority. When Homer allows us to know that Athena is deceiving Hector by making him think he is not facing Achilles alone, then the operation of the simple irony is adding to our pleasure in the narrative. Our sympathy for Hector is heightened, but we are also making our emotional preparations for his defeat, which becomes twice removed from us — once because we are not involved in this simulacrum of life, and again because our particular foreknowledge has forearmed us against this particular catastrophe. The uses of irony in narrative art range from a simple effect such as this to effects of extraordinary complexity; and the control of irony is a principal function of point of view.

If we consider the management of point of view in a historical perspective, two obvious conclusions present themselves to us. First, we can see that in the growth of narrative artists' awareness of, and exploitation of, the ironic possibilities inherent in the management of point of view we have one of the really developmental processes of literary history. Second, we can see that this has not been a steady and gradual process, but, like technological development, a matter of rapid proliferation over a period of a few centuries. The period of the rise of the novel as a literary form has also been the period of really great experimentation with, and development of, techniques in the management of point of view. As we shall see, this remarkable development is largely the result of the problems and opportunities presented to narrative artists seeking to achieve an effective combination of empirical and fictional techniques of narration.

We can begin to perceive the way in which the process worked if we consider for a moment just one aspect of the problem of point of view as it existed in ancient narrative and as it was modified historically: the problem of the authority of the narrator. In mythic or traditional narrative the events being narrated are always well back in the past and the tradition itself carries its own authority. The epic poet is a repository of tradition, fulfilling the functions of entertainer and historian simultaneously. The tradition provides him with his authority. It also limits his flexibility. The familiar invocation to the muse of Homeric epic may well represent an attempt on the part of the Greek epic poet to shift the authority from constricting tradition to inspiration, which is freer because personal and creative. The inspired bard must answer to his muse alone, and his muse can speak only through him. The invocation to the muse, with its concomitant shifting of authority from the tradition to the poet's creative ability, is not an indispensable feature of epic poetry. It is anything but this. In the epic of *Gilgamesh* and in the *Beowulf* epic, there is no such thing. It seems highly likely that the invocation is a sophisticated feature which developed late in Greek oral epic as a manifestation of the creative impulse toward a more fictional kind of narrative. Homeric epic, though it preserves many of the heroic features of primitive epic, is a more sophisticated form than either the earlier *Gilgamesh* or the later *Beowulf*, and has actually started to move toward romance. The artful construction of Homeric narrative is in itself a sign of this process; epic does not usually appear in so beautifully constructed and finished a form as either the *Iliad* or the *Odyssey*.

The Greek historians in their narratives substitute for the authority of tradition a new kind of authority. The *histor* as narrator is not a recorder or recounter but an investigator. He examines the past with an eye toward separating out actuality from myth.

Herodotus takes his authority not so much from his sources as from the critical spirit with which he means to approach those sources. Where the traditional poet must confine himself to one version of his story, the *histor* can present conflicting versions in his search for the truth of fact. Thucydides is the perfect type of the ancient *histor*, basing his authority on the accuracy of conclusions he has drawn from evidence he has gathered.

The principal other source of narrative authority which we would expect to find in empirical narrative is not so readily found there in the ancient world. This is the authority of the eye-witness. We have commented elsewhere on the rarity of first-person narration in pre-Roman narratives. This absence is nowhere more striking than in such a narrative as Xenophon's *Anabasis*. Here the author witnessed the events narrated and took a prominent part in them. Yet he not only narrates in the third person, casually introducing himself (Xenophon, an Athenian) in Chapter 8 of Book I, but originally caused his manuscript to be circulated under someone else's name. Thucydides also refers to himself bleakly in the third person in Book IV of *The Peloponnesian War*, striking the personal note of the eye-witness only momentarily — in Book V — and even there emphasizing his leisure for investigation rather than any immediacy of observation. Similarly, in the first century A.D. Josephus tells the story of the *Jewish War* from this apparently detached point of view, though identifying himself in the beginning as a participant in and witness to the events. And, of course, so does Caesar in his *Gallic War* adopt this ostensibly disinterested point of view (though at least one of his modern translators has elected to present the whole narrative in the first person). The reason for this employment of third-person narrative in historical works may be that the reliability of the *histor* seemed to the ancients clearly greater than that of the eye-witness. A document aspiring to achieve truth of fact had a better chance of being appreciated as factual if it did not seem too personal. This is another way of saying that history rather than mimesis dominated ancient empirical narrative. The important elements in classical history were the positions taken by sides in battle or debate, the events which occurred, the speeches which might have or should have been made. In modern empirical narrative we are interested — in history as well as in journalism and realistic fiction — in "the way it was." There are ancient writers who can and do give us a sense of the way it was, and we treasure them for it today; but they almost always give us this sense by accident or by the way, when they are concentrating on something else. Plato in the *Lysis,* presents Socrates as first-person narrator and gives us a surprisingly detailed picture of everyday life in a gymnasium. And Xenophon himself, though not narrating in the first person, enables us often in the *Anabasis* to have a sense of the way it must have been on that terrible and wonderful march. But the first-person narrative seems to have been used mainly in the ancient world not for factual or mimetic representation, but for highly unreliable and one-sided *apologiae,* as in the case of Josephus, whose *Life* of himself does not check well against his history, and is usually thought to be the least credible of all his writings. In Roman times the first-person narrative came to be used for fictions like those of Petronius and Apuleius, and finally, with St. Augustine, for the highly empirical *Confessions,* which set a standard of truth far removed from that of the earlier autobiographical mode, the *apologia.*

It must be remembered that thus far we have not been concerned with point of view in all its aspects but with the specific problem of the authority adduced for a given narrative. We can find a good deal of first-person narration in Greek romance. The *Aethiopica* of Heliodorus, for example, is full of it, divided among a large group of narrators. The *Leucippe and Cleitophon* of Achilles Tatius is almost entirely cast in the form of a first-person tale told by Cleitophon to the narrator proper, who disappears after the opening pages and never reappears. But we do not find in Greek romance the author-narrator claiming to have been an eye-witness to or participant in the events he is narrating, and founding his authority on his own testimony. For the most part these fictions are content to be fictional, without striving for either verisimilitude or authenticity. The statement of Longus, at the beginning of *Daphnis and Chloe,* while not a common device in the Greek romance expresses its spirit excellently. He has seen a charming picture, he tells us, of a love story (*historian erotos*), which he has had interpreted (by an *exegeten*), so that he could write it down. The story is vaguely referred to some past actuality represented in the picture, but its true reason for being is that it will instruct those unlearned in love and remind those who have experienced it, and will be a delightful possession (*ktema terpnon*) for all men. By resting the justification for his tale directly on its esthetic appeal to an audience, Longus showed that he understood his form perfectly; which may help account for his signal success in it.

In the last of the ancient Greek romances (ignoring Byzantine practitioners of a later age), the *Leucippe and Cleitophon,* we can see Achilles Tatius hovering between the approach of Longus and the idea of the autobiographical narrator. He begins, like Longus, with a description of a picture he has come upon that deals with love. But instead of telling us the story presented in that picture, he introduces a fellow spectator, Cleitophon, who is bursting to tell the story of his adventures, which, he says, are like fiction (*mythois eoike*). By the end of the story the author has forgotten that he began with his third-person narrator viewing a picture. He simply brings everything to a halt when Cleitophon finishes his tale. Thus this romance hovers between resting its authority on art, as Longus did, and on testimony; and it hovers between the standard romance technique of employing first-person narratives within the larger frame of the author-narrator's own presentation, and the technique of the true eye-witness narrative, as adopted by Apuleius and Petronius.

We have been working here toward a quite useful distinction between the first-person speaker in empirical narrative (the eye-witness narrator or the autobiographical confessor) and the first-person speakers of fictional narrative (the characters who tell the primary author-narrators their stories, often leading to stories within stories and narrators within narrations; and the self-apologists, who idealize their own lives for moral or esthetic purposes). As narrative art develops, new ways of handling point of view are conceived, and these new ways are quickly combined with older ones to allow still further refinements. As narrative art becomes sophisticated the artists continually strive to achieve the impossible — to have their empirical bread and eat their fictional cake too. On a fairly simple level we can see this process at work in Apuleius and Petronius, whose attempts to live in both worlds foreshadow those of the novelists of a later age, as they seek for compromises between an apparently empirical approach and a patently fictional or traditional one. In the *Golden Ass* and the *Satiricon* these Latin writers include not only what purports to be the eye-witness testimony of their protagonist narrators; they allow their narrators to report stories of interest that they have heard or overheard, such as the apparently Milesian tales of funereal fun at Miletus and Ephesus which appear in the two books. Apuleius includes in this manner also the beautiful romance of Cupid and Psyche. And ever since his time we have had romantic interludes in narratives otherwise of a different order — most notably in Cervantes and his followers.

Apuleius, in particular, was well aware of the difference between a tale like "Cupid and Psyche," which derives its authority from its own esthetic virtues, and a narrative such as his primary story of Lucius, which claims to be eye-witness testimony. When he wishes in Book X to give us a report of a trial at which Lucius was not present (being properly tethered in the stable), he allows Lucius to observe to the reader that though he was not present he offers what he has been able to piece together from such information as came to hand (or hoof) in the stable. Quite clearly Lucius operates as a kind of *histor* in this situation, and the events he recounts as *histor* or as eye-witness are intended to be of a different order from such a bed-time story as "Cupid and Psyche."

By the end of Roman times virtually all the possibilities for establishing the authority of a narrative had been employed in one way or another. A writer dealing with the past could adopt any of a number of postures: he could be a historian (Tacitus), inspired bard (Vergil, Ovid) or something in between (Lucan). A writer dealing with more recent times could present a personal eye-witness account in his own name (Augustine), a fictional account in a character's name (Petronius), or something in between (Apuleius). A writer more concerned with fictional than traditional, historical, or mimetic representation could offer a story with no justification (Xenophon of Ephesus' *Ephesian Tale*), one which carried its own esthetic and didactic justification (Longus' *Daphnis and Chloe*), or one which leaned toward eye-witness testimony (Achilles Tatius' *Leucippe and Cleitophon*). And a satirist like Lucian could turn most of the conventional kinds of authority on their ears by writing a "True History" in the form of an eye-witness narration which is a tissue of the incredible and the absurd.

With the writers mentioned here narrative literature as a living art form in the classical languages comes to an end. Change does not necessarily mean growth or progress, but without change there is no life in art. A literature which is alive is marked by continuous change in its literary forms. Though Latin in the West and Greek in the East continued to be read and written for a thousand years and more after the Roman Empire had declined and fallen, the forms of narrative did not change in this period and no important narratives in the classical languages have come to light from late Roman or post-Roman times. In the European vernacular languages an oral literature developed along the usual lines, gradually becoming aware of the written classical literature and gradually becoming itself a written literature. The existence of a variety of oral vernaculars, in the presence of the ubiquitous Latin, established conditions for literary development in Western Europe which were different from those that had prevailed in Greece and Rome. The awareness of the existence of writing as a medium for conveying narrative almost certainly resulted in Western European epic being reduced to writing before it had reached a stage of development comparable to Greek epic. And the existence of a multiplicity of languages, within the loose unity provided by the spread of Christianity and its Latin language, made translation from one language to another a major activity in narrative writing.

In terms of the question of authority for narrative works, the medieval situation resulted in a great prolongation and diversification of the authority of tradition. Narrative in oral tradition was justified naturally in terms of the tradition. But as oral narrative gave way to written in the later Middle Ages, tradition continued to be cited by most narrative writers as the authority for their narrations. We are familiar with Malory's "as the French book saith." Most of his great narrative predecessors said something similar. The major works of Chaucer, of Gottfried, of Wolfram, of Chrétien, and of countless lesser authors are all traditional narratives, and usually acknowledged as being such by their authors. The question of authority is not merely a matter of point of view, though we have been treating it as one; it is to a great extent related to the whole question of the development of narrative forms. In a literary culture dominated by traditional narrative, most of the narrative forms we know today cannot grow. In the Middle Ages history as we know it and as the Greeks knew it could not establish itself. Nor could truly fictional romance.

(We are entering a thicket of confused terminology here, but may find our way through it if we exercise some care. As the word romance is usually employed, the major narratives of Malory, Chaucer, Gottfried, Wolfram, and Chrétien would be called "medieval romances," and distinguished, as such, from the *chansons de geste*, which are closer to heroic epic in spirit and poetical techniques. But as we have been using the word romance in this discussion, it signifies a fiction composed by an individual author for esthetic ends, as opposed to traditional or historical narrative. Greek romance is romance in this sense. *Parzival* is not; it is mainly traditional, with the author figuring as embellisher and adaptor rather than as creator. No value judgment is implied here. The question is really one of a different approach to authorship. One of the original senses of the word novel is that of "a new thing." A traditional story is not "a new thing." A created fiction like *Daphnis and Chloe* is new. In Chaucer's *Canterbury Tales* the stories are traditional, and have their sources which can be located in the tradition; but the frame device of the pilgrims is quite novel, going well beyond previous known experiments in framing and dealing creatively with traditional types of character though not abandoning them. The freer a writer is with his sources, the further he is moving away from the traditional or mythic narrative, and the closer he is coming toward creative or romantic narrative. The Greek romances are not the last word in fictional independence from myth, obviously, but they are free to name their characters, to locate their story in time and space, to vary and diversify the events in their pattern of love, separation, adventure, and reunion. An adaptor of the Perceval story, or the Tristan story, is not so free. And stories such as these are not the fictional creations of individual authors but the result of slow accretions and modifications as the *mythos* passed from hand to hand in oral and written tradition.)

The so-called medieval romances, then, in our terms are not romances but elaborate mythic narratives (in contrast to the fictional French romances of the seventeenth century), and, as such, they derive their authority — usually quite openly — from tradition. The materials of medieval traditional narrative could, of course, be used in a more fictional way than a writer such as Malory found expedient. In a perfectly formed narrative like *Sir Gawain and the Green Knight* we are moving from traditional narrative toward true fiction. This is apparent in the exquisite shape and structure of the story, which makes nearly every other medieval narrative look like careless and sprawling work, and in the inability of scholars to find anything like a real source for the work. We have here a sample of creative activity in narrative well beyond the normal usage of the time. The *Gawain and the Green Knight* story is one of those phenomenal leaps made by individual creative genius (such as that made by Cervantes in *Don Quixote*) which are capable of revitalizing a literary culture which has ceased to find ways for fruitful change and growth. The failure of English literature to assimilate this tale — due no doubt to its having been written in an unpopular dialect — is partly responsible for the miserable state of English narrative in the fifteenth and early sixteenth centuries: a state of moribundity so profound that it required the introduction of Spanish picaresque, of Italian literary epic, and the revival and translation of Greek romance before signs of life began to reappear. Yet even this tale of Sir Gawain, which would seem to need no justification, is presented by its author as a traditional tale, which he has both heard and read before, so deeply engraved on the medieval mind was the formula of appeal to tradition in narrative, and so foreign to that mind was our modern concept of originality as a value in art.

For the *histor*, for the eye-witness, as for the author who feels his tale needs no justification, one searches with little success in medieval narrative. One of the most striking aspects of the new narrative forms which emerged in vernacular literature with the Renaissance is the appearance of the eye-witness narrator in contexts as different as Dante's *Commedia*, Cellini's *Autobiography*, and the picaresque tale of *Lazarillo de Tormes*. New stories, personal stories, stories with unusual pretensions to actuality tend, in both the ancient and the modern world, to take the form of eye-witness narrative. We can almost go so far as to say that the natural form of mimetic narrative is eye-witness and first-person. Circumstantiality, verisimilitude, and many more of the qualities which we recognize as identifying characteristics of realism in narrative are all natural functions of the eye-witness point of view. The fact that the European stage was unable to come to terms with realism until the drama of Ibsen, and then only for a moment, is in part explained by the fact that the stage had no such simple technical device as the eye-witness narrator to act as a realistic filter for events. The realistic elements we sense and respond to in such "unrealistic" narratives as the *Commedia* and *Gulliver's Travels,* as well as in the more realistic *Moll Flanders, Roderick Random,* and *Pamela,* are all partly due to the kind of coloring which an eye-witness or autobiographical narrator so readily imparts to the events he narrates.

The picaresque form of narrative, which played a crucial role in the development of the novel, tends to rely on the authority of the rogue narrator who is recounting his own experiences. The form of *Lazarillo de Tormes* is very like the form of the *Satiricon* (what we have of it) and the *Golden Ass,* though somewhat purged of the fantastic element which persists in both of these. We speak rather loosely, often, of any novel with a rogue for a protagonist as being "picaresque," and up to a point we are right to do so; but we ought not to let this obscure the fact that picaresque has had strong affinities with the autobiographical, eye-witness form of narrative from its beginnings to *Huckleberry Finn* and *Catcher in the Rye.* Picaresque itself is only one manifestation of the rapid evolution narrative forms underwent in the later Middle Ages and the Renaissance. After centuries of a tradition-centered narrative art, the empirical and the fictional spirits were at last gaining strength in Western Europe. What had passed for empirical narrative for centuries had been the Saint's Life and the Chronicle, both usually quite innocent of the historical attitude we found in Herodotus and Thucydides; and what had passed for fiction had been mainly great, traditionally oriented narrative cycles of chivalry; or short, often equally traditional fabliaux: the descendants of the Milesian tale as the chivalric cycles were descendants of oral legend, heroic epic, and *chansons de geste.*

As had happened in the ancient world, narrative artists began, at the close of the Middle Ages, to substitute for the authority of traditional narrative the authority of the eye-witness, the *histor,* or the creator. The resurgence of interest in classical literature made such formulas for departing from tradition as the invocation to the muse readily available once again. But the writer experimenting with prose forms of fiction in the Renaissance could hardly avail himself of the epic formulae. He was much more disposed to found his authority on devices imitative of the writers of established empirical prose narrative — the historians. The old distinction of Herodotus between lying poets and truthful prose historians arises again with the development of empirical thought in Europe. With a more sceptical attitude toward the veracity of narrative beginning to permeate the air, the authority for any narrative could no longer be laid safely to tradition. A tendency arose to abandon all pretense to verisimilitude and historicity and write in verse; or to insist on these qualities and write in prose. Romance became more fictional and more obviously fictitious. Fabliaux and novelle became more mimetic and less obviously fictitious. Two of the narratives produced in southern Europe in the first half of the sixteenth century can stand as typical of this new dissociation of the strands of narrative: *Orlando Furioso* in Italy, and *Lazarillo de Tormes* in Spain. The range of possibilities represented by these two works is extreme. The tension between the impulses they represent is responsible for the production of such a great mediator as *Don Quixote*. An examination of Cervantes' approach to the problem of authority in this narrative can be highly illuminating. And what such a consideration reveals is of enormous significance for the understanding of the rise of the novel as a literary form.

In the opening chapters of Part II of *Don Quixote* the question of authority is treated at some length in a discussion among the Don, Sancho, and the bachelor Sanson. The discussion rests in part on the distinction between poet and historian which is made by Sanson:

it is one thing to write as a poet, another as a historian: the poet can tell or sing of things not as they were but as they should have been, while the historian must write of them not as they should have been but as they were, without adding anything or taking anything away from the truth.

As the entire narrative turns on the interplay between a realistic and an idealistic view of life, the opposition between poet and historian is a crucial one to the whole conception of the book. In dealing with the matter of authority Cervantes assumes a number of conflicting postures which function so as to baffle the reader. He insists on the historical veracity of the record at times, and at times insists on his freedom to create. In the Prologue to the First Part of the story, he adopts the esthetic or fictional stance at first, acknowledging the book as "the child of my brain," which he should have liked "to be the fairest, the sprightliest, and the cleverest that could be imagined." But by the end of this prologue he has retreated from this position and is adopting the posture of the *histor*, presenting a "sincere and straightforward . . . account of the famous Don Quixote de la Mancha, who is held by the residents of the Campo de Montiel region to have been the most chaste lover and most valiant knight that had been seen in those parts for many a year."

At the beginning of the second episode of Part I, Cervantes introduces some narrative refinements which enable him thereafter to maintain his complete imaginative freedom while insisting on the historicity of his narrative. In Chapter 8 at the end of the first episode he indicates that up to this point he has been following a document (a mock appeal to tradition) which breaks off at a crucial point. He hopes that the "learned ones of La Mancha" will have found materials in their "archives and registry offices" (mock historical appeal) and that a continuing document will turn up. When the document does turn up, it is in Arabic, and its author, Cid Hamete Benengeli, is an Arabic historian. The narrator, with a Moorish translator assisting him, then continues the tale, pointing out that the author was an Arab, "and that nation is known for its lying propensities"; but because the author is of that hostile race, his trifling with the truth has probably taken the form of suppressing certain praises of Don Quixote rather than that of embellishing the chronicle with fictional materials. Cervantes goes on at this point (or his author-narrator does) to praise history in such fulsome terms that his praises themselves function ironically:

for it should be the duty of historians to be exact, truthful, and dispassionate, and neither interest nor fear nor rancor nor affection should swerve them from the path of truth, whose mother is history, rival of time, depositor of deeds, witness of the past, exemplar and advisor to the present, guide for the future.

Cervantes is usually presented to us as an anti-romancer primarily; and so, to a certain extent, he is. But he is also keeping the empirical spirit at ᵟₐ distance. He is well aware that his work stands between that of the poet and that of the historian — in our terms between fictional narrative and empirical. And though he attacks the excessive idealism of the romancers, he also continually fends off the historians, lest they encroach too much on his own fictional domain. In Chapter 47 of Part I, Cervantes has allowed the canon to present what must have been his own views on fiction — an attitude which has strong realistic overtones but is not fully committed to the empirical:

It is necessary to marry the deceitful fable to the understanding of the reader, writing in such a way as to make the impossible acceptable, smoothing over monstrosities, holding the attention suspended and wondering, pleased and amused all at once, so that admiration and entertainment march in step together; and all these things no one can accomplish if he avoids verisimilitude and the representation of nature [de la verisimilitud y de la imitación], in which consists the perfection of things written.

In this statement (which is a standard Renaissance esthetic view) the impossible itself is not ruled out, so long as it can be made to appear possible. In Cid Hamete Benengeli Cervantes found his ideal narrative device — a historian but an Arab historian and therefore an untrustworthy one. In Chapter 5 of Part II the author-narrator makes use of the historian's unreliability:

Getting ready to write, the translator of this fifth chapter of our history says that he considers it apocryphal, because in it Sancho Panza speaks in a style quite different from that suitable to his limited intellect, and says things so subtle that it does not seem possible that they could have occurred to him; but the translator does not want to abandon his task, the accomplishment of which is his official duty, and therefore has proceeded, saying:

This is one way in which Cervantes has his empirical bread and eats his fictional cake as well. And, of course, he allows his reader the same privilege. Faced with another problem which the narrator as *histor* must face, he solves it in a similar way. In Part II, the book version of Part I is assumed to be already in circulation and to have come into the hands of the characters (though Part I was previously supposed to have been written well after the events of Part II had taken place). Sancho poses to his master the question of how the historian could have told truly about those things that happened to the two adventurers when they were alone together — a problem peculiar to the *histor*. Don Quixote's answer provides for Cervantes a comic equivalent to the inspired bard's privileges: "I can assure you Sancho . . . that the author of our history must be some wise enchanter; for nothing that they choose to write about is hidden from those who practice that art." Don Quixote's explanation is as good as any other, for it is the truth; but Cervantes himself and not Cid Hamete Benengeli is the enchanter in question. He will make the most of his various historical postures but will relinquish none of his prerogatives as maker. To encompass as broad a domain as he can of the territory of narrative, to hold the mutually repellent poles of fiction and empiricism in nervous and vibrant conjunction — these are his aims, and these are the aims of many of his followers in the novel.

To explore these aims we must consider the major postures which the narrator may assume and the ways in which novelists have learned to deal with them. For convenience we shall divide this consideration into a discussion of eye-witness forms of narration and another category of other forms. We shall seek to give names to as many varieties of narrative posture as possible, not out of any delight in classification for its own sake, but so as to clarify the problems and conflicts which result from the novelists' desire to make the best of both the empirical and the fictional worlds.

THE EYE-WITNESS

The eye-witness can be employed in a wide variety of ways. His eyes can be turned inward so that he is his own subject matter or outward so that the other characters or the social scene itself become the dominant interest. In the eye-witness form of narration, considerations of character are intimately related to considerations of point of view. To the extent that the narrator is characterized he will dominate the narrative, taking precedence over event and situation. This is true whether the narrator is a real person like Benevenuto Cellini or a fictional one like Moll Flanders. But to the extent that the narrating character is differentiated from the author one ironic gap opens up, and to the extent that the narrating character is differentiated from himself as participant in events another ironic gap appears. In *Gulliver's Travels*, for example, the major disparity of viewpoint seems to lie between Gulliver and Swift, with the audience aware of the disparity and sharing Swift's view. In *Great Expectations*, on the other hand, the gap lies between Pip as participant and Pip as narrator, with Dickens and the reader sharing the viewpoint of the narrative Pip. In the autobiography of an actual person, the problem is complicated, as all our emotional responses to such works are complicated, by the outside knowledge that the reader may bring to bear on the work, and this is true whether the work is openly autobiographical, like Rousseau's *Confessions* or covertly so, like *David Copperfield*.

This distinction between real and fictional in the autobiographical form of eye-witness narrative makes discussions of this form difficult and sometimes confusing, but it must not be ignored. It bears to some extent on the whole question of when narrative is art and when it is not art but something else — social science, perhaps, or philosophy. There are always going to be borderline cases that will create problems if we try to make our dividing line coincide with some sort of division between fiction and non-fiction or between artful and factual narrative. Moreover, some actual lives, even as the fictional Cleitophon observed, will inevitably resemble fiction because they seem to have been shaped by circumstance with an esthetic eye. Our purpose here is not so much to establish a clear differentiation between factual and fictional autobiography as to observe the ways in which they are related and interact with one another. The principal differences in practice between the two can be considered under two aspects: the difference it makes to the reader and the difference it makes to the author if an autobiographical character in narrative has an existence in the world of actuality which lies outside the story. From the reader's side, the question is one of expectations. If he believes he is reading the life of a real person he is prepared to be interested by a narrative of less symmetry and significance than he would otherwise, consciously or not, expect. Simple, matter-of-fact things seem more exciting if we are convinced that they have had actual existence, and more meaningful as well. In an age like the eighteenth century which was just developing the modern yearning for the actual, it was natural that autobiography should flourish, and it was also natural that writers as different as Defoe and Richardson should go to great lengths to present their fictions in the form of actual autobiographical documents. The author of a fictional eye-witness narrative, whether it is inwardly or outwardly directed, wants to acquire for his narrative some of that passion for actuality which motivates the reader of any document that purports to contain the "real." The author of a fiction is not, of course, confronted by the same problems that face an author trying to present his own life and character in fictional form. A Defoe can take off from actuality very freely and make Robinson Crusoe's adventures much more prolonged and exciting than his model Alexander Selkirk's ever were. He has the whole world of imagination to choose from. His problem is only to choose with enough restraint to maintain that illusion of actuality which the form initially provides. The true autobiographer, on the other hand, must select and arrange the events of his life so as to give them a narrative shape and pattern. Even the diarist eliminates from his record countless trivial details. A diarist who makes a second draft of his diary, as Boswell did and as even Pepys may have done, is moving toward fiction already. The narrative impetus tends to bring factual and fictional autobiography closer together, though they may originate in quite separate ways and for quite different motives.

The eye-witness narrative in which the focus is outward rather than inward also has its factual and fictional polarity. This kind of eye-witness has been a favorite device for narrative satirists and utopists from Lucian to Swift and on to Butler. The more fantastic the story, the more the empirical aura which surrounds the eye-witness becomes desirable. One of the surest manifestations of the genius of Swift is to be found in his exploitation of Gulliver as eye-witness, bursting with matter-of-fact details. The author, on the other hand, who presents his eye-witness narrator as a legitimate memoirist, giving this narrator his own name, and naming actual people as the characters in his narrative — Boswell on the Grand Tour, for example — can count on an interest which will make mere fact exciting. But this does not prevent many of our memoirists from being singled out as notorious liars — Ford Madox Ford, Oliver Gogarty, George Moore, and Frank Harris, to name a few — by which we mean that they tend to give way to fictional impulses in their narratives. The impulse to shape, to improve, to present not what was said or what did happen but what should have been said or ought to have happened, inevitably makes itself felt. Narrative art is the art of story-telling, and the more literate and sensitive a man is, the more he feels creative pressures which drive him to seek beauty or truth at the expense of fact. Narrative art is an art of compromise, in which gains are always purchased at the expense of sacrifices. The story-teller is often faced with the choice of being either a bore or a charlatan. The great story-tellers inevitably choose the latter in preference to the former. But even the narrative artist who has avoided one kind of compromise by electing to present a made-up fiction, with no specific ties to actual persons living or dead (as the habitual disclaimer so often and so often untruthfully puts it), has not solved all his problems. Even such an apparently safe and convenient mode of narration as the eye-witness reporter presenting a totally fictitious sequence of events often involves the artist in problems and difficulties which only compromise or a touch of charlatanry can solve.

The powerful circumstantiality of eye-witness narration is purchased at the expense of accepting certain limitations. The eye-witness cannot see everything. And he can know only one mind — his own. We have observed Lucius Apuleius working around this problem, and the history of narrative is dotted with other examples. But the novelist's determination to have the benefits of eye-witness narration without accepting its limitations has been indefatigable. This determination illustrates as well as anything the nature of the compromise between empiricism and fiction on which the uneasy edifice of the novel has been reared. Consider some examples from the practice of a wide variety of novelists.

Tristram Shandy is a first-person narrator who should be an eye-witness, except that nearly everything he narrates seems to have taken place before he was in a condition to witness anything. Of course *Tristram Shandy* is no ordinary novel, and there is good reason to believe that Sterne's fast and loose treatment of the new literary form is deliberate parody, up to a point. But we can find much more serious novelists than Sterne refusing to accept the limitations of eye-witness narration. That most careful of novelists, Gustave Flaubert, begins *Madame Bovary* with an eye-witness account of Charles Bovary's arrival at school, but our eye-witness soon fades into a disembodied spirit who roams freely in time and space, revealing secret thoughts and actions of his characters. Flaubert wanted that eye-witness opening with its unduplicatable air of verisimilitude, and he did not hesitate to concoct an eye-witness for the moment and then cause him to dematerialize a

few pages later. Dickens's famous resort to a combination of disembodied omniscience and direct reporting in *Bleak House* is a
result of the same impulse, to some extent; but Dickens, who was
a genius of rhetoric primarily, was exploiting the contrast in language, tone, and understanding between the two narrators, while
Flaubert preferred to make a seamless connection between his
two points of view. Conrad, in *Victory*, employs the same device
as Flaubert in *Madame Bovary*. He begins with a localized eye-
witness, unnamed but obviously one of the veranda-sitters at
Schomberg's hotel, and he allows this person to wither away so
that the reader can be transported to the island where he hears
the private conversations of Lena, Heyst, and others, without even
realizing that his eye-witness guide through these events has disappeared. Proust, in *À la recherche du temps perdu*, has given us
some of the most flagrant cases in all literature of the novelist's
insistence on having things both ways. On countless occasions,
in fact habitually, the narrator Marcel tells us of thoughts and
actions of other people which the character Marcel could not
possibly have known. On the occasion of one of his most elaborate
transcendences of the eye-witness point of view, Proust offers,
through Marcel, a justification of his procedure. Often, Marcel
tells us, he thinks while lying in bed of old days in Combray and

of what, many years after leaving this little town, I had learned about
a love affair that Swann had had before my birth, with that precision
of details easier to obtain sometimes about the lives of people dead for
centuries than about those of our best friends; a thing which seems impossible, just as it used to seem impossible to converse from one town to
another — while we were still unaware of the device by which that
impossibility has been overcome.

Proust does not name for us here the device analogous to the
telephone which enables Marcel to know so accurately what mere
empirical means cannot provide; but we shall be safe in assuming
that this notion is of a piece with Proust's entire esthetic, which
continually mentions the limitations of the empirical and asserts
the extraordinary power of those insubstantial essences, memory

and imagination. He simply rejects the notion that "real" people can be apprehended without the assistance of these esthetic essences. Thus, conversely, as long as the eye-witness is imaginative enough he need not be hindered, like poor Lucius in the stable, by any merely physical bonds. Since we are all makers, he suggests, creating our lives as we go, there is no incompatability between the narrator as witness and the narrator as creator. Proust's esthetic enables the narrative artist to regain some of the ground he had lost when he abandoned his position as inspired bard for the more empirically oriented positions of eye-witness and *histor*. Few novelists have been able to work out so subtle an esthetic, however, and fewer still to generate so great a fictional edifice to embody and justify it. But other compromises have been developed in modern times.

One is the typical Conradian compromise, in which the eye-witness (Marlow) tells of a protagonist (Kurtz, Lord Jim) and attempts to understand the protagonist through an imaginative sharing of his experience. This has been a very fruitful device in modern fiction. The story of the protagonist becomes the outward sign or symbol of the inward story of the narrator, who learns from his imaginative participation in the other's experience. Since the imagination plays the central role, the factual or empirical aspect of the protagonist's life becomes subordinated to the narrator's understanding of it. Not what really happened but the meaning of what the narrator believes to have happened becomes the central preoccupation in this kind of narrative. Conrad's American followers have employed this mode of narration with some signal successes. Fitzgerald, Faulkner, and Warren have all worked variations on this basic tactic. In *The Great Gatsby*, Nick Carraway is the eye-witness to Gatsby's decline and fall, and he adds not merely circumstantiality to the narrative but understanding of the action which Gatsby himself could not provide. For American authors this sort of divided protagonist has been a great boon. The old tragic problem of presenting a character with enough crudeness for *hybris* and *hamartia* but enough sensitivity for ultimate discovery and self-understanding has always been a great one for the narrative artist. Because events in a play happen quickly, before our eyes, the sudden shifts of character from fool or brute or dupe to awareness or to that "ripeness" or "readiness" which, in tragedy, "is all" do not present the problems in consistency which shifts of the same nature present in the more continuous form of written narrative. Therefore, the division of protagonist into the simple, stark actor and the complex, sensitive sharer in the action solves for the novelist a great problem. Marlow can do the understanding for Kurtz or Jim; Carraway can do it for Gatsby; Jack Burden for Willie Stark in *All the King's Men;* and Quentin Compson and Shreve McCannon for Sutpen in Faulkner's *Absalom, Absalom!* Faulkner, more than any of these writers, has experimented with the eye-witness point of view. In his freest and most imaginative treatment of the problem he has simply ridden roughshod over the question of verisimilitude and presented characters like Jason Compson revealing themselves directly in a way which cannot be accounted for in realistic terms. To whom, under what circumstances, would Jason speak as he does? or Benjy? And in *As I Lay Dying* Faulkner even abandons any attempt to couch his characters' monologues in native idiom, but clothes all their speech with his own Faulknerian rhetoric.

The use of multiple narrators is another Conradian device which Faulkner adopted, with his own modifications, in *Absalom, Absalom!* Several points about this device should be noted. First, it was employed extensively by the Greek romancer Heliodorus and his European imitators (such as Mlle. de Scudéry). As narrators are multiplied, evidence becomes hearsay, empiricism becomes romance. The multiplication of narrators is characteristic of modern fictions which lean toward romance (as the fictions of Conrad, Faulkner, and Isak Dinesen clearly do); it is characteristic of earlier romantic novels of the Gothic variety, and of such a compromise between the novel and the Gothic tale as *Wuthering Heights.* The tendency of modern writers to multiply narrators or to circumvent the restrictions of empirical eye-witness narration are signs of the decline of "realism" as an esthetic force in narrative.

The multiplication of narrators has another interesting effect. It tends to place the primary narrator in the position of *histor*, seeking to find out the truth from the versions he is told, as Marlow does in *Lord Jim*. (The multiplication of eye-witness narrators is of course quite a different thing from the interlocking tale-tellers of frankly fictional narratives like Ovid's *Metamorphoses* or the *Arabian Nights*.) But even if the empirical posture of *histor* is retained for the primary narrator, in the modern fictions of Conrad or Faulkner emphasis will not be on factual truth but on truth of imagination. William Faulkner himself once indicated that in *Absalom, Absalom!* we move from the least reliable narration, that of Rosa Coldfield, the eye-witness, to the most reliable, that of Shreve and Quentin, who imagine those events for which they have no empirical evidence. In Conrad and Faulkner as in Proust, the superiority of imaginative truth over empirical truth is maintained.

Another variation on the basic device of the eye-witness narrator which has been exploited mainly in the modern novel is the device of the unreliable eye-witness. This device lends an especially ironical cast to an entire narrative, laying on readers a special burden of enjoyable ratiocination, as they seek to understand what the character telling the story cannot himself comprehend. Because of its intellectual possibilities, this has become a favorite device in didactic and satiric narratives such as *Castle Rackrent* and *Gulliver's Travels*. Picaresque narrative, in particular, easily accommodates satire based on the eye-witness narrator's inability to see or understand completely. The youthfulness of the picaro as narrator often aids in this process. When Smollett sends Roderick Random to the siege of Carthegena, Roderick's innocent attempt to justify the wisdom of his leaders operates ironically as satiric criticism of the British military mind. Similarly, the naïve Huck Finn can present damning criticism of Mississippi River folkways, which is all the more damning be-

cause of his apparent simplicity. By increasing or diminishing
the distance in time between the events in an eye-witness narrative and the supposed time of narration, an author can regulate
the quality of irony in the narrative. Pip in Dickens's *Great Expectations,* and George Ponderevo in Well's *Tono-Bungay* are both
eye-witness narrators, descendants of the picaresque type, as
softened from the Spanish originals by Le Sage and Smollett. But
Pip and Ponderevo tell their autobiographical tales with a mature
perspective on their deeds, opening an ironical gap between themselves as characters and themselves as narrators. Young picaros
who tell their stories without this temporal perspective tend to be
seen by the reader across the ironical gap. The reader gravitates
always to what seems the most trustworthy viewpoint, depending
on the criteria for trustworthiness which the narrative evokes. The
mature and sensible viewpoint of the narrator Pip in *Great Expectations* is shared easily by the reader, but the "sensible" views of
Lockwood and Nelly in *Wuthering Heights* do not seem to many
readers to be so adequate to the characters and events in that
story as Pip's view does to the story of *Great Expectations* or
Marlow's to the story of *Lord Jim.* More subtle variations on narrational unreliability are performed by such modern masters of
the technique as Gide and F. M. Ford. Gide in particular plays
with unreliability in *L'Immoraliste* and *La Porte étroite* and raises
it to the level of dominant principle in that esthetic tour de force
Les Faux-Monnayeurs, which is to the novel as Pirandello's *Six
Characters* is to the drama. In such works the ironic assurance of
a shared viewpoint is deliberately undercut, making the reader
not an accomplice to the ironic act but in part, at least, a victim
of it.

The unreliable or semi-reliable narrator in fiction is quite un-
characteristic of primitive or ancient narrative. The author of an
apologia is expected to be presenting himself in the best possible
light, and thus is to be taken *cum grano salis,* but the idea of
creating an unreliable fictional eye-witness is the sophisticated
product of an empirical and ironical age. Unreliability itself requires a fairly thoroughgoing conception of reliability before it

can be recognized and exploited in fiction. Its frequent use in modern fiction is also an aspect of the modern author's desire to make the reader participate in the act of creation. The Renaissance allegorist expected his readers to participate strenuously in his work, bringing all their learning and intellect to bear on his polysemous narrative. Similarly, the modern novelist often expects just such intense participation, but being empirically rather than metaphysically oriented he makes the great question that of what really happened inside and outside the characters he has presented; whereas the allegorists made the question of what these characters and events signified the primary question for their audience.

The eye-witness in narrative can be telling an ostensibly actual tale or a plainly made-up one. He can be protagonist or observer or both. He can be the inwardly directed autobiographer or the outwardly directed memoirist or both. He can be apologist or confessor or both. He can be limited to what his eyes have seen or he can supplement this by what as *histor* he can find out, or even by what he can confidently imagine. He may even dematerialize and become omniscient. He can be the repository of truth or be wholly or partially unreliable. He can report with perspective or immediacy or some compromise between the two. We must consider all these possibilities and more, not so as to devise new pigeonholes for narrative works, but so as to preserve our own flexibility of response to one of the most flexible aspects of the narrative art. The problem of point of view was largely neglected in literary criticism before the advent of Henry James. Since James a good deal has been written on the subject, often from an inadequate base of knowledge and understanding. On this subject, more than any other in the criticism of fiction, we must clear our minds of cant before approaching any literary work.

THE HISTOR AND OTHER NARRATIVE POSTURES

The *histor* is the narrator as inquirer, constructing a narrative on the basis of such evidence as he has been able to accumulate. The *histor* is not a character in narrative, but he is not exactly the author himself, either. He is a persona, a projection of the author's empirical virtues. Since Herodotus and Thucydides the *histor* has been concerned to establish himself with the reader as a repository of fact, a tireless investigator and sorter, a sober and impartial judge — a man, in short, of authority, who is entitled not only to present the facts as he has established them but to comment on them, to draw parallels, to moralize, to generalize, to tell the reader what to think and even to suggest what he should do. History from its beginning was closely allied with rhetoric, and the ancient *histor* knew that one of the first tasks of a speaker was to convince the audience of his authority and competence to deal with the subject at hand. The narrator as *histor* is a primary narrative ingredient of such novels as *Tom Jones, The Red and the Black, Vanity Fair, War and Peace,* and *Nostromo.*

The commentary, often labeled "intrusive," which is to be found in such works as these, is simply the *histor* going about his business. It is his business to be present whenever and wherever he wants to be, and to guide the reader's response to the events narrated. The *histor* has an ancient and natural affinity with his narrative predecessor, the inspired bard of Homeric epic. Because of the license afforded by his inspiration the bard was omniscient and could recount Hector's private thoughts before going into battle or private conversations between Helen and Paris. Herodotus, though distinguishing himself from the poets, did not hesitate to give us private conversation between Darius of Persia and his wife Atossa. But as history became more subject to empirical rigor in enlightened Europe, the historians had to part with the bardic privilege of omniscience. The novelists were quick to occupy the vacated narrative territory.

Henry Fielding in both *Joseph Andrews* and *Tom Jones* made it particularly plain that his narrator was modeling his authority on both that of the epic bard and that of the *histor.* This combination was of great importance for the history of the novel as a form. Fielding was not doing in these novels much more than

Cervantes had done in *Don Quixote*, in conflating a fictional and an empirical mode of narration, but his theoretical justifications of his practice have become major documents in the critical literature dealing with the novel. He called himself a historian and biographer, carefully distinguishing his narrative from traditional and fictional narratives such as the French imitations of Greek romance. He singled out for approval not only Cervantes but the French proto-realists of the late seventeenth and early eighteenth centuries: Scarron, Le Sage, and Marivaux. What is of great consequence for the novel is that, sharing as he did the new realistic spirit of his time, Fielding withstood the tendency of English empirical fiction to turn to eye-witness narration. We must remember that most of Defoe's, Richardson's, Sterne's, Smollett's and Fanny Burney's original fictions are cast in eye-witness form, either retrospective or the immediate form of letters and journals. (Smollett's justification for *not* using eye-witness form, in the opening chapter of *Ferdinand Count Fathom*, is less significant than the fact that he felt this practice needed justification.) Even Jane Austen's first essays toward *Sense and Sensibility* and *Pride and Prejudice* were apparently cast in the epistolary form. Fielding, the only really expert classicist in this gallery of early English novelists, preserved in the new English novel the elements of the *histor* and the bard of classical history and epic. To a certain extent he was merely following his continental predecessors: not only Cervantes but especially the narrator of Scarron's *Roman comique*. Still, his theoretical support for his practice and his enormous success in *Tom Jones* made his particular blend of *histor* and bard a major factor in English narrative and, via Byron and Stendhal, a factor in the great development of the European novel in the nineteenth century.

Fielding's narrative persona in *Tom Jones* and *Joseph Andrews* is not entirely an amalgam of *histor* and bard, however. Fielding also functions quite clearly as the maker of a purely fictitious narrative. In theory he has shifted the historical burden of his tale from the particular facts of person, place, and event to the

general facts of typical human nature. But in practice he sometimes adopts the role of *histor* (there are things he cannot find
out), of bard (he can reveal unspoken thoughts when he wants
to), and of maker (he admits he is making things up and brings
his artistic problems before the reader — as when he wonders
how he can rescue Tom Jones from jail and still not violate his
modern standards of probability). As maker he has authority over
his characters and can put them through their paces. As *histor* he
can only seek the truth. Like Cervantes, Fielding arranges to have
his empirical bread and eat his romantic cake, but he goes a step
farther and makes the reader not merely his accessory but his
accomplice. Later English novelists who have adopted Fielding's
posture of the narrator as maker — Thackeray, Trollope, and Meredith — have come in for some harsh criticism because of their
failure to play the game. The magician is not supposed to let the
audience see how he does his tricks. The novelist is not supposed
to call his characters puppets or pretend to bare his technical
problems through the narrator of the story. But it is quite all right
for him to call them *ficelles* in a preface and to impress the reader
there with the author's skill in solving problems. The assumption
that the reality of fiction depends on the reader's "belief" in it is
a highly dubious one. It is more likely that it depends on the complex interaction between the reader's partial belief and partial
disbelief. No one really believes in this age that a magician creates
an egg or a rabbit from nothing. We know it is a trick. Some
magicians acknowledge this as part of their performance and
some do not, but such acknowledgment is not the basis on which
we judge or enjoy them.

The great trick of modern literary magicians of the Jamesian
school is said to be the disappearance of the author. In English
fiction Henry James and James Joyce both adopted this as an aim,
having imbibed the notion from a reading of Flaubert's letters,
where it is written — and more than once — that the author
should be in his work like God in the universe: everywhere present but nowhere apparent. Joyce, the more precocious of the two

disciples, seems to have formulated his concept of the superiority of dramatic art over narrative quite early in his life — and then grown away from it. James, on the other hand, grew more and more preoccupied in his later works with making narrative art dramatic. Joyce began with a distinction among the three kinds of literary art: lyric, epic, and dramatic. He (or rather Stephen Dedalus) saw these three kinds of literary art as being arranged in an evolutionary order, reflecting the progress of the artist in refining himself out of existence in his art. In this view lyric art is the lowest kind because the most personal, and dramatic the highest because the most impersonal.

This conception of Joyce's may be useful, but it contains the seed of a confusion which has flowered in our day. Joyce's separation of the three kinds of art is not a *formal* one, though it unfortunately is presented as such. In reality it is possible for a narrative work to be lyric art. In Hemingway's *The Sun Also Rises*, for example, the artist, the narrator, and the protagonist are almost united and certainly share the same viewpoint on the action and the same attitude toward it. It is also possible — and much more usual, in fact — for a narrative work to be dramatic art. In Robert Penn Warren's *All the King's Men* the narrator makes it clear that he is a very different man from the man he was when the events narrated were actually taking place; and, of course, Jack Burden the character and Jack Burden the narrator are both very different from the artist Warren. But the confusion between the actual stage-drama and what Joyce called dramatic art still persists.

Henry James is responsible for a share of this confusion. He sought to translate the formal qualities of stage-drama to the novel in a similar attempt to refine the artist out of the art. For him this was undoubtedly the right method. But he explained and defended his method in prefaces which have become a powerful critical force today. The disciples of the master have collected and annotated his critical remarks and erected from them a system of rules, dealing primarily with the management of point of view, by which they propose to judge all narrative writing. But they are building on a very shaky foundation. The confusion between dramatic art and dramatic form is based on a confusion between the artist who is to be refined away and the narrator who is distinct from the artist and vital to narrative method. This confusion is both Jamesian and Joycean. But it was James who insisted on submerging the narrator in a character called the "central intelligence" in the belief that this was the most dramatic way of telling a story, while Joyce, though he often let his characters' thoughts speak for themselves, was capable of brilliant feats of truly narrative art, such as the "Cyclops" episode in *Ulysses*. We are often told that Joyce represents a dead end in the art of fiction. Actually, the influence of James, should it prevail, would be much more pernicious; for the Jamesian method leads inevitably to the death of narrative art by a kind of artistic suicide. The narrator is to eliminate himself for the good of his art.

The narrator who is neither *histor* nor eye-witness, and refuses the privileges of bard and maker, the self-effacing Jamesian narrator, may be termed the recorder. The impersonal, invisible creature who narrates a story like Hemingway's "Hills Like White Elephants" is a recorder, and so is the narrator of James's *The Spoils of Poynton*. Yet the difference between these two narrative essences is very great. James and Hemingway write in two of the most distinctive of English prose styles. In a Hemingway story not only the invisible narrator but the characters as well speak and think in that distinctive language, Hemingwayese. In a Jamesian novel all the language is annihilated to Jamesian thoughts in a Jamesian shade. The result of the disappearance of the narrator is not the refining away of the artist but a continual reminder of his presence — as if God were omnipresent and invisible, yet one could continually hear Him breathing.

James, in particular, complicated his problems in narration by refusing to resort to traditional narrative prerogatives. He not only would not comment in the manner of the *histor;* he accepted the constricting limits of the eye-witness point of view, which narrators since Apuleius had sought to circumvent, and accepted it without the compensating gain in verisimilitude of direct reporting. Joyce, it is true, did not really begin to exploit the purely narrational aspects of his medium until *Ulysses;* but in that work he felt free to present his characters' thought in interior monologue when he wanted to and to adopt in addition the greatest variety of narrative postures ever before assumed in a single literary work. Who wrote the headlines for "Aeolus"? Who asks the questions in "Ithaca," and who answers? Whose narrative excrescences are superimposed on the barfly's narration in "Cyclops"? Whose is the saccharine prose of "Nausicaa"? Who parodies all English prose styles in "Oxen of the Sun"? Whose enervated sentences limp and dawdle through "Eumaeus"? Joyce's narrator is a chameleon, always adapting himself to the situation, but not, like the real chameleon, merely for concealment. Joyce's various narrational postures are designed to exploit his material. Proust, in his great work, took the opposite direction from Joyce and accommodated everything to his single narrator. Marcel's ruminative narration, reminiscent at times of George Eliot's, is just as all-including as Joyce's. Time and space filter freely through his mind. Proust takes advantage of all the traditional narrative prerogatives. His narrator comments, he reveals the inner life, he presents as eye-witness both scenes he has attended and scenes he has not. Henry James can be seen as standing between the titans, Joyce and Proust, and making the least of both their worlds. Like Joyce, he does not intrude in his own person into the narrative, but the ineluctable rigidity of his style makes him always visible. He wears only one mask, and that one looks exactly like his face. Like Proust he filters his story through a central consciousness, but unlike Proust he anchors that consciousness in time and space, sacrificing huge areas of life to his desire for neatness. That his achievement, real and fine as it is, was made in the face of all his self-imposed restrictions is ample testimony to his literary skills. Our intention here is not to belittle those skills or that achievement but to indicate the way in which James's influence tends to run counter to the whole flow of narrative, creating not a wave of the future in narrative but a momentary eddy on the surface of narrative history.

The influence of James and his disciples on the criticism of fiction is not hard to explain. Like the French dramatic critics of the seventeenth century, they had apparently reduced to rules an essentially unruly art form. But unity of point of view is unlikely to stand up under such onslaughts as Joyce's and Proust's, any more than the dramatic unities could survive the growing prestige of Shakespeare. Criticism can never reduce art to rules. Its aim should be not to enact legislation for artists but to promote understanding of works of art.

THE CONCEPT OF OMNISCIENCE

We have been considering the *histor* and related narrative postures together with the Jamesian attack on omniscience. The kind of omniscient narration that James and his followers (especially Percy Lubbock in the influential *Craft of Fiction*) have attacked is that blend of bard, *histor*, and maker which characterizes the narrative voice in *War and Peace* and the similar voices of *Middlemarch, The Red and the Black, Vanity Fair,* and *Tom Jones.* But "omniscience" itself is not a descriptive term so much as a definition based on the presumed analogy between the novelist as creator and the Creator of the cosmos, an omniscient God. The analogy has a certain obvious relevance which has enabled it to maintain currency as a term in literary discussion. But it also, like most analogies, operates so as to prevent our seeing certain aspects of the thing analogized. In the case of omniscient narration in the novel, the analogy obscures an important duality in the fictional device. Omniscience includes the related god-like attribute of omnipresence. God *knows* everything because He *is* everywhere — simultaneously. But a narrator in fiction is imbedded in a time-bound artifact. He does not "know" simultaneously but consecutively. He is not everywhere at once but now here, now there, now looking into this mind or that, now moving on to other vantage points. He is time-bound and space-bound as God is not. Thus the narrator of the Tolstoyan kind is partly defined by his employment of a variety of separable perspectives, an attribute we may call his *multifariousness*. He is also defined by his resolution of those perspectives into a single, authoritative vision. Whereas, we conceive of God's omniscience and His omnipresence as being functions of an indivisible quality of godliness, we can separate the omniscient narrator in fiction into a multifarious element and a monistic element. The multiple perceptions of this kind of narrator coalesce into a single reality, a single truth.

The Jamesian attack on omniscience deals with these two attributes of the Tolstoyan mode of narration in somewhat different ways. James favors a single perspective over multiple perspectives, and he further insists that this single perspective be that of a character who is inside the frame of the action rather than that of a disembodied presence who addresses the reader from outside the action. James and Lubbock couch their criticism of these two attributes of Tolstoyan narration in a terminology that is purely esthetic. To employ more perspectives than are necessary for the "treatment of the subject" is seen by them as an artistic failure. (This judgment is probably itself based on an analogy with the logical principle known as Occam's razor, which assigns a superior validity to the simpler of two arguments.) And to resolve whatever perspectives are employed outside the frame of the action in some narrative persona is seen as a failure to dramatize, a reliance on telling rather than showing. Drama is showing, narration is telling; James's preference leads him in an inevitable circle to the point of condemning the narrative part of narrative literature. This purely esthetic argument can be met on its own grounds and has been effectively disposed of by Wayne Booth in *The Rhetoric of Fiction*. But James's instinctive withdrawal from the fully omniscient posture can be justified to some extent by arguments which he and Lubbock avoided because they were not esthetic, not matters of the craft of fiction.

We have suggested that James's avoidance of the multifarious
aspect of omniscience was in some sense idiosyncratic, an elevation of his personal preferences and limitations into a principle of
art. But his suspicion of the monistic and authoritative aspect of
omniscience is another affair altogether. A cogent justification
for James's reaction to this aspect of omniscience can be made,
though not without leaving the realm of esthetics, a departure he
would doubtless deplore. Esthetic criticism tends to separate the
artifact from its attendant circumstances: to see the artist as
making choices governed by artistic principles only, to see the
artist's *milieu* as providing raw material, perhaps, but not as influencing the artist's esthetic choices. This means that the closer a
particular art form is connected to its *milieu*, the less effective a
purely esthetic criticism can be in dealing with that form. Hence
the intractability of the realistic novel in the hands of esthetic
critics, and hence the hostility of the nineteenth-century esthetes
to realism as a literary mode. The configurations of the various
kinds of narrative art which have been associated to some extent
with the empirical impulse — from the epic to the novel — have
always been influenced by cultural conditions intruding into the
area of esthetic choices. This has been one of the great problems
and one of the great glories of narrative art, and it has been the
distinguishing feature of the novel. Just as the narrative device
of the eye-witness narrator is characteristic of picaresque and its
attendant forms of simple realism, the device of the omniscient
narrator — bard, maker, but mainly *histor* — is characteristic of
complex realism. These two novelistic strands interlock in their
historical development, but the simple, reliable eye-witness dominates realism from *Lazarillo* into the eighteenth century, and the
complex, omniscient *histor,* foreshadowed by Cervantes and
Fielding, belongs to the age of Hegel and Spengler — the nineteenth century. The tendency of modern novelists to shy away
from full omniscience in one direction or another is no more an
esthetic matter than these other historical developments in the
narrative tradition. It is tied to certain changes in the entire cul-

tural climate which have made some facets of this nineteenth-century device untenable in the twentieth century.

To understand more clearly what facets of omniscience have become untenable, and why they have become so, we must do two things. We must inquire a little more closely into the nature of point of view itself, especially to note what aspects of it are not susceptible to treatment as mere esthetic devices or tools of art; and we must take note of certain broad cultural developments which impinge on these non-esthetic aspects of point of view. First, as to the nature of point of view itself, we can observe that it is not the same thing for the creator and the beholder. If we think of a generalized "novelist" and his equally generalized "reader" we can see that, for the novelist, point of view is the primary way he controls and shapes his materials. Once made, his choice of point of view and the mode of language appropriate to it will influence his presentation of character, incident, and every other thing represented. For the reader, however, point of view is not an esthetic matter but a mode of perception. The point of view in a given novel controls the reader's impression of everything else. We do not perceive a novel with our eyes. The eye sees only the printer's inked shapes on the page. Yet a story impinges on our consciousness as a totality, with sights, sounds, smells, tastes, and feelings somehow smuggled into us through those inked shapes, and released into our perception without having passed through our sensory organs in the normal way. The ordering of this perceptive data in our consciousness is not controlled by our organs or by our will. We do not, in reading, create a story within ourselves. The story takes the shape its author has given it, a shape governed for us primarily by the point of view through which the characters and events are filtered. Because narrative point of view is so intimately and dynamically bound up with the reader's perception, it cannot be dealt with as a merely esthetic matter. Just as psychological knowledge impinges on the novelist's choices and the reader's expectations with regard to characterization, epistemological knowledge and notions about how we perceive and what we perceive inevitably impinge, for writer and reader, on the question of point of view. And the more realistic or representational a work is, the more insistent these non-esthetic pressures will be. The novelist, with his strong representational bias, is more at the mercy of the Time Spirit in these matters than most other literary artists.

The whole movement of mind in Western culture from the Renaissance to the present — the very movement which spawned the novel and elevated it to the position of the dominant literary form — has been a movement away from dogma, certainty, fixity, and all absolutes in metaphysics, in ethics, and in epistemology. The new philosophical realism, so closely connected with the rise of the novel (as Ian Watt has shown), has led inevitably to a cultural climate we may call relativism. In invoking "relativity" we need not lean too hard on Einstein's physics, which might prove a slender reed since even scientific knowledge is now generally conceived of as temporary and relative truth. For not only the physicists but all our non-literary sources of knowledge and understanding, which is to say the natural and social sciences with philosophy and theology trailing along behind, have led us to see truth, beauty, and goodness as relative rather than absolute matters. (The very words truth, beauty, and goodness seem old-fashioned in their claims to universality.) And the novel, as a major literary source of understanding, has played a vital role in the general movement, particularly in calling into question categorical imperatives which society seeks to impose on the ethical behavior of individuals.

With this broad cultural development in mind, we can see how the authoritarian monism of the fully omniscient mode of narration has become less and less tenable in modern times, while the multifarious relativism of that same mode has seemed increasingly appropriate. When James spoke, in his narrowly esthetic terminology, of bringing the point of view inside the frame of the action for dramatic reasons, he was arguing a weak case. The narrator does not need to be dramatized for the modern audience so much as he needs to be relativized. A narrator who is not in some way suspect, who is not in some way subject to ironic scrutiny is what the modern temper finds least bearable. It is not the narrator's narrating that disturbs the modern reader, nor his employment of multiple perspectives. We are willing to let Ford's Dowell or Conrad's Marlow or Faulkner's Quentin or Proust's Marcel go on and on, because all their attempts to resolve the multifarious facets of their tales are performed before our eyes. In this kind of fiction the author has not disappeared. He is often highly visible behind his surrogate. But by giving himself a fictional shape he has entered the ironic gap, which now lies not between author or narrator and characters but between limited understanding which is real, and an ideal of absolute truth which is itself suspect. This irony cuts in two directions simultaneously. The reader who tries to reduce a story like *The Good Soldier* to a single, absolute meaning becomes himself a victim of one blade of this irony. His only other choice is to accept a limited resolution of the work's meaning, holding part of this meaning in his mind as an unresolvable ambiguity — which is to enter the ironic gap, shake hands with Dowell and say, "I don't know either."

If Ford's way is one modern solution to the problem of point of view, Joyce's in *Ulysses* is another. The threads of his multifariousness lead out of the story, beyond the frame, but they are not held by a single authoritative hand. Unlike Thackeray's puppets in *Vanity Fair,* the marionette figures of *Ulysses* call into being whatever manipulators they need to put them through their paces, and no one is there to put them back in their box at the end of the show. By abandoning the old authoritative devices of narration the modern novelists drive themselves to new strategems, discover new possibilities in their art. This is not necessarily progress. It is simply a change as necessary and desirable as abandoning a played out mineral vein and digging somewhere else. Digging, of course, is not mining. It is more exciting, often, but not always as rewarding. But we need not choose between Tolstoy's way and Joyce's or Proust's. If the modern novelists seem to us to have reached a profitable vein of art, this does not mean that the achievements of George Eliot necessarily turn to dross. To condemn the great nineteenth-century realists for being so certain, so monistic in their omniscience would be as absurd as to condemn Dante for believing in a peculiarly medieval version of God. One reason we value works not immediately of our time or place is because of the way their vision differs from ours. They help to release us from the perceptual prison of our culture.

Yet to attack the modern writers for their relativistic fragmentation of the cosmos, for the irony and ambiguity which shape their fictions — as Wayne Booth has done in *The Rhetoric of Fiction* — is to betray nostalgia for a time when one was assured of certain certainties. It is to condemn modern literature for its ineluctable modernity. Such a condemnation is typical of that criticism which sees art in a narrow esthetic way, as a timeless field where every esthetic choice is open to every artist. Whereas, in practice all esthetic choices are conditioned by cultural factors which vary from one time and place to another. The neo-Aristotelian critics understand well the concept of genre. They would not blame a satire for not being a lyric. But they often seem less certain in their grasp of temporal and cultural conditions; their focus on the power of genre often leads them to neglect the pressure of history on an author's use of a genre. The artist, in other words, can only choose from what is available to him, and this is a matter partly of literary tradition and partly of moment and *milieu*. Greater sensitivity to these conditioning factors might prevent many a critic from elevating his private "I don't like it" into a categorical "It's no good." But such sensitivity need not inhibit criticism altogether. Even in this very matter of omniscient point of view, it should be possible to be both sensitive and critical. In fact, it should be quite appropriate for modern criticism to condemn a spurious omniscience in the contemporary novel as an empty imitation of an outmoded posture; or to focus on other failures to solve the constantly changing problem of point of view in modern fiction, such as the lifelong trouble D. H. Lawrence had with control of point of view, from the disastrous bungling of *The White Peacock* on through his finest novels. This problem in Lawrence's work is a function of his attempt to be rebel, prophet, and artist, attacking the old verities but accepting the notion of verity and offering new truths for old in narrative form. Thus he insists on omniscience in a world where omniscience is an anachronism. His art and his ethos converge and conflict in the handling of point of view. It is his weakest point, opening structural flaws in most of his long works which only his great skill with the texture of language could make tolerable. He fought with the Time Spirit, insisting on using esthetic materials which were not truly usable, and the Time Spirit was revenged by the failure of the tools. In an age of relativity the absolute posture of omniscience is likely to succeed only in a deliberately anachronistic work like *The Sot-Weed Factor,* or in works which otherwise abandon the novel's traditional empirical and representational predilections.

Having come so far, it might seem appropriate at this point to shift our attention from the recent past to the immediate contemporary scene, and even perhaps to cast a critical glance in the direction of the future. But to consider the contemporary scene with any justice to its complexity would require another work as long as this; and to consider the future would be to indulge in what Aristotle called deliberative rhetoric, leading us, ironically, into that legislative role which we have ourselves condemned as inappropriate for criticism. Still, there is one aspect of the contemporary scene so closely connected to our consideration of point of view and so likely to affect the future of narrative art that we must not close without mentioning it. The most powerful influence on contemporary narrative art is not esthetic or even cultural in any broad sense. The Time Spirit has quickened its music; the tradition's evolutionary dance has become almost frantic, with styles succeeding one another in a hectic confusion, paralleling the proliferation of styles in the visual arts. The novelistic union of the various conflicting strands of narrative is beginning to crumble as the crucial concept of realism loses its vitality. These are significant processes and could be investigated at length, but they are perhaps less important than a technological change which may leave a mark on the narrative tradition as profound as the invention of letters itself. We refer to the invention of the motion-picture film with its attendant devices of synchronous sound track and videotape, and with its flexible means of presentation in theater or home, direct or via television.

That the film is primarily narrative rather than dramatic in form may not be immediately obvious. We suggest that it is a form of narrative rather than dramatic art because it does not present a story directly, without narration, but always through the medium of a controlled point of view, the eye of the camera, which sharpens or blurs focus, closes up or draws off, gives the image its color and shading, and provides, through its synchronous sound track, a continuous commentary of words, music, noise or silence, along with the voices of the dramatis personae. To understand how the camera-projector point of view distinguishes film from stage drama, the reader need only remind himself of the difference between attending a football or baseball game in person and watching one on television. In the stadium the spectator responds to the total scene unfolding before him. His eye looks where it will, at whatever aspect of the scene catches its notice. But the televised game is seen through the camera eye, with its long shots and close-ups, the vocal commentary of the announcer, the time dislocation of the video-tape replay with its shifts in point of view. Sport is not art, of course, but we apprehend it either as drama or narrative, depending on whether we observe it directly or perceive it through a medium which filters it through a point of view.

Film form, then, is narrative, but the movie theater often competes directly with the stage play for the consumer's attention and financial support. Both play and book have much to fear from this new arrival on the literary scene, not merely in the competition for viewers and readers, but more importantly in the competition for artists. The great artistic question of "What next?", which the acceleration of tradition has made so overwhelming in the older literary forms, is an open invitation, a blank check, in the field of cinema. Whether the poet of the film plunders the older forms to feed his new medium, as Shakespeare and his contemporaries plundered chronicle and romance for plots, or simply allows this new technique to generate new kinds of story, just as the invention of writing helped to generate the complex romance plot, the new form offers open doors where the old has little left but mirrored walls. As in the early days of writing when bard and scribe existed side by side, we now have books and plays and films all apparently co-existing peacefully. But book and play are lambs co-existing with a lion cub that is just beginning to find its strength. The old MGM lion roaring so complacently under the battle cry of Gautier and the esthetes — *ars gratia artis* — used to seem an accidental irony, more joke than threat. But as the cinema begins to find artists like Renoir, Bergman, Truffaut, Resnais, Fellini, and Antonioni, we begin to see jest turn into prophecy before our astonished eyes. Thus we must face the possibility that book-narrative may dwindle to a rare and minor art. The monuments of the past will remain, as Homeric epic remains, to remind us of a vanished literary medium. But the older forms of story-telling, including the great achievements of the novel's golden age — the nineteenth century — may cease to be viable for the practitioners of narrative. It seems heretical now, or visionary, to suggest that written narrative may become, quite literally, a thing of the past. But so, in a very real sense, it may. The oral poet survives today in every travelling salesman who tells a traditional dirty joke. But this is a far cry from Homer. Intellectual prose and journalism will no doubt survive for ages. But the main impetus of narrative art may well pass from the book to the cinema, even as it passed from the oral poet to the book-writer long ago. Truly, all things flow. In no area is this more true than in the world of narrative literature. Both the lyric and the drama, perhaps because they are more perfect forms, have not changed greatly since Sappho and

Sophocles. But narrative literature is the most restless of forms, driven by its imperfections and inner contradictions to an unceasing search for an unattainable ideal. It is this terribly human struggle that makes the study of narrative art the most fascinating of literary studies.

8

Narrative Theory, 1966–2006: A Narrative

Focalization, prolepsis, analepsis homodiegetic, heterodiegetic, intradiegetic (are we having fun yet?), heteroglossia, the narrative audience, tensions and instabilities, disclosure functions, character zones, fuzzy temporality. Who else is ready to cry, "Hold, enough!"?

I begin with this eclectic and incomplete litany of terms introduced by narrative theorists over the last forty years in order, first, to indicate that narrative theory has been advancing on a number of fronts, and, second, to acknowledge that the large Terminological Beastie looming over the field is likely to be intimidating to the nonspecialist. My goal here is to do justice to the advances most relevant to *The Nature of Narrative*'s focus on literary narrative while keeping the Beastie at bay. Rather than proceeding through an inventory of narratological neologisms or even through an analysis of the interrelations between the history of critical theory and the study of narrative over the last forty years, I shall, in effect, construct a three-part narrative: a big picture account of major trends in the field, followed by a more detailed telling about work on elements of narrative, and then, finally, a brief look at the current scene. More specifically, Part One will (1) consider the expansion of narrative theory's focus over the past forty years—from literary narrative to narrative *tout court*—and the implications of that expansion for the study of literary narrative; and (2) describe three prominent general conceptions of narrative during this period: narrative as formal system, narrative as ideological instrument, and narrative as rhetoric. These conceptions authorize different theoretical and interpretive projects, though both the conceptions and the projects also overlap and influence each other at times. In a sense, this discussion will be an update of Scholes and Kellogg's chapter on Meaning. Part Two will then consider how these conceptions of narrative have influenced work on the three elements of narrative treated by Scholes and Kellogg: plot, character, and point of view—a topic I will modify to the broader category of narrative discourse. Part Three will briefly sketch some especially significant issues being addressed in current narrative theory.

Although this piece has minimal, or what Brian McHale might call "weak," narrativity, I deliberately refer to it as a narrative because I want to call attention to what I hope is a productive tension in it. On the one hand, the conventions of the genre dictate that this survey of scholarship be told from a perspective of Godlike omniscience. On the other hand, any narrative theorist with even a smidgen of self-awareness could not undertake such a survey without being acutely aware of all the selection it entails and the yawning gap between his own limited perspective and God's. In order to reflect this tension without making it dominate my discussion, I will observe the conventions of the genre but punctuate that observance with occasional reminders that I am writing only one of the many plausible narratives about the relation between narrative and narrative theory since 1966.[1]

PART 1: FOUR PROTAGONISTS AND MANY MORE PLOTS

I circulate endlessly throughout cultures and am invoked in countless claims—I explain experience; I frame beliefs, opinions, worldviews; I am central to the concept of identity; I am This, I am That, and I am most certainly the Other. I have become, to use a word favored by one of the great modernist practitioners of my art, a veritable avatar of postmodern identity.

Protagonist I: The Object of Study

We are living in the age of the Narrative Turn, an era when narrative is widely celebrated and studied for its ubiquity and importance. Doctors, lawyers, psychologists, business men and women, politicians, and political pundits of all stripes are just a few of the groups who now regard narrative as the Queen of Discourses and an essential component of their work. These groups acknowledge narrative's power to capture certain truths and experiences in ways that other modes of explanation and analysis such as statistics, descriptions, summaries, and reasoning via conceptual abstractions cannot. Phrases such as "narrative explanation," "narrative understanding," "narrative as a way of thinking," and "narrative identity" have become common currency in conversations inside and outside the academy. To take just one prominent example, after the 2004 presidential election in the United States, Democratic politicians contended that their candidate John Kerry lost to George W. Bush because Kerry failed to articulate his vision for an improved America in a clear and persuasive narrative.

As a result of the Narrative Turn, narrative theory now takes as its objects of study narrative of all kinds occurring in all kinds of media throughout history: personal, political, historical, legal, and medical narratives, to name just a few—in their ancient, medieval, early modern, modern, and postmodern guises, and in their oral, print, visual (film, sculpture, painting, performance), digital, and multi-media formats. In this way, narrative theory has gone much further down the road that Scholes and Kellogg travelled in 1966. While they persuasively located the then dominant object of narrative study, the novel, within a much broader history and understanding of literary narrative, contemporary narrative theory now locates literary narrative within a much broader conception of narrative itself. This change has two main consequences for the study of literary narrative. (1) Theories derived from a focus on literary narrative, including theories about plot, character, and narrative discourse, have a potentially greater significance even as they are subject to a more rigorous scrutiny. Such theories can contribute substantially to the conversation about how and why narrative is such a distinctive and powerful mode for explaining experience and organizing knowledge. But such theories are also subject to the test of whether they apply only to the special case of literary narrative. (2) Theories developed in connection with other kinds of narrative can cast new light on literary narrative, whether by highlighting similarities, emphasizing differences, or leading to revised understandings of literary narrative itself.

Protagonist II: Narrative as Formal System

Rules rule, but sometimes I rue rules; they make me feel cabin'd, cribbed, confined—framed.

Around the time that Scholes and Kellogg were completing the first edition, the rise of structuralism in France gave birth to the dream of a comprehensive description of narrative as a formal system on the model of a grammar. Although this dream never became a reality, structuralist narratology produced many valuable insights and fashioned many long-lasting tools for the study of narrative. In addition, structuralist narratology—now often called classical narratology—has provided a starting point for much subsequent narrative theory, even when that theory seeks to go in directions the structuralists would neither have anticipated nor approved. In particular, today's vibrant and still developing approach of cognitive narratology, while often noting its differences from structuralist narratology, shares the same goal of developing a comprehensive formal account of the nature of narrative. While classical narratology took structural linguistics as its model and therefore conceived of its desired formal system as a grammar, cognitive narratology is a more multi-disciplinary endeavor, and it conceives of its formal system as the components of the mental models that narratives depend on in their production and consumption. The most substantial contribution of structuralist narratology has been to the study of narrative discourse, especially through Gérard Genette's book *Narrative Discourse: An Essay in Method*, which I will discuss in some detail in the section on narrative discourse. Here I will focus on the larger context of the structuralist movement and sketch some of the similarities and differences between structuralist and cognitivist conceptions of narrative as a formal system.

Structuralism's first principle is that meaning-making is a rule-governed activity. Consequently, it seeks to identify the underlying rules—the codes and conventions—of the various domains of meaning-making (e.g., literature, fashion, even a specific culture). Structuralism's second principles are that language is the prototype of all sign systems and that, therefore, its disciplinary model should be linguistics. More specifically, the structuralists' approach to narrative, which Tzvetan Todorov labelled *narratologie* in his 1969 *Grammaire du Décaméron* is founded primarily on the structural linguistics of Ferdinand de Saussure and to a lesser extent on the work in poetics of the Russian Formalists.[2] Just as Saussure distinguished between the formal system of language (*langue*) and individual utterances (*parole*), so, too, the structuralists distinguish between identifying the formal system of narrative (its grammar or poetics) and the task of interpreting specific narratives. And just as Saussure's project was to analyze the components of the langue and the relationships among them, the main interest of the structuralists is to identify the basic elements of narrative and the relationships among them. Their goal in other words is a descriptive grammar of narrative, not a method for interpreting individual narratives (though a descriptive poetics inevitably has implications for interpretation).

An influential precursor of structuralist narrative theory is Vladimir Propp's *Morphology of the Folktale* (1928), a study of the common elements of a large corpus of Russian folktales. Saussure, Propp, and the classical narratologists all rely in their different ways on Saussure's distinction between rules of selection (paradigmatic rules) and rules of combination (syntagmatic rules). Paradigmatic rules stipulate, for example, that to find a subject for a sentence, we must choose from the set of nouns or noun phrases in the lexicon of the language, and to find a predicate we must choose from the set of verbs or verb phrases in that lexicon. Syntagmatic rules then stipulate (a) that the combination of subjects and predicates make sentences, and (b) which noun phrases can grammatically combine with which verb phrases. Thus, the sentence "the have is on the mat" does not form a grammatical sentence because it violates paradigmatic rules; the sentence "the mat the cat on sat ripped got up" does not form a grammatical sentence because it violates syntagmatic rules; and all the sentences in this edition of *The Nature of Narrative* (presumably) are grammatical because they observe both rules.

Propp's analysis of his corpus identifies the underlying paradigmatic and syntagmatic rules governing the Russian folktale. He finds that all the tales are built out of a small number of underlying character roles (Hero, Helper, Donor, Villain, and so on) that are themselves elements in 31 basic events (e.g., the Hero discovers a lack; the Hero is tested). What's more, although not all 31 events are in every folktale, they always occur in the same order. Thus, each of the 31 events represents a paradigmatic class, and their invariant order is testimony to the syntagmatic rules for their combination.

As we'll see below, Propp's study influenced structuralist ideas about both character and plot, but the structuralists also remain aware that the Russian folktale is a special rather than an archetypal case of narrative. More generally, their attention to the relation between paradigmatic and syntagmatic rules, to the Russian formalist distinction between *fabula* (the chronological order of a narrative's events) and *sjuzhet* (the order in which a narrative represents those events), and to a broader corpus of narratives than Propp's Russian folktales leads them to develop their most enduring insight: the distinction between the what and the how of narrative, which they labelled story (*récit*) and discourse (*discours*). In one sense the basic insight, though not articulated by the structuralists in this way, is that the Russian folktales are not typical but anomalous in presenting their events in an invariant order, because the rules for combining the selected events of a narrative turn out to be extraordinarily flexible. Genette's work on temporality, which I discuss below, can be understood as an account of the principles underlying these flexible combinations.

The story/discourse distinction is fundamental to narratology because it allows for (a) two distinct groupings of narrative elements with events, character, and setting (or alternatively, events and existents) under story and all the devices for presenting these elements under discourse; (b) a recognition that the relations between the elements of the two groups can vary widely from narrative to narrative; and (c) the comparison of versions of a single narrative across different media (what changes primarily in a narrative's move from one medium to another is discourse rather than story). In characterizing the story/discourse distinction as structuralism's most enduring insight, I do not mean to suggest that the distinction has never been questioned or contested. In fact, in the United States structuralism was followed so closely by post-structuralism that the move of deconstructing binary oppositions quickly became a habit.[3] Among the most intriguing such deconstructions of the story/discourse distinction is that proposed by Jonathan Culler. Culler argues that narrative has a double logic—a logic of action in the story and a logic of theme, genre, well-formedness in the discourse—and that attending to this double logic undoes the apparent priority of story over discourse. Do the lovers in romantic comedy get married because of their own actions or because the demands of thematic and generic coherence require them to? In Sophocles's *Oedipus*, Culler contends, Oedipus is considered guilty of killing Laius not because there is incontrovertible proof in the story but because the logic of the discourse requires that he be seen as fulfilling the prophecy that he would. In a historical rather than a deconstructive argument, Harry Shaw maintains that the absolute demarcation of story and discourse into separate spheres leads to a theory that is not able to describe adequately the role of narrators in the Victorian novel. In *Living to Tell About It* (2005) I argue that the distinction is better understood as a helpful heuristic than a rigid boundary between the elements of narrative. But none of these quarrels dislodges the story/discourse distinction from its useful place in narrative theory, and, indeed, each one recognizes the value of the distinction as at least a starting point for thinking about narrative as a formal system.

Cognitive narratology takes classical narratology's fundamental question, what are the underlying rules of narrative's textual system?, and revises it to ask, what are the mental tools, processes, and activities that make possible our ability to construct and understand narrative? In addition, cognitive narratology focuses on narrative itself as a tool of understanding, that is, on how narrative contributes to human beings' efforts to structure and make sense of their experiences. Thus, rather than taking structural linguistics as its disciplinary model, cognitive narratology draws on ideas from cognitive science, including (cognitive) linguistics, cognitive, evolutionary and social psychology, philosophy of mind, and other domains. In one of its variants, cognitive narratology emphasizes the importance of frames (or schemata) and scripts for both authors and audiences. Frames are general concepts that we employ as brackets or boundaries around experiences in order to be able to understand them better. Scripts are recurring patterns or sequences of action. Thus, frames refer to our knowledge of general domains of experience, while scripts refer to our knowledge of common scenarios or sequences of events within those domains. For example, when we enter a gourmet restaurant we employ a different frame from the one we employ when we enter a hardware store or even a fast food restaurant. We are able to order a meal in the gourmet restaurant and to purchase a tool in the hardware store because we know the relevant scripts. Frames provide conventional, default knowledge, which narratives can activate and then complicate by deviating from the standard models. As a relatively new field, cognitive narratology is still formulating and testing its proposals, but Monika Fludernik in *Towards a "Natural" Narratology* (1996) and David Herman in *Story Logic* (2002) present two valuable versions of cognitive narrative theory.

Fludernik argues for a broad theory of narrative that relies on the interrelations among three kinds of cognitive frames: (1) the ones we use for understanding conversational narrative, including our concern with their tellability and point; (2) the ones that follow from our experience of embodiedness in the natural world—what she calls experientiality; and (3) the ones that we use to "naturalize" or recuperate within a larger explanatory scheme initially puzzling textual data. Fludernik coins the terms "narrativize" and "narrativization" to refer to how readers naturalize texts by the use of narrative schemata. Among the many suggestive consequences of Fludernik's approach is its conception of narrativity (that which makes a text a narrative rather than something else) as grounded not in the presence of a teller and a sequence of events but rather in our embodied experience of the world, what she calls experientiality. Consequently, Fludernik puts greater emphasis on some standard elements of narrative and de-emphasizes others. Human protagonists who act and think are essential to narrative, but action sequences leading to a clear endpoint are not. The frame provided by our embodiedness makes acting and thinking crucial activities, while the frame of narrativization allows us to impose narrative schemata even on representations of consciousness that do not lead to any change in that consciousness or to any other traditional marker of narrativity. In this way, Fludernik moves away from a view of narrative as adequately grounded in the story/discourse distinction and toward one that emphasizes the importance of experientiality and the active role of the audience in framing a text as narrative.

In *Story Logic* Herman offers a different vision of a cognitively based narrative theory, one that emphasizes what he calls the storyworld. For Herman narrative analysis seeks to illuminate "the process by which interpreters reconstruct the storyworlds encoded in narratives" and by storyworlds he means "mental models of who did what to and with whom, when, where and why in what fashion in the world to which recipients relocate . . . as they work to comprehend a narrative" (5). He then divides his inquiry into detailed accounts of the principles underlying what he calls the "microdesigns" and the "macrodesigns" of storyworlds, by which he means the local and the global strategies of constructing and understanding such worlds. Microdesigns include our ability to sort textual data into states, events, and actions, our ability to apply scripts to action sequences, our ability to recognize the various roles that characters play in those sequences, and our ability to process dialogue. Macrodesigns include

our ability to conceptualize narrative temporality, space, and perspective as well as to anchor the storyworld in a particular context.
As even this brief summary suggests, Herman is more willing to
work with the story/discourse distinction and its division of elements
than Fludernik, but what emerges from Herman's analysis is a revi-
sionary account of just about every element in the standard inventory of a narrative's parts. I will have more to say about some specifics
of Fludernik's and Herman's theories when I turn to the elements
of narrative.

Protagonist III: Narrative as Ideological Instrument

*I am political and—or is it "because"?— personal. I reflect and trans-
form the social order. I interpellate and inculcate, resist and challenge.
I fall upon the thorns of life, I bleed; I am the thorns of life, I cut.*

After the post-1960s breakdown of the New Critical orthodoxy
with its insistence on the autonomy of the literary text and its celebration of what W. K. Wimsatt called the Verbal Icon, criticism in
the West began to focus on the interconnections between literature
and society, and especially the role of literature (and, in some cases,
literary theory) in inculcating, reinforcing, challenging, or transform-
ing cultural beliefs and value systems. In narrative studies, this development is evident in a range of projects, many of which
themselves overlap: (a) work by feminist and critical race theorists
emphasizing the difference that race, gender, and class make in the
writing, reading, and theorizing of narrative; (b) work influenced by
Michel Foucault about the novel's role in the disciplining of its readers; (c) work such as that of Fredric Jameson based in Marxist theory
that reads literary narrative in light of the larger economic and class
system existing at the time of its production; (d) queer theory's efforts to dislodge assumptions about normative heterosexuality that
tacitly guide many interpretations of individual narratives and some
understandings of character and plot; (e) postcolonial theory's various analyses of the way the condition of postcoloniality influences
the construction and reception of narrative; (f) new historicism's

approach to literary narrative as part of the larger network of cultural discourses at the time of its production, and, thus, inevitably influenced by and influencing that network.

Work in this mode is noticeably different from work that approaches narrative as a formal system because of its emphasis on politics and because the political commitments of the critic often provide the lens through which the critic views the object of study. Initially, theorists working on narrative as a formal system and those working on it as an ideological instrument worked along parallel tracks and even regarded each other with some suspicion. But over time, the tracks have intersected and the mutual suspicions have abated, as critics interested in both form and politics have demonstrated not only that there is no necessary opposition between those interests but also that they can be mutually reinforcing. Scholes's *Textual Power* (1986) was one of several mid-1980s studies to show how the study of a text's formal features could be linked with the study of texts as ideological instruments. Scholes identifies three main steps in a serious encounter with a text: (1) reading, which is especially concerned with identifying the binary oppositions upon which the text is built; (2) interpretation, which links the textual binaries to broader cultural codes, specifies the text's view of the relation between those binaries (e.g., does the text privilege one of the codes?), and determines its attitudes toward that relation (e.g., does it lament or celebrate the privileging?); and (3) criticism, which evaluates the text's attitudes toward those codes. The step of interpretation, with its linking of textual details to broader cultural codes, recognizes the text as an ideological instrument. But the particular way the instrument cuts depends on its selection and combination of specific binary oppositions. To put the point another way, since Scholes regards interpretation as grounded in reading, his approach contains no opposition between its interest in formal features of texts and its interest in texts as ideological instruments. At the same time, Scholes's approach insists that the reader not be a passive recipient of the text's ideological message but instead an active evaluator of that message. So much for the text as verbal icon whose formal perfection we admire. If there is a problem with the approach, it resides in the assumption that texts are built primarily on binary oppositions.[4]

Two other approaches that link form and ideology have been especially important to the ongoing development of narrative theory, and they will serve as my main illustrations of work that views narrative as an ideological instrument: Mikhail Bakhtin's focus on the novel as dialogic discourse and that branch of feminist criticism and theory known as feminist narratology. Bakhtin was part of a circle of Russian intellectuals who met between 1918 and 1929, a group that also included Pavel Medvedev and Valentin Voloshinov, two scholars whose books are sometimes attributed to Bakhtin. Bakhtin's work was not widely noticed in the West until the early 1980s when new translations of *The Dialogic Imagination* and *Problems of Dostoevsky's Poetics* appeared. Bakhtin's approach to narrative is radically different from the one taken by classical narratology because he has a radically different conception of language itself.

As noted above, one of the key distinctions in Saussurean linguistics is that between *langue* and *parole*, between, that is, the formal, abstract system of language, and language in use. For Saussure, *langue* makes *parole* possible, and parole leads to diachronic change in *langue*. Saussure was primarily interested in describing the elements and structure of *langue*, just as the structuralist narratologists were interested in writing the grammar of narrative. Bakhtin by contrast is primarily interested in *parole*, and, indeed, from his perspective, *parole* is so diverse that any attempt to capture *langue* in a comprehensive way is doomed to fail. Furthermore, the diversity of *parole* is a function not just of the range of semantic forms and syntactic structures used by speakers but also of the inseparable connection between language and ideology. The social nature of language means that different social groups develop characteristic patterns of diction and syntax and those patterns come to carry the ideological values of those groups. Thus, every utterance conveys both a semantic and an ideological meaning, because every utterance carries both a content and a set of values associated with its characteristic diction and syntax. No one speaker fully owns his or her utterance because the words of the utterance have been used by others and carry with them the marks of their previous uses. Consequently, Bakhtin regards any one language, say, English, as composed of an almost countless number of social dialects or mini-languages (or, in one meaning of the term, registers), each one shot through with ideology. For example, we could identify the language of the law, the language of the street, the language of the academy, the language of the popular media, and so on. Furthermore, a given society will often establish a hierarchy among its social dialects, with some more officially sanctioned and, thus, more authoritative than others. For Bakhtin, the task of establishing oneself as a mature speaker involves establishing one's relation to existing authoritative discourses by adopting what he calls internally persuasive discourses, ones that the individual values regardless of their place in the societal hierarchy.

Bakhtin argues that the novel is the highest form of literary art because it most effectively puts the multiple dialects of a society in dialogue with each other. This dialogue may occur through a sequential juxtaposition of dialects, or through what Bakhtin calls "double-voiced discourse," the use of more than one dialect within a single utterance. Some novels will orchestrate what Bakhtin calls the heteroglossia or the polyphony of these dialects so that one emerges as superior to the others. Other novels, such as those of Dostoevsky, which Bakhtin values above all others, orchestrate the polyphony so that no single dialect, and, thus, no single ideological position, emerges triumphant.

Bakhtin's influence on the study of narrative discourse has been extensive. His analyses of double-voiced discourse in Dickens and Turgenev in *The Dialogic Imagination* and of polyphony in *Dostoevsky's Poetics* provide models that have been widely followed. In addition, his ideas about the link between language and ideology have been taken up by just about every other mode of ideological criticism. I will include some Bakhtinian analysis of a passage from Ian McEwan's *Atonement* in the section on narrative discourse below.

Throughout the 1970s and into the mid-1980s, feminist theory and criticism produced valuable studies of the difference gender makes in the production and consumption of narrative at particular historical junctures. During this same period structuralist narratology gradually fell on hard times as post-structuralist theory, with its skepticism about the possibility and desirability of descriptive poetics, became the new orthodoxy. Then in 1986, Susan Lanser proposed joining the analytical precision of structuralist narratology with the political concerns of feminism as a way to contribute to the projects of both approaches. Although some narratologists initially felt that the study of form and the study of politics were incompatible projects and some feminist critics thought narratology to be an empty formalism, work by Lanser and others has now established feminist narratology as a significant movement within narrative theory. Its key theoretical principle is that gender—of authors, narrators, characters, and readers—is not just relevant to the study of narrative but something intrinsic to its form. Consequently, in this view, descriptions of narrative as a formal system that exclude gender are inadequate. At the same time, work in feminist narratology has also shown the importance of historicizing the interconnection between form and gender: while the connection itself is something that persists throughout the history of narrative, the precise nature of that connection is something that changes over time. Feminist narratology raises questions about all the elements of narrative, but its main contributions to date have been to the study of narrative discourse, and I will discuss those contributions in more detail below.

Protagonist IV: Narrative as Rhetoric

I am multi-layered, purposive, ethical. Or flat, univocal, and didactic.

In general terms, rhetorical approaches differ from structuralist, cognitive, and ideological approaches because they attend to the role of all three points of the rhetorical triangle—author, text, and reader—in the production of narrative meaning, and because they are less concerned with invariant rules or a priori political commitments. The three approaches I single out here put special emphasis on the reader's share in the production of meaning even as they retain a strong interest in the textual signals that guide the reader's role and acknowledge the author as the constructive agent of the text. In the first two of these approaches, gaps in the text are of special importance. Wolfgang Iser, who draws upon the phenomenology of Edmund Husserl and Roman Ingarden, views the relation among author, reader, and text as a dynamic one in which readers first follow the author's prestructured textual signals but then inevitably encounter gaps in those signals. Different readers then fill in those gaps in different ways, thus giving different concrete realizations to the potential meaning of the narrative text. This Ingarden-Iser model is one of the influences on Meir Sternberg's innovative approach to three interlocking kinds of narrative interest: suspense, which involves the reader's interest in what will be told; curiosity, which involves the reader's interest in gaps in what has been told; and surprise, which involves the reader's activity of recognition when gaps are filled in unexpected ways. In Sternberg's view, narrative is the mode of discourse in which the interplay among these three kinds of interests dominates.[5] The third approach is the one that I will give the most space to because it has made greater contributions to Scholes and Kellogg's categories of plot, character, and narrative discourse than the other two. This approach derives from Wayne C. Booth's revision of Chicago School neo-Aristotelian poetics into a rhetoric of narrative.

This method conceives of narrative as a purposive act of communication about characters and events: somebody telling somebody else on some occasion and for some purpose(s) that something happened. Given the emphasis on communicative action, the approach pays special attention to the relations among tellers, audiences, and the something that has happened. Furthermore, the focus on purpose(s) includes a recognition that narrative is a multi-layered communication, one in which tellers seek to engage and influence their audiences' cognition, emotions, and values. This method also stipulates that, in telling what happened, narrators tell about characters whose interactions with each other have an ethical dimension and that the acts of telling and receiving these accounts of characters and their actions also have an ethical dimension. Consequently, the approach attends to both an ethics of the told and an ethics of the telling.

The approach has its roots in Aristotle's *Poetics* with its definition of tragedy as the imitation of an action arousing pity and fear and leading to the purgation of those emotions. This definition makes rhetoric part of poetics by linking tragedy to its effect on its audience. The first generation neo-Aristotelian critics at the University of Chicago, who published their manifesto in 1953, also made rhetoric part of poetics in much the same way. R. S. Crane's seminal essay on "The Concept of Plot and the Plot of *Tom Jones*" assumes that the key to the form of Fielding's novel is its emotive effect, specifically, the pleasure the audience experiences in seeing Tom brought to the brink of fulfilling the prophecy that he was born to be hanged only to escape from the noose and be happily married to Sophia Western. Crane reasons back from this emotive effect to its causes in Fielding's specific choices about the sequence of the events and about his disclosures of who has the true knowledge of Tom's parentage. Crane's analysis of those choices, in turn, provides the basis for his definition of plot as a synthesis of character, action, and thought designed to affect the audience's emotions in a particular way.

Booth, a student of Crane's, inverts the relation between poetics and rhetoric in *The Rhetoric of Fiction* (1961), and in so doing paves the way for a broader rhetorical approach to narrative. *The Rhetoric of Fiction* starts out as a defense of certain narrative techniques that had fallen out of favor in the mid-twentieth century, particularly the use of overt authorial commentary such as that employed by Fielding, Dickens, Eliot and other eighteenth- and nineteenth-century novelists. Booth does not assume that such commentary is always effective but instead argues that any judgment of effectiveness should depend on the relation between the commentary and the novel's overall purpose of affecting its audience in a particular way. If the commentary advances the purpose, it is effective; if it detracts from the purpose, it is ineffective.

In developing this case, Booth argues that any technique will produce some effects on its audience rather than others and that, therefore, any technique is fundamentally rhetorical. Consequently, Booth's case about overt authorial commentary becomes just one part of his larger argument about the relation between rhetoric and fiction. The choice for the novelist is not *whether* to use rhetoric but rather about *which kind* to use—that associated with overt commentary or with the withholding of commentary, with the presentation of dramatic scenes or summaries of events, and so on.

This conception of narrative as fundamentally rhetorical influenced Booth's attention to the relations among authors, narrators, and audiences. The most important relation is that between the author, or to use the term Booth coined, "the implied author," the narrator, and the author's intended audience. (By the implied author, Booth means the version of himself or herself the author constructs in writing the narrative.) The implied author's communication can be direct or indirect, depending on the kind of narrator employed. Reliable narration, in which the narrator's reports and evaluations are endorsed by the implied author, is direct communication to the author's audience. Unreliable narration, in which the narrator's reports and evaluations are not endorsed by the implied author, is indirect. I will offer a fuller discussion of reliable and unreliable narration in the section on narrative discourse.

Booth's attention to the rhetorical exchanges among authors, narrators, and readers leads him at the end of *The Rhetoric of Fiction* to make an early foray into ethical criticism. He explores the ethical consequences of what he calls "impersonal narration," when employed in the representation of ethically reprehensible characters. By "impersonal narration" Booth means both narration by a character (first-person narration, or, as we will see below, what Genette more precisely labels homodiegetic narration) and center of consciousness narration. Booth notes that the very act of following a character's inner life typically generates at least some sympathy for that character, and he worries that such sympathy may override authorial signals about a character's ethical deficiencies. This portion of Booth's argument received the most resistance from his own audience in the 1960s—see, for example, the comments of Scholes and Kellogg on p. 278—and, as Booth notes in his Afterword to the second edition (1983), he himself soon felt that it was inadequate. Nevertheless, Booth maintained his conviction that ethics is an integral component of rhetoric, and in 1988, he returned to this general thesis in *The Company We Keep*. He argues there that because the rhetorical construction of a narrative invites its audience to follow a certain trajectory of desire, narrative inevitably has designs on its audience's values, if only to influence us to desire some things rather than others. More generally, Booth develops his concern with the complex exchanges between author and audience into the metaphor of books as friends—friends who can be either beneficial or harmful.

Booth's work has been revised and extended in many ways so that today it is possible to identify three key principles of the rhetorical approach in addition to its conception of narrative as a purposive communicative act. (I) It postulates a recursive relationship among authorial agency, textual phenomena (including intertextual relations), and reader response. Texts are designed by authors in order to affect readers in particular ways; those designs are conveyed through the words, techniques, structures, forms, and intertextual relations of texts; and reader responses are a function of and, thus, a guide to how authorial designs are created through textual phenomena.

(II) The approach recognizes multiple audiences in narrative communication. Peter J. Rabinowitz has persuasively argued for the existence of four distinct audiences in fictional narrative. In *Narrative as Rhetoric* (1996) I suggest one modification to Rabinowitz's model in order to differentiate his concept of the narrative audience from Gerald Prince's structuralist insight that the presence of a narrator implies the presence of a narratee. That modification leaves us with five audiences:

1. The flesh and blood or actual reader: each of us with our glorious (or not so glorious) individuality and common human endowments.
2. The authorial audience: the author's ideal reader. The rhetorical model assumes that the flesh-and-blood reader seeks to enter the authorial audience in order to understand the invitations for engagement that the narrative offers.
3. The narrative audience: the observer position within the narrative world that the flesh-and-blood reader assumes. In fiction, we are in this observer position when we respond to characters as if they were real people. Our ability to enter the narrative audience is one important reason why we respond affectively to fictional narratives.
4. The narratee: the audience addressed by the narrator, who may or may not be characterized.
5. The ideal narrative audience: the narrator's hypothetical perfect audience, the one he expects to understand every nuance of his communication. The ideal narrative audience may or may not coincide with the actual narratee, and it may or may not be an important part of a rhetorical interpretation.

(III) The rhetorical approach also notes that individual narratives explicitly or implicitly establish their own ethical standards and, therefore, it moves from the way those standards influence the authorial audience's judgments to its own assessment of both those ethical standards and the way they are deployed in the narrative. In this way, the rhetorical critic does ethical criticism from the inside out rather than the outside in. That is, rather than applying a pre-existing ethical system to the narrative, she seeks to discover the implicit value system of the text and how the author uses it to accomplish the communicative purposes of the narrative. Then, in a final step, the critic brings her own values into play as she evaluates the text's system and its use. By working from the inside out rather than the outside in, the rhetorical critic remains open to having her own values challenged and ultimately altered by the experience of reading.

PART 2: PLOT, CHARACTER, AND NARRATIVE DISCOURSE
        SINCE 1966

Plot's Progress

*Yes, oh dear, yes—you bet your life, yes—I have a plot. I never go
anywhere without at least one.*

"Quality of mind (as expressed in the language of characterization, motivation, description, and commentary), not plot is the soul
of narrative. Plot is only the indispensable skeleton which, fleshed
out with character and incident, provides the necessary clay into
which life may be breathed." (*The Nature of Narrative*, 239)

These concluding sentences of the 1966 chapter on plot reflect a
common attitude of that time, an attitude whose roots can be found
in E. M. Forster's preference for character over plot, in Henry
James's Prefaces with their attention to technique as the most important element of "the craft" of fiction, and in the then prevalent
New Critical orthodoxy, which viewed literature as a special use of
language. Over the past forty years plot has moved from this position as the Rodney Dangerfield of narrative theory to one where it
commands much more respect. This change in its fortunes is accompanied by an expansion of its reference: where Scholes and
Kellogg defined plot as "a more specific term" than story "intended
to refer to action alone, with the minimal possible reference to character" (208), most contemporary narrative theorists use plot as a
more encompassing term. In *Reading for the Plot* (1984), Peter
Brooks sees it, in the words of his subtitle, as the key to narrative's
"design and intention." Hayden White sees "emplotment," the transformation of a series of events into a coherent whole that expresses
a larger view of those events, as a fundamental task of writing history. Paul Ricouer uses the same term to refer to the way narrative
puts its various elements into meaningful relationships to one another and to the larger point of the narrative. Building on R. S. Crane's
conception of plot, I propose in *Reading People, Reading Plots* (1989)
a substitute term, "narrative progression," in order to refer to the
synthesis of the text's movement from beginning to end and the au-

thorial audience's developing response to that movement, and I argue that progression is a key to narrative form. I will shortly elaborate on Brooks's view and my own, but first I want to look at how plot fares when narrative is conceived as a formal system.

Structuralism's interest in the patterns underlying narrative and its privileging of descriptive poetics over interpretation significantly influence its approach to plot. Rather than using the story/discourse distinction as the basis for studies of plot as the transformation of story through discourse, structuralist studies of plot follow Propp's lead and seek to identify the deep structure of events beneath the various surface structures of individual narratives or recognizable genres. One of the most insightful analyses in this line is Tzvetan Todorov's analysis of the classic detective story in *The Poetics of Prose* (1977) as having two stories that need not even touch: the story of the crime and the story of the investigation. Furthermore, because the story of the crime is not immediately present, and because the detective is immune from serious harm, the story of the investigation serves as a mediator between the reader and the story of the crime.

The most extreme example of the structuralist approach to plot is found in the structural anthropologist Claude Levi-Strauss's mythic analysis of Sophocles's *Oedipus*. Levi-Strauss sees myth as a means by which cultures acknowledge and sometimes work through their underlying conflicts. He advances the view that the deep structure plot of Sophocles's *Oedipus* is built on four "mythemes" (beliefs central to a given culture): the overrating of blood relations (Oedipus's incest with his mother Jocasta); the underrating of blood relations (Oedipus's killing of his father Laius); the denial of our autochthonous roots (Oedipus's killing of the Sphinx) and the affirmation of those roots (Oedipus's swollen foot). Levi-Strauss's analysis, whatever else one might think of it, does support Peter Brooks's contention in *Reading for the Plot* that the structuralist approach tends to spatialize plot. More positively, Levi-Strauss's contention that myths are tools that help people deal with contradictory elements of their culture is a forerunner of cognitive narratology's understanding of narrative as a resource for structuring and comprehending the world.

We have seen above how Monika Fludernik's cognitive approach de-emphasizes plot while emphasizing experientality and narrativization, but other branches of cognitive narratology place more emphasis upon it. Following structuralist narratology's effort to find recurring patterns of events, Patrick Colm Hogan in *The Mind and Its Stories: Narrative Universals and Human Emotions* (2003) proposes that there are three story structures that are employed across cultures and that therefore deserve to be called universal: the romantic, the heroic, and the sacrificial. The romantic structure is about the relationships of lovers, especially their separations and coming together. The heroic is about conflicts over authority and their resolution within a particular group and about the group's defense from unwanted incursions by an external group. The sacrificial is about major injuries to the community and the healing of the community through acts of sacrifice by one or more of its members. Hogan does not claim that these recurring "story structures" are themselves plots or that all plots have at least one of these structures underlying them. He claims instead that these structures typically inform the plots of narratives that are frequently told, even as individual plots may invoke one or more of the structures only to deviate from them.

Emma Kafalenos in *Narrative Causalities* (2006) combines a function-analysis derived from Propp with cognitive narratology's interest in the processing of texts. Kafalenos identifies a set of ten functions that underlie a narrative's system of causality (e.g., an equilibrium is disrupted, an actant decides to rectify the situation, the actant takes action, equilibrium is restored) and the ways in which readers configure that system of causality. In addition to providing new insights into the structure of plots, Kafalenos's study reaffirms narrative's close connection with casual explanations.

David Herman's cognitive approach to plot follows from his ideas about the links among genres and preference rules. A preference rule has the form "prefer to see X as Y given a set of conditions Z," and Herman develops the sets of conditions that are associated with some broad generic distinctions. In other words, Herman's effort is to explain why a character performing such and such actions (X) in such and such a set of conditions (Z) will typically signal such and such a genre (Y). His cognitive orientation leads him to divide the sets of conditions into "process types" such as processes of doing, processes of sensing, and processes of being, categories that cognitive theory posits we use to make sense of actions. He then looks at how different process types typically combine in different genres. To extract just two simple examples from Herman's detailed and fine-grained analysis: in the epic, processes of doing are more important than processes of being, while in the psychological novel, processes of sensing are more important than processes of doing.

In *Reading for the Plot*, Brooks develops a psychoanalytical approach that emphasizes plot's temporal dimension. In an effort to link the temporality of plot to the temporality of life, he analyzes reading for the plot in terms of Freud's *Beyond the Pleasure Principle* and develops a model that describes narrative as a desire for the ending. Thus, he sees the beginning of plot as the introduction of desire, the middle as deferral and delay, largely through repetition, in its satisfaction, and the end as the satisfactory discharge of the tension built up through that arousal and delay. Thus, for example, in Jane Austen's *Pride and Prejudice*, the plot begins by introducing a desire for the marriage of Elizabeth and Darcy, and then the long middle defers the marriage through the complications of the plot and the repetitions with a difference of their various meetings and misunderstandings until, finally, the ending satisfies the desire with their engagement. While Brooks's model has been very influential, it has also been criticized, most notably by Susan Winnett, for its assumption that the trajectory of male sexual response is the underlying pattern of all plots.

In 1993, Susan Stanford Friedman proposed the concept of spatialization not as a way to revive structuralist approaches but as a way to complicate the idea of plot in another way. Her central point is that narrative has not only a horizontal movement through time but also a vertical dimension that brings back a spatial view of plot. The vertical dimension links the horizontal surface to literary, historical, and psychic intertexts. Literary intertexts include both generic patterns and specific prior narratives; historical intertexts involve the broader social order, including cultural narratives; and psychic intertexts involve the patterns of repression and return within the text itself as well as those involved in the author's relation to the material.

With *Pride and Prejudice*, then, Friedman would emphasize the way in which Austen's marriage plot interacts with previous marriage plots and makes Elizabeth both partly responsible for Darcy's reform and partly the fortunate beneficiary of his generosity of spirit. She would also emphasize the novel's commentary on the marriage market and the constrictions and restrictions that market places on female experience and choice. Charlotte Lucas's calculated decision to marry the vain and insensitive Mr. Collins rather than live her life as a single woman would figure prominently in a discussion of the historical intertext. Finally, Friedman would look for implied relations (both parallels and contrasts) between Austen's own experiences as a single woman and the horizontal unfolding of Elizabeth's fate.

Friedman's work on spatialization is one example of the ways in which feminist critics focus on the gender politics of plot patterns. Rachel Blau DuPlessis in *Writing beyond the Ending* (1985) succinctly articulates the assumption guiding much feminist work on plot: "ideology is coiled in narrative structure" (5). Plots reveal their ideologies of gender through such matters as how they limit or bequeath agency to male and female characters, set up some kinds of conflicts and ignore others, and imagine possible outcomes to those conflicts. History, both social and literary, has privileged certain plots and, in so doing, linked them with certain cultural values. *Pride and Prejudice*, for example, is one version of the marriage plot, a plot given great prominence in Anglo-American social and literary history, a plot that privileges heterosexuality, marriage, and the patriarchal order that sets up the rules of the marriage market, and defines women's proper place as in the domestic sphere. Experimentation with plot by women writers, gay and lesbian novelists, and novelists of color needs to be understood, as DuPlessis and many other feminist critics contend, as both formal innovation and political statement: breaking the sequence, as Virginia Woolf put it, is a way both to protest against the usual plot patterns and to find forms for experiences and values that those patterns have not attended to.

Jeanette Winterson's *Written on the Body*, for example, can be profitably read as breaking the sequence of the marriage plot. It traces not the coming together of a single couple but rather the unnamed character-narrator's multiple experiences of love and loss. Where the traditional marriage plot confines sex to the couple's untold life after the novel ends, Winterson's protagonist has multiple sexual partners. Winterson moves in the direction of the marriage plot by representing the character-narrator's temporary union with a lover named Louise, but Winterson then turns away from that plot to focus on the loss of Louise and the character-narrator's effort to come to terms with that loss. Furthermore, where the marriage plot reinforces heterosexuality, Winterson challenges that taken-for-granted position, first by showing that the character-narrator has sexual partners of both sexes, and second by refusing to identify the character-narrator's own sex. Meanwhile, as the title suggests, *Written on the Body* is also an allegory of reading, one that analogizes the relationship between the central lovers to that between author and narrator on one side, and implied reader and flesh and blood reader on the other. In this way, the formal choice not to identify the character-narrator's own sex has the political consequence of queering the experience of reading, of exposing the way desire in reading, like desire in general, cannot be readily confined to the clearly demarcated categories of gender and sexuality.

My rhetorical approach to plot, first proposed in *Reading People, Reading Plots* (1989) and recently elaborated through a fuller discussion of beginnings, middles, and endings in *Experiencing Fiction* (forthcoming), suggests, as I noted above, that we substitute the term progression for plot, with progression referring to the synthesis of the internal dynamics of the text's movement from beginning to end with the authorial audience's developing responses to that movement. The internal dynamics of the text are governed by the introduction, complication, and (often only partial) resolution of instabilities and tensions. Instabilities are unsettled matters involving elements of story, typically characters and their situations, while tensions are unsettled matters involving elements of discourse such as unequal knowledge among authors, narrators, and audiences (as in mysteries) or matters of different values and perceptions (as in narratives with unreliable narrators). As audiences follow the movement of instabilities and tensions, they develop three main kinds of interests: the mimetic, interests in the characters as possible people and their world as like our own; the thematic, interests in the narrative's ideas, values, and world views; and the synthetic, interests in the narrative as an artificial construct. As audiences develop these interests through following the internal dynamics of a narrative, they engage in many kinds of more specific responses: judging characters, developing hopes, desires, and expectations for them, and constructing tentative hypotheses about the overall shape and direction of the narrative. Indeed, *Experiencing Fiction* also explores the importance of the authorial audience's interpretive, ethical, and aesthetic judgments for narrative progressions.

An analysis of the progression of *Pride and Prejudice* would emphasize the interaction of Elizabeth's movement toward her happy union with Darcy and Austen's thematizing of Elizabeth's situation as a single woman of little fortune so that our pleasure in the mimetic story is deepened and deeply contextualized by that thematizing. To take just one salient example of this relationship, Collins's proposals, first, to Elizabeth, who refuses him, and then to Charlotte Lucas, who accepts him, are more than just deferrals or anticipations of Darcy's later proposals to Elizabeth. Instead, they represent an alternate fate for Elizabeth, the awareness of which strengthens our desire and satisfaction in her marriage to Darcy, even as it emphasizes that Elizabeth's good fortune is just that.

The analysis would also focus on the difference between Elizabeth's developing understanding of her situation and that of Austen's audience, a difference evident in Austen's handling of a secondary event, Lydia's elopement with Wickham. Elizabeth learns of this event from Darcy during her visit to Pemberley, several months after she has rejected Darcy's initial proposal and several months after she has realized, through her reflections on his post-rejection letter to her, that she has thoroughly misjudged him and Wickham. During this visit, through her viewing of the grounds, hearing Mrs. Reynolds's testimony about Darcy's character, and spending some time in his company, Elizabeth's understanding of Darcy's character deepens and she begins to fall in love with him. When Jane's letter tells her of Lydia's flight, however, Elizabeth believes that nothing can come of her feelings, since, to her mind, the disgrace Lydia has brought on the family must strengthen Darcy's negative judgment of it.

Austen, however, has given her audience a different set of expectations by establishing a pattern in which she provides enough knowledge of Darcy's character for us to judge the engagement as desirable and in which the threats to Elizabeth's happiness always dissipate. Elizabeth's successful refusal of Collins's marriage proposal despite the objections of her mother is the most salient example of this part of the pattern, though Jane's illness and subsequent return to good health and Elizabeth's own progress after Darcy's first proposal are also parts of it. Consequently, Austen's audience judges Lydia's behavior as a significant but temporary obstacle to Elizabeth's eventual happiness, even as we are invested in discovering how the obstacle will be overcome. Austen's genius is to use the obstacle as a means for demonstrating how Darcy has changed, thus leading us to even stronger positive ethical judgments of him. Rather than shunning the Bennets, Darcy takes it upon himself to deal with Wickham and make the best of the bad situation. When Elizabeth expresses her gratitude for his actions, Darcy feels emboldened to make his second, successful proposal. Austen's audience feels great satisfaction in the engagement precisely because we judge it to be the appropriate culmination of the growth of the two characters.

The Character of Character

*Am I person, idea, or word? All of these? None? If all, then what part
of me is story? If none, then who or what is speaking these words?*

"To suggest that one order of characterization is better than another is folly. To recognize that differences exist is the beginning of
wisdom." (*The Nature of Narrative*, 161)

Narrative theory's approach to character over the past forty years
has not always followed this wisdom—though the reasons for its
deviations are various. Structuralist narratology with its concern for
underlying rules tries to get beyond orders of characterization in
the surface structure of narratives and identify what all characters
have in common. Again Propp's work on the Russian folktale provides an influential model, as he focuses on the roles that characters
play in the deep structure plot. Just as he identifies 31 events, he
identifies 7 recurring roles: hero, false hero, villain, sought-for person and her mentor, dispatcher, donor, helper. The structuralists follow Propp's approach along two different, though compatible, tracks.
One follows in a direct line from Propp: A. J. Greimas has engaged
in an ongoing effort to develop a general taxonomy of roles performed by what he calls actants. At one point in his thinking, Greimas
proposes a six-item taxonomy: Subject, Object, Sender, Helper, Re-
ceiver, Opponent. (Greimas later revised the model by relabeling
Helper and Opponents positive and negative "auxiliants," but this
revision is not actually an improvement.)

The second track shares Propp's interest in getting at underlying
constituents of character, but it sees those constituents as fundamentally linguistic. Just as a particular semantic signifier, say, "man,"
can be broken down into underlying semantic markers such as +ani-
mate, +human, and +male, so too can character be broken down
into a set of predicates associated with a proper name. The two tracks
are ultimately compatible because both strip individuality away from
character and because predicates grouped under a proper name can
be further identified by the Proppian or Greimasan general roles
they perform.

Cognitive narratologists also move in two directions. David Herman revises Greimas's account of actants by drawing on recent linguistic theory about the intersection of syntax and semantics. This theory emphasizes that in order to give an adequate account of a sentence's meaning, the grammatical roles specified by syntax (noun phrase links with verb phrase) need to be supplemented by thematic roles or participant roles embedded in semantics (such as Agent, Patient, Instrument, Goal). Although the grammatical roles of the nouns in "The dog ate my homework" and "My homework was eaten by the dog" are different, their participant roles are the same (dog is Agent, homework is Patient). To take another example, the grammatical roles of "the dog" in "The dog ate my homework" and "The dog died" are the same, but their participant roles are different (Agent in the first, Patient in the second). In applying this work to cognitive narratology, Herman shifts from the term "actants" to the term "participants," deploys a taxonomy of ten different participant or thematic roles, and recognizes that the same participant can play multiple thematic roles in the course of a narrative just as different participants can share the same role. Furthermore, since, as we have seen above, Herman's cognitive perspective leads him to view stories as a means by which people conceptualize the world as involving various processes, he contends that characters will take on different roles as they participate in different kinds of processes. He then draws on the functional linguistics of M. A. K. Halliday to propose a taxonomy of process types, specifically material (e.g., "I put the ball in the basket again"), mental (e.g., "I pondered my options"), relational (e.g., "I am the walrus"), behavioral (e.g., "I cried"), verbal ("I repeated my advice"), and existential (e.g., "your car is in the driveway"), and uses this taxonomy as a way to identify participant roles.

Fludernik's emphasis on human consciousness and experientiality leads her to see *personhood* as not only essential to narrativity but also as a crucial frame that readers bring to narratives. This frame is a valuable aid in readers' efforts to narrativize texts, allowing us to deal with texts with minimal sequences of action or narrators who don't fall neatly into standard categories. We may not know, for example, the gender of the character narrator in *Written on the Body*, but we have no doubt about that figure's personhood. At the same time, the concept of personhood is not endlessly elastic. Narrations that continually revise the information they offer about characters or that use multiple, incompatible pronouns to refer to them go beyond what we understand to fall within the frame of personhood and therefore resist narrativization.

Under the rubric of narrative as ideological instrument, Bakhtin's theory has the potential for the most radical view of character. His preference for unresolved dialogue points to his underlying assumption that dialogism constitutes the essence of the novel, and that assumption in turn informs his view of both character and of plot. In effect, Bakhtin's emphasis on dialogism inverts the apparent logic of the story/discourse distinction. That logic, as noted above, suggests that characters and events have a kind of independence from their representation in discourse, but Bakhtin's approach makes both of these elements significant largely for their role in the author's orchestration of the dialogues. Consequently, characters are important less for their personalities than for their alignments with one or more of the novel's dialects and the ideological positions reflected in them. Similarly, plots are important less for their ordering of events into a larger design than for the way in which they trace the trajectory and resolution (or lack of resolution) of the dialogue among the dialects. Although Bakhtin has been a kind of universal donor among literary critics—that is, his ideas have been appropriated in the service of just about every major critical approach—his views of character and plot as subordinate to discourse have not been adopted by most narrative theorists.

Other ideological critics are typically concerned with how the representation of a character functions in relation to an individual narrative's ideological import. Thus, feminists such as Judith Fetterley in *The Resisting Reader* (1978) focus on (a) the relations between a given character's traits and the cultural assumptions about gender at the historical moment in which the narrative is constructed and (b) the specific roles in the plot performed by male and female characters and what those roles reveal about ideologies of gender. In her analysis of these relations, Fetterley argues that classic American fiction by men invites women readers to identify against themselves, and, therefore, she argues that women should resist those readerly positions.

Alex Woloch in *The One vs. the Many* (2003) offers another way to approach character within the larger perspective of narrative as an ideological instrument. Woloch starts with a helpful contribution to a formal theory of character, acknowledging first that there is often a tension between character as "reference" (that is, character as an imitation of a person) and character as "structure" (character as an element in a narrative design), and then introducing two related concepts, character-space and character-system. Character-space, the amount of textual space given to any character, is the result of the encounter between character as reference and character as structure: character as reference moves toward expansion, but character as structure curtails that movement. Character-system is the arrangement of all the character-spaces in a narrative in a larger structure. These concepts provide the basis for Woloch to address the structural relations among protagonists and other characters, and he argues that in the realistic novel, especially in the European realistic novel of the nineteenth century, these structural relations are conflicted. In Woloch's view, giving due justice to characters as imagined human beings entails recognizing that minor characters have the potential to take up more space and even become major, and that they are therefore sacrificed so that the protagonist may occupy center stage. Woloch then invokes the Marxist principle that narrative literature reflects the socioeconomic realities in which it is written and sees the sacrifice of the minor characters in the nineteenth-century novel as reflecting the processes of social stratification that follow from capitalism. Thus, when Woloch claims that *"minor characters are the proletariat of the novel"* (27, his emphasis), he is not employing a fanciful metaphor but asserting a strong connection between novelistic form and socioeconomic process.

In *Reading People, Reading Plots* (1989), I suggest a different conception of character and a different relationship between what

Woloch calls character as reference and character as structure. In my view, character has three components that correspond to the three main kinds of interest audiences develop in narrative progressions: mimetic (character as possible person, what Woloch refers to as reference), thematic (character as representative of a larger class or an embodiment of a set of ideas), and synthetic (character as artificial construct, what Woloch refers to as structure). Furthermore, different narrative progressions establish different relations among these components by guiding our developing interests in particular ways. In realist narrative, progressions typically foreground the mimetic and thematic components of character with the synthetic remaining in the background. In nonrealist modes, the mimetic tends either to go to the background or to be present through its violation; in either case, the synthetic then gets foregrounded. Like Scholes and Kellogg, I contend that the multiple possible relationships among the three components do not fall neatly into a hierarchy of aesthetic value.

Discourse about Narrative Discourse

I am the only reliable narrator I have ever known.

"In the relationship between the teller and the tale, and in that other relationship, between the teller and the audience, lies the essence of narrative art." (*The Nature of Narrative*, 240)

Perhaps because narrative theory has continued to subscribe to Scholes and Kellogg's dictum, its greatest advances in the past forty years have been in the study of narrative discourse. My discussions of Bakhtin and Booth have already indicated many of their contributions, so here I will focus on Genette, the feminist narratologists, and some revisions and extensions of Booth. I will then do an illustrative analysis of a passage from a post-1966 narrative, Ian McEwan's *Atonement*.

One reason for the enduring power of the story/discourse distinction is that Genette demonstrates its great utility in *Narrative Discourse* as he unpacks many of the complexities of the how of narrative. Genette subtitles his book "An Essay in Method" because he self-consciously conducts an unusual critical inquiry, one that is simultaneously theoretical and interpretive. His focus throughout is on both Proust's *A la recherche du temps perdu* and the principles of narrative discourse; he deploys the principles to illuminate Proust, even as he uses Proust to uncover new principles of narrative discourse or new powers and limits of existing ones. The most important contributions of Genette's rich study are his analyses of temporality and of voice and vision.

Genette's work on temporality treats it as a function of the relationships between the what and the how, more specifically between the events of the story and the way in which they are presented in discourse. Genette organizes his discussion of these relationships into three parts: order, duration, and frequency. Order refers to the relation between the actual chronological sequence of events and their sequence in the discourse. Narratives typically establish a primary temporal NOW. When the order of the discourse follows the chronological order of events, then the temporal NOW of the discourse follows the temporal NOW of the events. When the discourse narrates something that occurred prior to the temporal NOW, we have an analepsis (or flashback). Some narratives such as Kazuo Ishiguro's *The Remains of the Day* rely heavily on analepsis: as the character narrator Stevens recounts the details of his journey by automobile in the temporal NOW, he invariably leaves that narration and reports on events from his past. When the discourse narrates something that will occur after the temporal NOW, we have a prolepsis (or flashforward). In McEwan's *Atonement*, for example, the narrator reports about the protagonist Briony that "Six decades later she would describe how at the age of thirteen she had written her way through a whole history of literature, beginning with stories derived from the European tradition of folktales, through drama with simple moral intent, to arrive at an impartial psychological realism which she had discovered for herself, one special morning during a heat wave in 1935" (38). Since there are few examples of prolepsis in the novel, this one stands out.

Duration refers to the relationship between the amount of time an event or a series of events takes to happen and the amount of time it takes to read about that event (thus, duration is, in a sense, a matter of the relation between time and space—the temporal extent of the event and the space given to it in the narrative text). Henry Fielding's narrator in *Tom Jones* uses five paragraphs in Chapter 1 of Book III to set up his narration of twelve years of Tom's life in a single sentence, a narration that comically invites his sagacious readers to fill in the events of those twelve years. In *Missing*, Michelle Herman uses twenty pages to represent the event of her elderly protagonist Rivke Vasilevsky taking a bath. Frequency refers to the relation between the number of times an event occurs and the number of times it is narrated. Thus, the default frequency relation is one-to-one, and such narration is called singulative. But some events can happen many times and be narrated only once in what is called iterative narration. The opening to Proust's novel is a famous example: "Longtemps, je me suis couché de bonne heure" (For a long time I used to go to bed early). And some events can happen only once but be narrated many times in what is called repeated narration. For example, in Toni Morrison's *Beloved*, the event of Sethe's murdering her child rather than having her go back into slavery is narrated three times.

Genette's work on temporality has been usefully supplemented by David Herman's concept of fuzzy temporality, which he develops as part of his analysis of the "when" of the storyworld. Herman notes that Genette's approach assumes that we can always discern the underlying temporality of the story—the order, duration, and frequency of its events—but many narratives, especially ones dealing with trauma, do not allow such clear perceptions. Narratives with such fuzzy temporality are not necessarily ill-formed; such a judgment has to be deferred until after an examination of whether the fuzziness adds to or detracts from the narrative's effectiveness.

The key insight in Genette's approach to voice and vision is that the term "point of view" is inadequate because it conflates the two distinct elements of narrative discourse: who speaks (voice) and who sees, or, more broadly, who perceives (vision or what Genette calls focalization). Distinguishing the two allows us to get further insight into each. With voice, Genette points out that the traditional taxonomy of first person and third person (along with such refinements as first person observer, first person protagonist, third person omniscient, and third person limited) is inadequate because all individual narrators can—and often do—say "I." What the traditional taxonomy wants to capture, Genette notes, is the relation of the voice to the plane of the primary story events, what he calls the diegetic level of the narrative. Narrators traditionally called first person, whether protagonists or observers (e.g., Huck Finn and Nick Carraway), exist at that level and can interact or, depending on the time of the narration, could have once interacted with the other characters. Narrators traditionally called third person exist at another level within the storyworld, one from which they typically do not interact directly with the characters (for example, Fielding's narrator in *Tom Jones*, or George Eliot's narrator in *Middlemarch*). Thus, Genette proposes to replace the taxonomy based on grammatical person with one based on diegetic level: narrators such as Huck and Nick are homodiegetic; narrators such as those Fielding and Eliot employ are heterodiegetic. Genette does not give much attention to so-called second person narration, a matter I will return to at the end of this essay.

Genette's attention to the diegetic levels at which voices are located also allows him to mark "intradiegetic" and "extradiegetic" ones. Intradiegetic voices are those whose narration is embedded within the primary level of the action. Thus, for example, both Marlow's narration in Conrad's *Heart of Darkness* and the governess's narration in James's *The Turn of the Screw* are intradiegetic because they are contained within the narration of another voice, that of the frame narrator. Heterodiegetic narrators exemplify one kind of extradiegetic voice, but they are not the only kind: voices beyond the diegesis are also heard in titles (including chapter titles) and epigraphs.

With vision, Genette proposes a new term, focalization, and a taxonomy of three different kinds. Strikingly, Genette does not make this taxonomy parallel with the one based on voice. That is, he does not base it on the identity of the perceiver (character, narrator, hypothetical observer, etc.), but bases it instead on the ratio of knowledge between the narrator and the characters. In what he calls zero focalization (later helpfully amended to free focalization by William Nelles), the narrator knows more than the characters and exercises the privilege of moving freely about the story world to comment first on this scene and this character and then on that scene and that character. George Eliot has her narrator in *Middlemarch* call attention to her free focalization at the beginning of Chapter 29 by saying "One morning, some weeks after her arrival at Lowick, Dorothea— but why always Dorothea? Was her point of view the only possible one with regard to this marriage?" and then by moving to comment on Casaubon. In what Genette calls external focalization, the character knows more than the narrator because the narrator is restricted to reporting the character's observable behaviour. Genette's example is Dashiell Hammett's *The Maltese Falcon*; Hammett's narrator describes what Sam Spade looks like and what he does but he never adopts Spade's own perspective and never shows what Spade is thinking. In internal focalization, the narrator's knowledge and the character's knowledge are equal because the narrator is restricted to the character's perspective. Henry James's novels are perhaps the most celebrated examples of internal focalization, but it is a technique that, as Scholes and Kellogg's discussion of the interior monologue shows, can be found throughout the history of narrative going all the way back to the narratives of ancient Greece.

While Genette's distinction between voice and vision (or focalization) has been almost universally accepted, his specific proposals about focalization have been the source of considerable debate among narratologists. Those such as Seymour Chatman who are concerned with a strict division between story and discourse contend that heterodiegetic narrators (and even retrospective homodiegetic narrators) cannot be focalizers because they are not part of the story world and consequently their reports are of a different order from the perceptions of characters. Others such as Mieke Bal, however, argue that any verbal narration entails focalization because any narration entails not only speaking or writing (and thus a voice) but also speaking or writing from some perspective. As one especially interested in the experience of reading narrative, I find Bal's view to be more persuasive: the similarities in the perceptual activities of a narrator and a character are more significant for a reader's understanding of the distinction between voice and vision than the principle of keeping story and discourse neatly separated.

More recently, Manfred Jahn, who also subscribes to the "no-narration-without-focalization" position, has refined the concept of focalization further by approaching it from a cognitivist perspective and applying the metaphor of "windows" to it. Focalization opens one window and not another (e.g., a character's window rather than a narrator's) into the narrative world and thus leads readers to perceive some aspects of that world and not others. Furthermore, the windows may be more or less clearly located in relation to both the reader and the narrative world and may yield more or less sharp perceptions of that world. Jahn traces a continuum from "strict focalization" where the focalizer is in a clearly defined spatio-temporal position to "ambient focalization," where events or characters are perceived from more than one angle, to "weak focalization" where the spatio-temporal location cannot be specified to zero (or free) focalization where the perspective cannot be pinned down.

Another valuable revision of Genette's work on vision and voice from a cognitivist perspective can be found in Alan Palmer's work on fictional minds. Palmer argues that the structuralists' approach to the report of characters' speech and thought—as direct, indirect, or free indirect—is too piecemeal to offer an adequate account of the representation of thought in fiction. Palmer introduces the concept of a continuing consciousness frame as way to recognize the inadequacy of sentence-by-sentence tracings of shifts from reports of action to reports of thought (and the concomitant shiftings in vision and voice between narrators and character). As we'll see below, Palmer's concept allows us to recognize that such small fluctuations often do not alter the narration's basic frame of representing a character's mental activity.

Palmer's work also links up with the concept from cognitive psychology of Theory of Mind (ToM). ToM is another frame, the one we employ whenever we infer mental states behind physical actions. It is ToM that allows us to understand gestures as signifying others' mental intentions: to use an example from Lisa Zunshine's *Why We Read Fiction* (2006), teachers recognize a student's raising his hand as an expression of a desire to be called on rather than a sign that he has a pain in his armpit. A little reflection reveals that literary narrative relies heavily on ToM both because its characters must continually infer the mental states of other characters by observing their behavior and because readers must often do the same.

Feminist narratologists have productively built on structuralist analysis of narrative discourse by showing how that analysis can be tied to their concerns with gender politics. Robyn Warhol in her 1989 *Gendered Interventions* analyzes direct address to the narratee (the narrator's hypothetical audience) in the Victorian novels with heterodiegetic narrators and discovers that male and female writers typically employ different kinds. Victorian women writers most often use what Warhol calls "engaging" strategies in their addresses to the narratee, devices that bridge the distance between the narrator and the narratee, on the one hand, and the narratee and the actual reader on the other. Male authors, by contrast, typically have their narrators employ distancing strategies, devices that emphasize the gap between narrator and narratee and narratee and real reader. In her more recent book, *Having a Good Cry* (2003), Warhol looks more broadly at the interactions between narrative form, including narrative discourse, and cultural ideas about gender. She analyzes narrative discourse, formulaic plots, and bodily responses to reading narrative and explores their connections to cultural ideas about masculinity, femininity, and a third term that crosses the gender divide, effeminacy. The result is a provocative study of the connections between reading narrative and the development of gendered subjectivity.

Susan Lanser's 1992 *Fictions of Authority* focuses on voice as the element of narrative discourse in which women writers of fictional narrative confront the problem of claiming and establishing authority. Lanser's concept of authority illustrates the kind of connection feminist narratologists make between form and ideology: "the authority of a given voice . . . is produced from a conjunction of social and rhetorical properties" (6). The social properties come from the voice's relation to hierarchies of power that exist at the moment of its speaking (e.g., in nineteenth-century America white men's voices had more authority than white women's, and both white men and women had more authority than black men). The rhetorical properties of voice come from the skill with which the speaker employs specific textual strategies, which exist independently of the social hierarchies. Lanser postulates that, despite any individual woman writer's feeling of ambivalence about authority, the very act of writing itself signifies an implicit claim—or at least quest—for authority. She posits a basic formal distinction between public and private voices in fiction: narrators who address narratees external to the fictional world have public voices, while those who address narratees internal to the fictional world have private voices. She then identifies three main kinds of voice: the authorial, the personal, and the communal. Authorial voices are public; they are also heterodiegetic and may be self-referential. Personal voices may be public or private, but they belong to autodiegetic narrators self-consciously telling their own stories. A communal voice can belong to an individual who acts as a spokesperson for a community or to a group that narrates in the first-person plural or sequentially in mutually reinforcing ways.

Lanser does not set up a political or aesthetic ranking of the three kinds of voice but rather points out the claims and risks of each. Authorial voices claim the greatest authority, but that claim is also likely to encounter the greatest resistance because women have traditionally been in the lower ranks of the social hierarchy. This point helps explain why throughout the history of the novel many women writers who employed authorial voices took male pseudonyms. Personal voices claim a more limited authority, which makes them more inviting to those without pre-existing social authority. Nevertheless, even this more limited claim can meet with resistance, if either the narrator or the character "transgresses the boundaries of the acceptably feminine" (19). Communal voices get their authority through their connection with the communities they represent even as they implicitly challenge the dominant paradigm in the Western novel that associates authority with a single voice.

Alison Case, in a study that looks at the intersection of narration and plot called *Plotting Women* (1999) identifies and analyzes a kind of narrative discourse she calls feminine narration. Feminine narration comes from a narrator who is too naïve or inept to actively fashion the events into a coherent narrative with a set of thematic points. Case argues that in the eighteenth century such narration got marked as feminine, and this marking continued through the end of the nineteenth century. Whereas Warhol's and Lanser's ultimate concerns are with the gender of authors, Case's study makes the important move of separating the gender-linked technique from the gender of the author. As her definition indicates, it is not the gender of the author but the performance of the narrator (and cultural stereotypes about gender) that puts the feminine into feminine narration. Thus, both male and female authors employ feminine narration and both male and female narrators could be feminine.

Turning to rhetorical models, I noted above that for Booth reliable narration is a means of direct communication from implied author to authorial audience, and unreliable narration a means of indirect communication. But it is important to recognize that there are multiple kinds of unreliability and that narrators can be reliable in some ways and unreliable in others. In *Living to Tell about It* (2005), I suggest that narrators perform three main functions, which can be described as occurring along three different axes of communication: they report (along the axis of facts, characters, and events), they read or interpret (along the axis of perception/interpretation), and they make ethical judgments (along the axis of ethics/evaluation). Thus, they can be reliable or unreliable reporters, interpreters, or evaluators. Furthermore, they can be unreliable either by offering distorted reports, interpretations, and evaluations or by underperforming their functions (reporting less than they observe;

offering only partially correct interpretations of what they report; stopping too soon in their evaluations). These considerations lead to a taxonomy of two kinds of unreliability on each axis for a total of six kinds: misreporting, misreading (or misinterpreting), and misregarding (or misevaluating); underreporting, underreading (or underinterpreting), and underregarding (or underevaluating). This analysis suggests that the art of unreliable narration is an art of indirection: the author needs to make one text appropriate for two audiences and two purposes (narrator's and author's). My focus in *Living to Tell about It* is on how this art of indirection works in character narration, and I note that the single text actually communicates along two different tracks, that between narrator and narratee (the track of narrator functions) and that between author and authorial audience (the track of disclosure functions). Not surprisingly, sometimes authors cannot let a segment of the single text fully serve both purposes, and, in these cases, I suggest, disclosure functions typically trump narrator functions.

I also noted above that the rhetorical approach attends to both an ethics of the told and an ethics of the telling. More generally, the approach sees the ethical dimension of narrative as arising through the dynamic interplay of four distinct ethical positions: that of the characters in relation to each other; that of the narrator in relation to the characters and the narratee; that of the implied author in relation to the narrator, the characters, the narratee, and the authorial audience, and that of the flesh-and-blood audience in relation to the first three positions. Thus, the ethics of the told is found in the relation between the first and the fourth positions, while the ethics of the telling is found in the relations among the second, third, and fourth positions.

In order to show the interpretive consequences of this theoretical work on narrative discourse, I turn now to a close reading of a particular passage. Without denying the differences among the theorists I have just discussed, I will emphasize here the ways in which their different insights can complement each other. The passage is from Part One of Ian McEwan's *Atonement* (2001), and it describes the first physical union of two central characters, Cecilia Tallis and Robbie Turner. Cecilia is the elder daughter of the wealthy Tallis family, and Robbie is the son of their charwoman. They have known each other all their young lives but have just realized their mutual love—and begun to act on it. The scene takes place in the library in Cecilia's house.

Supported against the corner by his weight, she once again clasped her hands behind his neck, and rested her elbows on his shoulder and continued to kiss his face. The moment itself was easy. They held their breath before the membrane parted, and when it did, she turned away quickly but made no sound—it seemed to be a point of pride. They moved closer, deeper and then, for seconds on end everything stopped. Instead of an ecstatic frenzy there was stillness. They were stilled not by the astonishing fact of arrival but by an awed sense of return—they were face to face in the gloom staring into what little they could see of each other's eyes, and now it was the impersonal that dropped away. Of course there was nothing abstract about a face. The son of Grace and Ernest Turner, the daughter of Emily and Jack Tallis, the childhood friends, the university acquaintances, in a state of expansive, tranquil joy confronted the momentous change they had achieved. The closeness of a familiar face was not ludicrous, it was wondrous. Robbie stared at the woman, the girl he had always known, thinking that the change was entirely in himself, and was as fundamental, as fundamentally biological, as birth. Nothing as singular or as important had happened since the day of his birth. She returned his gaze, struck by the sense of her own transformation and overwhelmed by the beauty in a face which a lifetime's habit had taught her to ignore. She whispered his name with the deliberation of a child trying out the distinct sounds. When he replied with her name, it sounded like a new word—the syllables remained the same, but the meaning was different. Finally he spoke the three simple words that no amount of bad art or bad faith can ever quite cheapen. She repeated them, with exactly the same slight emphasis on the second word, as though she had been the one to say them first. He had no religious belief, but it was impossible not to think of an invisible presence or witness in the room, and that these words spoken aloud were like signatures on an unseen contract. (128-29)

Let us start with temporality. Part One loosely follows the chronological order of the events on a hot June day in 1935. I say "loosely follows" because the narration does employ analepses that function to provide context for our understanding of the events of that day, and there is the prolepsis that I quoted above. In addition, within the temporal boundaries of this June day, there are some temporal shifts that accompany spatial shifts: the narration will follow one or more characters in one spatial location for a while, and then, when the spatial location shifts, move back in time and pick up the actions of another character. Within the passage itself, however, Robbie's and Cecilia's thoughts shift from present to past and back again, as they register how the vitality and wonder of the present is dependent on that past. The sentence "The son of Grace and Ernest Turner, the daughter of Emily and Jack Tallis, the childhood friends, the university acquaintances, in a state of expansive, tranquil joy confronted the momentous change they had achieved" exemplifies this movement. It starts with their identity as infants, then moves to divide their previous relationship into its two main temporal and spatial frames (childhood at the Tallis estate; young adulthood at Cambridge) and ends with the present moment. The next two sentences trace the movement of Robbie's thought from the present to the recent past and then all the way back to his birth. Cecilia, for her part, is aware of her "lifetime's habit" of ignoring his face, and, as she re-names Robbie, she relocates herself in a time before that habit had taken hold and speaks "with the deliberation of a child trying out the distinct sounds."

As for frequency, the scene is narrated only once. Shortly after this scene and before their lovemaking is complete, the lovers will be interrupted by Cecilia's younger sister Briony, who later that night will mistakenly identify Robbie as the man who sexually assaults her cousin Lola. That identification will lead to Robbie's being sent to prison and then, as a way to modify his sentence, to his joining the British army. As a soldier he participates in the retreat to Dunkirk in 1939, which is narrated in Part Two. In their correspondence after this night, Cecilia and Robbie use the phrase "a quiet corner in the library" but that is the only time the narration returns explicitly to the scene. The result, to adapt a phrase from the passage itself, is to highlight its singularity and importance in the narrative.

There are two salient dimensions of duration in the passage. I have already touched on the first, which is about the relation between order and duration. Though the characters' consciousnesses frequently return to the past, the duration of those returns is minimal: many years are summed up in short phrases such as "the childhood friends, the university acquaintances," while the descriptions of the present instant of stopped time are drawn out: "in a state of expansive, tranquil joy confronted the momentous change they had achieved." The second dimension is the duration of the period of stopped time itself in relation to the duration of the narration about it. One way to appreciate the extended duration of the narration is to compare the length of time it would take for Cecilia and Robbie, while physically joined, to exchange gazes, say each other's names, and then "I love you" and the length of time it takes to read the passage. Another way to appreciate the extended duration is to pause over the first sentence of the next paragraph: "They had been motionless for perhaps as long as half a minute."

Turning to narrative perspective, we can see that this passage illustrates the value of Palmer's concept of the continuing consciousness frame, and its advantages over an exclusive attention to sentence-by-sentence movements of focalization. In a classical, grammatical analysis we would note how the focalization shifts as the passage moves from descriptions of physical action (the first sexual intercourse between the two characters) to reports of their thoughts and other mental activity. We'd assign the focalization of the reports of action to the narrator and the focalization of the rest of the passage to the relevant characters. Palmer's concept enables us to recognize the limitation of that approach because it offers a more encompassing and more adequate account of how the discourse is working here. Everything that is reported—the sexual intercourse, its accompanying sensations, emotional responses and thoughts, including the inferences each character makes about the other—falls within the continuing consciousness frame of Cecilia and Robbie. The passage does move from their joint consciousness to their individual consciousnesses, but that movement offers variations on a theme rather than an exposure of significant gaps between them. Consider some elements of the first four sentences. The description of Cecilia's physical movement in the first sentence, though given in the heterodiegetic narrator's voice, is very much within the characters' consciousness frame. "The moment itself was easy" may initially appear to be another external description by the narrator, but a little reflection reveals that "easy" describes how the physical act of penetration felt to Cecilia and to Robbie. "It seemed to be a point of pride" may initially appear to be only a sign of the narrator's lack of omniscience, but the clause is better understood as Robbie's inference about Cecilia's turning away. Perhaps the best evidence of how attention to the continuing consciousness frame transforms the sentence by sentence analysis of focalization is in the phrase "everything stopped." It is clearly not the narrator's objective report through his window on the events as privileged observer of the scene but rather a way of rendering the joint mental experience of the two characters.

Their joint consciousness is represented down through the sentence, "The closeness of a familiar face was not ludicrous, it was wondrous," but when the narration shifts to their individual consciousnesses, the passage works by repetition with a difference, and it shows that their mental activity goes beyond thought to include their emotions of joy and of wonder at each other and what they are sharing. Each one's line of mental activity is mirrored by the other's: Robbie stares at Cecilia contemplating the magnitude of the change in his perception of her; she returns his gaze and is "struck by her own transformation." They take turns whispering each other's names and then saying "I love you." Finally, although the passage ends with Robbie's consciousness, he is contemplating their mutual covenant before a quasi-sacred, invisible witness.

Turning now to voice, we can see that the passage provides excellent grounds for Genette's distinction between voice and vision/ perception as well as for Bakhtin's attention to heteroglossia. While we can confidently identify the characters' continuing consciousness frame as governing the passage, we must also recognize that their voices are not the only ones in the passage. The heterodiegetic narrator's voice is also present on its own and mingled with theirs in the multiple sentences of indirect discourse. (For the sake of convenience and relying on the principle that the default gender of such a narrator is the gender of the author, I will for now refer to the narrator as "he." But, as we will see shortly, one of the striking things about *Atonement* is the way in which revelations in its plot have consequences for our understanding of voice.) Sometimes the mingling means that we cannot separate the narrator's voice from the characters', as, for example, in "the closeness of a familiar face was not ludicrous, it was wondrous." We also cannot separate these voices because, in Bakhtin's terms, they share the same register, that of the well-educated upper middle class. Robbie's sharing this register with the narrator and with Cecilia is a sign of the difference his education at Cambridge has made. The son of the charwoman has become, in at least this one respect, the equal of the daughter of her employers. But this representation of Robbie's equality contrasts with the role that class plays in the readiness of almost everyone to believe Briony's identification of the charwoman's son as Lola's rapist.

At other points in the passage, we can identify the characters' voices with a high degree of probability, thus bringing us closer to their actual thoughts. The "of course" in "Of course there was nothing abstract about a face" seems to belong to both Robbie and Cecilia, while "as fundamental, as fundamentally biological, as birth," with its quick movement from one phrase to a second that refines the first, belongs to Robbie, and "like a new word—the syllables remained the same, but the meaning was different," with its quick movement from the analogy to the explanation of the analogy's meaning, belongs to Cecilia, as does the phrase "lifetime habit." Similarly, "nothing as singular or important," "an invisible presence or witness," and "signatures on an unseen contract" also seem to belong to Robbie's voice,

Furthermore, the language of the passage sets up a Bakhtinian dialogue among the language of the body, the language of voicing itself, and the language of religion. The language of the body is obviously there in the references to "their breath," "the membrane," "each other's eyes," and "the face." But it is also there in Robbie's comparison of this moment with his birth, since in both cases something fundamentally biological is going on, and that something involves the connection between his body and that of a woman. This dimension of the passage also links it with the language of Robbie's letter to Cecilia in the version that he never meant her to see but mistakenly asked Briony to deliver. In that letter, he wrote "In my dreams I kiss your cunt, your sweet wet cunt. In my thoughts I make love to you all day long" (80). The direct vulgarity of that letter led Cecilia to recognize that she had been repressing her feelings for Robbie, and that recognition led them to this scene. The language of the letter, though not repeated in this passage, nevertheless provides an undercurrent to the more refined language of the body here, a refinement seen most clearly in the way the "ecstatic frenzy" of bodies coupling is mentioned only as a contrast to the stillness they felt. The implicit dialogue between the vulgar and the refined conveys the physical desire driving Robbie and Cecilia's coupling while emphasizing that their sexual union transcends the physical.

The relation between these languages of the body and the languages of voice and of religion magnifies this effect. By the language of voice I mean McEwan's descriptions of the way Robbie and Cecilia utter each other's names and the way each one pronounces the three simple words. Underneath these descriptions, we hear the direct discourse of "Robbie Turner," "Cecilia Tallis," "I love you," and "I love you," while the descriptions, through their attention to each speaker's now defamiliarized relation to the utterances, also defamiliarize them for us. The sequence of utterances adds to this effect. Cecilia's impulse to name Robbie itself highlights the implied mental activity conveyed by the passage: now that her perception of him has been transformed, she feels compelled to name him anew—as if she were learning his name for the first time. Similarly, now that her perception of him has changed, she hears his utterance of her name in a fresh way. They are like Adam and Eve in the Garden of Eden naming the wonders of creation, but what they name is each other. The implied mental activity and the defamiliarization effect for both the characters and McEwan's audience carry over to the next logical step in the sequence, the exchange of "the three simple words." The transformation in their mutual perception leads to their re-naming, the re-naming leads to the exchange of "I love yous," and that exchange simultaneously gives voice to and enacts their transformed perceptions. "I love you" cannot be cheap within this context of mutual understanding—either for the two characters or for the members of the narrative and authorial audiences. Indeed, the exchange is so satisfying that it evokes the language of religion, even for the nonbeliever Robbie, who cannot help thinking of "an invisible presence or witness in the room." The dialogue of languages emphasizes the mingling of the physical, the mental, and the spiritual in the sexual union of Robbie and Cecilia.

Often the techniques McEwan uses here, especially the representation of characters' consciousnesses, lead to a discrepancy between their perceptions and those of the authorial audience. But in this case the techniques lead us to marvel at what is being revealed. The passage is a part of a remarkable scene representing the power, wonder, and beauty of newly discovered love. As noted above, it is the high point in that love story, one that sustains the lovers after they are separated and one that underlines for us the absolutely devastating consequences for Cecilia and Robbie of Briony's mistaken identification of him as Lola's sexual assailant.

But if we were to stop the analysis here we would be stopping too soon, because McEwan's late revelation that, within the world of the novel, Briony is the author of this passage, complicates our understanding of it. And here the emphases of the rhetorical approach to narrative discourse become especially relevant. McEwan reveals, in the last section of the novel, by means of a diary entry Briony writes after the celebration of her seventy-seventh birthday in 1999, that (a) Briony's novel is her effort to atone for what she did to Robbie and Cecilia and (b) she intends Parts One and Two of her novel to be truthful representations of actual events, while she deliberately alters history in Part Three. Those alterations are major: Part Three represents Cecilia and Robbie as reunited and Briony

herself on the verge of some measure of atonement as she prepares
to confess her mistaken identification of Robbie to all the relevant
parties. But within the storyworld, the reality is that Robbie dies in
the retreat from Dunkirk, and Cecilia dies when the Balham Underground Station is blown up a few months later. Briony's only
direct effort at atonement takes the form of her novel, Parts One,
Two, and Three of McEwan's *Atonement*.

The first issue then in reconsidering this passage involves recon-
figuring our understanding of the relations among McEwan as implied author, Briony as character in both her novel and McEwan's,
and Briony as author of Part One. In both McEwan's novel and Briony's
novel, Briony as character, at the age of 13 in 1935, is a budding writer
with a limited imagination, someone who is only dimly beginning to
realize that other people have consciousnesses as alive as her own:
"though it offended her sense of order, she knew it was overwhelm-
ingly probable that everyone else had thoughts like hers. She knew
this, but only in a rather arid way; she didn't really feel it" (34). Furthermore, Briony's limited ability to recognize the complexity of other
minds fuels her misidentification of Robbie: having read his letter to
Cecilia, she has labelled him a "maniac" and then fit him into her own
simplified narrative of what a maniac would do, after she sees a figure
retreating from Lola. Thus, McEwan shows Briony the author clearly
representing the limitations of Briony the character, and asks his audience to recognize that her critical self-representation is one part of
her effort to atone through her novel. Furthermore, he asks us to recognize her authorial act of constructing the scene between Robbie
and Cecilia in the library before she interrupted them as another crucial part of her effort at atonement. Through its mastery of many of
the techniques of modernist fiction for representing consciousness,
the passage gives vivid and enduring life to Robbie, to Cecilia, and to
their union, even as it implicitly acknowledges what she as character
took from them.

The second issue in reconsidering the passage goes beyond its
specifics to the larger ethical dimensions of both Briony's narrative
and McEwan's. If Briony's representation of herself and of Robbie

and Cecilia in Part One shows her taking responsibility for her
misidentification and its horrible consequences, does her altering
history in Part Three become an effort to avoid taking ultimate responsibility for that crime and its consequences? Is this alteration
of the historical record a sign of her falling back into a more sophisticated version of the sentimental romances she loved—and wrote—
when she was 13? Or is her authorial decision to change the historical
outcome in her fiction a justifiable choice to reject what she calls
the "bleakest realism" in her diary entry, a better way to honor the
memory of Robbie and Cecilia? For McEwan's part, what is the ethical dimension of the unusual relation he sets up between disclosure
functions and narrator functions, a relation that keeps his audience
so long in the dark about the nature of the reading they are engaged
in? More specifically, what kind of ethical act is it to ask readers to
engage emotionally and ethically with a plot of grave error and earnest atonement only to disclose after an extended trajectory of that
engagement that, within the storyworld, the error was real but the
atonement was not? What do we make of the apparent analogy between Briony's misidentification of Robbie and McEwan's misidentification of the nature of his narrative? Attempting to answer these
ethical questions in a responsible way would require another long
essay, and I have no doubt that the answers would themselves be
contested. But the specifics of my answers matter less than the recognition that these questions arise directly out of McEwan's handling of his narrative discourse.[6]

These questions are also related to the kind of ideological questions about McEwan's techniques that feminist narratologists would
pose. What do those techniques suggest about his view of the relation between gender and authority? If we think McEwan guides us
to find Briony's choice to alter history as an evasion of her responsibility, then we would conclude that he gives Briony the author tremendous authority in Parts One, Two, and Three only to undermine
that authority with the inclusion of the diary entry. On the other
hand, if we find McEwan guiding us to accept Briony's justification
for altering history, then we would conclude that he is granting her
a rare kind of authority, one that links her act of fictional narrative

with her act of atonement. More generally, feminist narratologists would raise questions about McEwan's choice to tell this story about error and possible atonements by focusing on the mistakes of a young girl and the choices of a mature woman novelist. They also would focus on the choice of the central event—the sexual assault of a young woman, who, it turns out, falls in love with and marries her assailant—as another site for questions about the gender politics of McEwan's choices. Again, working through the possibilities in a responsible way would require a separate essay, but the point is that the questions arise directly out of McEwan's narrative.

PART 3: UNRESOLVED INSTABILITIES

I am large, I contain multitudes.

As I hope is now evident, the narrative of the relation between narrative and narrative theory has many plots, and the dynamics of those plots can be affected in multiple ways. Consequently, as I come to the end of my version, I want to avoid gestures toward completeness, indeed, any signals that this narrative is approaching a state of equilibrium in which theory and narrative, like two lovers in a romantic comedy, will live in a perpetual state of mutual understanding and happiness. Instead, this narrative not only has many unresolved instabilities but it is also one in which new instabilities continually emerge. New instabilities emerge because, as Scholes and Kellogg so amply demonstrate, narrative itself continues to evolve as changes in history and culture (including literary history and culture) prompt innovations in narrative form. New instabilities also arise because any theoretical framework worthy of the name will, in solving some problems, either reveal or neglect others. As theorists then propose solutions to these problems, the larger theoretical frameworks get revised, and the cycle starts again. Finally, new instabilities materialize because interdisciplinarity generates new approaches to narrative, and these approaches either address new problems or old problems in a substantially different way. Recently, a number of critics have been developing an approach to literary narrative derived from the principles of Darwin's *The Origin of Species*. This approach looks at both the behavior of characters and the behavior of authors and readers in evolutionary terms, explaining their motivations and activity by the principles that govern natural selection (e.g., Elizabeth Bennet wants to marry Darcy because, as the leading male in her social circle, he provides the best chance for her genes to survive into future generations). At this stage in its own evolution, "literary Darwinism" strikes me as being too much of an a priori scheme in which the complex relations between nature and culture get reduced to the single pattern of nature trumping culture. The approach works much better in explaining why Elizabeth marries Darcy than it does in explaining why she initially rejects him. But if "literary Darwinism" eventually proves to be a productive new approach to narrative, it will at the very least propose new understandings of character and plot.

Rather than speculate about the fate of literary Darwinisim or otherwise predict the future of narrative theory, I'd like to end my telling by highlighting four currently unresolved instabilities, the first two involving the relation between narrative and narrative theory and the second two within narrative theory itself.

1. Narrative theory and the tradition of nonmimetic narrative. In *Unnatural Voices* (2006) Brian Richardson persuasively argues that most existing narrative theory is derived from the study of narratives with a mimetic orientation, which leads it to misleading generalizations about the nature of narrative, and especially the nature of narrative discourse. Richardson shows that there is a long tradition of narrative that deliberately eschews such a mimetic orientation, and he proposes many valuable extensions and revisions of current theory. Among other issues, he analyzes second-person (or direct address) narration, "we" narration, and multi-person narration. Beyond these specifics, Richardson's work opens up a new vein of theoretical exploration.

2. Narrative theory and digital narrative. The advent of digital technology and the development of early hypertext narratives led to

many extravagant claims about the differences between digital and print narratives. But as digital technology continues to evolve, and as narrative artists continue to work in the new medium, the likelihood that the differences will become more significant increases. As those differences develop, narrative theory will need to be revised so that it can do justice to the distinctiveness of each kind of narrative. Marie-Laure Ryan in *Narrative as Virtual Reality* (2001) provides an excellent foundation for work on these developments precisely because she places digital narrative and the interactivity it often encourages within the context of the virtual reality generated by print narrative and the immersion it encourages.

3. Narrative theory, the borders between fiction and nonfiction, and cross-border traffic. Spurred by the work of Hayden White on the similarities between the techniques of writing history and writing fiction, including the necessity of emplotment, some theorists argue that the borders between fiction and nonfiction are illusory. Dorrit Cohn advances the counterargument that there are distinctive "signposts of fictionality," such as its freedom to employ internal focalization and unreliable narration. Richardson's work could also be marshalled in support of Cohn's case. In my rhetorical view, preserving the borders has the major advantage of helping us account for the differences in the ways we respond to particular narratives, even as the debate calls attention to various kinds of border-crossing—of technique, of character, of place, and so on. Susan Lanser offers a promising proposal for looking at another kind of border crossing: the similar "attachments" that authors of fiction and nonfiction can have to their statements. Lanser persuasively argues that much commentary within the borders of fiction—e.g., a narrator's generalizing statements about the nature of the world—is as directly attached to their authors as if that commentary occurred outside the borders of fiction.

4. Narrative space. Genette, Ricoeur, Brooks, Herman, and others have all done significant work on narrative time, and though there

has been some significant work on narrative space throughout the history of narrative theory, it has not received the same amount of attention. Recently, however, the situation is changing as critics of various orientations turn their attention to the importance of space within narrative. To cite just two examples: Susan Friedman has recently followed her work on "spatialization" with a provocative proposal for the development of a "spatial poetics." Such a poetics would recognize space's intimate connection with time and its capacity to be not just a static background but a dynamic element of narrative structure. From a cognitivist perspective, Marie-Laure Ryan has proposed a project of "literary cartography," the analysis of strategies that readers employ for reconstructing mental maps of narrative space.[7]

Although the narrative of the relation between narrative theory and its object of study remains very much *in mediis rebus*, my version of the last forty years of that narrative must, thankfully for all, come to a close. In order to pay tribute to the groundbreaking work of Scholes and Kellogg and to underline once again the intimate and evolving connection between narrative and narrative theory, I would like to quote and then adapt their conclusion. They end with a short and suggestive narrative about their subject: "narrative literature is the most restless of forms, driven by its imperfections and inner contradictions to an unceasing search for an unattainable ideal. It is this terribly human struggle that makes the study of narrative art the most fascinating of literary studies" (282). Shifting the subject from narrative to narrative theory, I end thus: At its best narrative theory is the most restless of pursuits, driven by its own imperfections and by the wonders and the variety of its object of study to an unceasing search for an unattainable ideal: the comprehensive account of the pervasiveness and power of stories and storytelling, in short, for the nature of narrative itself. It is this simultaneously daunting and exhilarating challenge that makes narrative theory one of the most vital and valuable enterprises of contemporary intellectual inquiry.

Appendix

These materials are the documentation for part of the discussion of soliloquies and monologues as devices of characterization (Ch. 5). For a number of reasons we have thought it advisable to include fresh translations (by R. Scholes) of the classical texts. We offer them not as attempts to outdo previous translators, whose expertise is in general far beyond our own, but because some aspects of the problem we are considering are quite properly hidden in most translations. A translator of a classical text is not merely taking things from one language and putting them into another. He is also taking things from one time and adapting them to another. He not only translates but modernizes as well. In practice this usually means introducing certain consistencies, eliminating a certain repetitiveness and floridity, and, in passages such as those we are concerned with, substituting "She thought" for "She said." Modern notions of effectiveness in language and of the relation of language to thought make modern translations dangerous aids for a student of literary history. No translation which is effective as a work of *modern* literature has not paid a price. And the price involves an inevitable sacrifice of the pastness of the past.

1. Apollonius Rhodius, *The Argonautica*, Bk. III, 772–801.

"Δειλὴ ἐγώ, νῦν ἔνθα κακῶν ἢ ἔνθα γένωμαι;
πάντῃ μοι φρένες εἰσὶν ἀμήχανοι· οὐδέ τις ἀλκὴ
πήματος· ἀλλ' αὔτως φλέγει ἔμπεδον. ὡς ὄφελόν γε
Ἀρτέμιδος κραιπνοῖσι πάρος βελέεσσι δαμῆναι,
πρὶν τόνγ' εἰσιδέειν, πρὶν Ἀχαιίδα γαῖαν ἱκέσθαι
Χαλκιόπης υἷας. τοὺς μὲν θεὸς ἤ τις Ἐρινὺς
ἄμμι πολυκλαύτους δεῦρ' ἤγαγε κεῖθεν ἀνίας.
φθίσθω ἀεθλεύων, εἴ οἱ κατὰ νειὸν ὀλέσθαι
μοῖρα πέλει. πῶς γάρ κεν ἐμοὺς λελάθοιμι τοκῆας
φάρμακα μησαμένη; ποῖον δ' ἐπὶ μῦθον ἐνίψω;   780
τίς δὲ δόλος, τίς μῆτις ἐπίκλοπος ἔσσετ' ἀρωγῆς;
ἦ μιν ἄνευθ' ἑτάρων προσπτύξομαι οἶον ἰδοῦσα;
δύσμορος· οὐ μὲν ἔολπα καταφθιμένοιό περ ἔμπης
λωφήσειν ἀχέων· τότε δ' ἂν κακὸν ἄμμι πέλοιτο,
κεῖνος ὅτε ζωῆς ἀπαμείρεται. ἐρρέτω αἰδώς,
ἐρρέτω ἀγλαΐη· ὁ δ' ἐμῇ ἰότητι σαωθεὶς
ἀσκηθής, ἵνα οἱ θυμῷ φίλον, ἔνθα νέοιτο.
αὐτὰρ ἐγὼν αὐτῆμαρ, ὅτ' ἐξανύσειεν ἄεθλον,
τεθναίην, ἢ λαιμὸν ἀναρτήσασα μελάθρῳ,
ἢ καὶ πασσαμένη ῥαιστήρια φάρμακα θυμοῦ.   790
ἀλλὰ καὶ ὧς φθιμένῃ μοι ἐπιλλίξουσιν ὀπίσσω
κερτομίας· τηλοῦ δὲ πόλις περὶ πᾶσα βοήσει
πότμον ἐμόν· καί κέν με διὰ στόματος φορέουσαι
Κολχίδες ἄλλυδις ἄλλαι ἀεικέα μωμήσονται·
ἥτις κηδομένη τόσον ἀνέρος ἀλλοδαποῖο
κάτθανεν, ἥτις δῶμα καὶ οὓς ᾔσχυνε τοκῆας,
μαργοσύνῃ εἴξασα. τί δ' οὐκ ἐμὸν ἔσσεται αἶσχος;
ᾧ μοι ἐμῆς ἄτης. ἦ τ' ἂν πολὺ κέρδιον εἴη
τῇδ' αὐτῇ ἐν νυκτὶ λιπεῖν βίον ἐν θαλάμοισιν
πότμῳ ἀνωίστῳ, κάκ' ἐλέγχεα πάντα φυγοῦσαν,   800
πρὶν τάδε λωβήεντα καὶ οὐκ ὀνομαστὰ τελέσσαι."

How miserable I am. Must I find evil whichever way I turn? Every alternative leaves my heart sick, and there is no help for this pain — it will burn forever. I wish I had been killed by the swift arrows of Artemis before I had seen him [Jason], before Chalciope's sons had gone to Achaea. Some God or some Fury brought them here with grief and tears for us. Let him fall in the attempt if he is fated to die in the new-ploughed field. For how could I brew some magic potion without my parents' knowledge? What story can I tell them? What trick, what cunning device will help him? How can I speak to him alone, away from his comrades? How ill-fated I am. I cannot even hope that my sorrows would die with him; his death would only make me unhappier. Farewell, my modesty; farewell, my good name. Protected from harm by me, he might go as he pleases and leave me to die. Yes, on the day he succeeds in his task I could die by hanging myself from a rafter or by taking some medicine to still my heart. Yet even so they would gossip about me after I was dead; my fate would be bruited about in distant cities; and here the Colchian women would whisper my name with low mockery: the one who died for love of a stranger, the one who disgraced home and parents, overcome by lust. Oh, what disgrace would not be mine, thanks to this foolish passion. Better for me to die here in my room this very night by some accident and escape all this dishonor than to succeed in a scheme too low to name.

Medea's speech is presented as a spoken soliloquy, introduced by φώνησέν τε (she said) and closed by Ἦ (she spoke, or she finished speaking). Dido's monologue is quite different in this respect.

2. Vergil, *The Aeneid*, Bk. IV, 534–552.

> "en, quid ago? rursusne procos inrisa priores
> experiar, Nomadumque petam conubia supplex,   535
> quos ego sim totiens iam dedignata maritos?
> Iliacas igitur classis atque ultima Teucrum
> iussa sequar? quiane auxilio iuvat ante levatos
> et bene apud memores veteris stat gratia facti?
> quis me autem, fac velle, sinet ratibusque superbis   540
> invisam accipiet? nescis heu, perdita, necdum
> Laomedonteae sentis periuria gentis?
> quid tum? sola fuga nautas comitabor ovantis?
> an Tyriis omnique manu stipata meorum
> inferar et, quos Sidonia vix urbe revelli,   545
> rursus agam pelago et ventis dare vela iubebo?
> quin morere ut merita es, ferroque averte dolorem.
> tu lacrimis evicta meis, tu prima furentem

his, germana, malis oneras atque obicis hosti.
non licuit thalami expertem sine crimine vitam   550
degere more ferae, talis nec tangere curas;
non servata fides cineri promissa Sychaeo."

Now what can I do? Turn back, a laughing-stock, to my former
suitors and beg for a marriage among the Numidians whom I have so
often scorned as bridegrooms? Or follow the Trojan ships and every
last Trojan command? What good is it that they have been strength-
ened by my aid? Will they remember gratefully my helpfulness in the
past? And who would let me (even if I wanted to), who would allow
this hateful wretch on his proud ship? Now you see, lost creature, you
finally understand the treachery of these sons of Laomedon. But then
if I cannot accompany those triumphant sailors as a lone fugitive, can
I join them attended by all my own citizens and soldiers? Can I get
those whom I could scarcely tear away from the city of Sidon to venture their sails before the winds again? No, die as you deserve to, fend
off grief with a dagger. Why did you, my sister [Anna], listen to my
tears and expose me to the enemy to be weighed down with all these
evils that are driving me mad? Why wasn't I left unmarried as the wild
things are, untouched by such worries. My vows to your ashes have
not been kept, Sychaeus!

This begins definitely as an unspoken soliloquy, an *interior*
monologue. It is introduced, in the preceding line, by the expression *secumque ita corde volutat* (and thus she turns [things]
over in [her] heart). The end of the soliloquy may be regarded in
two ways. The phrase in the line which succeeds the monologue
is *Tantos illa suo rempebat pectore questus* (She burst out with
such lamentations from her breast). *Corde volutat* (she turns
over in her heart) does not seem quite equivalent to *rumpebat
pectore* (she bursts out from her breast). Perhaps Vergil was
using the two phrases mechanically, without considering the sort
of question we are raising here, but it seems more in keeping
with his carefulness and sensitivity for us to assume that he meant
to indicate a progression from an internal consideration of her
situation to such painful thoughts as cannot be retained in the
heart but must burst forth as a cry of anguish. Most of the ancient

monologues are introduced and closed by such formulas as "She said" and "She spoke." Vergil, in going beyond the formulas, is making use of the resources open to one who composes at leisure, in writing. Such attention to detail is the main justification for the supersession of oral narrative by written, as it is for our two-thousand-year veneration of the Mantuan poèt.

(The last part of the translated passage is quite difficult and contains an unresolved textual problem or two. This translation has thus, of necessity, been made with a bit more boldness and freedom than any of the others, but the disjointedness of the last sentences, the hopping from topic to topic and thought to thought — these are faithfully rendered. They are part of the characterization and show Vergil combining a psychological approach to the language of thought with the very effective rhetoric of the first part of Dido's monologue.)

3. Ovid, *Metamorphoses*, Bk. X, 319–333.

illa quidem sentit foedoque repugnat amori
et secum "quo mente feror? quid molior?" inquit
"di, precor, et pietas sacrataque iura parentum,   321
hoc prohibete nefas scelerique resistite nostro,
si tamen hoc scelus est.   sed enim damnare negatur
hanc Venerem pietas: coeunt animalia nullo
cetera dilectu, nec habetur turpe iuvencae   325
ferre patrem tergo, fit equo sua filia coniunx,
quasque creavit init pecudes caper, ipsaque, cuius
semine concepta est, ex illo concipit ales.
felices, quibus ista licent! humana malignas
cura dedit leges, et quod natura remittit,   330
invida iura negant.   gentes tamen esse feruntur,
in quibus et nato genetrix et nata parenti
iungitur, ut pietas geminato crescat amore."

She herself senses the vileness of her passion and resists it; where am I headed, what do I intend, she demands of herself. Oh gods, I pray, Oh filial devotion and the sacred rights of parents, forbid this crime and keep this evil away from me — if it really is evil. But piety need not condemn this kind of love: other animals mate indiscriminately; it is no shame for a heifer to be mounted by her father, nor for a horse to mate with his daughter. A goat has the run of she-goats he has sired, and even the birds grow big with the seed from which they sprang. Happy creatures who are allowed to live thus. Human meddling has made such spiteful laws; what nature allows, the jealous laws deny. Yet they say that there are even human tribes among whom mothers mate with sons, fathers with daughters so that filial devotion increases through a double love. . . . [Twenty additional, highly rhetorical lines follow.]

The inwardness of this soliloquy is not a concern of Ovid's. The *inquit* of line 320 almost suggests a legal cross-examination, in which Myrrha is both prosecutor and defendant (as is Stephen Dedalus in some passages of *Ulysses*). The soliloquy ends at line 356 with a conventional *Dixerat* (She finished speaking). Where Vergil moved inward with his *corde volutat* and a pattern of thought which tended toward the personal and irrational, Ovid maintains his logic-chopping argument and verbal play right to the end, with such expressions as *quia iam meus est, non est meus* (because he is already mine, he is not mine), delighting in the patterns of language which the situation generates. In the last lines, however, with a brilliant *coup de rhétorique*, he shows us that he too is a psychologist, as the legal argument is resolved one way, the woman herself the other. And it is the woman who has the last word:

> velle puta: res ipsa vetat; pius ille memorque
> moris — et o vellem similis furor esset in illo.

Even if you still want this, everything is against it; he is a good, law-abiding man — and O how I wish he loved me as I love him.

Myrrha's passion bursts through her rhetorical scheme of argument much as Dido's cry of anguish bursts forth to climax her silent monologue. The general form of the Ovidian monologue, then, is very like the Vergilian. But precisely because Ovid is employing a device or *topos* which has become conventional, he must push the convention to the point of mannerism; he must overexploit its possibilities almost, transferring interest from the object represented to the form of representation. The inevitable change from classical to mannered or rococo in artistic form can be seen here in the difference between Vergil and Ovid as it can be seen in modern literature in the difference between Tolstoy and Joyce.

4. Xenephon of Ephesus, *Habrocomes and Anthia*, Book I, Part IV, 1–3, 4, 6–7.

IV (1) Λαβὼν δὴ τὴν κόμην ὁ Ἀβροκόμης καὶ σπαράξας τὴν ἐσθῆτα «φεῦ μοι τῶν κακῶν» εἶπε, «τί πέπονθα δυστυχής; ὁ μέχρι νῦν ἀνδρικὸς Ἀβροκόμης, ὁ καταφρονῶν Ἔρωτος, ὁ τῷ θεῷ λοιδορούμενος ἑάλωκα καὶ νενίκημαι καὶ παρθένῳ δουλεύειν ἀναγκάζομαι, καὶ φαίνεταί τις ἤδη καλλίων ἐμοῦ καὶ θεὸν Ἔρωτα καλῶ. (2) Ὦ πάντα ἄνανδρος ἐγὼ καὶ πονηρός· οὐ καρτερήσω νῦν; οὐ μενῶ γεννικός; οὐκ ἔσομαι καλλίων Ἔρωτος; νῦν οὐδὲν ὄντα θεὸν νικῆσαί με δεῖ. (3) Καλὴ παρθένος· τί δέ; τοῖς σοῖς ὀφθαλμοῖς, Ἀβροκόμη, εὔμορφος Ἀνθία, ἀλλ', ἐὰν θέλῃς, οὐχὶ σοί. Δεδόχθω ταῦτα· οὐκ ἂν Ἔρως ποτέ μου κρατήσαι.»

Habrocomes pulled his hair and tore his clothing. Ah me, what pain! he said. What is happening to me? The manly Habrocomes, the despiser of Eros, who used to insult the god regularly, now is defeated and captured, forced to be the slave of a girl, and now someone seems handsomer than I, and I call Eros god. I am the least manly of men, now. Can't I fight back? Can't I be brave and prove myself better than Eros? Now I shall humble this petty divinity. The girl is pretty? So what. Only your eyes, Habrocomes, find Anthia pretty, not, unless you wish it, your true self. If I keep this in mind, Eros will never be my master.

(4) Ταῦτα ἔλεγε, καὶ ὁ θεὸς σφοδρότερος αὐτῷ ἐνέκειτο καὶ εἷλκεν ἀντιπίπτοντα καὶ ὠδύνα μὴ θέλοντα. Οὐκέτι δὴ καρτερῶν, ῥίψας ἑαυτὸν εἰς γῆν «νενίκηκας», εἶπεν, «Ἔρως, μέγα σοι τρόπαιον ἐγήγερται κατὰ Ἀβροκόμου τοῦ σώφρονος. ἱκέτην ἔχεις . . . .»

He spoke thus, but the god pressed him harder and harder, dragging him against his will to that torment which he wanted no part of. When he could stand it no longer, he threw himself on the ground, saying,

You have beaten me, Eros, and deserve a great trophy for your victory over the chaste Habrocomes. . . .

Habrocomes' soliloquy, spoken out loud apparently, (εἶπε, ἔλεγε), at this point becomes a prayer to Eros in which the young man goes on to ask the god to be merciful now and give him Anthia. Anthia's own soliloquy follows immediately; she too, we are told, has been engaged in a similar struggle:

(6) . . . «Τί» φησὶν «ὦ δυστυχὴς πέπονθα; παρθένος παρ' ἡλικίαν ἐρῶ καὶ ὀδυνῶμαι καινὰ καὶ κόρῃ μὴ πρέποντα. Ἐφ' Ἀβροκόμῃ μαίνομαι καλῷ μέν, ἀλλ' ὑπερηφάνῳ.

(7) Καὶ τίς ἔσται ὁ τῆς ἐπιθυμίας ὅρος καὶ τί τὸ πέρας τοῦ κακοῦ; Σοβαρὸς οὗτος ἐρώμενος, παρθένος ἐγὼ φρουρουμένη· τίνα βοηθὸν λήψομαι; τίνι πάντα κοινώσομαι; ποῦ δὲ Ἀβροκόμην ὄψομαι;»

. . . Ah, she said, what is happening to me? For a maiden I love beyond my years; I suffer from a malady strange and unbecoming to a young girl. I am mad with love for Habrocomes, who is as proud as he is handsome. Where will this passion end? How will my pain be eased? he is unapproachable, this man I love, and I am a well-chaperoned maiden. Who can I find to help me? Who can I tell everything? Where will I see Habrocomes?

Anthia's situation resembles that of Medea and the other unhappy females, but it is really different in that it can be resolved, whereas the "tragic" or epic soliloquy presents a problem that is unsolvable, a true dilemma. Habrocomes and Anthia, of course, after many trials and tribulations, are finally united. The same conventions operate in Longus' *Daphnis and Chloe;* the same set pieces appear at the same moments. But Longus is a superior artist. His soliloquies are enriched with telling details and something like a truly internal approach to character. Still, the linguistic convention which presides over the soliloquies in Longus is mainly a rhetorical one. The artlessness of Chloe, for example, is very artfully presented.

5. Longus, *Daphnis and Chloe*, Book I, Parts 14 and 18.

(14) "Νῦν ἐγὼ νοσῶ μέν, τί δὲ ἡ νόσος ἀγνοῶ· ἀλγῶ, καὶ ἕλκος οὐκ ἔστι μοι. λυποῦμαι, καὶ οὐδὲν τῶν προβάτων ἀπόλωλέ μοι· κάομαι, καὶ ἐν σκιᾷ τοσαύτῃ κάθημαι. πόσοι βάτοι με πολλάκις ἤμυξαν, καὶ οὐκ ἔκλαυσα· πόσαι μέλιτται κέντρα ἐνῆκαν, ἀλλ᾽ οὐκ ἔκραγον. τουτὶ δὲ τὸ νύττον μου τὴν καρδίαν πάντων ἐκείνων πικρότερον. καλὸς ὁ Δάφνις, καὶ γὰρ τὰ ἄνθη· καλὸν ἡ σύριγξ αὐτοῦ φθέγγεται, καὶ γὰρ αἱ ἀηδόνες· ἀλλ᾽ ἐκείνων οὐδείς μοι λόγος. εἴθε αὐτοῦ σύριγξ ἐγενόμην, ἵν᾽ ἐμπνέῃ μοι· εἴθε αἴξ, ἵν᾽ ὑπ᾽ ἐκείνου νέμωμαι. ὦ πονηρὸν ὕδωρ, μόνον Δάφνιν καλὸν ἐποίησας, ἐγὼ δὲ μάτην ἀπελουσάμην. οἴχομαι, Νύμφαι, καὶ οὐδὲ ὑμεῖς σώζετε τὴν παρθένον τὴν ἐν ὑμῖν τραφεῖσαν. τίς ὑμᾶς στεφανώσει μετ᾽ ἐμέ; τίς τοὺς ἀθλίους ἄρνας ἀναθρέψει; τίς τὴν λάλον ἀκρίδα θεραπεύσει; ἣν πολλὰ καμοῦσα ἐθήρασα, ἵνα με κατακοιμίζῃ φθεγγομένη πρὸ τοῦ ἄντρου, νῦν δὲ ἐγὼ μὲν ἀγρυπνῶ διὰ Δάφνιν, ἡ δὲ μάτην λαλεῖ."

I am surely sick, but what kind of sickness is this? I ache but have no bruise. I worry but have not lost a sheep. I burn though I'm sitting in a very shady place. How many thorns have scratched me without my crying? How many bees have stung me without my groaning. But whatever is pricking my heart now is worse than any of those. Daphnis is lovely but so are the flowers. His pipe sounds lovely, but so do the nightingales and I don't care about them. I wish I were a pipe so that he might blow through me, or a goat with him for my herdsman. O cruel water, to make Daphnis so lovely but leave me just as I was. O Nymphs, I'm dying and you are doing nothing to help me, a girl who grew up among you. Who will make your garlands when I'm dead and gone? Who will look after my poor lambs. Who will take care of my chirping cricket? I had a lot of trouble catching it to sing lullabyes outside my cave, but now I can't sleep on account of Daphnis, and it chirps away for nothing.

Chloe's love soliloquy is presented here as a lamentation uttered aloud. In it the girl's artlessness comes through beautifully. The rich and precise details and the sweet, simple tone are all hers; but the artful repetitions of structure for emotional effect reveal the hand of the artist, shaping his carefully selected materials. In the soliloquy of Daphnis, which follows soon after, the echoes and reminders of Chloe's lament show Longus carefully building a cumulative effect where a lesser artist might have been satisfied to invoke a formula.

(18) "Τί ποτέ με Χλόης ἐργάζεται φίλημα; χείλη μὲν ῥόδων ἀπαλώτερα καὶ στόμα κηρίων γλυκύτερον, τὸ δὲ φίλημα κέντρου μελίττης πικρότερον. πολλάκις ἐφίλησα ἐρίφους, πολλάκις ἐφίλησα σκύλακας ἀρτιγεννήτους καὶ τὸν μόσχον ὃν ὁ Δόρκων ἐδωρήσατο· ἀλλὰ τοῦτο φίλημα καινόν. ἐκπηδᾷ μου τὸ πνεῦμα, ἐξάλλεται ἡ καρδία, τήκεται ἡ ψυχή, καὶ ὅμως πάλιν φιλῆσαι θέλω. ὦ νίκης κακῆς· ὦ νόσου καινῆς, ἧς οὐδὲ εἰπεῖν οἶδα τὸ ὄνομα· ἆρα φαρμάκων ἐγεύσατο ἡ Χλόη μέλλουσά με φιλεῖν; πῶς οὖν οὐκ ἀπέθανεν; οἷον ᾄδουσιν αἱ ἀηδόνες, ἡ δὲ ἐμὴ σύριγξ σιωπᾷ· οἷον σκιρτῶσιν οἱ ἔριφοι, κἀγὼ κάθημαι· οἷον ἀκμάζει τὰ ἄνθη, κἀγὼ στεφάνους οὐ πλέκω. ἀλλὰ τὰ μὲν ἴα καὶ ὁ ὑάκινθος ἀνθεῖ, Δάφνις δὲ μαραίνεται. ἆρά μου καὶ Δόρκων εὐμορφότερος ὀφθήσεται;"

What on earth is Chloe's kiss doing to me? Her lips are softer than roses and her mouth is sweeter than honey, but her kiss hurts worse than a bee-sting. I have often kissed kids, and I've often kissed puppies and the calf that Dorcon gave her, but this kiss is something new. My breath comes in gasps, my heart leaps up and down, my soul melts away — but I still want to kiss her again. O what an unlucky triumph, O what a strange disease, which I can't even give a name. Did Chloe take poison before she kissed me? Then why did she not die? How sweetly the nightingales sing, while my pipe is silent. How gaily the kids frisk, while I sit still. How sweetly the flowers grow, but I weave no garlands. The violets and the hyacinths flourish; Daphnis withers. Won't Dorcon finally seem handsomer than I?

6. Chaucer, *Troilus and Criseyde*, Book I, stanzas 58–62; Petrarch, Sonnet 88; Boccaccio, *Filostrato*, Part I, stanzas 38–39; Chaucer, *Troilus and Criseyde*, Book II, stanzas 100–116.

Chaucer

58

"If no love is, O god! what fele I so?   CANTUS TROILI
And if love is, what thing and which is he?   401
If love be good, from whennes comth my woo?
If it be wikke, a wonder thynketh me,

Whenne every torment and adversite
That comth of hym may to me savory thinke;   405
For ay thurst I the more that ich it drynke.

59

"And if that at myn owen lust I brenne,
From whennes cometh my waillynge and my pleynte?
If harme agree me, wherto pleyne I thenne?
I noot, ne whi unwery that I feynte.   410
O quike deth! O swete harme so queynte!
How may of the in me swich quantite,
But if that I consente that it be?

60

"And if that I consente, I wrongfully
Compleyne, iwis; thus possed to and fro,   415
Al steereles withinne a boot am I
Amydde the see, bitwixen wyndes two,
That in contrarie stonden evere mo.
Allas! what is this wonder maladie?
For hete of cold, for cold of hete, I dye."   420

61

And to the god of love thus seyde he,
With pitous vois: "O lord, now youres is
My spirit, which that oughte youres be.
Yow thanke I, lord, that han me brought to this;
But wheither goddesse or womman, iwis,   425
She be, I not, which that ye do me serve;
But as hire man I wol ay lyve and sterve.

62

"Ye stonden in hir eyen myghtily,
As in a place unto youre vertu digne;
Wherfore, lord, if my service or I   430
May liken yow, so beth to me benigne;
For myn estat roial here I resigne
Into hire hond, and with ful humble chere
Bicome hir man, as to my lady dere."

Petrarch

> S'amor non è, che dunque è quel ch'io sento?
>   Ma, s'egli è Amor, per Dio che cosa e quale?
>   Se bona, ond' è l'effetto aspro mortale?
>   Se ria, ond' è si dolce ogni tormento?
>
> S'a mia voglia ardo, ond' è 'l pianto e lamento?
>   S'a mal mio grado, il lamentar che vale?
>   O viva morte, o dilettoso male,
>   Come puoi tanto in me, s'io no'l consento?
>
> E s'io'l consento, a gran torto mi doglio.
>   Fra si contrari venti in frale barca
>   Mi trovo in alto mar, senza governo,
>
> Sí lieve di saver, d'error sí carca,
>   Ch'i' medesmo non so quel ch'io mi voglio;
>   E tremo a mezza state, ardendo il verno.

Boccaccio

38
> E verso Amore tal fiata dicea
> con pietoso parlar: — Signor, omai
> l'anima è tua che mia esser solea;
> il che mi piace, però che tu m'hai,
> non so s'io dica a donna ovvero a dea,
> a servir dato, che non fu giammai,
> sotto candido velo in bruna vesta,
> si bella donna, come mi par questa.

39
> Tu stai negli occhi suoi, signor verace,
> si come in loco degno a tua virtute;
> per che, se 'l mio servir punto ti piace,
> da quei ti priego impetri la salute
> dell'anima, la qual prostrata giace
> sotto i tuoi piè, sí la ferir l'acute
> saette che, allora, le gittasti,
> che di costei 'l bel viso mi mostrasti. —

Like the monologue of Habrocomes (No. 4 above), that of Troilus falls into two parts, one soliloquy and one direct address to the god of love. Such striking similarity, combined with the absence of evidence of any direct borrowing, suggests that we are confronted, here, with a very powerful convention or *topos*. Of the two parts of the monologue in Chaucer, only the second is found in Chaucer's source, the *Filostrato* of Boccaccio. Apparently Chaucer felt the conventional form here so urgently as an artistic necessity that he was not content to follow Boccaccio but looked about for some material to complete the *topos*. Taking a hint from Boccaccio's observation that Troilo broke into song for joy, Chaucer caused Troilus to go to work on a sad song which he might use in his wooing. Rather than make up his own song, Chaucer went to Petrarch's Sonnet 88, which is full of echoes of the soliloquy tradition we have been examining. Chaucer's choice was strikingly appropriate.

Between Troilus, who naturally expresses himself in the Petrarchan idiom, and Criseyde, whose speech (especially in 108–109) reminds us of the Wife of Bath, there is a great and ironic gulf of sensibility: a chasm which can be measured partly in literary and cultural terms. He is a man as shaped by literary convention as his great successor in disillusionment, Don Quixote de la Mancha. She, on the other hand, is both a realist and a realistic characterization. Like the great narrative of Cervantes, Chaucer's *Troilus and Criseyde* gains its main strength through its employment of the cultural tension generated by the conflict between romantic and realistic visions of the world. For the whole passage presented here only a few, scattered lines from the *Filostrato* can be adduced as a source. The astonishing range and virtuosity demonstrated in these two monologues must be the kind of quality which drew from Dryden those undying words of praise: Here, indeed, is "God's plenty."

(Note that in keeping with its other realistic qualities, this soliloquy is clearly intended to be unspoken thought from beginning to end; but Chaucer still uses "seyde" and "seide" to refer to her process of verbalization.)

Chaucer

100

And, lord! so she gan in hire thought argue
In this matere of which I have yow tolde,   695
And what to don best were, and what eschuwe,
That plited she ful ofte in many folde.
Now was hire herte warm, now was it colde;
And what she thoughte, somwhat shal I write,
As to myn auctour listeth for tendite.   700

101

She thoughte wel, that Troilus persone
She knew by syghte, and ek his gentilesse,
And thus she seyde: "al were it nat to doone,
To graunte hym love, yit, for his worthynesse,
It were honour with pleye, and with gladnesse,   705
In honestee with swich a lord to deele,
For myn estat and also for his heele.

102

"Ek wel woot I, my kynges sone is he;
And sith he hath to se me swich delit,
If I wolde outreliche his sighte flee,   710
Paraunter he myghte have me in despit,
Thorugh which I myghte stonde in worse plit;
Now were I wis, me hate to purchace,
Withouten nede, ther I may stonde in grace?

103

"In every thyng, I woot, ther lith mesure;   715
For though a man forbede dronkenesse,
He naught forbet that every creature
Be drynkeles for alwey, as I gesse.
Ek sith I woot for me is his destresse,
I ne aughte nat for that thing hym despise,   720
Sith it is so, he meneth in good wyse.

104

"And ek I knowe, of longe tyme agon,
His thewes goode, and that he is nat nyce.

Navauntour, seith men, certein he is noon;
To wis is he to doon so gret a vice;   725
Ne als I nyl hym nevere so cherice,
That he may make avaunt, by juste cause,
He shal me nevere bynde in swich a clause.

105

"Now sette a cas: the hardest is, ywys,
Men myghten demen that he loveth me;   730
What dishonour were it unto me, this?
May ich hym lette of that? why nay, parde!
I knowe also, and alday heere and se,
Men loven wommen al biside hire leve,
And whan hem list no more, lat hem leve.   735

106

"I thenk ek how he able is for to have
Of al this noble towne the thriftieste,
To ben his love, so she hire honour save;
For out and out he is the worthieste,
Save only Ector, which that is the beste;   740
And yit his lif al lith now in my cure.
But swich is love, and ek myn aventure.

107

"Ne me to love, a wonder is it nought;
For wel wot I my self, so god me spede,
Al wolde I that no man wiste of this thought,   745
I am oon the faireste, out of drede,
And goodlieste, whoso taketh hede,
And so men seyn, in al the town of Troie.
What wonder is, though he of me have joye?

108

"I am myn owene womman, wel at ese,   750
I thank it god, as after myn estat,
Right yong, and stonde unteyd in lusty leese,
Withouten jalousie or swich debat;
Shal noon housbonde seyn to me 'chek mat.'
For either they ben ful of jalousie,   755
Or maisterful, or loven novelrye.

109

"What shal I doon? to what fyn lyve I thus?
Shal I nat love, in cas if that me leste?
What, pardieux! I am nat religious.
And though that I myn herte sette at reste   760
Upon this knyght, that is the worthieste,
And kepe alwey myn honour and my name,
By alle right it may do me no shame."

110

But right as whan the sonne shyneth brighte,
In March, that chaungeth ofte tyme his face,   765
And that a cloude is put with wynd to flighte,
Which oversprat the sonne as for a space,
A cloudy thought gan thorugh hire soule pace,
That overspradde hire brighte thoughtes alle,
So that for feere almost she gan to falle.   770

111

That thought was this: "allas! syn I am free,
Sholde I now love, and putte in jupartie
My sikernesse, and thrallen libertee?
Allas! how dorste I thenken that folie?
May I nat wel in other folk aspie   775
Hire dredful joye, hire constreynte, and hire peyne?
Ther loveth noon, that she nath wey to pleyne.

112

"For love is yit the moste stormy lyf,
Right of hym self, that evere was bigonne;
For evere som mystrust, or nice strif,   780
Ther is in love; som cloude is over that sonne.
Therto we wrecched wommen nothing konne,
Whan us is wo, but wepe and sitte and thinke;
Oure wreche is this, oure owen wo to drynke.

113

"Also thise wikked tonges ben so preste   785
To speke us harm; ek men ben so untrewe,
That right anon, as cessed is hire leste,
So cesseth love, and forth to love a newe;
But harm ydoon is doon, whoso is rewe;

For though thise men for love hem first to-rende,   790
Ful sharp bygynnynge breketh ofte at ende.

114

"How ofte tyme hath it yknowen be,
The tresoun that to wommen hath ben do!
To what fyn is swich love, I kan nat see,
Or wher bycometh it, whan it is ago.   795
Ther is no wight that woot, I trowe so,
Wher it bycometh; lo, no wight on it sporneth;
That erst was no thing, into nought it torneth.

115

"How bisy, if I love, ek moste I be
To plesen hem that jangle of love, and dremen,   800
And coye hem, that they seye noon harm of me.
For though ther be no cause, yit hem semen
Al be for harm that folk hire frendes quemen;
And who may stoppen every wikked tonge,
Or sown of belles whil that thei ben ronge?"   805

116

And after that, hire thought bygan to clere,
And seide: "he which that nothing undertaketh,
No thyng acheveth, be hym looth or deere."
And with an other thought hire herte quaketh;
Than slepeth hope, and after drede awaketh;   810
Now hoot, now cold; but thus bitwixen tweye,
She rist hire up, and wente hire for to pleye.

(The editions used for the texts quoted in this appendix are as follows: For Apollonius, Ovid, and Longus — the Loeb Classical Library; for Vergil — R. G. Austin's edition of Book IV of the *Aeneid;* for Xenophon — the Collection des Universités de France; for Chaucer and Petrarch — R. K. Root's edition of *Troilus;* for Boccaccio — Scrittori D'Italia. In these texts, as in most modern editions of earlier works, the printer's device of quotation marks or inverted commas has been intruded, carrying with it modern assumptions about the nature of thought and discourse, which are often quite at odds with the spirit of the texts.)

Notes

GENERAL NOTES AND ACKNOWLEDGMENTS

The notes for specific chapters which follow this general note have been prepared with several purposes in mind. We have cited "authorities" not so much to support our argument, which must make — or fail to make — its own case, but so as to acknowledge, wherever we could, such works as helped us to formulate our concept of narrative art. We have also had in mind the reader who might wish to pursue some aspects of this subject beyond our formulations. For this reader we have tried to indicate useful texts, especially such as are now widely available in less expensive reprints. We have not provided direct numerical references connecting particular passages in the text to particular notes (except for chapter 8), since our indebtedness is usually broad and general rather than precise and specific. The notes do follow, however, roughly the order in which topics are treated in the text.

In this general note we wish to mention some other kinds of indebtedness and to explain somewhat the nature of our collaborative relationship, beginning with our mutual indebtedness as it relates to the genesis of this book. The book developed out of a long, informal sequence of discussions, centering mainly around a college course in narrative literature which we designed together. Our ideas might have remained in their own, private oral tradition but for the intervention of the Institute for Research in the Humanities at the University of Wisconsin, which awarded R. Scholes a visiting fellowship in 1963 to begin putting these ideas on paper. Thus, the discussions of several years, augmented and refined by translation to the medium of the

U. S. Mail, began to be recorded. First drafts of Chapters 3, 5, 6, 7, and finally 1 were thus written at Madison, under ideal working conditions, where they benefited from conversations with Marshall Clagett, Julius Weinberg, and Stanley Rosen, from discussions during the brief visits of Nathalie Sarraute and Rev. Walter Ong, and where finished parts of the manuscript were read and criticized by Emmet Bennett, Friederich Solmsen, Alain Renoir, and Germaine Brée. All this discussion and criticism was immensely helpful, but the most memorable piece of advice we got was from Mlle. Brée, who said, "Wow! You can't say that about Proust." (We didn't.) Meanwhile, first drafts of Chapters 2 and 4 were being composed by R. Kellogg in Charlottesville, where they benefited from the critical scrutiny of Oliver Lee Steele. In the following year the laborious process of exchanging chapters for revision, and re-exchanging for re-revision, was completed. In the final preparation of manuscript, proofs, and index we have been excellently assisted by Constance Merker, Patricia Laidlaw, and Christopher Parker. And along the way we have received some financial aid from the Universities of Iowa and Virginia.

The book, then, is a collaboration in a very real and full sense, rather than a collection of separate pieces by two individuals. It is, we feel, a better thing than either of us could have done alone. We are glad it is done and grateful to all those who helped us do it, including those many friends and colleagues whose contributions to our thinking have become so habitual as to pass unnoticed.

A NOTE ON TRANSLATIONS

All extended translations in our text have been made by the authors (Medieval Latin in Chapter 2 and all Icelandic passages by R. Kellogg, others by R. Scholes). Our rationale is partly explained in the Appendix. To that argument we can add a further item here, which applies to our translations from the modern languages as well as the ancient ones. A collection of translations by diverse hands would necessarily be more divergent than they needed to be. We have restricted our translating to one hand, insofar as we could, so that all our translated passages would at least have passed through the same medium, sharing the same sorts of fidelity and infelicity, felicity and infidelity. Insofar as it lay in our power, we have chosen the literal over the graceful, subordinating our love for our native idiom to our care for the foreign.

CHAPTER 1

The kind of indebtedness hardest to assay is also the most profound. A fact or an idea can often be traced through the working of one's thoughts, but those verbal structures which have influenced the very way in which one thinks are so pervasive as to be sometimes untraceable. In the notes to later chapters we have tried to indicate our more specific and limited indebtedness. Here we wish to name some scholars whose work we are aware of as having provided the indispensable scaffolding for our thought. We must begin with the names of Erich Auerbach and Northrop Frye. In our text we may seem frequently to quarrel with these two great teachers, but we quarrel as one quarrels with one's masters. *Mimesis,* trans. by Willard R. Trask (Princeton University Press, 1953 [Anchor, 1957]), and *Anatomy of Criticism* (Princeton University Press, 1957) provided the co-ordinates which shaped our first discussions of the narrative tradition and have continued to influence both the texture and the structure of our work.

We have also learned much from René Wellek and Austin Warren's *Theory of Literature* (rev. ed. Harcourt, Brace, 1955 [Harvest paperback]), which offers in addition to its balanced and compendious text an excellent bibliography; and from Ian Watt's perceptive *Rise of the Novel* (University of California Press, 1960 [paperback, 1964]. Important theoretical materials from these four studies and others were collected by R. Scholes for *Approaches to the Novel* (Chandler paperback, 1961) at the time that our discussions began.

CHAPTER 2

Man's fascination with the origin of language has generated a vast literature on the subject, all of it speculative and most of it touchingly naïve by modern standards; see Alf Sommerfelt, "The Origin of Language: Theories and Hypotheses," *Journal of World History,* I (1953–54), 885–902. A discussion of the origin of language and the biological evolution of man, as well as of the role of literature in primitive cultures, is to be found in Charles F. Hockett, *A Course in Modern Linguistics* (Macmillan, 1958), pp. 553–86. The early stages of the scientific study of primitive literature are well illustrated in the voluminous writings of Franz Boas, especially *Race, Language and Culture* (Macmillan, 1940) and *Primitive Art* (Harvard University Press, 1927). Two books on primitive literature that are of interest to the general reader are Sir Maurice Bowra's *Primitive Song* (World Publishing Company, 1962) and Joseph Campbell's *The Masks of God: Primitive Mythology* (Viking, 1959). North American Indian tales are excellent exemplars of primitive narrative; a 65-page survey is included in the best general guide to the folktale: Stith Thompson, *The Folktale* (Holt, Rinehart and Winston, 1946).

On Minoan writing see Sterling Dow, "Minoan Writing," *American Journal of Archaeology*, LVIII (1954), 77–129; Michael Ventris and John Chadwick, *Documents in Mycenaean Greek* (Cambridge University Press, 1956); and John Chadwick, *The Decipherment of Linear B* (Cambridge University Press, 1958 [Modern Library paperback]).

Parry's statement that the two great parts of literature are oral and written is to be found in his article "Whole Formulaic Verses in Greek and Southslavic Heroic Song," *Transactions and Proceedings of the American Philological Association*, LXIV (1933), 180. When Milman Parry died in 1935 he was an assistant professor of classics at Harvard. His writings had been confined to the pages of scholarly journals and to his doctoral thesis, *L'Épithète traditionelle dans Homère* (Paris, 1928). Fortunately, the tragedy of Parry's death did not bring to an end the investigation he had begun in Yugoslavia. His student, Albert B. Lord, now a professor of Slavic and comparative literature at Harvard, who accompanied Parry to Yugoslavia and was from the beginning an important collaborator in his work, undertook a massive collection of Yugoslav oral narrative, the texts and translations of which, under the title *Serbocroation Heroic Songs*, are being published jointly by the Serbian Academy of Sciences and the Harvard University Press. A list of Parry's writings is to be found in A. B. Lord, "Homer, Parry, and Huso," *American Journal of Archaeology*, LII (1948), 43–4.

For the student of narrative literature in general, Lord's book, *The Singer of Tales* (Harvard University Press, 1960 [Atheneum paperback, 1965]), is even more important than his collection of texts. Lord goes beyond Parry in analyzing every conceivable aspect of the relationship between oral and written poetry, applying his results to the criticism of the Homeric epics. Although in the present work we depend heavily on *The Singer of Tales* for our characterization of oral tradition, it would be erroneous to leave the impression that the oral composition of heroic poetry had gone unnoticed by scholarship until Parry and Lord. Especially important are V. V. Radlov, *Proben der Volkslitteratur der türkischen Stämme*, 10 vols. (St. Petersburg, 1866–1904); Hector M. and Nora K. Chadwick, *The Growth of Literature*, 3 vols. (Cambridge University Press, 1932–40); R. Trautmann, *Die Volks-*

dichtung der Grossrussen. I, *Das Heldenlied* (Heidelberg, 1935); and
C. M. Bowra, *Heroic Poetry* (Macmillan, 1952). A scaled-down and
handier, but necessarily more limited, study than these is Jan de Vries,
Heroic Song and Heroic Legend, trans. B. J. Timmer (Oxford University Press, 1963 [paperback]).

Two recent contributions to the study of the diverse modes of
thought characteristic of oral and written literary cultures are Eric A.
Havelock, *Preface to Plato* (Harvard University Press, 1963) and Jack
Goody and Ian Watt, "The Consequences of Literacy," *Comparative
Studies in Society and History,* V (1963), 304–45. Of the two, Havelock comes closer to defining an oral tradition in terms of the "grammar" it superimposes on the everyday language of non-literary discourse. Such oral grammars are most noticeable in poetic narrative;
see *The Singer of Tales,* pp. 35–46; and Frederic G. Cassidy, "How
Free Was the Anglo-Saxon Scop?" in *Franciplegius: Medieval and
Linguistic Studies in Honor of Francis Peabody Magoun, Jr.,* edd. J. B.
Bessinger, Jr., and R. P. Creed (New York University Press, 1965).

Lord's analysis of the repetition of the pattern "abuse," "rebuke,"
"recognition" in the *Odyssey* occurs in *The Singer of Tales,* pp. 174–7.
For two theoretical studies of the structure of oral narrative see Vladimir Propp, *Morphology of the Folktale,* trans. Laurence Scott, Publication of the Indiana University Research Center in Anthropology,
Folklore, and Linguistics 10 (Bloomington, 1958) and Alan Dundes,
The Morphology of North American Indian Folktales, Folklore Fellows
Communications 195 (Helsinki, 1964). One of the papers in a stimulating symposium on myth that was published in the October-December
1955 issue (no. 270) of the *Journal of American Folklore* is especially
interesting for its study of the structure of traditional plots: Claude
Lévi-Strauss, "The Structural Study of Myth," LXVIII (1955), 428–44.

For the role of the Homeric epics in the transmission of Greek cultural ideals see Werner Jaeger, *Paideia: The Ideals of Greek Culture,*
trans. Gilbert Highet, 2nd ed. (Oxford University Press, 1945), I, 3–56.
Alcuin's evidence for the singing of heroic songs in the abbey in Lindisfarne is discussed in Eleanor S. Duckett, *Alcuin, Friend to Charlemagne* (Macmillan, 1951). A convenient translation of Bede's *Historia
Ecclesiastica Gentis Anglorum* ("Ecclesiastical History of the English
People") by John Stevens and revised by L. C. Jane is published with
an index in Everyman's Library. The story of Cædmon is told in IV. 24
(pp. 205–8).

The earliest applications of the Parry-Lord hypothesis of oral-formulaic composition to the study of medieval vernacular narrative were made by Professor F. P. Magoun, Jr. His important article, "Oral-Formulaic Character of Anglo-Saxon Narrative Poetry," *Speculum*, XXVIII (1953), 446–67, was followed by "Bede's Story of Cædmon: The Case History of an Anglo-Saxon Oral Singer," *Speculum*, XXX (1955), 49–63; "The Theme of the Beasts of Battle in Anglo-Saxon Poetry," *Neuphilologische Mitteilungen*, LVI (1955), 81–90; a translation of *The Kalevala, or Poems of the Kaleva District*, compiled by Elias Lönnrot (Harvard University Press, 1963); and several more detailed studies of Finnish and Anglo-Saxon oral tradition. A list of Magoun's writings through 1964 appears in *Franciplegius*, pp. 3–16.

An investigation of the use of oral-formulaic diction in the poems attributed to Cynewulf has been made by Robert Diamond, "The Diction of the Signed Poems of Cynewulf," *Philological Quarterly*, XXXVIII (1959), 228–41. Our discussion of *Heliand* is indebted to Magoun's convenient edition and translation of the *Præfatio* and *Versus* in the essay "The *Præfatio* and *Versus* Associated with Some Old-Saxon Biblical Poems" in *Medieval Studies in Honor of J. D. M. Ford*, edd. Urban T. Holmes, Jr., and Alex. J. Denomy, C. S. B. (Harvard University Press, 1948), pp. 107–36. For a study of the usefulness of the *Heliand* in attesting to some Germanic formulas which go unrecognized as such in the surviving body of Anglo-Saxon poetic narrative where they occur only once, see Robert Kellogg, "The South Germanic Oral Tradition," *Franciplegius*, pp. 66–74. Two quite technical analyses of the traditional character of the diction of *Beowulf* are to be found in unpublished doctoral dissertations: Robert P. Creed, "Studies in the Techniques of Composition of the Beowulf Poetry" (Harvard, 1955) and Godfrey L. Gattiker, "The Syntactic Basis of the Poetic Formula in *Beowulf*" (Wisconsin, 1962). The diction of *Beowulf* is also the subject of several published papers, among them Jess B. Bessinger, Jr., "*Beowulf* and the Harp at Sutton Hoo," *University of Toronto Quarterly*, XXVII (1958), 148–68; Robert P. Creed's two papers, "The Making of an Anglo-Saxon Poem," *ELH*, XXVI (1959), 445–54, and "The Singer Looks at His Sources," *Comparative Literature*, XIV (1962), 44–52; and William Whallon, "The Diction of *Beowulf*," *PMLA*, LXXVI (1961), 309–19.

Other studies of oral-formulaic composition in Anglo-Saxon poetic narrative include: Robert P. Creed, "The *andswarode*-System in Old English Poetry," *Speculum*, XXXII (1957), 523–8, and "On the Possibility of Criticizing Old English Poetry," *Texas Studies in Literature and Language*, III (1961), 97–106; Stanley B. Greenfield, "The Formulaic Expression of the Theme of 'Exile' in Anglo-Saxon Poetry," *Specu-*

lum, XXX (1955), 200–206; Wayne A. O'Neil, "Another Look at Oral Poetry in *The Seafarer*," *Speculum*, XXXV (1960), 596–600; Lewis E. Nicholson, "Oral Techniques in the Composition of Expanded Anglo-Saxon Verses," *PMLA*, LXXVIII (1963), 287–92; and Robert E. Diamond, *The Diction of the Anglo-Saxon Metrical Psalms*, Janua Linguarum, Series Practica X (The Hague: Mouton, 1963).

For evidence of oral-formulaic composition in traditional narrative other than Homeric, Yugoslav, Finnish, and Anglo-Saxon, see Stephen G. Nichols, Jr., *Formulaic Diction and Thematic Composition in the "Chanson de Roland,"* University of North Carolina Studies in the Romance Languages and Literatures 36 (Chapel Hill, 1961); James Ross, "Formulaic Composition in Gaelic Oral Literature," *Modern Philology*, LVII (1959), 1–12; R. A. Waldron, "Oral-Formulaic Technique and Middle English Alliterative Poetry," *Speculum*, XXXII (1957), 792–801; and Paul Beekman Taylor, "The Structure of *Völundarkviða*," *Neophilologus*, XLVII (1963), 228–36.

A post-Parry-Lord-Magoun investigation of the traditional ballads of the Faroe Islands has not yet been made, nor are very detailed earlier descriptions available in English. These ballads, some of which are more than 1500 lines long in present-day performances, where they are sung by large groups of dancers, preserve heroic legends from the fifth and sixth centuries as well as stories of considerably more recent origin. The best study, and one which thoroughly documents the formulaic quality of these important narrative poems, is still Helmut de Boor, *Die Färöischen Lieder des Nibelungenzyklus* (Heidelberg, 1918). A large body of Faroese ballads collected by Svend Grundtvig and J. Bloch, of which four volumes have so far appeared, is being published with a commentary in German by Professor Christian Matras: *Føroya Kvæði: Corpus Carminum Færoensium* (Copenhagen: Munksgaard, 1941–54).

Einhard's *Vita Caroli Magni* ("The Life of Charlemagne"), itself an interesting example of medieval historiography as well as a valuable source of information about the Gascon attack on Charlemagne's rear guard in the Pyrenees, has been translated by Samuel Epes Turner (University of Michigan Press, 1960). A convenient summary of the historical documents and legendary materials which shed light on the growth of the Roland epic is contained in Jan de Vries, *Heroic Song and Heroic Legend*, pp. 22–43.

In relation to their variety and interest the sagas of medieval Iceland have suffered comparative neglect in the criticism of narrative art. The surviving corpus is large. The task of editing, translating, and classifying these works has been a difficult one. Of the many narrative types, the *Islendinga sögur* ("family sagas"), which most critics now regard as the highest achievement of Icelandic literature, have seemed to be neither fish nor fowl generically; they mediate between works which pass for sober history on one hand and those which frankly acknowledge themselves to be flights of the romance imagination on the other. Not until a similarly mimetic prose fiction had evolved in nineteenth-century Europe was a suitable esthetic theory available with which to approach the *Islendinga sögur* as narrative art. And even when the theory has been available the will to use it has often been thwarted by a desire to use the sagas as documentation for this or that preconceived notion about Scandinavian history or culture. All of this is changing under the influence of a generation of deeply learned and sophisticated native Icelandic scholar-critics, the most prominent of whom are Sigurður Nordal and Einar Ólafur Sveinsson. Some of the finest fruits of this modern school of Icelandic literary scholarship are contained in the monograph-length introductions to the saga editions produced by the Íslenzka Fornritafélag (Ancient Icelandic Text Society). Especially noteworthy are Nordal's edition of *Egils Saga* and Sveinsson's *Brennu-Njáls Saga*. Under the editorship of Professor Guðni Jónsson nearly the entire corpus of Icelandic narrative prose is being issued by the Íslendingasagnaútgáfa in inexpensive, unannotated editions, of which 34 volumes have so far appeared.

The idea that the *Islendinga sögur* are the direct product of an oral tradition is an old one. Its classic statement was made by Knut Liestøl in *The Origin of the Icelandic Family Sagas* (Oslo, 1930). Since then, however, the tide of scholarly opinion has swung away from notions of oral composition to what can only be described as a theory of individual authorship in the modern sense of the words. Not without trepidation we have returned to a view similar to Liestøl's in the present work. We cannot believe on purely external grounds that authorship in thirteenth-century Iceland could have been "individual" in anything like the modern sense; and we can see far too much evidence in the texts themselves for a highly stereotyped diction and structure of *topoi* that would have made the oral composition of long narrative works entirely feasible. We assume that this question, whether it be raised in connection with the Homeric epics, the Anglo-Saxon narrative poems, or the Icelandic sagas, cannot be settled by an appeal to esthetic worth. The sagas — or rather the best of them — are superbly controlled and masterfully narrated works of the very highest quality. But such a fact has no bearing on the question of their authorship. In purely formal terms they exemplify the characteristics of a traditional, oral art. Recently, the somewhat heretical ideas about the *Íslendinga sögur* found in the present work have been expressed by a young American scholar, Theodore M. Andersson, in *The Problem of Icelandic Saga Origins*, Yale Germanic Studies 1 (New Haven, 1964). The cultural isolation of thirteenth-century Iceland was in many ways more apparent than real. The twelfth century had been an age of considerable scholarly activity in the church schools. The knowledge of Latin was if not widespread at least not a rarity, and the strong rationalizing tendency of medieval scholarship must have impressed the best minds. The thirteenth century inherited a book culture and the habits of scholarship. At the same time, however, both the *Heimskringla* and the *Prose Edda* of Snorri Sturluson represent a clear rejection of the matter of Latin book culture, while the techniques it taught were put to the service of vernacular tradition. We have to do, therefore, with an extremely complex phenomenon in the intricate relationship between the two cultural forces. The best treatment of this relationship (but one that is marred by its easy equivalence of "oral" with "formless") is Gabriel Turville-Petre, *The Origins of Icelandic Literature* (Oxford University Press, 1953).

For a general survey in English of both medieval and modern Icelandic literature, see Stefán Einarsson, *A History of Icelandic Literature* (The Johns Hopkins Press for the American-Scandinavian Foundation [ASF], 1957). The fullest survey is still Finnur Jónsson, *Den Oldnorske og Oldislandske Litteraturs Historie*, 2nd ed., 3 vols. (Copenhagen, 1920–24). Peter Hallberg, *The Icelandic Saga*, trans. with a valuable bibliographical essay by Paul Schach (University of Nebraska Press [paperback], 1962) is a handy guide to the *Íslendinga sögur*. The best critical appreciation of Icelandic prose narrative is still W. P. Ker, "The Icelandic Sagas," Chapter III in *Epic and Romance* (London, 1897 [Dover paperback ed., 1957]). For the serious student and scholar the *Catalogue of the Icelandic Collection*, 3 vols. (1914, 1927, 1943) and the bibliographies of *Islandica*, an annual publication of the Fiske Icelandic Collection in Cornell University Library, both published by Cornell University Press, are invaluable. They are almost entirely the work of a single man, the late Halldór Hermansson.

The thirteenth-century anthology known as the *Poetic Edda* (or as tradition would have it, the *Edda* of Sæmundur the Wise, hence *Sæmundar Edda*) was translated by Henry Adams Bellows (New York: The American-Scandinavian Foundation, 1926). The thirteenth-century treatise on mythology, literary allusion, and poetics by Snorri

Sturluson (*Snorra Edda*), often called the *Prose Edda* or *Younger Edda*, was translated in part by Arthur Gilchrist Brodeur (New York: ASF, 1929). The origin of the name Edda is not known with certainty. It is, however, a proper name, not the designation of a literary genre. Snorri called his book *Edda*, and tradition has since given the same name to the poetic anthology. The two Eddas do constitute the chief repositories of pre-Christian myth and legend, although in other respects they are works of quite different sorts. A convenient and reliable guide to Norse mythology is E. O. Turville-Petre, *Myth and Religion of the North: The Religion of Ancient Scandinavia* (Holt, Rinehart and Winston, 1964).

The whole of *Sturlunga Saga* has regrettably not yet been translated into English. A translation of one major part, *Íslendinga Saga*, is in progress, and another excellent, but very small, section has been translated by Anne Tjomsland, *The Saga of Hrafn Sveinbjarnarson, Islandica*, XXXV (1951). Two translations of Snorri Sturluson's *Heimskringla* are available: Lee M. Hollander (University of Texas Press [ASF], 1964) and Samuel Laing, revised by Peter Foote and Jacqueline Simpson, 3 vols. (Everyman's Library, 1964, nos. 717, 722, 847). One of the greatest sagas of the Norse kings outside of those in *Heimskringla* is *The Saga of King Sverri of Norway*, trans. John Sephton (London: David Nutt, 1899). Two sagas relating to the Icelandic discovery of North America have been translated by Magnus Magnusson and Hermann Pálsson, *The Vinland Sagas* (Penguin, 1965). Further extracts from historical writings are available in two anthologies, Jacqueline Simpson's *The Northmen Talk* (University of Wisconsin Press, 1965) and Henry Goddard Leach's *A Pageant of Old Scandinavia* (ASF, 1946).

A series of editions of Icelandic sagas with facing translations and useful introductions and notes in English was begun in 1957 by Thomas Nelson and Sons Ltd. as Nelson's Icelandic Texts, under the general editorship of Sigurður Nordal and Gabriel Turville-Petre. Four volumes have appeared so far: *The Saga of the Jomsvikings*, ed. N. F. Blake; *The Saga of Gunnlaug Serpent-Tongue*, edd. P. G. Foote and R. Quirk; *The Saga of King Heidrek the Wise*, ed. Christopher Tolkien; and *The Saga of the Volsungs*, ed. R. G. Finch. The parallels and analogues to the story of the Volsungs in the surviving relics of Germanic antiquity are comparatively numerous. In addition to Finch's introduction and notes above, see the best critical monograph in English on the *Nibelungenlied* by A. T. Hatto in his translation of the Middle High German poem (Penguin, 1965). A selection from other recent English translations of the sagas might include the following:

Njal's Saga, trans. Magnus Magnusson and Hermann Pálsson (Penguin, 1960); *The Laxdoela Saga*, trans. A. Margaret Arent (University of Washington Press [ASF], 1964); *Egil's Saga*, trans. Gwyn Jones (Syracuse University Press [ASF], 1960); *The Saga of Grettir the Strong*, trans. G. A. Hight, ed. Peter Foote (Everyman's Library, no. 699, 1965); *Eirik the Red and Other Icelandic Sagas*, trans. Gwyn Jones (Oxford World Classics, 1961); *The Sagas of Kormák and The Sworn Brothers*, trans. Lee M. Hollander (Princeton University Press [ASF], 1949); *The Saga of Gisli*, trans. George Johnston (J. M. Dent, 1963); *Eyrbyggja Saga*, trans. Paul Schach and Lee M. Hollander (University of Nebraska Press [ASF], 1959); and *The Vatnsdaler's Saga*, trans. Gwyn Jones (Princeton University Press [ASF], 1944).

The idea of non-traditional, written narrative as an *imitation* of a teller narrating his story to an implied audience was suggested to us by Paul Gray, "James Joyce's *Dubliners:* A Study of the Narrator's Role in Modern Fiction" (unpublished doctoral dissertation, University of Virginia, 1965). For Northrop Frye's use of the term "radical of presentation" to distinguish between epos and fiction in his theory of genres, see *Anatomy of Criticism* (Princeton University Press, 1957), pp. 246–9. A rich and learned study of ballads and of their relationship to the longer forms of traditional narrative is William J. Entwistle, *European Balladry* (Oxford University Press, 1939).

CHAPTER 3

The view of classical literature presented in Chapter 3 is itself an amalgam of notions from some orthodox and some unorthodox classicists, information from some standard sources, and ideas generated by interaction between our own experience of classical literature and the views of expert critics and scholars in the field. For stimulation, then, we must cite Rhys Carpenter's *Folk Tale, Fiction, and Saga in the Homeric Epics* (University of California Press, 1946 [paperback, 1958]), though we have not accepted his terminology; and F. M. Cornford's *Thucydides Mythistoricus* (E. Arnold, 1907). For information on Greek historiography, J. B. Bury, *Ancient Greek Historians* (Macmillan, 1909); and on other aspects of early Greek culture John Forsdyke, *Greece Before Homer* (Parrish, 1956 [Norton paperback, 1964]); and Jan de Vries, *Heroic Song and Heroic Legend*, trans. by B. J. Timmer (Oxford University Press, 1963 [paperback]); and on Greek literature in general Moses Hadas, *A History of Greek Literature* (Columbia University Press, 1950 [paperback, 1962]).

We must also express here our appreciation of two great humanistic publishing ventures, the Loeb Classical Library and the Penguin Classics. The Penguin translations are generally more "modern" and spritely; the Loeb more literal, enabling those familiar with the classical languages but not expert in them to magnify their powers and come to grips with the original texts. For much varied and continuing usefulness we are grateful to all those who have contributed to these two ventures.

For general information on the Roman historians we have found M. L. W. Laistner's book useful: *The Greater Roman Historians* (University of California Press, 1947 [paperback, 1963]). Concerning a form of early narrative which we have somewhat neglected, hagiography, we are pleased to refer the reader to a work by Hippolyte Delahaye, S. J.: *The Legends of the Saints*, trans. V. M. Crawford (Longmans, Green, 1907 [University of Notre Dame paperback, 1961]) — a work which is illuminating about many aspects of narrative history as they impinge on its central subject matter. Another venture which we wish to commend to the reader is the Dutton Paperback sequence of translations of medieval historical narratives, which includes Geoffrey of Monmouth's *History of the Kings of Britain*, Sir John Froissart's *Chronicles of England, France, and Spain*, and the *Crusade Memoirs* of Villehardouin and de Joinville. Also in this series is an excellent anthology of *Medieval Russia's Epics, Chronicles, and Tales* with a very full and illuminating introduction by the translator, Serge A. Zenkovsky. For the literature of Eastern Europe from Hellenistic times to the rise of Russian literature, we have found no satisfactory work in English, but can recommend the chapters on literature in two broadly historical works which are now widely available: W. W. Tarn's *Hellenistic Civilization* revised by G. T. Griffith (World, 1952 [Meridian paperback, 1961]); and A. A. Vasiliev's *History of the Byzantine Empire* (University of Wisconsin Press, rev. ed., 1952 [paperback, 2 vols., 1961]). For post-classical developments in Western European narrative we should mention the two somewhat dated but very full volumes on *Italian Literature* by John A. Symonds (now available in Capricorn paperback); Erich Auerbach's *Introduction to Romance Languages and Literatures*, trans. by Guy Daniels, 1948 (Capricorn); W. P. Ker's *Epic and Romance* (cited in notes to Chapter 2); and Charles H. Haskins's *The Renaissance of the Twelfth Century* (Harvard University Press, 1927 [Meridian paperback, 1957]) — especially the section on historical writing.

CHAPTER 4

Throughout this chapter we have been guided by the notions of historical criticism set forth by D. W. Robertson, Jr., in "Historical Criticism," *English Institute Essays, 1950,* ed. Alan S. Downer (Columbia University Press, 1951), pp. 3–31. For a stimulating analysis of what we have called the illustrative aspect of medieval narrative art see Robertson's *A Preface to Chaucer* (Princeton University Press, 1962). A major contribution to the history of art and ideas, Professor Robertson's work has relevance to the study of European narrative from the fifth to the seventeenth centuries. We are indebted to it for our discussion of Chaucer's Wife of Bath and for our treatment of the medieval rhetorical conception of "wheat" and "draf." For these terms and similar ones see Bernard F. Huppé and D. W. Robertson, Jr., *Fruyt and Chaf: Studies in Chaucer's Allegories* (Princeton University Press, 1963), Chapter I, "An Approach to Medieval Poetry." A recent study of Chaucer as poet-rhetorician is Robert O. Payne, *The Key of Remembrance: A Study of Chaucer's Poetics* (Yale University Press, 1963). See especially Chapter II, "Chaucer on the Art of Poetry," for the roles of experience and authority.

Our survey of Homeric allegoresis in antiquity is especially indebted to a series of articles in *The Classical Quarterly* by John Tate, XXIII (1929), 41–5, 142–54; XXIV (1930), 1–10; and XXVIII (1934), 105–14. See also E. R. Curtius, *European Literature and the Latin Middle Ages,* trans. Willard R. Trask (Pantheon Books for the Bollingen Foundation, 1953 [Harper Torchbooks, 1963]), index under "allegory"; and Jean Pépin, *Myth et allégorie; les origines grecques et les contestations judéo-chrétiennes* (Paris, 1958).

A fine introduction to the concept of typology in biblical exegesis and the features which distinguish it from Greek methods of allegoresis is Jean Daniélou, *From Shadows to Reality,* trans. Walston Hibbard (London: Burns and Oates, 1960). The most detailed authority on fourfold interpretation of Scripture is Henri de Lubac, *Exégèse médiévale: les quatre sens de l'Écriture,* 4 vols. (Paris, 1959–64 [in progress]). See also Beryl Smalley, *The Study of the Bible in the Middle Ages,* 2nd ed. (Oxford: Basil Blackwell, 1952). On Augustine as exegete see D. W. Robertson, Jr.'s translation of *De doctrina christiana* (Library of Liberal Arts, 1958), with introduction and bibliography.

Probably the best introduction to medieval allegoresis of classical narrative is Charles G. Osgood, *Boccaccio on Poetry: Being the Preface and the Fourteenth and Fifteenth Books of Boccaccio's* Genealogia

Deorum Gentilium *in an English Version with Introductory Essay and Commentary* (Princeton University Press, 1939 [Library of Liberal Arts, 1956]). On allegoresis of Vergil see D. Comparetti, *Virgilio nel medio evo*, ed. G. Pasquali, 2 vols. (Florence, 1937–1941). On Ovid see E. K. Rand, *Ovid and His Influence* (Boston: Marshall Jones, 1925). For a lively discussion of the proper uses of allegorical interpretation, especially typological exegesis, in the criticism of medieval narrative see the essays by E. Talbot Donaldson, Robert E. Kaske, Charles Donahue, and Richard H. Green in *Critical Approaches to Medieval Literature,* Selected Papers from the English Institute, 1958–59, ed. Dorothy Bethurum (Columbia University Press, 1960).

We are indebted for the idea of a narrative image as analyzable into a *motif* and a *theme* to the similar conception as it is applied to the plastic arts by Erwin Panofsky in *Studies in Iconology* (Oxford University Press, 1939 [Harper Torchbooks, 1962]), pp. 3–31. In addition to Panofsky's work, two other books by art historians are as valuable to the student of medieval and renaissance allegory as anything written by literary scholars: Jean Seznec, *The Survival of the Pagan Gods,* trans. Barbara F. Sessions (Pantheon Books for the Bollingen Foundation, 1953 [Harper Torchbooks, 1961]); and Emile Mâle, *Religious Art in France of the Thirteenth Century,* trans. Dora Nussey (E. P. Dutton, 1913 [reprinted as *The Gothic Image* by Harper Torchbooks, 1958]).

For the distinction between the sacred and the profane in the study of myth see Mircea Eliade, *The Sacred and the Profane,* trans. Willard R. Trask (Harcourt, Brace, 1959 [Harper Torchbooks, 1961]). The various manifestations of Arthurian myths, legends, and romances are studied by a large group of specialists in *Arthurian Literature in the Middle Ages: A Collaborative History,* ed. Roger Sherman Loomis (Oxford University Press, 1959). Professor Loomis's most recent study of the progress from myth to allegorical romance is *The Grail: From Celtic Myth to Christian Symbol* (Columbia University Press, 1963) Hugh Kenner's essay, "Art in a Closed Field" has been collected in R. Scholes, *Learners and Discerners* (University Press of Virginia, 1964).

CHAPTER 5

Chapter 5 is perhaps the most purely inductive in the book. Very little of its material is derived from any kind of synthesis of ideas presented by experts and specialists. It is mainly the result of a prolonged confrontation of the primary materials by the authors. However, some

works and editions can be cited as relevant, corroborative, or supple-
mentary. Essays by James, Trilling, and Frye mentioned in the text
can be found in R. Scholes, *Approaches to the Novel* (Chandler, 1961).
The two chapters on character in Forster's *Aspects of the Novel* (Har-
vest paperback) have stood the test of time very well and seem now
to be the best things in that book.

For excellent translations of Gottfried's *Tristan* and of *Njal's Saga*
we can refer the reader to the Penguin Classics. The new translation
and introduction to Wolfram's *Parzival* mentioned in this chapter is in
the Vintage Book edited by Mustard and Passage. Fairfax's translation
of Tasso, an important English poem in its own right (as Dryden understood), has been made available in a Capricorn paperback.

For the Plato cited (and all other Plato) we must warn the reader
away from all translations. A reader with even a smattering of Greek
should use the Loeb text and translation along with the Liddell and
Scott *Lexicon* so that he can begin to confront crucial words and
phrases directly.

For a full and sympathetic treatment of the French romances of the
seventeenth century, we can recommend George Saintsbury's *History
of the French Novel*, Vol. I (Macmillan, 1917). On the predecessors
of the English novel a useful book has recently appeared: Margaret
Schlauch's *Antecedents of the English Novel 1400–1600 (from Chaucer
to Deloney)*, (Oxford University Press, 1963).

With respect to primary materials on the short narrative forms in
circulation during the transition from romance to realism, the lot of
the reader confined to English has recently improved considerably.
The *Gesta Romanorum* in the Swan-Hooper translation is now available in a Dover paperback. Several editions of later European and
English short narratives are also available in paperback: *The Palace of
Pleasure*, ed. by Harry Levtow and Maurice Valency, an excellent collection of novelle, mainly fourteenth-century (Capricorn, 1960); *A
Hundred Merry Tales and Other Jestbooks of the Fifteenth and Sixteenth Centuries*, ed. by P. M. Zall, a collection of strictly English
materials (Bison, 1963); *The Hundred Tales*, trans. by R. H. Robbins,
the first English version of the fifteenth-century French collection, *Les
Cent Nouvelles Nouvelles* (Crown Publishers, 1960 [hard cover]).
Boccaccio himself has been crisply translated (and quite accurately
where we have checked) by Richard Aldington in an edition recently
reprinted in the Laurel paperback series. For information on the
sources of Boccaccio's tales we have consulted A. C. Lee's *The Decameron; its Sources and Analogues* (D. Nutt, 1909).

On the failure of the interior monologue and other devices to pene-

trate the ultimate secrets of consciousness, Nathalie Sarraute has commented shrewdly in her essay "From Dostoievski to Kafka" in *The
Age of Suspicion,* trans. Maria Jolas (G. Braziller, 1963). Additional
material related to Chapter 5 may be found in the Appendix.

CHAPTER 6

For some of the concepts presented in this chapter we have drawn
upon the following works: Bronislaw Malinowski's *Myth in Primitive
Psychology* (New York University Press, 1926); Theodore H. Gaster's
Thespis (Revised edition for Anchor paperback, 1961); his *Oldest
Stories in the World* (Viking, 1952 [Beacon paperback, 1958]); and
his edition of F. M. Cornford's *Origins of Attic Comedy* (Anchor,
1961). We have also been influenced by the discussion of time in
Mircea Eliade's *Myth of the Eternal Return* (Pantheon Books, 1954
[published as a Harper Torchbook under the title *Cosmos and History,*
1959]). And at some point well back in the development of our ideas,
the thought of Henri Focillon was seminal. His *Life of Forms in Art*
(Yale University Press, 1942) should be made more widely available.

CHAPTER 7

Like Chapter 5, this chapter is relatively independent of earlier critical
formulations. But it treats a much narrower topic and operates, necessarily, within a fairly tight framework of critical theory. Serious critical
discussions of point of view begin with Henry James's Prefaces. Any
list of subsequent discussions would start with Percy Lubbock's *Craft
of Fiction* (Jonathan Cape, 1921 [Viking Compass, 1957]) and end
with Wayne C. Booth's *Rhetoric of Fiction* (University of Chicago
Press, 1961 [now in paperback]). For a full bibliography on the subject
see Norman Friedman's essay on "Point of View in Fiction" in *PMLA,*
December 1955.

CHAPTER 8

1   For a different approach to the problem of comprehensive cover-
age of the field, see *The Routledge Encyclopedia of Narrative Theory*
(2005), a 718-page tome by more than 200 diverse hands, containing
entries on approximately 450 topics, ranging from "actant" to "writerly
text." For a recent snapshot of the state of the field, see the Blackwell
Companion to Narrative Theory (2005), a 571-page volume containing

35 essays on topics ranging from the history of narrative theory to the relations between narrative and music.

2   Related work, also influenced by the Russian formalists and by structuralist linguistics, was being done by the Moscow-Tartu group that included Juri Lotman and Boris Uspensky, but this work has not been as influential as that of the French structuralists—yet. Another important branch of structuralist inquiry, one that preceded much of the work done in France, was carried out by the Prague School, a group that included Jan Mukarrovský and Nikolai Trubeckoi. For excellent overviews of these bodies of work, along with essential bibliographies, see the entries in the second edition of the *Johns Hopkins Guide to Literary Theory and Criticism* by Uri Margolin (on the Moscow-Tartu group) and Lubomir Dolezel (on the Prague School group).

3   Significant deconstructive work has been done on narrative primarily by Paul de Man, J. Hillis Miller, and Barbara Johnson, and much of that work is brilliant in its individual analyses and its posing of theoretical challenges to nondeconstructive methods. But I do not feature that work in this narrative because I do not see it as having had an enduring effect on narrative theory's understandings of plot, character, and narrative discourse. Deconstruction would loom larger in my story of literary criticism since 1966 than it does in my story of narrative theory since that time. To put this point another way, although deconstruction has amply established that all narratives, narrative elements, and narrative theories are susceptible to deconstruction, narrative theory has nevertheless continued to pursue what it regards as substantial, if provisional, understandings of narrative, narratives, and the elements of both.

4   For more on this potential problem, see my discussion in Chapter 2 of *Reading People, Reading Plots*.

5   Also noteworthy is Sternberg's work on the relation between narrative elements and techniques, on the one side, and their functions on the other. He persuasively develops a "Proteus Principle," which stipulates that "in different contexts . . . the same form may fulfill different functions and different forms the same function" ("Proteus," 148).

6   I offer my answers in my chapter on *Atonement* in *Experiencing Fiction*.

7   Important earlier work includes Juri Lotman's *The Structure of the Artistic Text* and Bakhtin's essay on "Forms of Time and the Chronotope in the Novel" in *The Dialogic Imagination*. Other useful, more recent work includes Manfred Jahn's overview in his entry on "Space" in the *Routledge Encyclopedia of Narrative Theory* and David Herman's chapter on "Spatialization" in *Story Logic*.

Bibliography

Aristotle. *Poetics*. Oxford: Clarendon Press, 1968.

Austen, Jane. *The Complete Novels*. Oxford: Oxford Univ. Press, 1994.

Bakhtin, Mikhail. *The Dialogic Imagination*. Edited by Michael Holquist, translated by Caryl Emerson and Michael Holquist. Austin: Univ. of Texas Press, 1981.

Bal, Mieke. *Narratology*. Second Edition. Translated by Christine van Boheemen. Toronto: Univ. of Toronto Press, 1998.

Booth, Wayne C. *The Rhetoric of Fiction*. Chicago: Univ. of Chicago Press, 1961.

———. "Afterword." In *The Rhetoric of Fiction*. Second Edition. Chicago: Univ. of Chicago Press, 1983.

———. *The Company We Keep*. Berkeley: Univ. of California Press, 1988.

Brooks, Peter. *Reading for the Plot*. New York: Knopf, 1984.

Case, Alison. *Plotting Women*. Charlottesville: Univ. Press of Virginia, 1999.

Chatman, Seymour. *Coming to Terms*. Ithaca Cornell Univ. Press, 1990.

Chomsky, Noam. *Syntactic Structures*. Paris: Mouton, 1957.

Cohn, Dorrit. *The Distinction of Fiction*. Baltimore: Johns Hopkins Univ. Press, 1999.

Conrad, Joseph. *Lord Jim; Heart of Darkness; Nostromo*. Oxford: Oxford Univ. Press, 1994.

Crane, R. S. "The Concept of Plot and the Plot of *Tom Jones*." In *Critics and Criticism*. Edited by R. S. Crane. Chicago: Univ. of Chicago Press, 1952, pp. 616–647.

Culler, Jonathan. "Story and Discourse in the Analysis of Narrative." In *The Pursuit of Signs*. Ithaca: Cornell Univ. Press, 1981, pp. 169–187.

Darwin, Charles. *The Origin of Species and The Voyage of the Beagle*. New York: Alfred A. Knopf, 2003.

De Man, Paul. *Allegories of Reading*. New Haven: Yale Univ. Press, 1979.

Dolezel, Lubomir. "Prague School Structuralism." In *Johns Hopkins Guide to Literary Theory and Criticism*. Second edition. Edited by Michael Groden, Martin Kreiswirth, and Imre Szeman. Baltimore: Johns Hopkins Univ. Press, 2005, pp. 773–777.

DuPlessis, Rachel Blau. *Writing Beyond the Ending*. Bloomington: Indiana Univ. Press, 1985.

Eliot, George. *Middlemarch*. Edited by David Carroll. New York: Oxford Univ. Press, 1986.

Fetterley, Judith. *The Resisting Reader*. Bloomington: Indiana Univ. Press, 1978.

Fielding, Henry. *Tom Jones*. Edited by Fredson Bowers. New York: Modern Library, 1985.

Fitzgerald, F. Scott. *The Great Gatsby*. New York: Scribner's, 1953.

Fludernik, Monika. *Towards a "Natural" Narratology*. New York: Routledge, 1996.

Forster, E. M. *Aspects of the Novel*. New York: Harcourt, Brace & World, 1964.

Foucault, Michel. *Discipline and Punish*. Translated by Alan Sheridan. London: Allen Lane, 1977.

Freud, Sigmund. *Beyond the Pleasure Principle*. Translated by James Strachey. New York: Bantam, 1963.

Friedman, Susan Stanford. "Spatial Poetics and Arundhati Roy's *The God of Small Things*." In *A Companion to Narrative Theory*. Edited by James Phelan and Peter J. Rabinowitz. Oxford: Blackwell Publishing, 2005, pp. 192–205.

———. "Spatialization: A Strategy for Reading Narrative." *Narrative* 1 (1993), pp. 12–23.

Genette, Gérard. *Narrative Discourse*. Translated by Jane E. Lewin. Ithaca, New York: Cornell Univ. Press, 1980.

Greimas, Algirdas Julien. "Actants, Actors, and Figures." In *On Meaning: Selected Writings in Semiotic Theory*. Translated by Paul J. Perron and Frank H. Collins. Minneapolis: Univ. of Minnesota Press, 1987, pp. 106–120.

———. *Structural Semantics*. Translated by Danielle McDowell, and Alan Velie. Lincoln: Univ. of Nebraska Press, 1983.

Hammett, Dashiell. *The Maltese Falcon*. New York: Knopf, 1957.

Halliday, M. K. *An Introduction to Functional Grammar*. Second edition. London: Edward Arnold, 1994.

———. "Types of Process." In *Halliday: System and Function in Language*. Edited by Gunther Kress. Oxford: Oxford Univ. Press, 1976, pp. 159–73.

Herman, David. *Story Logic*. Lincoln: Univ. of Nebraska Press, 2002.

Herman, David, Manfred Jahn, and Marie-Laure Ryan, eds. *The Routledge Encyclopedia of Narrative Theory*. New York: Routledge, 2005.

Herman, Michelle. *Missing*. Columbus: Ohio State Univ. Press, 1990.

Hogan, Patrick Colm. *The Mind and Its Stories: Narrative Universals and Human Emotions*. New York: Cambridge Univ. Press, 2003.

Iser, Wolfgang. *The Act of Reading*. Baltimore: Johns Hopkins Univ. Press, 1978.

———. *The Implied Reader*. Baltimore: Johns Hopkins Univ. Press, 1974.

Ishiguro, Kazuo. *The Remains of the Day*. London: Faber and Faber, 1989.

Jahn, Manfred. "The Mechanics of Focalization: Extending the Narratological Toolbox." *GRAAT* 21 (1999), pp. 85–110.

———. "Windows of Focalization: Desconstructing and Reconstructing a Narratological Concept." *Style* 30 (1996), pp. 241–67.

James, Henry. *The Art of the Novel: Critical Prefaces*. New York: Scribner, 1962.

James, Henry. *The Turn of the Screw and Other Stories*. Edited by T. J. Lustig. New York: Oxford Univ. Press, 1998.

Jameson, Fredric. *The Political Unconscious*. Ithaca: Cornell Univ. Press, 1981.

Johnson, Barbara. *The Critical Difference*. Baltimore: Johns Hopkins Univ. Press, 1980.

Kafalenos, Emma. *Narrative Causalities*. Columbus: Ohio State Univ. Press, 2006.

Lanser, Susan. *Fictions of Authority*. Ithaca: Cornell Univ. Press, 1992.

———. "The 'I' of the Beholder: Equivocal Attachments and the Limits of Structuralist Narratology." In *A Companion to Narrative Theory*. Edited by James Phelan and Peter J. Rabinowitz. Oxford: Blackwell Publishing, 2005, pp. 206–219.

———. "Toward a Feminist Narratology." *Style* 20 (1986), pp. 341–63.

Levi-Strauss, Claude. "The Structural Study of Myth." Translated by Claire Jacobson and Brooke Grundfest Schoepf. In *Myth*. Edited by Thomas Sebeok.Bloomington: Indiana Univ. Press, 1958, pp. 81–106.

Lotman, Juri. *The Structure of the Artistic Text*. Translated by Gail Lenhoff and Ronald Vroon. Ann Arbor: Dept. of Slavic Languages and Literature at the Univ. of Michigan, 1977.

Margolin, Uri. "Moscow-Tartu School." In *Johns Hopkins Guide to Literary Theory and Criticism*. Second edition. Edited by Michael Groden, Martin Kreiswirth, and Imre Szeman. Baltimore: Johns Hopkins Univ. Press, 2005, pp. 660–665.

McEwan, Ian. *Atonement*. New York: Doubleday, 2001.

McHale, Brian. "Weak Narrativity: The Case of Avant-Garde Poetry." *Narrative* 9 (2001), pp. 161–67.

Miller, J. Hillis. *Reading Narrative*. Norman: Univ. of Oklahoma Press, 1998.

Morrison, Toni. *Beloved*. New York: Knopf, 1987.

Nelles, William. "Getting Focalization into Focus." *Poetics Today* 11 (1990), pp. 365–82.

Palmer, Alan. *Fictional Minds*. Lincoln: Univ. of Nebraska Press, 2004.

Phelan, James. *Experiencing Fiction*. Columbus: Ohio State Univ. Press (forthcoming).

———. *Living to Tell about It*. Ithaca: Cornell Univ. Press, 2005.

———. *Narrative as Rhetoric*. Columbus: Ohio State Univ. Press, 1996.

———. *Reading People, Reading Plots*. Chicago: Univ. of Chicago Press, 1989.

Phelan, James and Peter J. Rabinowitz, eds. *A Companion to Narrative Theory*. Oxford: Blackwell Publishing, 2005.

Prince, Gerald. "Introduction a l'étude du narrataire." *Poetique* 14 (1973), pp. 178–96.

Propp, Vladimir. *Morphology of the Folktale*. Translated by Laurence Scott and Svatava Pirkova-Jakobson. Austin: Univ. of Texas Press, 1968.

Proust, Marcel. *A la recherche du temps perdu*. Translated by C.K. Scott Moncrieff and Terence Kilmartin. New York: Modern Library, 1992.

Peter J. Rabinowitz . *Before Reading*. Second Edition. Columbus: Ohio State University Press, 1998.

———. "Truth in Fiction: A Reexamination of Audiences." *Critical Inquiry* 4 (1977), pp. 121–41.

Richardson, Brian. *Unnatural Voices*. Columbus: Ohio State Univ. Press, 2006.

Ricouer, Paul. *Time and Narrative*. 3 volumes. Translated by Katherine Blamey and David Pellauer. Chicago: Univ. of Chicago Press, 1984–88.

Ryan, Marie-Laure. "Cognitive Maps and the Construction of Narrative Space." In *Narrative Theory and the Cognitive Sciences*. Edited by David Herman. Stanford, CA: Center for the Study of Language and Information, 2003, pp. 214–42.

————. *Narrative as Virtual Reality*. Baltimore: Johns Hopkins Univ. Press, 2001.

Saussure, Ferdinand de. *Course in General Linguistics*. Edited by Charles Bally and Albert Sechehaye, translated by Roy Harris. London: Duckworth, 1983.

Scholes, Robert. *Textual Power*. New Haven: Yale Univ. Press, 1985.

Shaw, Harry. "Loose Narrators: Display, Engagement, and a Search for a Place in History." *Narrative* 3 (1995), pp. 95–116.

Sternberg, Meir. "Proteus in Quotation-Land: Mimesis and the Forms of Reproted Discourse." *Poetics Today* 3 (1982), pp. 107–56.

————. "Telling in Time (II): Chronology, Teleology, Narrativity." *Poetics Today* 13 (1992), pp. 463–541.

Todorov, Tzvetan. *Grammaire du Décaméron*. The Hague: Mouton, 1969.

————. *The Poetics of Prose*. Translated by Richard Howard. Ithaca: Cornell Univ. Press, 1977.

Twain, Mark. *Adventures of Huckleberry Finn*. Edited by Emory Elliott. New York: Oxford Univ. Press, 1999.

Warhol, Robyn. *Gendered Interventions*. New Brunswick: Rutgers Univ. Press, 1989.

————. *Having a Good Cry*. Columbus: Ohio State Univ. Press, 2003.

White, Hayden. *Metahistory*. Baltimore: Johns Hopkins Univ. Press, 1973.

Wimsatt, W. K. *The Verbal Icon*. Lexington: Univ. of Kentucky Press, 1954.

Winnett, Susan. "Coming Unstrung: Women, Men, Narrative, and Principles of Pleasure." *PMLA* 105 (1990), pp. 505–18.

Winterson, Jeanette. *Written on the Body*. New York: Knopf, 1992.

Woloch, Alex. *The One vs. the Many*. Princeton: Princeton Univ. Press, 2003.

Zunshine, Lisa. *Why We Read Fiction*. Columbus: Ohio State Univ. Press, 2006.

Index

Note: This is an index of writers, works, and terminology. All works by known writers are indexed under the names of the authors. In indexing the terminology we have tried especially to locate passages of definition and illustration so that the index may be used as a kind of glossary. The various forms of narrative (novel, legend, and so on) are under the general heading, Narrative forms. Except for the item "acknowledgments" the Notes have not been indexed.

380